PRACTICAL METABOLIC NUTRITION

A Systems Approach to Vitamins and Minerals

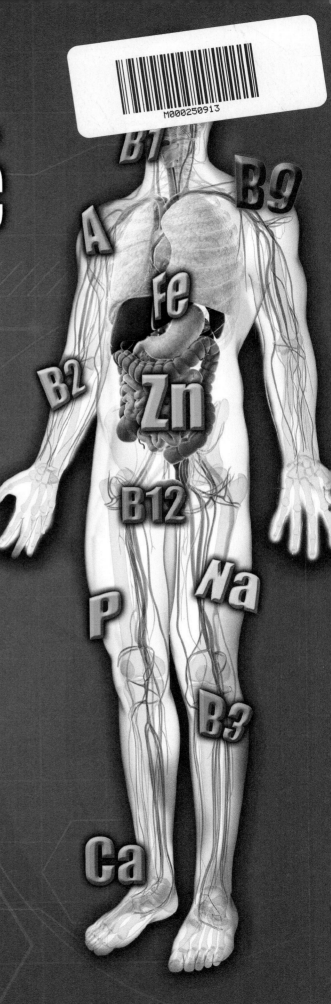

Deborah J. Good, Ph.D.

Kendall Hunt
publishing company

M000250913

Cover Image © Shutterstock.com

Kendall Hunt
publishing company

www.kendallhunt.com
Send all inquiries to:
4050 Westmark Drive
Dubuque, IA 52004-1840

Copyright © 2017 Deborah J. Good, Ph.D.

ISBN 978-1-4652-6824-2

Kendall Hunt Publishing Company has the exclusive rights to reproduce this work,
to prepare derivative works from this work, to publicly distribute this work,
to publicly perform this work and to publicly display this work.

All rights reserved. No part of this publication may be reproduced,
stored in a retrieval system, or transmitted, in any form or by any
means, electronic, mechanical, photocopying, recording, or otherwise,
without the prior written permission of the copyright owner.

Printed in the United States of America

CONTENTS

FORWARD

This is not your average vitamins and minerals textbook.

Several years ago I was asked to teach a large lecture class in Vitamins and Minerals. I was told that I needed to take over teaching this course, not for my expertise in the subject area per se, but because of my experience in teaching other large lecture courses. I contacted the previous professor of the class and got her notes, and reviewed these. Then, since this was the second semester course of a two-semester Metabolic Nutrition course, I contacted the current professor of the first semester course to find out what textbook he was using. For the first two years, we used the same textbook, and for the micronutrients section, the vitamins and minerals were discussed in the traditional vitamins by vitamins, and minerals by minerals methods. I taught the course this way, too, starting with the water-soluble vitamins, and ending the semester with the ultra-trace minerals.

However, I tend to look at things and learn material in a "big picture" sort of way, so skipping around and talking about energy metabolism and the TCA cycle and the electron transport chain over and over again throughout the semester, as we went through thiamine, then riboflavin, then niacin, and then again for iron and copper in the minerals section seemed very disjointed from a whole body/physiology perspective. Also, because of the interaction of vitamins and minerals with each other during digestion, energy metabolism—well just about every system—the deficiencies and toxicities also felt like just more things to memorize, rather than affecting systems and metabolic processes leading to the symptoms.

In my third year of teaching the course, I decided to mix things up. Rather than teach each vitamin and each mineral as separate classes, I took a systems-based approach. Energy metabolism was taught as a whole, looking at carbohydrate, protein, and fat metabolism and the interrelationships between them, and the vitamins and minerals acting in and on the pathways. Embryogenesis, the skeletal system, and digestion were taught as processes, where deficiency of one vitamin could lead to disruptions in several vitamins or minerals due to their interdependence.

Some students have voiced strong opposition to this method, as they have been taught in the traditional ways (vitamin by vitamin and mineral by mineral) and perhaps want to simply memorize the foods sources, DRI, toxicity, deficiency, and processes as a single entity. However, most students have embraced the new method, and feel that they have a better overall understanding of the intimate relationship of the micronutrients in whole body physiology.

The downside to teaching this subject in a new way is that there was no available textbook, and in their "end of year" teacher evaluations, several students asked for additional resources for the course, feeling that the vitamin and mineral textbooks I recommended did not provide the type of background material that they needed for the course, since those textbooks were all organized in the traditional vitamin by vitamin and mineral by mineral way. Thus, when I was approached by Kendall-Hunt to write a textbook, I agreed. While there are many online sources and other textbooks on vitamins and minerals, I really felt that mine would be unique, and give students a go-to volume for additional information. My hope is that students will find the book easy to follow and stimulating to read. I welcome suggestions for improvements, as well as any comments you, the reader, may have.

I would like to thank my husband Danny Miglia, for his support and encouragement during the writing (and before—in urging me to get started!!). Of course I couldn't have done this textbook without my publisher, Kendall-Hunt, my acquisitions editor, Curtis Ross, and the project coordinator, Elizabeth Cray.

Deborah J. Good, Ph.D.
March 9, 2015

CHAPTER 1

Let's Get Started!
An Introduction to Vitamins and Minerals

Table of Contents

Every living thing eats. Nutrients are substances, both organic and inorganic that are required by living organisms for life—such as those nutrients that sustain growth, health, and reproduction. Complete absence of any nutrient will result in characteristic symptoms, and usually death, making these nutrients absolutely required in the diet of healthy individuals.

We can group the nutrients into organic and inorganic compounds, and then further classify them into macro- and micronutrients. The macronutrients include inorganic water, as well as the organic or carbon-containing carbohydrates, fats, and proteins. Micronutrients include the organic vitamins and the inorganic minerals (Table 1.1). Neither micro- nor macronutrients alone can fuel the body in isolation—both are needed to be healthy. Since this book focuses on the micronutrients, let's get started with them.

What makes one substance essential, even in minute amounts, and another substance required but not essential? Why are dietary vitamins and minerals considered essential to life? These are the questions each of you should ask yourselves as you start learning about vitamins and minerals.

Did you KNOW...?

Sufficient daily vitamin intakes range from 2.4 µg (vitamin B12) to 16 mg (niacin), while macronutrient intakes range from 31 grams/day of fats to 130 grams/day of carbohydrates. That's an 8,000-fold difference in intake!

Vitamins—13 total

Water soluble: **Vitamin C, B1 (thiamine), B2 (riboflavin), B3 (niacin), B5 (pantothenic acid), B6 (pyridoxine), B7 (biotin), B9 (folate), B12 (cobalamin)**

Fat Soluble: **Vitamin A, Vitamin D, Vitamin E, Vitamin K**

Minerals—16 total

Major (range >100 mg/day): **Calcium, Chloride, Magnesium, Phosphorus, Potassium, Sodium**

Trace (range 1 mg-100mg/day): **Fluoride, Iron, Manganese, Zinc**

Ultra-Trace (range < 1 mg/day): **Chromium, Cobalt, Copper, Iodine, Molybdenum, Selenium**

WHAT IS A VITAMIN?

Vitamins are water- or fat-soluble substances that are needed in our diet in small quantities (usually in the range of micrograms to milligrams). While some micronutrients we can make ourselves from starting materials that we ingest, we usually get vitamins by eating a variety of foods, including meats, dairy products, fruits, vegetables, and whole grains.

The list of vitamins (Table 1.1) is only a list for humans. Each animal has its own list of required vitamins (and minerals). For example, cats and in fact many vertebrates can make vitamin C, so it is not considered a vitamin for them. What?! Why can't humans make vitamin C when other animals can? I mean, it makes sense…you don't see cats and dogs eating oranges or begging for red peppers—right? It turns out that even fish and frogs and reptiles make vitamin C so what makes humans so different?

Most mammals make vitamin C (which is more scientifically known as ascorbic acid, or ascorbate) in their livers, using glucose as a starting material. The process requires several steps, with all but one of the steps needed for other pathways—thus essential enzymes. An enzyme called gulonolactone oxidase (we'll call this enzyme Gulo for short) performs the final step in the reaction to make 2-keta-L-gulonolactone, which spontaneously converts to L-ascorbate. In humans, the Gulo gene is inactive [1]. All humans (and some other primates, guinea pigs, birds, and bats) have the genetic disease hypoascorbemia, meaning that while we can and do utilize glucose in other ways, we can't use it to make vitamin C. So, vitamin C is a vitamin for humans. Most mammals have a functional Gulo gene, which means that they don't have to rely on dietary intake for vitamin C. This means, that for other mammals, vitamin C is *not* a vitamin (Figure 1.1).

Likewise, dogs and cats seem to produce sufficient vitamin K via bacteria in their guts, meaning that vitamin K is also not considered an essential vitamin for them (Figure 1.1). Wait…so now I'm telling you that some vitamins can be synthesized in our guts? Yes, that is true for cats, dogs, and other mammals with gut bacteria. In addition to processing some of our macronutrients, bacteria in our guts can

13 essential vitamins

11 vitamins, not including Vitamin C and Vitamin K

© Alemon cz/Shutterstock.com, © LANTERIA/Shutterstock.com

FIGURE 1.1: **Vitamins are specific to the organism.** For humans there are 13 essential vitamins, while many other mammals, including cats and dogs, require only 11 vitamins. This leads to differences in the dietary foods eaten by different organisms, with humans requiring fruits and vegetables, that are rich in Vitamins C and K, while dogs and cats do not.

synthesis vitamin K, as well as some other vitamins. In cats and dogs, the amount of vitamin K synthesized is enough, so they don't have to go around eating green leafy veggies very often—although for cats, perhaps that occasional nibble on catnip and grass gives them an extra boost. For humans, we still need to eat some green leafy veggies daily to get our vitamin K—anyone for a kale smoothie? (Figure 1.2).

Getting back to the original question—what makes a vitamin, a vitamin, and some other nutrient not a vitamin…?

Hopefully, you have come to the conclusion that vitamins are essential substances that are needed in small quantities, from the diet. Period. Even though the bacteria in humans can make vitamin K, it is still a dietary vitamin for us, because the bugs in our gut don't make enough of it. Humans can also make vitamin D, and niacin in small quantities, but again, not enough for our needs, so both of these are vitamins as well. Substances like coenzyme Q (CoQ) are not vitamins because humans can synthesize enough of these to support body needs.

So, the answer to "What is a vitamin" is "it is a substance, that cannot be obtained by an individual organism in sufficient quantities to sustain health, from any other source but dietary ingestion."

FIGURE 1.2 **Kale is an excellent source for vitamin K.** This smoothie is a recipe developed by the author, and her husband. Blend fruit of your choice (we use apples, strawberries, blueberries—whatever we have on hand) with about 3 large stalks of kale, and a handful of carrots. Blend on high speed, and add water to desired thickness. Enjoy!

Fat and water do not mix

The essential vitamins can be further classified as belonging to the water- or fat-soluble class. Water-soluble vitamins, including all of the B vitamins, and vitamin C, need to be ingested daily, as excess water-soluble vitamins that are not used are excreted in the urine. We'll talk more about that when we discuss digestion of vitamins and minerals in Chapter 3. The one exception to this rule (and aren't there always exceptions to the rules in biology?) is the storage of vitamin B12 in the liver. Vitamin B12 has a half-life of approximately 1 year in the liver [2], meaning that if you eat some today, it will likely be there next year at this time. The recommended daily allowance (RDA) for B12 is also one of the lowest of the vitamins at 2.4 µg/day [3], and as expected, most people don't need to worry about a B12 deficiency. For water-soluble vitamins, including B12, there are rarely side effects or toxicities for ingesting too much, and thus few have upper tolerable limit levels from the Food and Nutrition Board (more about them later). Water-soluble vitamins C, B6, niacin, and folate have upper tolerable limit recommendations [3, 4], which are rarely exceeded by diet intake. Rather, supplement users need to be cautious when taking high-dosage pills containing these water-soluble vitamins.

Fat-soluble vitamins, on the other hand are ingested, and then can be stored in readily available forms for future use. While the Food and Nutrition Board recommends a daily intake of these vitamins, most of the fat-soluble vitamins can be obtained intermittently and then utilized as needed from storage. An example of this is vitamin A, which is given at a dose well in excess of the recommended tolerable upper limit, to children in developing countries to prevent blindness and neonatal death [5]. This treatment has prevented some infant mortality and reduced childhood blindness, but is controversial because of the possibility of toxicity [6]. Vitamins A, D, and E have upper tolerable recommended limits [4, 7, 8], meaning that there can be toxicity if these vitamins are consumed at too high of a level. While there is no established upper limit for vitamin K [7], due to no known adverse effects of ingesting large amounts, the Food and Nutrition Board does caution individuals to monitor their intake—but hey, how much kale and spinach can a normal person really eat???

What do you THINK...?

Take a look at the editorial by Haider and Bhutta (2014) Lancet S0140-6736(14)62342-4. Do you think WHO should stop vitamin A supplementation? If not, what additional safeguards should be put in place? Does additional research need to be done?

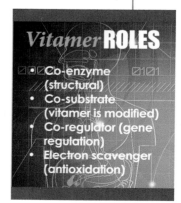

Vitamer ROLES

- Co-enzyme (structural)
- Co-substrate (vitamer is modified)
- Co-regulator (gene regulation)
- Electron scavenger (antioxidation)

Vitamins have vitamers with different bioactivities

The vitamins each have different forms, called "vitamers," each with overlapping and sometimes distinct activities from each other (Table 1.2). So, when someone refers to, let's say vitamin A, they are actually talking in broad terms about the group of vitamers that each have some level of vitamin A activity. For example, retinoic acid is the vitamer that functions in the gene regulation activities of vitamin A—such as during embryogenesis, in immune cells, and generally getting involved in a lot of cellular processes, while the other vitamers of vitamin A have varying activity with gene regulation or vision (Table 1.3).

TABLE 1.2: Vitamins and their vitamers

Vitamin	Vitamers
B1	Thiamine, thiamine pyrophosphate (TPP)
B2	Riboflavin, Flavin mononucleotide (FMN), Flavin adenine dinucleotide (FAD)
B3	Niacin, Nicotinamide, NAD+, NADP+, NADPH, NADH, Nicotinic Acid
B5	Pantothenic acid, panthenol, pantethine, Coenzyme A
B6	Pyridoxine (PN), pyridoxine 5-phosphate (PNP), pyridoxamine (PM), pyridoxamine 5-phosphate (PMP), pyridoxal (PL), pyridoxal 5-phosphate (PLP)
B7	Biotin (this is the only vitamer, although biocytin is a derivative made of biotin covalently linked to lysine in proteins)
B9	Folic acid, folinic acid (rare), 5-methyl tetrahydrofolate (5-methyl-THF), dihydrofolate (DHF), and others
B12	Cyanocobalamin, hydroxocobalamin, methycobalamin, adenosylcobalamin, cobalamin
Vitamin A	Retinol, retinal, retinyl ester, retinoic acid Carotenoids: alpha-carotene, beta-carotene (major), gamma carotene, xanthophyll, and beta-cryptoxanthin
Vitamin C	Ascorbic acid (AA), dihydroascobic acid (DHA), other salts that we won't discuss
Vitamin D	Calcitriol (1, 25 hydroxy D3), Calcidiol (25 hydroxy D2), cholecalciferol (D3), ergocalciferol (D2)
Vitamin E	Alpha-, beta-, gamma- and delta-tocopherol, alpha-, beta-, gamma-, and delta-tocotrienol
Vitamin K	Phylloquinone (K1, food), menaquinone (K2-bacteria), menadione (K3, synthetic)

TABLE 1.3: Typical roles of the major bioactive vitamers

Vitamin	Bioactive Vitamers	Typical Role (enzymatic role)
B1	TPP	Aldehyde transfer (co-enzyme)
B2	FMN, FAD	Oxidation-reduction (co-substrate)
B3	NAD+, NADP+	Oxidation-reduction (co-substrate)
B5	Coenzyme A	Acyl-group transfer (co-enzyme)
B6	PLP	Aminotransferase (amination) reactions (co-enzyme)
B7	Biocytin	Biotinylation, carboxylation (prosthetic group)
B9	5-methyl-THF, 5, 10'-methylene THF,	Transfer of one-carbon/methyl groups (co-substrate)
B12	Cobalamin, methycobalamin	Transfer of methyl groups; intramolecular rearrangements (co-enzyme)
Vitamin A	Retinol, retinal, retinoic acid	Vision (co-enzyme), gene expression (co-regulator)
Vitamin C	AA, DHA	Water soluble electron scavenger, electron transfer (co-enzyme)
Vitamin D	Calcitriol	Gene expression (co-regulator)
Vitamin E	γ-tocopherol	Lipid soluble peroxyl radical scavenger
Vitamin K	K1, K2, K3	Gamma carboxlyation reactions (co-substrate)

CHAPTER 1: Let's Get Started! An Introduction to Vitamins and Minerals

5

Many of the vitamers have coenzyme activities. While enzymes are proteins that perform, accelerate, or catalyze chemical reactions, coenzymes are nonprotein molecules that assist the enzymes in their reactions, and many coenzymes are vitamins. Binding of a coenzyme vitamer to its enzyme converts the empty enzyme (or apoenzyme) into a "whole enzyme" (or holoenzyme). In their coenzyme roles, vitamers can serve many different functions (see Table 1.3). For example, TPP forms a substrate-binding pocket for enzymes such as pyruvate dehydrogenase, where it interacts with pyruvate leading to acetyl formation for downstream reactions. The pyruvate dehydrogenase enzyme is part of a larger complex called the pyruvate dehydrogenase complex, which also contains niacin, in the form NAD/NADH, and riboflavin in the form FAD/FADH (Figure 1.3). Both NAD and FAD are PDH complex coenzymes, acting in a cosubstrate role. This is differentiated from a simple structural coenzyme like TPP, in that NAD and FAD are involved in oxidation-reduction reactions involving the transfer of electrons, changing these cosubstrates to NADH and FADH. In addition to structural coenzyme, and co-enzyme/cosubstrate roles for vitamers, those vitamers that act in gene regulation are referred to as co-regulators. An example of this type is vitamin A (retinoic acid vitamer) which must bind to the retinoic acid receptor in order for the receptor to have the ability to actively direct gene expression.

FIGURE 1.3:
Bioactive vitamers in the pyruvate dehydrogenase complex. The PDH complex is composed of three different enzymes, each with its own set of vitamer requirements. TPP acts as a substrate binding co-enzyme for the E1 subunit. CoA acts as a co-substrate acyl acceptor in E2 subunit, while both FAD and NAD act in co-substrate electron transfer reactions for E3.

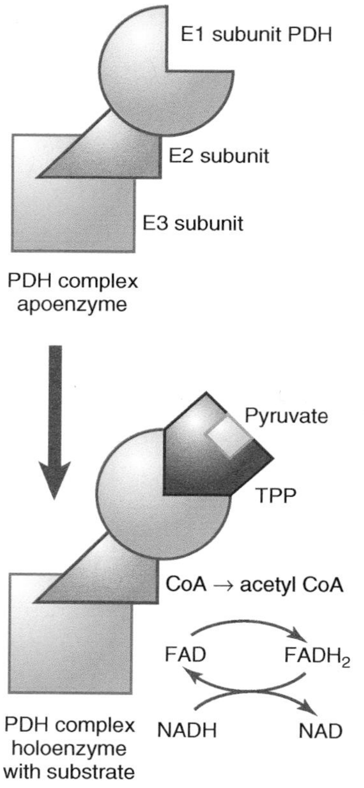

E1 subunit PDH

E2 subunit

E3 subunit

PDH complex apoenzyme

Pyruvate

TPP

CoA → acetyl CoA

FAD   FADH$_2$

PDH complex holoenzyme with substrate

NADH   NAD

To summarize this introduction to vitamins… humans currently require 13 water-soluble and fat-soluble vitamins to be included in their diet, even in cases like vitamin D and niacin, where we can make a little of these ourselves, or in cases like vitamin K where the bugs in our gut make some of the vitamin for us to use. Vitamins are essential to the normal functioning of our bodies because of their roles as co-enzymes for many enzymatic reactions, and in free-radical neutralization. Before we leave our intro to vitamins section, consider this…thousands of enzymatic reactions are going on in our bodies right now… did you get enough of your vitamins today?

YOU MEAN TO SAY WE ARE MINERALIZED?

Well, the truth is that minerals only make up about 4% of our total body weight, but their importance to human health cannot be understated. Calcium alone constitutes up to 2% of our body

© Kendall Hunt Publishing

weight, mainly from the skeleton, but did you know that calcium is also an important signaling molecule in all of the cells our body? Without calcium, fertilization could not take place because the waves of calcium flux activate pathways leading to formation of the zona pellucida (the "shell" around a fertilized egg which prevents more sperm from getting in after the first one has), as well as the initial events in cell division.

The list of 16 nutritional minerals (see Table 1.1), also known as "dietary elements," includes ones that you probably heard about, such as calcium, sodium, and fluoride, and perhaps some that you didn't know were needed in our bodies, such as zinc, copper, molybdenum, and chromium. These elements are the same ones found on the periodic table of the elements that you should have learned about in elementary school (at least my daughter did)—yes, individual atoms with electrons buzzing around their nucleus containing protons and neutrons (Figure 1.4). In some cases, such as fluorine, which is a noble gas, and not stable as a nutritional element, electrons are stolen (resulting in F⁻, fluoride), or in the case of iron, donated (resulting in Fe^{+2}, ferrous iron).

As shown in Table 1.1, the nutritional minerals can be further divided into three categories—macrominerals, trace minerals, and ultratrace minerals—and these categories are defined by the amounts needed by our bodies' daily. Minerals come from rocks—and are part of the mineral ecology that biologists refer to as biogeochemical processes. We can get all of the minerals that

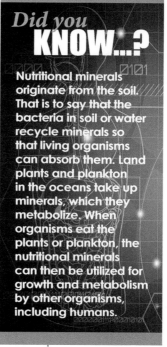

Did you KNOW...?

Nutritional minerals originate from the soil. That is to say that the bacteria in soil or water recycle minerals so that living organisms can absorb them. Land plants and plankton in the oceans take up minerals, which they metabolize. When organisms eat the plants or plankton, the nutritional minerals can then be utilized for growth and metabolism by other organisms, including humans.

H																	He
Li	Be											B	C	N	O	F	Ne
Na	Mg											Al	Si	P	S	Cl	Ar
K	Ca	Sc	Ti	V	Cr	Mn	Fe	Co	Ni	Cu	Zn	Ga	Ge	As	Se	Br	Kr
Rb	Sr	Y	Zr	Nb	Mo	Tc	Ru	Rh	Pd	Ag	Cd	In	Sn	Sb	Te	I	Xe
Cs	Ba	* Lu	Hf	Ta	W	Re	Os	Ir	Pt	Au	Hg	Tl	Pb	Bi	Po	At	Rn
Fr	Ra	** Lr	Rf	Db	Sg	Bh	Hs	Mt	Ds	Rg	Cn	Uut	Fl	Uup	Lv	Uus	Uuo

	*	La	Ce	Pr	Nd	Pm	Sm	Eu	Gd	Tb	Dy	Ho	Er	Tm	Yb
	**	Ac	Th	Pa	U	Np	Pu	Am	Cm	Bk	Cf	Es	Fm	Md	No

The four organic basic elements   Macrominerals   Essential trace elements
Possible structural or functional role in mammals

FIGURE 1.4:
Dietary elements...i.e. nutritional minerals. Shown here, some of the most prevalent minerals in our bodies, as elements from the periodic table with their elemental numbers (upper left corner) and molecular weights (center). From top left, fluorine (used by our body in the form fluoride, which has an extra electron and a negative charge), sodium, magnesium, calcium, iron and zinc.

© Kendall Hunt Publishing

we need for metabolism from plants and seeds. Even minerals, such as calcium, which we usually associate with eating dairy products and bony fish, can be obtained in sufficient amounts with a good diet of leafy green vegetables, nuts, seeds, and soybeans. So, you don't have to eat dirt to get your nutritional minerals, but just make sure you eat plenty of things that grow in dirt!

Mineral forms and functions

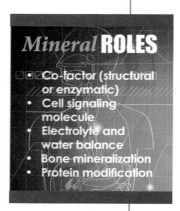

Mineral ROLES

- Co-factor (structural or enzymatic)
- Cell signaling molecule
- Electrolyte and water balance
- Bone mineralization
- Protein modification

Just like the vitamins and their vitamers, minerals come in different forms and perform different functions (Table 1.4). For example, many minerals are necessary to constrain the structure of proteins in a certain conformation. These minerals use their positive or negative charges to hold on to amino acid side chains within a protein, bringing together portions of the protein that might otherwise be very far apart on the amino acid chain. As you can see in Figure 1.5A, one good example of this Zn working as a structural bridge between different parts of the amino acid chain of a zinc-finger transcription factor [9]. By interacting with four cysteine amino acids, zinc squeezes together a loop or "finger" which can then contact the DNA helix and interact with nucleotides, directing mRNA expression of the target genes. Without Zn, the fingers would be floppy and the transcription factor inactive.

TABLE 1.4: Minerals—forms and functions

Mineral	Common Bioavailable Form	Function
Calcium	Ca^{+2} (fluids) Hydroxyapatite (bones)	Cell signaling, bone mineralization
Chloride	Water soluble ion (Cl^-)	Water and electrolyte balance
Chromium	Cr^{+3}	Controversial-involved in glucose/insulin metabolism
Cobalt	Bound to Vitamin B12	Structural vitamin co-factor
Copper	Cupric (Cu^{+2}), Cuprous (Cu^+)	Structural or Enzyme co-factor
Fluorine	Fluoride (F^-)	Bone and teeth mineralization
Iodine	Iodide (I^-)	Structural component of thyroid hormone
Iron	Ferric (Fe^{+3}), Ferrous (Fe^{+2})	Structural or Enzyme co-factor
Magnesium	Mg^{+2}	Structural or Enzyme co-factor
Manganese	Mn	Enzyme co-factor
Molybdenum	Complexed with molybdepterin	Enzyme Co-factor
Phosphorus	H_2PO_4 (fluids) Hydroxyapatite (bones)	ATP, protein modification (co-factor), bone mineralization
Potassium	Water soluble ion (K^+)	Water and electrolyte balance, nerve transmission
Selenium	Selenocysteine and selenomethionine	Enzyme co-factor
Sodium	Water soluble ion (Na^+)	Water and electrolyte balance
Zinc	Zn^{+2} (bound to albumin or transferrin in circulation)	Protein structural co-factor

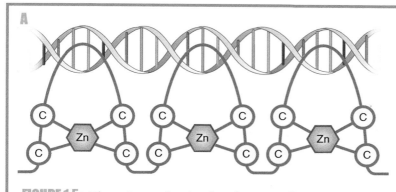

FIGURE 1.5: **Minerals are structural and enzymatic co-factors.**
A. Zinc is a structural component of zinc-finger transcription factors. Zn complexes with four cysteine amino acids, allowing a finger-like extension to be formed in the protein. This so-called "zinc finger" contacts the DNA double helix, allowing the zinc finger transcription factor to wrap around the DNA, and then direct gene expression. **B.** Cytochrome oxidase C uses zinc (Zn) and magnesium (Mg) as structural cofactors, and copper (Cu) and iron (Fe) as enzymatic cofactors. Electrons move through the enzyme complex, from cytochrome c to copper, to heme (with iron), and then back to a second copper ion. H+ ions move in the opposite direction, forming a proton gradient.

© Kendall Hunt Publishing

Other minerals perform enzymatic functions as cofactors in enzymes. A good example of this is copper in the cytochrome oxidase. Two copper ions, in the form Cu^+, are bound within cytochrome c oxidase by three histidine amino acids each, and work to transfer electrons from copper to a heme molecule containing iron, and then back to the second copper ion (hence, the "electron transport chain") [10]. In cytochrome c oxidase, zinc and magnesium are structural co-factors, while copper and iron are enzymatic co-factors (Figure 1.5B). Dietary deficiency of any of the nutritional metals disrupts the cytochrome c oxidase complex, and disrupts the electron transport chain, causing energy deficiencies in the organism.

Summing up the rocks in our bods…we require 16 nutritional minerals (also called dietary elements) to be supplied in our diverse diets of meats, dairy products, fruits, vegetables, seeds, grains, and nuts. Minerals can be categorized into macrominerals, which we need the most of, trace minerals, which we need a little of, and ultratrace minerals, which we need minute amounts of. Regardless of the category, minerals play important structural and cofactor enzymatic roles in our body processes. Without minerals, we would essentially be a bag of nonfunctional goo, as we would lack a skeletal, cell signaling, enzymatic activity, and water balance (all of which we will learn about in later chapters).

CHAPTER 1: Let's Get Started! An Introduction to Vitamins and Minerals

9

HOW MUCH OF THESE VITAMINS AND MINERALS DO WE ACTUALLY NEED?

I hope by now you agree that vitamins and minerals are absolutely necessary for the functioning of all processes in our body. But how much do we need? And who figures this sort of thing out? The quick answer to this question is that government committees, along with private sector institutes, make recommendations and mandate laws based on specific scientific criteria regarding what, when, and how much you should eat. The Institute of Medicine (IOM), a private, nonprofit (and nongovernment) organization is responsible for scientifically evaluating and making informed decisions in the area of health and healthcare. In 1940, the IOM established the Food and Nutrition Board (FNB), which was charged with determining scientifically sound guidelines for good nutrition (it also has other duties food safety, and the food supply). A standing committee of the FNB serves to scientifically evaluate studies and establish the dietary reference intakes. The current Dietary Reference Intakes (DRIs) were originally introduced in 1994, replacing the more limited Recommended Daily Allowances (RDAs) from previous years. IOM reports were issued for 1997–2004 (total of six reports) to establish the DRIs for the vitamins, minerals and macronutrients and water, and then most recently, were updated in 2011 for calcium and vitamin D [8, 11]. For the micronutrients, the DRIs provide reference values for the estimated average requirement (EAR), the RDA, adequate intake (AI), and Tolerable Upper Intake Level (UL) (Figure 1.6) (IOM, 2006). These values allow clinicians, dieticians, and other health professionals to make informed decisions about dietary intake in various groups of people. The bottom line is that intake of micronutrients is different for different ages, genders, and even for those with different health conditions.

Take a look at the DRI values for micronutrients, which can be found at the Institute of Medicine website (www.iom.edu). Are these numbers helpful to you in determining what foods to choose for a healthy diet? Probably not…which is why the government stepped in. Of course the government had to get involved in some way! Since 1977, arms of the government, including the United States Department of Agriculture (USDA), the United States Department of Health and Human Services (HHS), and the Food and Drug Administration (FDA) have developed guidelines that help consumers follow nutritional guidelines. The Current Guidelines for Americans: 2015-2020, published jointly by the USDA and HHS is in its eight edition online and available at https://health.gov/dietaryguidelines/2015/ [12]. The USDA also developed a visual guide for healthy eating—MyPlate (www.ChooseMyPlate.gov), and the FDA mandates nutrition labeling guidelines for food products.

Dietary Reference Intakes

A.
- **Recommended Dietary Allowance (RDA)** is the average daily dietary intake of a nutrient that is sufficient to meet the requirement of nearly all (97–98%) healthy persons.
- **Adequate Intake (AI)** for a nutrient is established when available data are insufficient to set an RDA but are sufficient to estimate an intake that would maintain nutritional adequacy in most people. The AI is based on observed intakes of the nutrient by a group of healthy persons.
- **Tolerable Upper Intake Level (UL)** is the highest daily intake of a nutrient that is likely to pose no risks of adverse health affects (toxicity) for almost all individuals. As intake above the UL increases, risk increases.
- **Estimated Average Requirement (EAR)** is the amount of a nutrient that is estimated to meet the requirement of half of all healthy individuals in the population.

B.

FIGURE 1.6:
A visual, adapted from The Food and Nutrition Board's "Dietary Reference intakes for Energy, Carbohydrates, Fiber, Fat, Fatty Acids, Cholesterol, Protein and Amino Acids. This figure shows the relationships between the dietary reference intakes. Source: *Dietary Reference Intakes for Energy, Carbohydrate, Fiber, Fat, Fatty Acids, Cholesterol, Protein, and Amino Acids*, pp. 3, 23. Food and Nutrition Board, Institute of Medicine of the National Academies. The National Academies Press: 2002/2005.

© Kendall Hunt Publishing

How are these guidelines established?

The various government and non-government entities use committees composed of scientific experts to review all available published information, scientifically and hopefully in an unbiased fashion, then weigh all of the information and make recommendations. For the newest guidelines on vitamin D and calcium [8], as an example, there were four major steps for the process. First, the committee used systematic evidence-based reviews to pull together data from various published reports, used expert opinions, and made scientific conclusions on the roles (requirements for) of vitamin D and calcium in skeletal health. Next the committee asked what the dose-response values were for intake—in other words, how did low, medium, and high intakes affect skeletal health? Third, the committee evaluated the current intake data for Americans to determine the current dietary levels being obtained, and finally compared the dietary levels, to determine the prevalence of inadequate intake in the population, as well as the health implications. As you might imagine, this process takes a long time, and for the 2011 DRI for vitamin D and calcium, the process took two years. The *Dietary Guidelines for Americans*, on the other hand, is reviewed and revised every five years by the USDA and HHS. They basically start the new set of reviews as soon as they finish the previous ones.

Fun FACT

Nutrition labels use percentages of macro- and micronutrients based on a 2000-calorie diet. Of the micronutrients, only vitamins A and C, and the minerals calcium and iron are required listings, mandated by the Food and Drug Administration. Sometimes other micronutrients are included—especially if a company is trying to show increased levels of B vitamins, for example. Check out a nutrition label near you!

CHAPTER 1: Let's Get Started! An Introduction to Vitamins and Minerals

11

So, next time you sit down for a meal, consider all that goes into defining a healthy diet and ask yourself—are you getting your recommended intakes?

Multivitamin and mineral supplement use in the United States

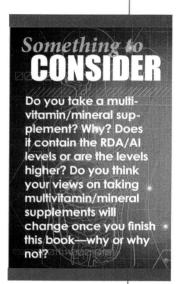

Something to **CONSIDER**

Do you take a multi-vitamin/mineral supplement? Why? Does it contain the RDA/AI levels or are the levels higher? Do you think your views on taking multivitamin/mineral supplements will change once you finish this book—why or why not?

According to a CDC brief, based on the National Health and Nutrition Examination Survey III (NHANES III), up to 39% of individuals without known nutritional deficiencies take a multivitamin and mineral supplement daily, and this percentage has increased since the previous survey period, which occurred between 1988 and 1994 [13]. Daily multivitamin and mineral supplements are usually formulated to provide the RDA or AI (when an RDA is not available) for some combination of vitamins and minerals. According to the federal government's current *Dietary Guidelines for Americans, 2010* (website reference), Americans should get their nutrients from foods, and this recommendation did not change with the new 2015 guidelines. Why? Because recent papers in the scientific literature have failed to support multivitamin/mineral supplement use as a preventative in otherwise healthy people. For example, a December 2013 study, and an editorial response to this study, also published in December 2013 concluded that we should "Stop Wasting Money on Vitamin and Mineral Supplements" with the statement "The case is closed—supplementing the diet of well-nourished adults with (most) mineral or vitamin supplements has no clear benefit and might even be harmful" [14, 15]. The study by Fortmann and colleagues went as far as to show that in some cases, supplements were not only ineffective, but for those containing beta-carotene, could actually increase lung cancer incidence, providing a true negative for taking that type of supplement if you are at risk [14]. In response to the article, some scientists and clinicians called for more data and more controlled studies in which the actual circulating levels and dietary intakes for micronutrients would be considered, and scientifically measured, in addition to having control (placebo) and test (long-term use) groups taking supplements. As you might imagine, these types of studies would require large numbers of individuals who would have to comply with taking a pill every day for multiple years—at a large cost to the government or whomever funds that research—so it is not clear that these types of well-controlled, long-term studies will be conducted.

In the meantime, what is the dietary status of Americans, in terms of micronutrient intake? Is there a nutritional deficiency epidemic? One might have to say yes here… even though there are the *Dietary Guidelines for Americans:2015–2020* and many public service announcements about MyPlate [16] and healthy eating campaigns, according to an assessment of NHANES data from 2001–2008, most adults appear NOT to be getting the recommended levels of vitamins A, D, and E, and minerals calcium, potassium, and magnesium from diet alone [17]. Those individuals included in the study who were taking multivitamin/mineral supplements improved their total micronutrient intakes such that fewer were now in the deficient range [17]. In other words, for those individuals not getting sufficient amounts of a single vitamin or mineral by diet alone, it may be prudent to target intake to the deficient micronutrient, rather than just take a single multivitamin/mineral supplement which could risk oversupplementation of those micronutrients where the individual has sufficient intake. To do this, consumers must make a conscience effort to track dietary intake and use nutritional calculators (available now in the form of smartphone apps and online web programs) to determine what micronutrients they are not getting enough of.

CHAPTER SUMMARY

There are 13 nutritionally-essential vitamins and 16 minerals for humans with specific needs for different genders, ages, and health issues.

- Vitamers function as parts of proteins in co-enzyme, co-regulatory, and co-substrate roles, and as water and fat-soluble antioxidants.
- Minerals are categorized as major (six of these), trace (four of these), and ultratrace (six of these).
- Minerals function as structural or enzymatic cofactors for proteins, as cell-signaling molecules. They are also used in electrolyte and water balance, bone mineralization, and protein modifications.
- The Institute for Medicine's Food and Nutrition Board, the U.S. Department of Agriculture, the U.S. Department of Health and Human Services, and the U.S. Food and Drug Administration all work to define and promote dietary guides for vitamins and minerals.

POINTS TO PONDER

- In the future, with highly personalized medicine, do you think dietary guidelines will be tailored individually, rather than by groups such as age and gender? What are the implications for that from a policy standpoint?
- Are there likely to be newly identified required vitamins or minerals?
- Could a person be eating a well-balanced diet, according to MyPlate and other guidelines, and still not get enough of certain micronutrients?
- Do you think more or fewer people should be taking vitamin or mineral supplements? Why?

CHAPTER 1: Let's Get Started! An Introduction to Vitamins and Minerals

13

References

1. Nishikimi, M., and K. Yagi. (1991). Molecular basis for the deficiency in humans of gulonolactone oxidase, a key enzyme for ascorbic acid biosynthesis. *Am J Clin Nutr* **54**(6 Suppl): 1203S–1208S.

2. Grasbeck, R. (2013). Hooked to vitamin B12 since 1955: A historical perspective. *Biochimie* **95**(5): 970–975.

3. Institute of Medicine. Standing Committee on the Scientific Evaluation of Dietary Reference Intakes; Panel on Folate, Other B Vitamins and Choline; Subcommittee on Upper Reference Levels of Nutrients. (1998). *Dietary reference intakes for thiamin, riboflavin, niacin, vitamin B_6, folate, vitamin B_{12}, pantothenic acid, biotin, and choline.* Washington, D.C.: National Academy Press, pp. xxii, 564.

4. Institute of Medicine. Panel on Dietary Antioxidants and Related Compounds. (2000). *Dietary reference intakes for vitamin C, vitamin E, selenium, and carotenoids: A report of the Panel on Dietary Antioxidants and Related Compounds, Subcommittees on Upper Reference Levels of Nutrients and of Interpretation and Use of Dietary Reference Intakes, and the Standing Committee on the Scientific Evaluation of Dietary Reference Intakes, Food and Nutrition Board, Institute of Medicine.* Washington, D.C.: National Academy Press, pp. xx, 506.

5. World Health Organization. (2011). *Guideline: Neonatal vitamin A supplementation.* Geneva, Switzerland: WHO.

6. Haider, B.A., and Z.A. Bhutta. (2014). Neonatal vitamin A supplementation: Time to move on. *Lancet.*

7. Institute of Medicine. Panel on Micronutrients. (2001). *DRI: Dietary reference intakes for vitamin A, vitamin K, arsenic, boron, chromium, copper, iodine, iron, manganese, molybdenum, nickel, silicon, vanadium, and zinc: A report of the Panel on Micronutrients ... and the Standing Committee on the Scientific Evaluation of Dietary Reference Intakes, Food and Nutrition Board, Institute of Medicine.* Washington, D.C.: National Academy Press, pp. xxii, 773.

8. Institute of Medicine. (2011). *Dietary reference intakes for calcium and vitamin D.* Washington, D.C.: National Academy Press.

9. Evans, R.M., and S.M. Hollenberg. (1988). Zinc fingers: Gilt by association. *Cell* **52**(1): 1–3.

10. Wikstrom, M. (1989). Identification of the electron transfers in cytochrome oxidase that are coupled to proton-pumping. *Nature* **338**(6218): 776–778.

11. Institute of Medicine. (2006). *Dietary reference intakes: The essential guide to nutrient requirements.* Washington, D.C.: National Academy Press.

12. *Dietary Guidelines for Americans, 2015–2020 (ePub)* Health and Human Services Dept. and Agriculture Dept., ISBN: 9780160934650 Available at : https://bookstore.gpo.gov/products/sku/017-300-00039-3

13. Gahche, J., et al. (2011). Dietary supplement use among U.S. adults has increased since NHANES III (1988-1994). *NCHS Data Brief* (61): 1–8.

14. Fortmann, S.P., et al. (2013). Vitamin and mineral supplements in the primary prevention of cardiovascular disease and cancer: An updated systematic evidence review for the U.S. Preventive Services Task Force. *Ann Intern Med* **159**(12): 824–834.

15. Guallar, E., et al. (2013). Enough is enough: Stop wasting money on vitamin and mineral supplements. *Ann Intern Med* **159**(12): 850–851.

16. *MyPlate.* Online March 12, 2015. www.choosemyplate.gov/

17. Agarwal, S., et al. (2015). Comparison of prevalence of inadequate nutrient intake based on body weight status of adults in the United States: An analysis of NHANES 2001-2008. *J Am Coll Nutr*: 1–9.

crossword

Active Vitamers

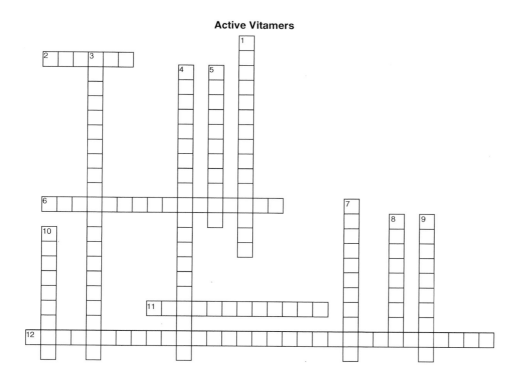

Instructions: Use the broad name of the vitamin to find the specific vitamers for each which fits into the crossword puzzle

ACROSS		ANSWER
2	B7	
6	B9	
11	Vitamin A	
12	B3	
DOWN		
1	B5	
3	B1	
4	B2	
5	Vitamin E	
7	Vitamin K	
8	B6	
9	Vitamin D	
10	B12	

CHAPTER 1: Let's Get Started! An Introduction to Vitamins and Minerals

15

NOTES

_____
_____
_____
_____
_____
_____
_____
_____
_____
_____
_____
_____
_____
_____
_____
_____
_____
_____
_____
_____
_____
_____
_____
_____
_____
_____
_____
_____

CHAPTER 2

The History of Vitamins and Minerals
200+ Years in the Making

Discovery is seeing what everybody else has seen, and thinking what nobody else has thought.
—*Albert Szent-Gyorgyi* [2]

Table of Contents

Did you KNOW...?

While cod liver oil and animal liver are traditional sources of vitamin A (just 3 oz of beef liver can provide about 440% of your daily value or DV of vitamin A), leafy or orange vegetables can also serve as vitamin A sources as these are rich in beta carotene, which can be converted to retinol. These include carrots (1 medium carrot can provide up to 200% of your vitamin A needs for the day), sweet potatoes (1 medium = ~560% DV), and even spinach (1/2 cup cooked spinach gives ~220% DV) [1].

While you are most certainly itching to get into the nitty-gritty of vitamin and mineral actions in your body's organs, it's important to know the history of an issue before embarking on a new journey. So, when did we first know there were nutritional micronutrients that we needed to get from our diet? The answer to this question depends on your interpretation of the question…when did we know that food has nutrients? When was the first nutritional vitamin or mineral identified? When was the term *vitamin* first used? These questions will be answered as we go through this chapter. The timeline is messy and in some cases filled with discrepancies in time/place/people—like most of history, in my opinion, the accuracy is only as good as the original recorder of the material. But the plan is to present the known facts, figures, and events in a logical order (Figure 2.1), to bring us up to present day and acknowledge the contributions of men, women, and animals in our current knowledge of vitamins and minerals.

THE EARLY DAYS OF NUTRITION RESEARCH

There is no doubt that early humans understood the importance of a good diet. Many individuals studying the importance of food attribute the quote "Let Food Be Thy Medicine and Medicine Be Thy Food" to Hippocrates, the Father of Medicine. However, while the attribution to Hippocrates is probably incorrect [4], the quote itself rings true in suggesting that a proper diet can cure illness. This knowledge has likely been practiced since ancient times, and even Hippocrates and his followers used diet to treat or relieve symptoms of disease [4]. For example, the Egyptians, in 1300 BC, well before Hippocrates, who was born ~460 BC, knew that eating liver could cure a person of night blindness [5]. We now know that liver is an excellent source of vitamin A, as it is a storage site for this fat-soluble vitamin, and while liver may not be your favorite dietary source for vitamin A, I think all of us would rather eat a little liver than have night blindness!

Scurvy—the bain of the British Navy

The need for certain fruits, vegetables, meats, and grains—in other words, a balanced and varied diet—has been evident throughout history, with many of the vitamin and mineral deficiencies showing themselves in the poorer populations. However, the diseases were thought to be caused by infection, or "bad humors," and oftentimes individuals had both poor hygiene and poor nutrition. As we move up in our timeline (see Figure 2.1) and long sea voyages become more commonplace, scurvy—also called scuvie, skyrvie, scorbie, and *Purpura nautica*, to distinguish the "sea" version of the disease, also flourished. Scuvy, caused by a deficiency in vitamin C, had actually been recognized since the time of the Cruisades, especially the Fifth Cruisade, when even wealthy participants died or came down with diseases in great numbers—night blindness and scurvy prevalent among them [6]. Fresh fruits and vegetables are packed with vitamin C and it can take up to 6 months for a deficiency in vitamin C to manifest itself as scurvy—which is why scurvy was so prevelant on

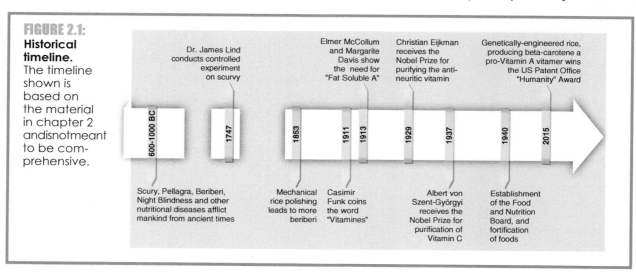

FIGURE 2.1:
Historical timeline. The timeline shown is based on the material in chapter 2 andisnotmeant to be comprehensive.

600-1000 BC — Scury, Pellagra, Beriberi, Night Blindness and other nutritional diseases afflict mankind from ancient times

1747 — Dr. James Lind conducts controlled experiment on scurvy

1853 — Mechanical rice polishing leads to more beriberi

1911 — Casimir Funk coins the word "Vitamines"

1913 — Elmer McCollum and Margarite Davis show the need for "Fat Soluble A"

1929 — Christian Eijkman receives the Nobel Prize for purifying the anti-neuritic vitamin

1937 — Albert von Szent-Györgyi receives the Nobel Prize for purification of Vitamin C

1940 — Establishment of the Food and Nutrition Board, and fortification of foods

2015 — Genetically-engineered rice, producing beta-carotene a pro-Vitamin A vitamer wins the US Patent Office "Humanity" Award

© Kendall Hunt Publishing

long journeys by land and by sea. Vasco da Gama's famous trip around the horn of Africa was marred by scurvy, but some of his sailors recovered, at least briefly when eating citrus fruits during brief landfalls [7]. However, providing citrus fruits on long voyages did not become prevalent in the 15th through 18th centuries, due to problems of storage and fruit sources, so the scourge of scurvy continued.

The turning point in the battle on scurvy, and what is now considered the first controlled clinical research trial, came in 1747, when Dr. James Lind, a British Naval surgeon, was posted to the HMS *Salibury* under the command of Admiral Geroge Edgecumbe [7]. Lind felt that tests for possible remedies for scurvy needed to be conducted and is quoted as saying, "I shall propose nothing dictated from theory, but shall confirm all by experience and facts, the surest and most unerring guides." Lind selected 12 men with advanced scurvy (obviously a low "N" for any experiment!), and divided them into six groups of two: Group 1—cider, Group 2—sulphuric acid in water, Group 3—vinegar before each meal, as a gargle, Group 4—sea water, Group 5—two oranges and one lemon per day, and Group 6—a mixture of nutmeg, garlic, horseradish, and mustard seed. While one could say those getting the sea water were the controls, Lind actually had a control group of men receiving nothing additional, but for some reason did not include these in this paper on the finidngs [7]. Given that there were only a small group of participants, statistics were not run, but the results were still quite conclusive, with only Group 5 showing a complete cure in 6 days. Interestingly, Lind did not publish his findings until 1753 [7]. However, the British Navy did not immediately institute the use of citrus fruits on long voyages, and scurvy continued to be a problem aboard vessels until, in 1794, Sir Dr. Gilbert Blane conducted a long-term trial of lemon juice with sailors on the HMS *Suffolk* [7]. Sailors on board got a daily ration of 2/3 oz of lemon juice, which it turns out gave the daily level of ~10 mg vitamin C; and no cases of scurvy were found on the 6-month journey. After that, the British Navy continued to include citrus fruits or juice on long journeys.

THE DISCOVERY OF VITAMINS

Fastforward about 100 years, and the opening of Japan to outsiders. Also happening around that time, mechanized rice milling machines became available, meaning that the Japanese could eat more refined white rice, rather than the hand milled rice, which left some of the husk. European doctors entering Japan after this time found that many Japanese were suffering from a malady called kakke, which included numbness, difficultly breathing, heart failure, and death [7]. Kakke was recongized to be similar to another condition called beriberi, which was prevelent in the Dutch East Indies (now Indonesia). It was thought by scientists at the time that this disease was caused by a microorganism. In the late 19th and early 20th centuries, scientists were experimenting with possible disease-causing microorganisms, as Robert Koch, who was awarded the Nobel Prize in 1905, showed in 1876 that anthrax and Micobacteria tuberculosis could cause disease [8]. Along

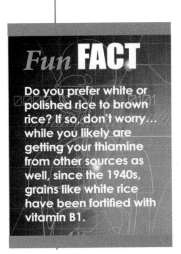

Fun **FACT**

Do you prefer white or polished rice to brown rice? If so, don't worry... while you likely are getting your thiamine from other sources as well, since the 1940s, grains like white rice have been fortified with vitamin B1.

Fun FACT

McCollum and Davis worked at the University of Wisconsin. McCollum started working with rats because he used to catch them on his farm in Kansas, and found that rats were cheap, easy to house, and experiments could be done more quickly than with farm animals, which were the animal model of choice for nutrition experiments. The Dean at the University of Wisconsin opposed this work, and so his initial experiments were done using "secret rat colonies." He then convinced the Dean to allow him to purchase albino rats for nutritional research. McCollum and Davis are credited with setting up the first research rat colonies [3].

came Christiaan Eijkman who was mentored by Dr. Koch, and at age 30 was named director of the Research Laboratory for Pathology and Bacteriology in Indonesia/Dutch East Indies. Eijkman was also convinced that beriberi was caused by an infectious microorganism, and began working with chickens as an experimental model for the disease. However, no matter what type of agent—bacterial cultures or blood from infected patients—Eijkman tried to inject into the chickens, the injected birds were showing no signs of illness. While this seems to have been leading nowhere, Eijkman didn't give up and ordered a new batch of chickens for experimentation, dividing the animals into control and experimental groups. Surprisingly, some of the control birds started getting a disease called polyneuritis, which resulted in paralysis of the legs similar to the paralysis seen in beriberi. Even when the sick birds were kept away from the healthy ones, birds were continuing to get sick, with even the experimental animals then showing signs of the so-called infection. As elegantly put by Kenneth Carpenter in his article on the discovery of thiamine, "This, I think, is where Eijkman showed his brilliance" [9]. Instead of giving up or being frustrated, Eijkman systematically tried to uncover what was wrong with the chickens, questioning everything about their living conditions, including their diet. He found that around the same time that the control chickens started coming down with polyneuritis, the cook had switched their diet to leftover polished rice, which was missing the hull, and therefore the thiamine. While many historical accounts of this story state that Eijkman still felt that beriberi likely had an infectious cause [7, 9], he continued to systematically test milled or polished versus unmilled rice and found that the animals fed unmilled rice were "cured" or did not develop the disease. To make a longer story short, Eijkman received the Nobel Prize for this work on the "discovery of the antineuritic vitamin" in 1929 [8].

Eikman shared his Nobel prize with another scientist, Sir Frederick Hopkins, who also used animals to study nutrition [8]. He showed that rats cannot thrive on artificial diets containing only protein, carbohydrates, fats, and some minerals, but needed "essential accessory factors" that could be found in cow milk [7]. While he never physically identified this accessory factor in cow milk, it was likely either vitamin A, D, or E. Vitamin A was discovered and purified as an ether extract by Elmer Verner McCollum and his assistant, Marguerite Davis, in 1913 using cow milk as the source. In most accounts they are credited with identifying "fat-soluble factor A" as a growth-promoting nutrient found in cow milk, butter, and eggs [3, 10]. There is little information on what Davis did after this period, but McCollum went on to discover that cow milk also contained a substance that prevented rickets (vitamin D), and that fluoride could prevent tooth decay. McCollum was prolific in his micronutrient studies on thiamine, vitamin C, riboflavin, magnesium, sodium, and potassium (examples [3, 10-17]). He is also credited with proposing that micronutrients be given letter designations by the solubility of the factor—that is, fat-soluble A and water-soluble B [11]; however, his discoveries were clouded by the fact that he never fully purified vitamin A alone, and butter, milk, and eggs actually contain

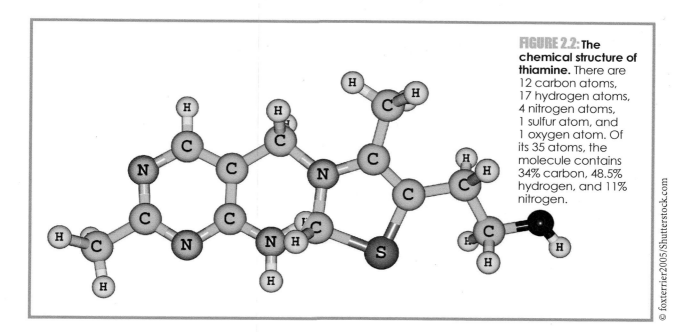

© foxterrier2005/Shutterstock.com

FIGURE 2.2: **The chemical structure of thiamine.** There are 12 carbon atoms, 17 hydrogen atoms, 4 nitrogen atoms, 1 sulfur atom, and 1 oxygen atom. Of its 35 atoms, the molecule contains 34% carbon, 48.5% hydrogen, and 11% nitrogen.

three vitamins (A, D, E), which could have contributed to the findings in his study [18]—a fact that likely led to his failure to receive a Nobel Prize for this work.

What's in a name?

Did you ever wonder how the term *vitamin* came about? Casimir Funk, a Polish-born biochemist coined the word *vitamine* in 1911, as a combination of the Latin *vita* for "life" and *amine*—the chemical name for a nitrogen-containing compound [19]. The original term, *vitamine* was controversial, and especially not accepted by Elmer McCollum as he did not like the use of a word that did not describe all of the micronutrients—remember McCollum had been working on "fat-soluble A" around that time. In Funk's first paper on the subject, showing the purification of what would later be called vitamin B1 or thiamine, he was not allowed to even use the word *vitamine* in the title of the paper, which read "On the chemical nature of the substance which cures polyneuritis in birds induced by a diet of polished rice" [20]. In this publication, Funk writes, "Reasons for provisionally regarding the active substance as a body giving a crystalline nitrate which has the percentage composition of 55-63% C, 5-29 % H and 7-68 % N…" [20]. We now know that the actual chemical structure of thiamine does contain amine groups, but that Funk's percentages of each of the elements in the molecule were a bit off (Figure 2.2). His book, *Die Vitamines* [21], was published in 1914 and is credited by some for instilling new interest into micronutrient research, leading to the discovery of 13 vitamins in the next 35 years, ending with the purification of B12 in 1948. The name *vitamin*, without the final *e*, was eventually accepted by the scientific community, and McCollum is even quoted as saying, "Funk's investigations created a new interest in studies of nutrition" [19]. Since 1928, six Nobel prizes have been awarded for the discovery, isolation, synthesis, and structure of vitamins (Table 2.1).

NAME	YEAR	TYPE	DESCRIPTION	VITAMIN
Adolf Otto Reinhold Windaus	1928	Chemistry	"for the services rendered through his research into the constitution of the sterols and their connection with the vitamins".	Vitamin D
Christiaan Eijkman and Sir Frederick Hopkins	1929	Physiology or Medicine	Divided equally between Christiaan Eijkman "for his discovery of the antineuritic vitamin" and Sir Frederick Gowland Hopkins "for his discovery of the growth-stimulating vitamins"	B1
Albert von Szent-Györgyi Nagyrapolt	1937	Physiology or Medicine	"for his discoveries in connection with the biological combustion processes, with special reference to vitamin C and the catalysis of fumaric acid".	Vitamin C
Walter Norman Haworth and Paul Karrer	1937	Chemistry	Divided equally between Walter Norman Haworth "for his investigations on carbohydrates and vitamin C" and Paul Karrer "for his investigations on carotenoids, flavins and vitamins A and B2".	Vitamins C, A, and B2
Richard Kuhn	1938	Chemistry	"for his work on carotenoids and vitamins".	Vitamin A
Henrik Carl Peter Dam and Edward Adelbert Doisy	1943	Physiology or Medicine	Divided equally between Henrik Carl Peter Dam "for his discovery of vitamin K" and Edward Adelbert Doisy "for his discovery of the chemical nature of vitamin K".	Vitamin K

THE NUTRITIONAL MINERALS

The need for certain minerals in our diets has been known for centuries. For example, the Chinese in ~3600 BC used ground-up seaweed to prevent goiter, and the early Romans understood the healing properties of their baths for "curing" symptoms such as pallor and weakness that we would now associate with iron deficiency anemia [22, 23]. Like vitamin research, much of the information on nutritional minerals starting coming into focus near the turn the 20th century. For iodine, these data came from the French scientist Adolphe Chatin who showed that goiter was associated with iodine deficiency [22], while for iron, Daniel Davies confirmed the association of iron deficiency with hypochromic anemia [23]. However, despite it being 100 to 130 years from these original publications, the incidence of goiter and iron deficiency anemia worldwide is still problematic [8].

Elmer McCollum again enters the picture, at the forefront of studies on nutritional minerals. He moved in 1917 from the University of Wisconsin to Johns Hopkins University, Baltimore, Maryland [11]. McCollum actually began work on phosphorus at Wisconsin, showing that hens needed orthophosphate added to their feed to produce eggs [24]. After a large grant from the Rockefeller Foundation in 1936, McCollum studied and published many papers on nutritional requirements for sodium, potassium, phosphorus, iron, zinc, magnesium, calcium, and boron, again using rats [24]. He also studied the effects of fluoride on both teeth and bones, and is credited with being one of the first to show that excess fluoride could be harmful to incisors, while also showing that deficient diets could have deleterious effects on both bones and teeth [24]. Fluoride is a somewhat controversial inorganic mineral, and one of particular personal interest.

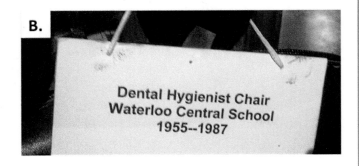

**Dental Hygienist Chair
Waterloo Central School
1955--1987**

FIGURE 2.3: **Dentist hygienist chair.** Pictures were taken by the author at the Waterloo Terwilliger Museum in Waterloo, New York (July 2014). **A.** The inscribed handle of the chair. **B.** The museum's description of the chair. This is the very chair that the author sat in for her weekly fluoride rinses.

Fluoride—my story

I grew up in a small farming community in Upstate New York and attended the public school system. We were on well water, which was nonfluoridated, and so I took an orange-flavored fluoride tablet almost every morning. My parents also took me to a dentist yearly. I also remember going often to my school's dental hygienist for rinses and checks of my teeth. Last year when I visited my parents back home, I took a picture of the dental hygienist's chair that I used to sit in (Figure 2.3). It turns out I might have been part of a larger study on using fluoride rinses in school programs [25]. I remember going weekly or perhaps every other week to the school's hygienist, and doing a rinse with a purple colored fluid. I would then spit the rinse back into the cup, wipe my mouth, and put the napkin in the cup for disposal. Sometimes, I would use chewable tablets that turned all of the plaque in my mouth blue, and I remember sitting in that chair to be examined by the hygienist during that time. It turns out that there were no real control groups—data for these studies were compared to historical data from the community, rather than having some students rinse and others not rinse, or use nonfluoride-containing rinses. New York State began its Supplemental Fluoride Program in 1978 [8], with some of the data being published showing a reduction in plaque, caries, and tooth extractions (for example [26]). While fluoridation programs remain controversial, I did not have a single cavity until well into adulthood, and for this I am thankful!

PUBLIC POLICY AND FORTIFIED FOOD

> *"He has done more than any other man to put vitamins back in the nation's bread and milk, to put fruit on American breakfast tables, fresh vegetables and salad greens in the daily diet."* [24]

The quote refers to Elmer McCollum, who in addition to his research studies on vitamins and minerals, was also strongly influential on public policies regarding

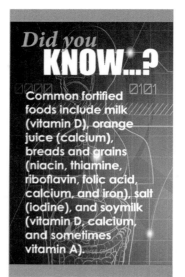

Did you KNOW...?

Common fortified foods include milk (vitamin D), orange juice (calcium), breads and grains (niacin, thiamine, riboflavin, folic acid, calcium, and iron), salt (iodine), and soymilk (vitamin D, calcium, and sometimes vitamin A).

fortification of foods and in ensuring proper nutrition for the public. Mc-Collum was originally part of the Food and Nutrition Board, in 1941, as they were considering legislation to add fortification of niacin, thiamine, riboflavin, calcium, and iron to bread and flour grains [24]. At that time, the United States was engaged in World War II, and some of the enlisted solders showed signs of improper nutrition, so this step was part of a government-sponsored program to increase micronutrient intake, originally proposed during a National Nutrition Conference for Defense, which was convened by President Roosevelt in May 1941 [27].

While many of our grains, milk, salt, and other foods have fortification or enrichment, did you know that enrichment never was, and still is not, mandatory? Enrichment refers to adding back vitamins or minerals, which may have been lost during processing, while fortification refers to adding in vitamins or minerals that were not necessarily there in the first place. The FDA establishes the standards for fortification/enrichment of grains and other foods, which corresponds to whether the food can be labeled "enriched" or not. However, back in 1942, the FDA made the decision that it would not require the enrichment of food—rather there are standards that specify whether a food can be labeled enriched/fortified, or not [27].

We've talked about adding in micronutrients after the food was grown and harvested, but what about the process of genetically engineering food? Genetically engineered foods contain an added gene to make a nutrient or other substance that

FIGURE 2.4:
Comparison of rice.
A. Rice husks, which are removed during the milling process. **B.** Brown rice is rice with just the husk removed. **C.** White rice is processed further, removing the bran and the germ, and with it, thiamine. **D.** Golden rice is genetically engineered to contain beta-carotene.

© nbriam/Shutterstock.com

© Stepan Popov/Shutterstock.com

© Sakarin Sawasdinaka/Shutterstock.com

© zcw/Shutterstock.com

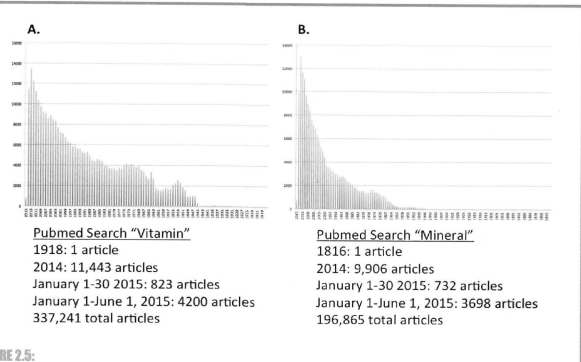

A.

Pubmed Search "Vitamin"
1918: 1 article
2014: 11,443 articles
January 1-30 2015: 823 articles
January 1-June 1, 2015: 4200 articles
337,241 total articles

B.

Pubmed Search "Mineral"
1816: 1 article
2014: 9,906 articles
January 1-30 2015: 732 articles
January 1-June 1, 2015: 3698 articles
196,865 total articles

FIGURE 2.5:
Vitamin and mineral research is going strong. Graph of total number of journal articles listed in PubMed (y-axis) for the terms "vitamin" **(A)** and "mineral **(B)**, with 2015 data from January 2015 on left-most side of x-axis, to 1918 (vitamin), and 1816 (mineral) on right-most side of x-axis.

wouldn't ordinarily be there. Today controversy surrounds genetically engineering rice to make beta-carotene—the so-called "golden rice" (Figure 2.4). Recall from Chapter 1 we discussed the fact that vitamin A is sometimes given in very large doses in countries where that deficiency is endemic. Well, one way that scientists thought to combat this problem is by supplementing the food with vitamin A—hence, golden rice. It turns out that rice plants normally can make beta-carotene, but do so in their leaves, not in the grain. Two genes were added to the plant (i.e., genetically engineered into the plant), resulting in beta-carotene to be produced in the rice grains [28]. In 2015, the golden rice project was one of seven patented projects to be awarded the United State Patent Office's "Patents for Humanity Awards" [8]. There are other ongoing projects that could easily be found in a PubMed database search, including engineering soybeans to produce more vitamin E [29], creating grains with higher folate content [30], and growing multivitamin-enriched corn containing vitamins C and B9 along with beta-carotene [31]. The debates on fortification of foods started over 75 years ago. A search of the terms "vitamin" and "mineral" in the NCBI PubMed database reveals hundreds of thousands of articles with these search terms, with the numbers of publications growing each year (Figure 2.5), so these debates will likely continue through our lifetimes and beyond.

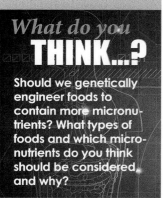

What do you
THINK...?
Should we genetically engineer foods to contain more micronutrients? What types of foods and which micronutrients do you think should be considered, and why?

CHAPTER SUMMARY

The need for nutrients from food has been known since antiquity, but the recognition and purification of nutritionally important vitamins and minerals is more recent—within the last 100 years or so.

- Christiaan Eijkman is credited with discovering thiamine, through his work on beriberi and chicken polyneuritis.
- Scurvy once led to more sailing deaths than war, but was cured in some of the first controlled clinical trials, conducted by James Lind.
- Elmer McCollum made many contributions to vitamin and mineral nutrition research, but was never awarded the Nobel Prize. He is credited with discovering fat-soluble A and with establishing the first rat colonies for nutrition research.
- Casimir Funk is credited with coining the term *vitamines*, which was later shortened to *vitamin*, to reflect the fact that not all vitamins are amines, like thiamine.
- Fortification of grains occurred in the 1940s as a result of the finding that many soldiers applying for active duty in World War II were unfit for service.
- The FDA oversees the regulations governing whether a food can be considered enriched or fortified.
- Golden rice and other genetically modified foods may be the 21st century's answer to vitamin and mineral deficiencies—or may be too controversial.

POINTS TO PONDER

- Do a search to find other scientists not mentioned in this chapter who contributed to our current knowledge of micronutrients. Where were they trained? What did they do? What is their legacy?
- Considering water fluoridation, do you think water should be fluoridated, or do children and adults already get enough fluoride from toothpaste and food sources (such as mechanically deboned chicken, boney seafood, and some cereals made with fluoridated water)?
- Many animals can make vitamin C, although humans cannot due to a single missing enzyme. Should we consider genetically engineering ourselves to replace that missing enzyme?

References

1. *USDA National Nutrient Database for Standard Reference, Release 24*, A.R.S. (2011). U.S. Department of Agriculture, Editor.
2. ASzent-Gyorgyi, A. Online May 21, 2015. www.brainyquote.com/quotes/authors/a/albert_szentgyorgyi.html - 5xy9VYfZtDk2Crr
3. Frankenburg, F.R. (2009). *Vitamin discoveries and disasters: History, science, and controversies*. Praeger Series on Contemporary Health and Living. Santa Barbara, Calif.: Praeger/ABC-CLIO, pp. xiii, 143.
4. Cardenas, D. (2013). Let not thy food be confused with thy medicine: The Hippocratic misquotation. *e-SPEN Journal* **8**(6): e260–e262.
5. Al Binali, H.A. (2014). Night blindness and ancient remedy. *Heart Views* **15**(4): 136–139.
6. Powell, J.M. (1986). *Anatomy of a crusade, 1213-1221. The Middle Ages*. Philadelphia: University of Pennsylvania Press, pp. xix, 287.
7. Gratzer, W.B. (2005). *Terrors of the table: The curious history of nutrition*. Oxford/New York: Oxford University Press, pp. ix, 288.
8. Online at www.uspto.gov/patent/initiatives/patents-humanity/2015-award-recipients
9. Carpenter, K.J. (2012). The discovery of thiamin. *Ann Nutr Metab* **61**(3): 219–223.
10. McCollum, E.V., and M. Davis. (1913). Tne necessity of certain lipins in the diet during growth. *J. Biol. Chem* **15**: 167–175.
11. Simoni, R.D., R.L. Hill, and M. Vaughan. (2002). Nutritional biochemistry and the discovery of vitamins: The work of Elmer Verner McCollum. *J. Biol. Chem* **277**(19): e8.
12. McCollum, E.V., et al. (1921). Studies on experimental rickets: I. The production of rachitis and similar diseases in the rat by deficient diets. *J. Biol. Chem* **45**: 333–341.
13. Orent, E.R., and E.V. McCollum. (1931). Effects of deprivation of manganese in the rat. *J. Biol. Chem* **92**: 651–678.
14. Itter, S., E.R. Orent, and E.V. McCollum. (1935). The possible role of the sulfhydryl group in vitamin B2 deficiency. *J. Biol. Chem* **108**: 585–594.
15. Orent-Keiles, E., and E.V. McCollum. (1940). Mineral metabolism of rats on an extremely sodium-deficient diet. *J. Biol. Chem* **133**: 75–81.
16. Orent-Keiles, E., and E.V. McCollum. (1941). Potassium in animal nutrition. *J. Biol. Chem* **140**: 337–352.
17. McCollum, E.V., and N. Simmonds. (1917). A biological analysis of pellagra-producing diets. II. The minimum requirements of the two unidentified dietary factors for maintenance as contrased with growth. *J. Biol. Chem* **32**: 181–193.
18. Semba, R.D. (2012). The discovery of the vitamins. *Int J Vitam Nutr Res* **82**(5): 310–315.
19. Piro, A., et al. (2010). Casimir Funk: His discovery of the vitamins and their deficiency disorders. *Ann Nutr Metab* **57**(2): 85–88.
20. Funk, C. (1911). On the chemical nature of the substance which cures polyneuritis in birds induced by a diet of polished rice. *J. Physiol* **43**: 395–400.
21. Funk, C. (1914). *Die vitamine*. Wiesbaden: J. F. Bergmann, pp. viii, 193.
22. Leung, A.M., L.E. Braverman, and E.N. Pearce. (2012). History of U.S. iodine fortification and supplementation. *Nutrients* **4**(11): 1740–1746.
23. Poskitt, E.M. (2003). Early history of iron deficiency. *Br J Haematol* **122**(4): 554–562.
24. Day, H.G. (1974). *Biographical memoir of Elmer Verner McCollum* (vol. 45). Washington, D.C.: National Academy of Sciences.
25. Miller, A.J., and J.A. Brunelle. (1983). A summary of the NIDR community caries prevention demonstration program. *J Am Dent Assoc* **107**(2): 265–269.
26. Leverett, D.H., O.B. Sveen, and O.E. Jensen. (1985). Weekly rinsing with a fluoride mouthrinse in an unfluoridated community: Results after seven years. *J Public Health Dent* **45**(2): 95–100.

27. Institute of Medicine (U.S.). Committee on Use of Dietary Reference Intakes in Nutrition Labeling. (2003). *Dietary reference intakes: Guiding principles for nutrition labeling and fortification*. Washington, D.C.: National Academy Press, p. 1. Online resource available (1 PDF [xiii, 205 pages]).

28. Paine, J.A., et al. (2005). Improving the nutritional value of golden rice through increased pro-vitamin A content. *Nat Biotechnol* **23**(4): 482–487.

29. Kramer, C.M., et al. (2014). Vitamin E levels in soybean (Glycine max [L.] Merr.) expressing a p-hydroxyphenylpyruvate gene from oat (Avena sativa L.). *J Agric Food Chem* **62**(15): 3453–3457.

30. Blancquaert, D., et al. (2014). Present and future of folate biofortification of crop plants. *J Exp Bot* **65**(4): 895–906.

31. Arjo, G., et al. (2012). Mice fed on a diet enriched with genetically engineered multivitamin corn show no sub-acute toxic effects and no sub-chronic toxicity. *Plant Biotechnol J* **10**(9): 1026–1034.

Scientists and Others in Micronutrient Research

Active Vitamers

```
V  V  Z  B  K  B  M  D  M  S  I  V  A  D
M  O  S  M  L  N  N  U  T  Y  K  Y  D  X
C  C  N  R  G  I  U  B  L  P  W  O  M  P
C  H  I  S  L  E  Z  F  L  L  I  X  B  Q
O  A  K  N  Z  L  I  Z  M  S  O  R  Z  Y
L  T  P  H  R  E  M  J  Y  T  O  C  V  Y
L  I  O  U  L  R  N  Y  K  O  X  M  C  R
U  N  H  K  J  L  Q  G  S  M  Y  M  R  M
M  K  A  R  R  E  R  E  Y  S  A  P  N  D
E  N  I  A  P  L  V  J  E  O  K  N  B  B
L  R  R  G  N  E  N  I  Z  D  R  M  L  W
G  K  K  Z  L  T  V  R  R  R  B  G  J  R
N  M  T  T  P  A  G  D  J  W  Y  T  Y  L
L  B  M  Z  D  M  N  N  Y  T  Z  J  Z  I
```

Instructions: Each clue refers to the last name of a person named in Chapter 2. Use the clues and then search for the name in the word search puzzle above.

	CLUE	ANSWER
1	Sea captain with first clinical study	
2	Female scientist who helped discover vitamin A	
3	Secret rat colonies at the University of Wisconsin	
4	Nobel prize for antineuritic factor	
5	Coined the word "vitamins"	
6	Discovered the antiscorbic vitamin	
7	Discovered carotinoids	
8	Discovered the quinone chemistry of fat-soluble vitamin	
9	Discovered growth stimulating role of thiamine	
10	Worked on flavins	
11	Goiter is caused by iodine deficiency	
12	Iron deficiency causes anemia	
13	A member of the 1941 Food and Nutrition Board	
14	Convened the National Nutrition Conference for Defense	
15	Created golden rice	

NOTES

CHAPTER 3

Digestion
A Healthy Tract Promotes Micronutrient Balance

Table of Contents

Most individuals should get all of their micronutrients by eating a well-balanced diet. For those who need a little more, supplements are taken. Regardless of the source, both the micronutrients in food and those in pills need to go through the digestive tract to be absorbed and used by the body. As you will see in this chapter, the digestive tract has very regionalized areas where food is systematically broken down, and nutrients released (Figure 3.1). Absorption can take place passively, by diffusion between the cells lining our gut and then out to the bloodstream, or actively, using specific receptors that recognize the micronutrient, bind to it, and pull it into the cell for transport back out on the other side into the bloodstream. In some cases, vitamins and minerals help each other get through the gut, while in other situations, they compete with each other for specific receptors or form insoluble compounds, which pass through the gut and are excreted. There are also genetic and physiological conditions that can affect how vitamins and minerals get absorbed and transported throughout the body. Let's take a look at these conditions now.

REGIONAL SPECIFICITY OF THE DIGESTIVE TRACT

As food or fluids are taken into the body, they enter the mouth, which is the first place that the food is broken down into small pieces and mixed with salivary gland digestive juices. We will talk about the process of taste and the papillae on the tongue in later chapters. For now, the mouth and teeth masticate every piece of food to break it down into smaller pieces so that it can pass into the esophagus. Then the stomach is the next stop, and an important one for some vitamins—especially B12, as we'll see later in this chapter.

In the stomach, strong muscular contractions combined with an acidic environment from the gastric enzymes that are secreted by the stomach break food into smaller and smaller pieces, producing chyme. Chyme is essentially a slurry of food bits, which is then exposed to the hydrochloric acid and pepsin in the stomach and is further broken down. While all vitamins and minerals need this step to be released from food, none of our micronutrients are absorbed in a normal stomach. Rather, the stomach muscles push the chyme into the duodenum where absorption of micronutrients starts to occur.

The approximately 20-foot-long duodenum is where the bulk of the action takes place. As chyme enters the duodenum, pancreatic enzymes and bile from the gallbladder break it down even further. Micronutrient absorption takes place here, and in the jejunum and ileum before the unused material is pushed into the large intestine. The small intestine is where many of the vitamin and mineral receptors are located, and we'll talk about these further along in the chapter. It is also where passive diffusion of our micronutrients takes place, leaving between the intestinal cells (called enterocytes) and directly entering the bloodstream.

The large intestine, which can be up to 6 feet in length, receives the undigested bulk waste, in a slightly liquid form, and has two main functions—to extract water from the waste, maintaining water balance in the body; and to harbor bacteria, some of which can synthesize vitamins they use for their own processes, and allow us to gather up the excesses in a completely symbiotic relationship. The bacterially synthesized vitamins are then absorbed in the large intestine through specialized receptors. After ~39 feet of digestive track, and 24 to 48 hours, the rest of the material that started out as your lunch is finally excreted as waste.

MICRONUTRIENTS THAT PROMOTE A HEALTHY DIGESTIVE TRACT

The cells lining the main route through the digestive tract have some of the highest turnover rates of any cells in the body. It is estimated that just the cells in your digestive tract weight up to 1.5 lb, and are completely renewed (and recycled) every 5 days [1]. Thus, micronutrients that are needed for cell division and energy production are those that also promote a healthy digestive tract. For example, as we

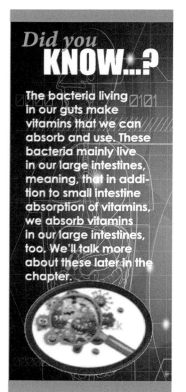

Did you KNOW...?

The bacteria living in our guts make vitamins that we can absorb and use. These bacteria mainly live in our large intestines, meaning, that in addition to small intestine absorption of vitamins, we absorb vitamins in our large intestines, too. We'll talk more about these later in the chapter.

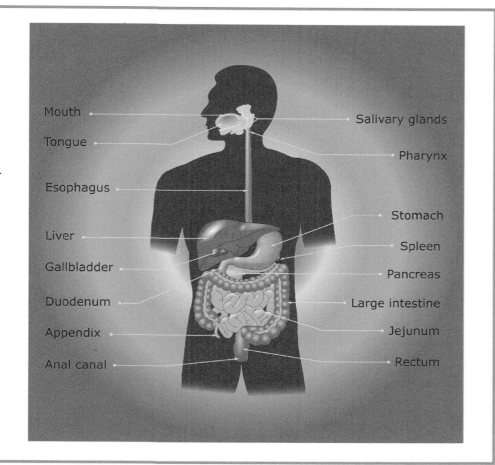

FIGURE 3.1: The human digestive system, with areas labeled. Micronutrient absorption takes place mainly in all three parts of the small intestine—the duodenum, the jejunum and the ileum (not shown, but follows the jejunum).

Mouth

Tongue

Esophagus

Liver

Gallbladder

Duodenum

Appendix

Anal canal

Salivary glands

Pharynx

Stomach

Spleen

Pancreas

Large intestine

Jejunum

Rectum

© dr OX/Shutterstock.com

will see in Chapter 4, niacin, riboflavin, and thiamine all play key roles in energy production, and deficiency of any of these results in diarrhea and gastrointestinal upset. Folic acid, as part of the folate cycle in proliferating cells, contributes to the formation of nucleic acids and amino acids—all of which are needed by dividing and actively metabolizing cells. Some of the first signs of deficiency of B9 include nausea and diarrhea, suggesting a direct effect on the GI system. Finally, as we will see in a later chapter on immunity, vitamin A in the form retinoic acid is important in maintaining mucosal immunity through the recruitment of B cells producing IgA antibodies [2]. Retinoic acid works through its receptor, the retinoic acid receptor (RAR), which is a zinc-finger containing protein. Zinc is a key mineral for gut health. Deficiency of zinc initially leads to loss of appetite, and with increasing severity, diarrhea. As zinc is also needed for the salivary gland protein gustin, zinc deficiency can lead to taste abnormalities, including ageusia, which is the complete loss of taste, and hypogeusia, which is the partial loss of taste. Maintaining a healthy tract is necessary before we can even discuss how micronutrients can be absorbed. Without a healthy tract, a vicious cycle of diarrhea and nausea may lead to further nutritional deficiencies, and impair the ability to absorb the micronutrients for repair and regeneration of the gut cells.

DIGESTION AND ABSORPTION OF VITAMINS

As we discuss the digestion and absorption of vitamins, you will see that some can leak between the enterocytes and directly enter the bloodstream, while others have specialized vitamin receptors that are even regulated in response to vitamin need by the body; and many of the water-soluble vitamins can get into the bloodstream using both methods. Any vitamin that doesn't get absorbed passes through the small intestine and in some cases could get absorbed in the colon, or just excreted. Think about this when you are taking high levels of water-soluble vitamins in supplements or water-infused beverages—you might just be flushing most of it down the drain!

Vitamins that are passively diffused

Passive diffusion refers to the ability of a molecule to go from one side of a membrane to another, usually along a concentration gradient (Figure 3.2). For passive diffusion to be effective in the small intestine, this means that the concentration of the vitamin must be high in the lumen and relatively low in the enterocytes and their surrounding extracellular matrices. For example, nicotinic acid (niacin) can be absorbed directly via passive diffusion between the enterocytes when high levels, such as that obtained from taking supplements, are present in the gut lumen (Figure 3.3) [3, 4], although, as we will discuss below, the mechanism for niacin uptake is still controversial. Other water-soluble vitamins require some modification to be passively absorbed, while fat-soluble vitamins absorb by incorporation into bile-salt coated micelles. Let's look at each of these types of passive diffusion individually.

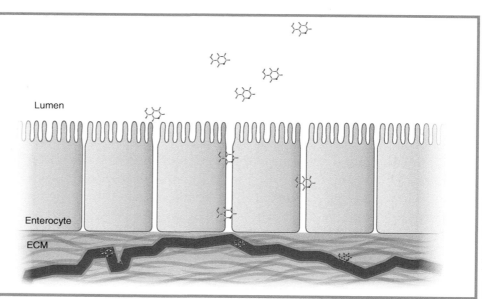

FIGURE 3.2: Passive diffusion. Niacin, as represented by its chemical structure, diffusing between enterocytes, and into the capillaries in the extracellular matrix (ECM) (not to scale).

Lumen

Enterocyte

ECM

© Kendall Hunt Publishing

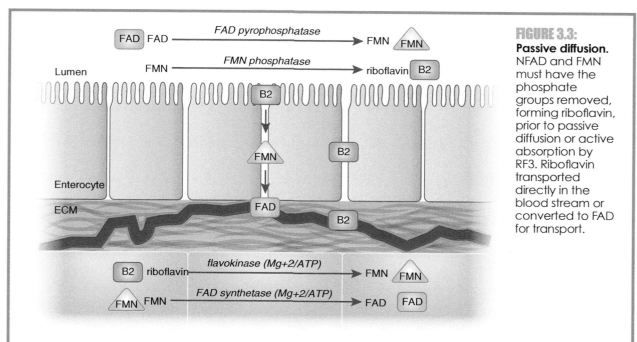

© Kendall Hunt Publishing

FIGURE 3.3:
Passive diffusion. NFAD and FMN must have the phosphate groups removed, forming riboflavin, prior to passive diffusion or active absorption by RF3. Riboflavin transported directly in the blood stream or converted to FAD for transport.

DIRECT PASSIVE DIFFUSION ALONG A CONCENTRATION GRADIENT

True passive diffusion of vitamins along concentration gradients is rare, and still controversial, with the latest review paper on the subject still contending that most if not all vitamins have carrier-mediated mechanisms of transport. That being said, older papers exist that show convincing data for direct passive diffusion of nicotinic acid using rat small intestine tissue strips [3, 4], and 5-methyl-tetrahydrofolic acid using rat "gut sacs" [5]. When we talk about passive diffusion in this section, we are only talking about food forms of a vitamin—not synthetic forms that might be modified for faster or more efficient uptake. Nicotinic acid can be obtained in foods such as meats (liver, chicken, beef), eggs, some fruits at low concentrations, and nuts/seeds. The 5-methyl-tetrahydrofolic acid is the predominant B9 form in food sources, with the exception of synthetic folic acid additives to fortified foods. The remaining food forms of all of the water-soluble vitamins require either modification for passive diffusion or the utilization of specific receptors for transport, or both.

PASSIVE DIFFUSION FOLLOWING MODIFICATION

Vitamers of five of the water-soluble vitamins can utilize passive diffusion only after they are modified enzymatically. As shown in Table 3.1, these include the vitamers of thiamine, riboflavin, B5, B6, and B7. All of these also have specific receptors and along with the rest of the water-soluble vitamers, including vitamin C, require active transport for absorption. These will be discussed later.

The food form of thiamine is TPP, which is also the active vitamer of B1. This form, also called thiamine diphosphate (ThDP), has two phosphate molecules attached. These phosphate groups must be removed by intestinal phosphatases, because with

Needs more
research...

Most of our information on passive diffusion comes from experiments done more than 30 years ago. It is still not clear how pure the enzymatic preparations were, or if crude intestinal preparations were the best model for studying passive diffusion, especially since the receptors for thiamine, riboflavin, and the other water-soluble vitamins had not yet been identified. For example, early studies on thiamine absorption used the term "thiamine pyrophosphatase" to describe the enzyme that removes the phosphate groups from thiamine, but later studies talk about intestinal alkaline phosphatases as doing the job—perhaps implying that there wasn't a specific thiamine phosphatase. To this author, after hours of searching the literature, my conclusion is that the area needs more research, especially with the newer tools now available.

the phosphate groups attached, thiamine is too large to diffuse between the cells [6]. However, passive diffusion of thiamine only occurs at high concentrations of thiamine, usually after a supplement or fortified cereal.

FAD and FMN, which would be two of the main riboflavin forms in foods, must be converted to free unphosphorylated riboflavin for passive absorption, the levels of which are high. FAD pyrophosphatase converts FAD to FMN, and then FMN phosphatase converts FMN to riboflavin for absorption (Figure 3.4) [7].

Like thiamine, the phosphorylated forms of B6, PLP, PNP, and PMP require intestinal alkaline phosphatase for phosphate removal before passive diffusion (see Table 3.1). This was shown directly for the pyridoxine (PN) form of B6 using perfused rat small intestine [8]. For B6, PN is the predominant form of this water-soluble vitamin when obtained from plants, while pyridoxal (PL) and pyridoxamine (PM) are primarily found in animal sources. Once the phosphate groups are removed, all three are said to show passive uptake via simple diffusion when concentrations are high on the luminal side of the intestine, although the review paper by Gropper and Smith does not directly reference any additional articles showing PL and PM diffusion rates [9].

Biotin is found bound to proteins in food sources, and as such needs to be removed from these proteins for passive diffusion. Proteases in the stomach separate biotin from biotinylated proteins, forming biocytin. Biocytin is an amide composed of biotin and the amine group of the amino acid lysine, to which biotin was attached in the biotinylated proteins. Once formed, biocytin travels to the small intestine, where the brush border enzyme biotinidase cleaves biocytin, forming lysine and biotin, both of which can be absorbed by passive diffusion, although this only occurs at high concentrations [10]. As we'll see later in the chapter, once freed, biotin usually binds to its receptor—which it shares with pantothenic acid, for active uptake by enterocytes. Like biotin, pantothenic acid occurs in food in the form of coenzyme A (CoA) that also needs to be proteolyzed prior to uptake in the small intestine. This requires several steps. First, coenzyme A is hydrolyzed to 4-phosphopantetheine, and then dephosphorylated to pantothenic acid [11]. This form of B5 can be absorbed passively at high concentrations, or uses active transport, sharing a receptor with biotin, when at lower levels.

To date, it appears that most water-soluble vitamins (some with modifications) can be passively absorbed when ingested at pharmacologically high levels. There is no evidence that either the ascorbic acid or dehyroascorbate forms of vitamin C can be passively absorbed, and its route of absorption will be discussed later in the chapter. Furthermore, to date, the receptor for niacin has not been definitively identified—although evidence suggests that there are both saturable (i.e., receptor-mediated) and nonsaturable (i.e., passive absorption) methods for B3 uptake. Obviously more research is needed, with modern tools and model systems to clarify these processes.

Food Form	Conversion	Enzyme	Vitamin form absorbed	Reference
TPP	Removal of phosphate	Intestinal phosphatases (alkaline phosphatase requires Zn)	thiamine	Hoyumpa, A M, et al., 1982
FAD FMN	Removal of phosphates	FAD diphosphatase FMN phosphatase	Riboflavin	Akiyama et al., 1982
CoA, Acyl carrier protein	Hydrolysis	Pantetheine hydrolase	Pantothenic acid	CoA: Shibata et al., 1983
PLP, PMP	Removal of phosphate	Alkaline phosphatase (requires Zinc)	PL, PM	PLP: Buss et al., 1980; Gropper and Smith (2013)
Biocytin	proteolysis	Biotinidase	Biotin (+lysine)	Biocytin: Dakshin-amurti et al., 1987

Fat-soluble vitamins are incorporated into bile-salt micelles

Fat-soluble vitamins are absorbed once they are incorporated into micelles, but newer research suggests that this does not always occur by simple diffusion across the enterocyte membrane. Micelles are formed within the lumen of the small

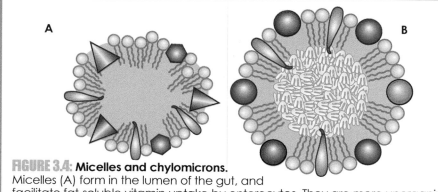

FIGURE 3.4: **Micelles and chylomicrons.**
Micelles (A) form in the lumen of the gut, and facilitate fat-soluble vitamin uptake by enterocytes. They are more unorganized than chylomicrons, but still contain lipids, cholesterol and bile salts. See the text for specific components that help absorption of each of the fat-soluble vitamins. Chylomicrons (B) form in the enterocyte to facilitate fat-soluble vitamin transfer through the serum. They have apoproteins incorporated into their phospholipid coat, and tryglycerides and cholesterol within their cores.

© Kendall Hunt Publishing

intestine, and are composed of bile salts, cholesterol, and phospholipids. Previous studies seemed to indicate that micelles were randomly formed with available dietary lipids. Newer research suggests that the formation of micelles is more complex, with specific fat-soluble vitamins incorporated into types of micelles that facilitate their uptake by enterocytes.

VITAMIN A

When food containing vitamin A vitamers, mainly in the form of dietary retinyl esters and esterified carotinoids, are absorbed, the retinyl esters and esters of carotinoids are hydrolyzed in the intestine by pancreatic triglyceride lipase and phospholipase B. Then, both are incorporated into micelles for absorption. For retinyl-containing micelles, the absorption process may involve the Stra6 binding protein, or another active transport process. For carotinoids, the lipid-binding protein, Scavenger Receptor class B type I (SR-BI) appears to be necessary for micellar uptake by enterocyte. Once inside the enterocyte, retinol is bound by the cellular retinol transport protein (CRBP), and eventually incorporated into chylomicrons for transport in circulation. For carotinoids, there has not been a carotinoid cellular binding protein isolated for mammals, although there has been one identified in the silkworm in 2010, making it likely that the mammalian homolog will eventually be identified. This and all of the work on the intestinal absorption of vitamin A vitamers has been summarized in a nice review by Emmanuelle Reboul [12].

VITAMIN D

The food forms of vitamin D (D$_2$, calcidiol; and D$_3$, calcitriol) require no further modification prior to micellar incorporation. However, calcitriol requires bile salts within the mixed micelle molecule for efficient uptake by enterocytes, while calcidiol uptake is not influenced by bile salt concentration. Interestingly, many different types of lipid molecules make up mixed micelles, but high levels of cholesterol within the micelle can inhibit calcitriol absorption. Micellar vitamin D appears to also use SR-BI protein or the Niemann Pick C1-like 1 protein (NPC1L1) to enter the enterocyte, to be then transported across the enterocyte by vitamin D binding protein (DBP) prior to chylomicron incorporation [13].

VITAMIN E

Food forms of vitamin E, α- and γ-tocopherol can be directly incorporated into micelles, and it appears that there is a preference for cholesterol-containing micelles to contain vitamin E tocopherols. The micelles are bound nonspecifically by the lipid scavenger proteins SR-B1 and NPC1L1. A recent paper suggests that Cluster determinant 36 protein (CD36) is essential for tocopherol uptake by enterocytes, and routing through cells for incorporation into chylomicrons [14]. However, more research on vitamin E is needed to ascertain if this pathway is unique to vitamin E, or used by other fat-soluble vitamins as well.

Vitamin K

Like the other fat-soluble vitamins, vitamin K is sequestered into micelles to begin the absorption process. The food form of vitamin K is phylloquinone, which is also called K_1 and is the form found in leafy greens such as kale. Phylloquinone, along with K_3 or menadione, the synthetic form, are the two main types of vitamin K that are found and absorbed in the small intestine. There, the NPC1L1 and the CD36 scavenger receptors appear to be the main proteins responsible for facilitated uptake [15]. It has been known for a long time that excess vitamin E uptake can interfere with vitamin K "activity," causing excessive bleeding. Goncalves and colleagues speculate that the use of similar transporters by vitamins K and E may result in the long-known problem of excess bleeding (due to lack of vitamin K) in individuals with his vitamin E levels [16]. One issue that has not been sufficiently investigated is how colon-synthesized K_2 or menaquinone uptake is regulated or if additional proteins are needed for facilitated uptake from the colon. Both CD26 and NPC1L1 RNA are found in small intestine and colon total RNAs, according to information in the GeneCards Database (www.genecards.org). Thus, the possibility exists that the RNA is translated into protein, and that vitamin K absorption in the colon occurs via the same mechanism as in the small intestine.

Fun FACT

An understanding of vitamin K intestinal absorption pathways is so new, that in a late 2014 article the pathway was described as "not understood" [15].

Vitamins utilizing specialized intestinal receptors

While some vitamins can use passive diffusion, many additionally use active diffusion. This means that they use a receptor or carrier to actively (using ATP) transport the vitamin through the enterocyte membrane, to the inside of the cell. The solute carrier protein family is an important family of proteins in this respect—there are over 300 different genes in this large family, and luckily for us, only a few of these are vitamin transporters. You can see examples of these in the list found in Table 3.1. Let's talk about these SLC family members that are vitamin transporters in a little more detail.

Thiamine and folate both use SLC19 family members for transport, along with a second, distinct SLC family member. For thiamine, the SLC19A2 and SLC19A3 protein products are involved in uptake for dietary thiamine and there does not appear to be a substrate difference in what is recognized by the SLC19 transporters. However, the SLC25 gene codes for a transporter, which is only in mitochondria where it is responsible for transporting thiamine into mitochondria—and it is needed there, as we'll find out in the next chapter! For folate, the SLC19A1 gene, which shares only 55% to 60% homology with the SLC19 thiamine transporters [17] is responsible for transporting 5-methy-THF, but not folic acid, which uses SLC46A1, also called the proton-coupled folate transporter, meaning that two different receptors have distinct roles in absorption of dietary folate.

The SLC23 family is responsible for vitamin C transport. There are two forms, terms A1 and A2, but only the SLC23A1 gene codes for an intestinal vitamin C transporter. It is important to note that this transporter only recognizes ascorbic acid, and not DHA, which is only absorbed from the diet, and that cotransport of sodium occurs with ascorbic acid. Interestingly, as we saw in an earlier chapter, humans and some other animals cannot make vitamin C, and thus need to absorb it from the diet. Other animals make ascorbic acid in the liver or kidneys, and therefore do not need to spend time or energy absorbing it. When the SLC23 protein, also called the sodium-dependent vitamin C transporter (SVCT), was originally cloned in mice it was thought to be involved more in kidney retention of vitamin C than intestinal uptake, which makes sense since mice normally would synthesize their own vitamin C [18].

Another sodium-dependent member of this vitamin transporter family is the SLC5A6 gene (sodium multivitamin transporter protein, SMVT). SMVT is the transporter responsible for uptake of both biotin and pantothenic acid. When this transporter was originally cloned, and expressed in nonexpressing cells by cDNA transfection, it was found to increase biotin absorption by 15-fold over nontransfected cells, and pantothenic acid absorption by 4-fold over nontransfected cells [19]. Recently SMVT was found to require the association of another protein, called PDZD11, for full activity [20]. Unfortunately, this study only looked at the effect of knockdown of PDZD11 on biotin absorption, so it is not clear what role, if any, PDFD11 plays in pantothenic acid absorption by SMVT.

Finally, riboflavin transporters also belong to the SLC superfamily of transporters, and specifically to the SLC52 subfamily. There are three known riboflavin transporters (RF1, SLC52A1; RF2, SLC52A3; RF3, SLC52A2) to date, which each of these only identified within the last 5 to 7 years [21]. I remember teaching the Vitamins and Minerals course one year and stating that there was one riboflavin transporter, and by the next year, there were two more to discuss. Each of these transporters for riboflavin is both sodium and chloride dependent, with RF2 being the main intestinal transporter. Only riboflavin is transported by the RF transporter proteins—with conversion to FMN and FAD taking place either extra- or intra-cellularly, as shown in Figure 3.3.

As shown in Table 3.2, the SLC superfamily is key to vitamin absorption for a number of the water-soluble vitamins. Some of the other similarities include the necessity for sodium in many of these processes, as a cotransporter, and as we will see in the minerals section, use of the SLC superfamily to transport other positively charged minerals, such as zinc.

B12—THE MOST COMPLEX ABSORPTION ROUTE

Vitamin B12, structurally, is unlike any of the other B vitamins. This vitamin is quite complex, and as you know from previous chapters, even contains a mineral, cobalt. The absorption of B12 is complex because it needs to be protected—its

TABLE 3.2: The Solute Carrier Protein (SLC) Family of Vitamin Transporters

VITAMINS	Gene Names	Protein Names	Mineral or Co-transporter protein
Thiamine	SLC19A2 SLC19A3 SLC25	ThTr1 ThTr2 Mitochrondrial thiamine transporter	Sodium (all forms of transporter)
Folate	SLC19A1 SLC46A1	Methy-THF transporter Proton-coupled folic acid transporter	Likely sodium Sodium and protons
Vitamin C	SLC23	Sodium Dependent Vitamin C Transporter	Sodium
PA, Biotin	SLC5A6	Sodium Dependent Multi-Vitamin Transporter	Sodium and PDZD11
Riboflavin	SLC52A1 SLC52A2 SLC52A3	RF1 RF3 RF2	Sodium (all forms)

functionality would be destroyed if it were broken down during gastric digestion process. Thus, to digest vitamin B12 nondestructively, a salivary protein called haptocorrin (a member of the salivary "R" proteins) strongly binds and protects the B12 molecules from stomach acid once it is cleaved from their protein complexes. Once the B12-haptocorrin complexes pass from the stomach, pancreatic proteases remove the haptocorrin from the B12 molecules, and B12 is immediately rebound by intrinsic factor (IF), which is synthesized in the stomach and secreted there for the purpose of transporting B12. The B12-IF complexes travel to the ileum portion of the small intestine where the IF receptor, called cubin, binds to the B12-IF complex for absorption. Thus, unlike many of the vitamins we've just discussed, which are absorbed in the duodenum, B12 is targeted by gut proteins and transported further down the GI track and absorbed primarily in the ileum. To finally enter circulation, B12 is transported across the enterocyte where it binds to transcobalamin 2, which can exit the cell and travel where needed in the body.

DE NOVO PRODUCTION OF VITAMINS IN OUR DIGESTIVE TRACT

While this author believes there is still a lot that needs to be uncovered in regular foodborne vitamin absorption, many scientists are now focusing their attention on the vitamins being synthesized in our lower digestive tract—namely in the colon. Our gut microorganisms synthesize both water- and fat-soluble vitamins. While it was previously known that gut bacteria synthesize water-soluble vitamins for their own use, it was only recently discovered that these vitamins may also be available for host absorption from the colon. A good review on the subject of bacterially synthesized water-soluble vitamins was published by Hamid Said [22]. According to Said, more water-soluble vitamins are produced by our colon microbiota following a complex carbohydrate meal than following either a simple carbohydrate meal or a high-protein meal, and in some cases, the amount of biotin and B6 can actually be higher in fecal matter (i.e., waste) than was eaten in the diet, indicating that de novo synthesis at least equal to or more than what was eaten occurred via colon bacteria. While the mechanism for B6 absorption by colonocytes is still not known, absorption of thiamine, niacin, riboflavin, biotin, pantothenic acid, and folate take place using the same absorption mechanisms as in the small intestine [22]. B12 has long been known to be produced by enteric bacteria, with meat products being a good food source of this vitamin [23]. However, whether the complex B12 absorption mechanisms used in the small intestine are also present in the colon is not clear at this time.

DIGESTION AND ABSORPTION OF MINERALS

Food for **THOUGHT**

☑ Why do you think fluoride is the only mineral that currently doesn't have a known transporter? Do you think all fluoride is taken up passively, or do you believe the data showing a possible anion antiporter for fluoride? If so, how do these data fit with what is known about fluoride toxicity?

Dietary intake is the only source of nutritional minerals that we need for our bodily processes. That is to say, unlike some vitamins, there is no "de-novo synthesis" of minerals, which makes sense, because in their most basic sense they are elements, not molecules.

Most mineral absorption occurs via specific intestinal receptors, likely due to the fact minerals are needed in very small amounts, and unregulated passive diffusion could result in toxicity. The exception occurs for both the food and water forms of fluoride, as well as dietary magnesium. For fluoride, paracellular absorption (between the cells) appears to predominate, at least in a study using a human colon cell line [24]. However, that same study produced data to suggest that fluoride may share an anion antiporter (negative ion/OH-) with chloride. For dietary magnesium, especially when intake is high, up to 90% of the ingested magnesium may be absorbed paracellularly in the duodenum and jejunum [25]. However, as we will see below, magnesium, like calcium, also uses an inducible receptor in case of normal to low intake to prevent hypomagnesemia.

The major known mechanisms for mineral absorption in the small intestine and colon (where we also absorb minerals) are shown in Table 3.3. While we will not cover all of these mechanisms in detail, we will discuss the role of the divalent metal transporter (DMT1), which can transport several different metal-type minerals, ion channels, which are involved in transport of sodium and other ions, and Zip4, a member of the SLC superfamily, like the vitamin transporters.

DMT1—the major iron transporter

Iron absorption is well studied, likely because iron-deficiency anemia has had such a high prevalence around the world. In fact, the first published study on iron absorption, using the rat as a model, occurred in the April 1894 issue of the *Journal of Physiology* [26]. The figures in this article, which is available free on PubMed Central, are hand drawn, and the conclusion is more about the area in which iron absorption occurs in the guinea pig (the small intestine), than how it is absorbed. No speculation

Mineral	Uptake Route in Small Intestine	Other Notes
Calcium	TRPV6	Transient receptor potential cation channel, member 6, Vitamin D regulated gene expression of TRVP6. Some evidence that calcium can passively diffuse between enterocyte at high levels
Chloride	Na/Cl- channel	May also work through a Cl-/OH- antiporter
Chromium	Not known	
Cobalt	Along with B12	May use DMT1
Copper	Ctrl1	Ctrl1 is a member of the SLC superfamily. DMT1 is not a major transporter-in vitro confirmation only
Fluoride	Passive diffusion	No known intestinal receptors, but some evidence of a F-/OH- antiporter
Iodine	Na/I channel	Can also be absorbed as part of thyroid hormone, taken orally
Iron	DMT1 (free iron) HCP1 (heme)	Requires Vitamin C
Magnesium	TRPM6 TRPM7	Transient receptor, potential melastatin, members 6 and 7, At very high concentrations, up to 90% can be passively diffused
Manganese	DMT1	In vitro only
Molybdenum	Not known	
Phosphorus	Na/P channel	
Potassium	Na/K channel	
Selenium	Through selenoprotein/amino acid transporters	Selenite transporter uses sodium/Se channels
Sodium	Sodium channels (many!)	NHE3 is the main Na+/H+ channel for absorption

is made as to whether this is receptor-mediated or passive. It was not until 100 years later that the divalent metal transporter-1 (DMT1) was cloned and characterized [27]. When originally cloned, the protein was known as divalent cation transporter 1 or DC1, and found to be a large protein of 561 amino acids, composing a membrane protein with 12 transmembrane domains [27]. Interestingly, the initial characterization of DMT1 (DC1) showed that it could transport Fe^{2+}, Cd^{2+}, Co^{2+}, Cu^{2+}, Ni^{2+}, Mn^{2+}, Pb^{2+}, and Zn^{2+}. However, subsequent work has questioned some of these affinities, as the initial study was done in oocytes microinjected with the DMT1 cDNA. One of the newest studies from 2015 using a knockout mouse model shows that Cu^{2+}, Zn^{+2}, and Mn^{+2} do not use DMT1 [28].

Dietary iron is usually found in the form Fe^{3+} (ferric) from food sources, and must be reduced to Fe^{+2} (ferrous) which can then be absorbed by DMT1. One of the main ways this is done in the intestine is through the action of the duodenal cytochrome b protein (DCYTP), which requires vitamin C in the form of ascorbic acid to convert the ferric ion to the ferrous ion that can be absorbed [29]. Once in the enterocyte, iron is either stored in ferritan or is transported out, using other proteins that we'll discuss in the blood and body fluids section.

Of **NOTE**

The Shawki and colleagues study [28] used a special type of knockout mouse, called a conditional knockout, in order to delete the DMT1 gene just in intestinal villi of the mouse. While the animals still showed iron-deficiency anemia, the condition was not as severe as when the there was a global knockout of DMT1. Intestine-specific deletion allowed for the animals to live up to 186 days, while whole body deletion results in animals that die by 7 days due to the severity of the anemia. These types of data are what scientists use to then study the role that DMT1 plays in iron transport for nonintestinal cells.

Ion channels—a major mechanism for mineral absorption

Ion channels within the small intestine are responsible for uptake of sodium, calcium, chloride, magnesium, potassium, phosphorus, and iodine (see Table 3.3). Many of these channels couple with sodium uptake (as cotransporters), or something like those channels for calcium and magnesium, and simply work with an electrochemical gradient. There are multiple types of sodium channels, and many of these are coupled with other molecules such as protons, amino acids, glucose and other nutrients [30]. However, for sodium itself, the majority of luminal small intestinal transport occurs through the Na+/H+ exchanger-form 3 (NHE3) [30]. Mice with a targeted deletion of the NHE3 gene, SLC9A3 (yes, it is another SLC family member!), show the expected phenotype of diarrhea and reduced blood pressure [31]. Thus, sodium coupled with chloride and bicarbonate transport are also linked to water absorption and release in the gut.

Zip4-absorbing zinc in a jiffy

After iron, zinc is the second most abundant trace mineral in our diets, and zinc deficiency remains a global problem today. Some even say that with the dietary emphasis on reducing red meat intake, where zinc is readily bio-available for absorption, even countries such as the United States may see a rise in zinc deficiency in their population. So, how does the body make sure to get adequate (but not too much) zinc from the diet? Zinc homeostasis mechanisms in humans can regulate excretion and intake over a tenfold concentration, and does so through the action of zinc transporters [33]. As zinc does not participate in redox reactions, it is absorbed in its dietary Zn^{2+} form. There are 14 Zip transporter family members with different tissue distributions and slightly different regulation, but the main intestinal zinc transporter is Zip4 [33]. However, the actual mechanism of transport is not well understood, and may involve a channel function as well as an electrochemical gradient with bicarbonate. The requirement of Zip4 as the primary zinc transporter in the intestine was confirmed, both from its expression pattern, mainly in the gut tissues, and by using both global and conditional knockout mice, which are embryonically lethal early in gestation due to the lack of zinc uptake; [33]. Animals were only able to live ~2 weeks without excess dietary zinc supplementation, which could only compensate somewhat, as animals on zinc-heavy diets thrived up to 4 weeks following induction of the deletion. Even the enterocyte-specific DMT1 knockout (remember, this is the dietary iron receptor) did not have as great of an effect, indicating a major role for zinc in many proteins and physiological processes.

Complex KNOCKOUTS

Building on the ability to knock out a gene in a specific tissue, a study by (Geiser, Venken, De Lisle, & Andrews, 2012) showed the lifelong importance of zinc absorption by making a small-intestine-specific and timing-specific knockout mouse for Zip4. In other words, when the mice were given a drug, a deletion of Zip4 would occur, only in enterocytes, and the role of Zip4 at that time and place could be studied. These are complex knockout animals which allow scientists to study genes that would otherwise be lethal in total or even tissue-specific knockouts.

In summarizing mineral absorption, there appears to be regulated processes for each of our minerals, with the exception of fluoride, which predominantly uses passive absorption, although there may be an as-yet unidentified transporter.

The regulated uptake of minerals from our diet is thought to be due to the fact that we only need minerals in small quantities, and toxicity can result if we get too much of any of these individually, or, in the case of the sodium-coupled transporters, as a group. Many of the individual receptors and mechanisms for mineral absorption were only recently discovered, or need more research in order to fully understand, and so are active areas of research. As you will see in the next section, full understanding is important when we start to consider how mineral (and vitamin) deficiencies can occur via abnormal or interfered with absorption.

WHEN THINGS GO WRONG—CAUSES OF ABNORMAL MICRONUTRIENT ABSORPTION

While in many people, a healthy diet means one in which all nutrients are optimally absorbed with little waste, and ideal health, things can go wrong, even in the healthiest individual. In addition, some individuals are born with a predisposition to abnormal absorption of specific nutrients, meaning that they must deal with the consequences or find ways to alleviate the malabsorption on a daily basis. Let's talk about what can go wrong!

Food interactions

Sometimes the best intentions can lead to food interactions. Think about a delicious sushi/sashimi dinner, complete with tuna rolls, made using long-grain brown rice. You should get a lot of thiamine out of that, especially since you chose the brown rice, which hasn't been stripped of its entire husk, and still contains about 0.19 mg of B1 per cup. You also know that tuna is a great source of thiamine, with 0.38 mg available in just about 2 ounces. You could get most of your daily thiamine requirement in just this meal, right? Not so fast… what you might not have thought about is that the fish you are about to eat is raw, and still has active enzymes in it. One of those enzymes is thiaminase, which basically will cleave thiamine from the rest of your dinner, making it inactive. Cooked tuna is an excellent thiamine source, but raw tuna, not so much (sorry). In addition, thiamine intake isn't your only problem with this meal, as some mineral absorption might be blocked as well, including iron, calcium, and zinc absorption. That's because the brown rice that you picked is a great source of phytic acid. As shown in Table 3.4, phytic acid and some fibers complex with calcium, iron, magnesium, and zinc to form insoluble compounds cannot be absorbed. This is a pity since nori, the seaweed wrapping for sushi, is a good source of iron. Other food components can also interfere with micronutrient absorption, so Table 3.4 is not meant to be exhaustive. Certain foods also enhance micronutrient absorption, such as juice or an orange with vitamin C and your eggs with iron. In Table 3.5 we compare the types of micronutrients that interact to help absorption—such as vitamin C helping iron absorption, and those that when digested together, may impair one another's absorption, such as iron with any of the other divalent metals that can bind to DMT1 transporter, iron's

Meal PLANNING

Can you come up with other meals where the components in one food may interfere with absorption of micronutrients found in the rest of the meal? How might what you eat throughout the day influence when you should take a vitamin or mineral supplement?

main route for intestinal absorption. The list in Table 3.5 also is not exhaustive, so it's important to consider other combinations of vitamins and minerals that might help or inhibit each other. So, the next time you are planning to eat a meal with more than one food type in it (which is likely for most meals), think about how those foods might interfere or enhance each other's digestion and absorption. Can you come up with a meal that is "perfect" in this regard?

TABLE 3.4: Some foods that interfere with vitamin and mineral absorption. This list is not meant to be exhaustive.

Food	Substance	What goes wrong	What can you do?
Sushi and Shellfish	Anti-thiamine factors: thiaminases	Cleave thiamine- making it inactive	Don't expect to get thiamine when you eat sashimi (rice/rolls), even if it is brown rice
Raw egg whites	Avidin, a heat labile glycoprotein	Irreversibly binds to biotin, and prevent its absorption	Cook your eggs
Egg yolks	Phosvitin, a phosphoprotein	Metal chealtor, interferring with Fe, P, Ca absorption	Don't eat a lot of eggs if you are iron deficient. Calcium-fortified juice won't do you much good if you have eggs for breakfast!
Bok choy, brocccoli, cabbage	Goitrogens	Block or interfere with iodine update	Avoid these foods if you have a thyroid problem
High Fiber/whole grains	Phytic acid or the fiber itself	Interferes with calcium, iron, zinc and magnesium absorption by forming complexes that are unable to be absorbed	Balance your fiber and mineral intake, or eat at different times.

TABLE 3.5: Micronutrient interactions during absorption. Left hand column shows combinations that improve absorption for the micronutrient listed, while right hand column shows combinations that reduce absorption. This table is not meant to be exhaustive.

Micronutrient	Micronutrient absorption helper(s)	Micronutrient absorption inhibitor(s)
Iron	Vitamin C (ascorbate reduces iron for absorption)	Metals (such as Cu^{2+}, Zn^{2+}, Fe^{2+}, Mn^{2+})-competes for DMT1 transporter to some extent
All micronutrients	Niacin (promotes a healthy GI tract) Riboflavin (promotes a healthy mouth	
Calcium	Vitamin D (increases intestinal Ca^{2+} receptor)	Ca^{2+} & Mg^{2+} (use same transport systems in the kidney $\rightarrow$ may compete for re-absorption) Ca^{2+} + F (insoluble precipitate CaF_2)

Drug complications

It's probably no wonder that drugs, including caffeine and alcohol, can interfere with micronutrient absorption. The list in Table 3.6 is just a sampling of some of the interactions that can occur. Caffeine is one that most of us are exposed to at some time during the day, usually in the morning with our first cup of "joe." Do you take yours with milk? Perhaps that milk is even vitamin D enriched, and you figure that putting that milk in your coffee gives you a bit of an edge with respect to calcium absorption? Not so fast…Caffeine, in the amounts that you would have in a normal cup of coffee can increase calcium excretion (due to caffeine's effect on water balance—more on that in a later chapter), and at the same time, promote reduced bone mineral density, in some people. Are you that person? A study in the *American Journal of Clinical Nutrition*, published in 2001, clearly shows that elderly individuals who drank ~3 cups of coffee per day, and were carriers of a polymorphism in their vitamin D receptor gene, had a significantly lower bone mineral density than those with the "normal" allele [34]. The polymorphism isn't even in a coding region of the vitamin D receptor gene, so it is unclear how it affects metabolism through calcium and caffeine, but the results are striking—take a look at the original article and see for yourself. As shown in Table 3.6, alcohol affects many different vitamins and minerals, not only through its diuretic effects, but in some cases, such as with thiamine, directly modulates the level of thiamine receptor expressed in intestinal cells [35]. Again, the mechanism by which this happens is not yet defined—is it through water balance sensing or is there a signaling pathway activated by alcohol that leads to transcriptional changes in the thiamine receptor (THTR-1) gene expression? More research in this area is really needed to help us understand how caffeine, alcohol, and other drugs/chemicals interact with micronutrient absorption. That Irish coffee drink isn't looking so good now, huh?

TABLE 3.6: Drugs and chemicals that interfere with vitamin and mineral absorption. This list is not meant to be exhaustive.

Substance	What goes wrong	What can you do?
Caffeine	• Increases Calcium and B-vitamin excretion • Reduces Vitamin D receptor expression (reduced calcium absorption)	Coffee with milk won't help your calcium absorption
Alcohol	Reduces absorption of riboflavin, thiamine, folate, B12, Vitamin A, Vitamin C	Consider this when combining alcoholic drinks with meals
Acid-reflux drugs (Proton inhibitors)	Reduce B12 absorption	Increase B12 supplementation
Orlistat (diet drug)	Reduces Fat Soluble vitamin absorption	Combine a healthy diet with dieting in any form

TABLE 3.7: Examples of digestive-system conditions in the left hand column that affect the absorption of specific micronutrients (listed in right hand column).

Condition	Effect
Pancreatic Insufficiency	B12 deficiency (pancreatic enzymes needed to release B12 from R-proteins)
Lack of IF production (can be caused by age or autoimmune disease)	B12 deficiency
Tapeworms	Effects on many vitamins and minerals, but especially B12
Diarrhea	Increased loss of Vitamin C and fat soluble vitamins, minerals, especially iron
Achlorhydria (low gastric acid production)	Reduced absorption of vitamin C, K, B vitamins, Zn, Mg
Gastric Bypass surgery	Shifting of all vitamin/mineral absorption to lower in SI, but major effects on B12
Inflammatory bowel disease or celiacs disease	Iron deficiency anemia

Diseases or conditions that affect absorption

When one isn't feeling well, their diet sometimes suffers too, and they don't get sufficient vitamins and minerals. On top of that, it turns out that some of these conditions that cause us to feel sick also can impede micronutrient absorption of the few nutrients that do make it down our digestive tract. As shown in Table 3.7, conditions affecting the digestive tract directly, or conditions that impair the organs responsible for enzyme production, such as the pancreas, also directly affect micronutrient absorption. This shouldn't be surprising to you, but something that you should keep in mind when considering vitamin and mineral absorption. Of those conditions listed in Table 3.7, let's look at what happens during a (nowadays) routine gastric bypass, which was likely brought on by obesity. First of all, morbidly obese individuals, who are the candidates for bariatric surgery, such as the gastric bypass, are many times themselves deficient in both vitamins and minerals—perhaps due to poor diet or malabsorption, or both. In a meta-analysis conducted by de Lima and colleagues, close to, and in some cases more than 25% of morbidly obese individuals, were found to be already severely deficient in vitamin D, thiamine, iron, selenium, zinc, copper, and folic acid [36]. When these individuals then elect to have bariatric/gastric bypass surgery, the very nature of the surgery, in removing or bypassing parts of the stomach and upper small intestine, directly interferes nutrient absorption. The most severely affected is B12 absorption, which requires intrinsic factor production in the stomach, as well as cleavage by stomach acid to release it from foods. Thus, most individuals undergoing bypass or bariatric surgery will now be required to have a B12 supplement for life. However, the patients may also experience changes and malabsorption for other nutrients as well. Those other micronutrients include (but probably are not limited to) thiamine (~49% found to be deficient), vitamin D (up to 73% found to be deficient), iron (up to 49% deficient), and zinc (up to 91% found to be deficient following bariatric surgery) [37]. It is of concern to health professionals and dieticians, and this author, that those obese individuals trying to become healthier by undergoing surgery in some cases may make their overall health worse by disrupting the absorption of needed micronutrients. Other conditions listed in Table 3.7 are less of a choice than surgery, but still have consequences, and some will require supplementation to ameliorate the deficiencies.

Genetics

As our knowledge of vitamin and mineral needs increased during the past century, concurrently, we began to understand that some individuals can do everything right—eating diets with a full RDA of each vitamin and mineral, and yet still not be able to absorb the micronutrients. For some of these individuals, genetic variances in their DNA cause vitamin and mineral receptors, or regulators of those receptors, not to work properly. This then leads to genetic conditions that result in vitamin and mineral deficiencies. Together, humans share genetic identify of about 99.9%, but even within the cells of our own body, only 99.999998% of the bases are correctly copied with each division. To put this differently, within just hours of conception, ~50 mutations have occurred in the developing embryo [38]. Some of these are meaningless and occur in parts of our genome that don't code for proteins, or are silent in not affecting the function of the protein. But, some of these mutations can lead to abnormalities with vitamin and mineral metabolism, and if occurring early enough, can become part of the germ cells (egg and sperm) of the organism and be passed on to the next generation. Usually when this happens, the original mutation is in a heterozygous state, meaning that there is still a functional "normal" copy of the gene, and therefore does not affect the function. But when two people with the mutation have offspring, there is a possibility that the child inherits only the mutant copies of the gene—showing a recessive trait. These so-called "inborn errors of metabolism" lead to life-threatening conditions or result in a less-than-optimal lifestyle for that person. In addition to recessive inborn errors of metabolism are mutations that can be dominantly acting, meaning that only one copy of the mutant gene is sufficient to cause a problem. Thus any individual inheriting or through early mutation carrying a single mutation will show signs of the condition. These inborn errors of metabolism can affect many different metabolic enzymes, but for the purpose of this chapter, we will discuss only those affecting vitamin and mineral absorption from the digestive tract to the blood, or de novo synthesis, and of those, only a few of the key changes that occur (Table 3.8). In later chapters, other mutations will be discussed that might affect enzyme action or regulation.

Online Mendelian
Inheritance in Man

Take a look at http://omim.org/ and put the word "vitamin" in the search box. At this writing, 438 entries related to a genetic condition affecting "vitamins" are listed. The OMIM site catalogues genes and disorders affecting humans. Take a look around the site and see what you can find on it! And look for "OMIM" reference numbers for conditions we'll talk about.

Gene	OMIM	Vitamin/Mineral Affected	Condition
SLC19A2	249270	Thiamine	Roger's Syndrome
SLC46A1	611672	Folate	Hereditary Folate Malabsorption Syndrome
SLC27A5	603314	Fat Soluble Vitamins	Unnamed
MTTP	200100	Fat Soluble Vitamins	Bassen-Kronzweig syndrome
ApoB	615558	Fat Soluble Vitamins	Familial Hypobetalipoproteinemia
TTP	277460	Vitamin E	Acquired Vitamin E Deficiency
DMT1	600523	Iron	Microcytic anemia with iron overload
HFE	235200	Iron	Classic Hereditary Hemochromatosis
Zip4	201100	Zinc	Acrodermatitus Enteropathica
ENaC	177200	Sodium	Liddle Syndrome
SLC6A19	234500	Niacin (de novo synthesis)	Hartnup Syndrome

GENETICS OF VITAMIN ABSORPTION

Vitamins that can be passively diffused intact, without any additional processing, usually are not affected by any genetic conditions affecting absorption. Vitamin B6 is one of these, and to this author's knowledge, there are no known genetic conditions that affect the ability of vitamin B6 to be absorbed by the enterocytes and passed into the bloodstream. For other B vitamins, this is not the case. For example, mutations in the SLC19A2 gene codes for the main thiamine transporter in the intestine, THTR1, and results in a condition of thiamine-responsive megaloblastic anemia, also called "Roger's syndrome" (OMIM 249270) [39]. The condition is "thiamine responsive" because thiamine in very large doses can diffuse passively; high doses of B1, in the range of 25 to 50 mg per day, taken orally, can alleviate most if not all of the manifestations of the condition. Look up the current RDA for B1 and see how much more patients with Roger's syndrome need, compared to the average American.

There are five inborn errors of metabolism that can affect folate, but only one of these has to do with folate absorption during digestion. Mutations in the proton-coupled folate transporter (SLC46A1) lead to hereditary folate malabsorption syndrome (OMIM 611672). There are several different variants in humans, each resulting in slightly different intensities of the condition, from either full malabsorption or some partial but impaired absorption of folate. Without supplementation with

5-formyltetrahydrofolate , which can bind to the other folate receptor (reduced folate carrier) in intestinal cells, the condition results in a general failure to thrive, anemia, diarrhea, developmental delays, cognitive and motor impairment, behavioral disorders, and, frequently, seizures [40]. Interestingly, carriers of one particular SLC46A1 mutation are found in about 0.2% of the Puerto Rican population [41], while only the first case on the Chinese mainland was reported in 2015 [42]. That is a great example of population genetics for you!

Several genetic conditions affect fat-soluble vitamins, including two of which primarily affect chylomicron formation, which is needed for transport out of the enterocyte and into blood circulation. Since fat-soluble vitamin uptake is rather similar for vitamins A, D, E, and K, and involves formation of micelles containing these vitamins, any condition that would affect formation of the micelles would also affect absorption of all fat-soluble vitamins. This is the case with genetic defects in the bile acid CoA ligase gene (SLC27A5). While not discovered and characterized until 2013, patients with mutations in this gene show reduced absorption of all fat-soluble vitamins, leading initially to vitamin D–deficient rickets, but eventually conditions related to deficiencies in the other fat-soluble vitamins as well [43]. Similarly, genetic conditions that affect chylomicron formation will impede transport of the fat-soluble vitamins to tissues that need them. Two genetic conditions fit this category: Bassen-Kornzweig syndrome and familial hypobetalipoproteinemia. For Bassen-Kornzweig syndrome (OMIM 200100), a mutation in the gene encoding the microsomal triglyceride transfer protein (MTTP) results in the lack of any lipoprotein formation, and thus no chylomicrons, giving this syndrome the more common name of abetalipoproteinemia. In familial hypobetalipoproteinemia (OMIM 615558), a mutation in the gene coding for the apoB protein, which is an integral protein in the membrane of chylomicrons, leads to impaired transfer of fat-soluble vitamins to tissues that require them. Finally the last condition that we'll talk about in the vitamin area is that which only affects a single fat-soluble vitamin—vitamin E. In "acquired vitamin E deficiency" syndrome, or AVED (OMIM 277460), a mutation in the tocopherol transport protein (alpha TTP) leads to the inability of vitamin E to be transferred from the enterocyte to tissues in the body. TTP appears to be important in attaching tocopherols to very low-density lipoproteins (VLDLs). The resulting condition leads to ataxia, or an unsteady gait and neurological symptoms. In some cases, this condition can be treated with high doses of oral vitamin E.

In this section, only a few of the genetic conditions are listed and described, and others exist…if there is a protein involved in the absorption or transport process, then you can assume that there likely is a mutation that can disrupt that process. Take a look for yourself, by going back through the vitamin absorption section of this chapter and then searching for a receptor or protein on OMIM. What did you find? Isn't it fascinating what a single nucleotide change can do to vitamin absorption? With that in mind, let's look at the minerals.

GENETICS OF MINERAL ABSORPTION

Just like vitamin absorption, if there is a protein involved, there is a possibility that genetic mutation can result in mineral malabsorption. Interestingly, that might not always be the case...try to search in OMIM for Dcytb, the iron/DMT1 co-molecule. It's there (OMIM gene number 605745), but there are no listed mutations for this—at least not yet! Not so for DMT1 as an OMIM search indicates that there are five known allelic variants (OMIM 600523), which all lead to a micro-cytic anemia with iron overload. Iron overload, you say? That doesn't make sense. You are right, since DMT1 should be responsible for iron uptake by enterocytes, if DMT1 is mutant, then there should be low iron uptake. However, the authors speculate that in humans, the heme-iron uptake pathway might be upregulated, with DMT1 mediating liver release of iron, and red blood cell uptake, hence the phenotype. As an aside, increased intestinal absorption of iron is also the phenotype of another genetic condition, classic hereditary hemochromatosis (OMIM 235200). In this condition, genetic mutation of an iron sensor molecule called HFE leads to upregulation of DMT1 in enterocytes, and iron overload. Either way, as too much in some tissues or too little iron in other tissues is a problem, either of these genetic conditions can have severe consequences for the carriers.

A simpler case, where the polymorphism in the gene gives rise to the expected condition, involves mutations affecting Zip4, the intestinal zinc transporter. Mutations in Zip4 result in a condition called acrodermatitus enteropathica (OMIM 201100). The individuals with homozygous mutations in the SLC39A4 gene, which codes for Zip4, show low serum zinc levels leading to severe skin rash, alopecia, and diarrhea. Lifelong supplementation with zinc can "cure" this condition to some extent, depending on the severity of the disease. Similarly, mutations in the epithelial sodium channel ENaC results in a condition called pseudoaldosteronism, or Liddle syndrome (OMIM 177200). However, in this situation, the mutation is usually dominant and results in *increased* sodium uptake by the ENaC channel. This leads to increased sodium overall in body fluids, and as expected, hypertension. A low-salt diet is necessary for these individuals in order to limit sodium uptake on a daily basis.

GENETICS OF DE NOVO VITAMIN SYNTHESIS

We now know that bacteria synthesize several of our B vitamins, and certainly there are mutations in these bacteria that could lead to low colonic synthesis. At this time, it appears that bacterial mutagenesis is not a major contributing factor to vitamin deficiency. However, we can make niacin in the liver and vitamin D in the skin, and mutations in production of the starting materials for both of these processes can affect overall vitamin status.

Approximately 9% of the tryptophan that we take in from our diet goes to synthesize niacin. While we still need to get niacin in our diet, which is why individuals with insufficient dietary niacin get pellagra, our own de novo synthesis appears to be needed as well. A condition called Hartnup disease (OMIM 234500) results in pellagra-like symptoms, including a rash, ataxia, and seizures. However, this condition is not due to the so-far elusive niacin receptor, but to the receptor for neutral amino acids, including tryptophan, which, as stated above, is the starting material for de novo niacin synthesis. While Hartnup disease is rarely seen in the United States, probably due to niacin supplementation of our grains, according to one study the frequency of mutations in SLC6A19, which codes for the neutral amino acid transporter, is similar to that of phenylkentonuria [44]. When identified, a high-protein diet is usually recommended to make sure sufficient neutral amino acids are absorbed for both protein and niacin synthesis.

As of late, the news reports seem to indicate that there is an epidemic of vitamin D deficiency in humans. Many reports link deficiency to various conditions, and whether this linkage is causative or a resultant effect, more research needs to be done. What is of note and relevant to this chapter (although it is not listed in Table 3.8 because it is not a specific syndrome, just suspicious linkage) is the link between de novo vitamin D synthesis, through sunlight, and mutations that may affect the ability of the body to initite the de novo synthesis in the first place. In a 2015 study, elderly adults were genotyped and phenotyped with respect to vitamin D metabolic genes and vitamin D serum status. Interestingly, individuals carrying a polymorphism in an enzyme that converts 7-dehydrocholesterol (7DHC) to cholesterol were *more likely* to have low vitamin D levels, perhaps due to a lack of 7DHC, which is the starting material for de novo vitamin D synthesis [45]. However, mutations that inactivate the 7DHC converting enzyme leading to higher levels of 7DHC, and low cholesterol levels, do not result in abnormally high vitamin D levels either [46]. I feel a little like a broken record saying this, but obviously more work needs to be done to figure out the contribution of de novo vitamin D synthesis to the body's needs, with a particular emphasis on how mutations in the genes involved contribute to low vitamin D status.

CHAPTER SUMMARY

Eating a healthy well-balanced diet is the cornerstone to ensuring that you get enough vitamins and minerals daily. As you can see from this chapter though, the process of getting micronutrients into your body can range from simple passive diffusion (e.g. fluoride) to complex transfers bewteen proteins and receptors (e.g. B12).

- Vitamins and minerals can either help each other get absorbed (e.g. iron and vitamin C), or can use the same receptor and compete for uptake (e.g. B5 and B7).
- Surgery involving the GI tract can impair absorption for some vitamins and minerals (e.g. gastric bypass surgery), and conditions that impair the GI system can impair absorption (i.e. pancreatitis).

- Genetic mutation can lead to malabsorption that affects both vitamins and minerals. In the case of genetics, we are really only just skimming the surface of our understanding of how polymorphisms that only have minor consequences might result in subtle changes in absorption, with the real possibility that the RDA for one person may not be the RDA for another, based solely on their genotype.

POINTS TO PONDER

- Celiac disease is known to affect iron absorption, but do you think it might affect other micronutrients? Can you do a PubMed search to determine this?
- Metformin is a first-line treatment for Type 2 diabetes. However, a recent paper by shows that it is taken up in the intestine by, but also interferes with the thiamine transporter, THTR2. What are the implications of this for patients taking metformin?
- In a person who has undergone gastric bypass surgery, they can take supplements to increase B12 absorption. What dietary changes might you also recommend (as related to micronutrient absorption)
- How would you design an experiment to test whether or not DMT1 can transport copper in vivo?
- How well are you doing with micronutrient intake? For one day, or even one week, record your food intake and use USDA's MyPlate Supertracker resource (https://www .choosemyplate.gov/tools-supertracker) to see if you met any or all of your RDAs. Look back on your choices—did you have any meals where micronutrients might have competed with each other for absorption? Did you have any where micronutrients could have helped each other get absorbed (i.e. Vitamin D and calcium)?

References

1. Wilson, T.H. (1962). *Intestinal absorption*. Philadelphia: Saunders.
2. Cassani, B., E.J. Villablanca, J. DeCalisto, S. Wang, and J.R. Mora. (2012). Vitamin A and immune regulation: Role of retinoic acid in gut-associated dendritic cell education, immune protection and tolerance. *Mol Aspects Med* **33**(1): 63–76. doi:10.1016/j.mam.2011.11.001
3. Elbert, J., H. Daniel, and G. Rehner. (1986). Intestinal uptake of nicotinic acid as a function of microclimate-pH. *Int J Vitam Nutr Res* **56**(1): 85–93. Online www.ncbi.nlm.nih.gov/pubmed/3710722

4. Sadoogh-Abasian, F., and D.F. Evered. (1980). Absorption of nicotinic acid and nicotinamide from rat small intestine in vitro. *Biochim Biophys Acta* **598**(2): 385–391. Online www.ncbi.nlm.nih.gov/pubmed/6445756

5. Strum, W., P.F. Nixon, J.B. Bertino, and H.J. Binder. (1971). Intestinal folate absorption. I. 5-Methyltetrahydrofolic acid. *J Clin Invest* **50**(9): 1910–1916. doi:10.1172/JCI106683

6. Hoyumpa, A.M., Jr., R. Strickland, J.J. Sheehan, G. Yarborough, and S. Nichols. (1982). Dual system of intestinal thiamine transport in humans. *J Lab Clin Med* **99**(5): 701–708. Online www.ncbi.nlm.nih.gov/pubmed/6279749

7. Akiyama, T., J. Selhub, and I.H. Rosenberg. (1982). FMN phosphatase and FAD pyrophosphatase in rat intestinal brush borders: Role in intestinal absorption of dietary riboflavin. *J Nutr* **112**(2): 263–268. Online www.ncbi.nlm.nih.gov/pubmed/6120218

8. Buss, D.D., M.W. Hamm, H. Mehansho, and L.M. Henderson. (1980). Transport and metabolism of pyridoxine in the perfused small intestine and the hind limb of the rat. *J Nutr* **110**(8): 1655–1663. Online www.ncbi.nlm.nih.gov/pubmed/7400856

9. Gropper, S.A.S., and J.L. Smith. (2013). *Advanced nutrition and human metabolism* (6th ed.). Belmont, CA: Wadsworth/Cengage Learning.

10. Dakshinamurti, K., J. Chauhan, and H. Ebrahim. (1987). Intestinal absorption of biotin and biocytin in the rat. *Biosci Rep* **7**(8): 667–673. Online www.ncbi.nlm.nih.gov/pubmed/3122856

11. Shibata, K., C.J. Gross, and L.M. Henderson. (1983). Hydrolysis and absorption of pantothenate and its coenzymes in the rat small intestine. *J Nutr* **113**(10): 2107–2115. Online www.ncbi.nlm.nih.gov/pubmed/6619987

12. Reboul, E. (2013). Absorption of vitamin A and carotenoids by the enterocyte: Focus on transport proteins. *Nutrients* **5**(9): 3563–3581. doi:10.3390/nu5093563

13. Reboul, E. (2015). Intestinal absorption of vitamin D: From the meal to the enterocyte. *Food Funct* **6**(2): 356–362. doi:10.1039/c4fo00579a

14. Goncalves, A., S. Roi, M. Nowicki, I. Niot, and E. Reboul. (2014). Cluster-determinant 36 (CD36) impacts on vitamin E postprandial response. *Mol Nutr Food Res* **58**(12): 2297–2306. doi:10.1002/mnfr.201400339

15. Goncalves, A., M. Margier, S. Roi, X. Collet, I. Niot, P. Goupy, . . . E. Reboul. (2014). Intestinal scavenger receptors are involved in vitamin K1 absorption. *J Biol Chem* **289**(44): 30743–30752. doi:10.1074/jbc.M114.587659

16. Traber, M.G. (2008). Vitamin E and K interactions—a 50-year-old problem. *Nutr Rev* **66**(11): 624–629. doi:10.1111/j.1753-4887.2008.00123.x

17. Ganapathy, V., S.B. Smith, and P.D. Prasad. (2004). SLC19: The folate/thiamine transporter family. *Pflugers Arch* **447**(5): 641–646. doi:10.1007/s00424-003-1068-1

18. Burzle, M., Y. Suzuki, D. Ackermann, H. Miyazaki, N. Maeda, B. Clemencon, . . . M.A. Hediger. (2013). The sodium-dependent ascorbic acid transporter family SLC23. *Mol Aspects Med* **34**(2-3): 436–454. doi:10.1016/j.mam.2012.12.002

19. Prasad, P.D., H. Wang, R. Kekuda, T. Fujita, Y.J. Fei, L.D. Devoe, . . . V. Ganapathy. (1998). Cloning and functional expression of a cDNA encoding a mammalian sodium-dependent vitamin transporter mediating the uptake of pantothenate, biotin, and lipoate. *J Biol Chem* **273**(13): 7501–7506. Online www.ncbi.nlm.nih.gov/pubmed/9516450

20. Nabokina, S.M., V.S. Subramanian, and H.M. Said. (2011). Association of PDZ-containing protein PDZD11 with the human sodium-dependent multivitamin transporter. *Am J Physiol Gastrointest Liver Physiol* **300**(4): G561–G567. doi:10.1152/ajpgi.00530.2010

21. Yonezawa, A., and K. Inui. (2013). Novel riboflavin transporter family RFVT/SLC52: Identification, nomenclature, functional characterization and genetic diseases of RFVT/SLC52. *Mol Aspects Med* **34**(2-3): 693–701. doi:10.1016/j.mam.2012.07.014

22. Said, H.M. (2013). Recent advances in transport of water-soluble vitamins in organs of the digestive system: A focus on the colon and the pancreas. *Am J Physiol Gastrointest Liver Physiol* **305**(9): G601–G610. doi:10.1152/ajpgi.00231.2013

23. Roth, J.R., J.G. Lawrence, and T.A. Bobik. (1996). Cobalamin (coenzyme B12): Synthesis and biological significance. *Annu Rev Microbiol* **50**: 137–181. doi:10.1146/annurev.micro.50.1.137

24. Rocha, R.A., V. Devesa, and D. Velez. (2013). In vitro study of intestinal transport of fluoride using the Caco-2 cell line. *Food Chem Toxicol* **55**: 156–163. doi:10.1016/j.fct.2012.12.037

25. Lameris, A.L., P.I. Nevalainen, D. Reijnen, E. Simons, J. Eygensteyn, L. Monnens, . . . J.G. Hoenderop. (2015). Segmental transport of Ca(2)(+) and Mg(2)(+) along the gastrointestinal tract. *Am J Physiol Gastrointest Liver Physiol* **308**(3): G206–G216. doi:10.1152/ajpgi.00093.2014

26. Macallum, A.B. (1894). On the absorption of iron in the animal body. *J Physiol* **16**(3-4): 268–318. Online www.ncbi.nlm.nih.gov/pubmed/16992166

27. Gunshin, H., B. Mackenzie, U.V. Berger, Y. Gunshin, M.F. Romero, W.F. Boron, . . . M.A. Hediger. (1997). Cloning and characterization of a mammalian proton-coupled metal-ion transporter. *Nature* **388**(6641): 482–488. doi:10.1038/41343

28. Shawki, A., S.R. Anthony, Y. Nose, M.A. Engevik, E.J. Niespodzany, T. Barrientos, . . . B. Mackenzie. (2015). Intestinal DMT1 is critical for iron absorption in the mouse but is not required for the absorption of copper or manganese. *Am J Physiol Gastrointest Liver Physiol.* doi:10.1152/ajpgi.00160.2015

29. Lane, D.J., D.H. Bae, A.M. Merlot, S. Sahni, and D.R. Richardson. (2015). Duodenal cytochrome b (DCYTB) in iron metabolism: an update on function and regulation. *Nutrients* 7(4): 2274–2296. doi:10.3390/nu7042274

30. Kato, A., and M.F. Romero. (2011). Regulation of electroneutral NaCl absorption by the small intestine. *Annu Rev Physiol* **73**: 261–281. doi:10.1146/annurev-physiol-012110-142244

31. Schultheis, P.J., L.L. Clarke, P. Meneton, M.L. Miller, M. Soleimani, L.R. Gawenis, . . . G.E. Shull. (1998). Renal and intestinal absorptive defects in mice lacking the NHE3 Na+/H+ exchanger. *Nat Genet* **19**(3): 282–285. doi:10.1038/969

32. Geiser, J., K.J. Venken, R.C. De Lisle, and G.K. Andrews. (2012). A mouse model of acrodermatitis enteropathica: Loss of intestine zinc transporter ZIP4 (Slc39a4) disrupts the stem cell niche and intestine integrity. *PLoS Genet* **8**(6): e1002766. doi:10.1371/journal.pgen.1002766

33. Kambe, T., T. Tsuji, A. Hashimoto, and N. Itsumura. (2015). The physiological, biochemical, and molecular roles of zinc transporters in zinc homeostasis and metabolism. *Physiol Rev* **95**(3): 749–784. doi:10.1152/physrev.00035.2014

34. Rapuri, P.B., J.C. Gallagher, H.K. Kinyamu, and K.L. Ryschon. (2001). Caffeine intake increases the rate of bone loss in elderly women and interacts with vitamin D receptor genotypes. *Am J Clin Nutr* **74**(5): 694–700. Online www.ncbi.nlm.nih.gov/pubmed/11684540

35. Subramanya, S.B., V.S. Subramanian, and H.M. Said. (2010). Chronic alcohol consumption and intestinal thiamin absorption: Effects on physiological and molecular parameters of the uptake process. *Am J Physiol Gastrointest Liver Physiol* **299**(1): G23–G31. doi:10.1152/ajpgi.00132.2010

36. de Lima, K.V., M.J. Costa, C. Goncalves Mda, and B.S. Sousa. (2013). Micronutrient deficiencies in the pre-bariatric surgery. *Arq Bras Cir Dig* **26**(Suppl 1): 63–66. Online www.ncbi.nlm.nih.gov/pubmed/24463902

37. Stein, J., C. Stier, H. Raab, and R. Weiner. (2014). Review article: The nutritional and pharmacological consequences of obesity surgery. *Aliment Pharmacol Ther* **40**(6): 582–609. doi:10.1111/apt.12872

38. Kohlmeier, M. (2013). *Nutrigenetics: Applying the science of personal nutrition* (1st ed.). Oxford/Waltham, MA: Academic Press.

39. Brown, G. (2014). Defects of thiamine transport and metabolism. *J Inherit Metab Dis* **37**(4): 577–585. doi:10.1007/s10545-014-9712-9

40. Diop-Bove, N., D. Kronn, and I.D. Goldman. (1993). Hereditary folate malabsorption. In R.A. Pagon, M.P. Adam, H.H. Ardinger, S.E. Wallace, A. Amemiya, L.J.H. Bean, T.D. Bird, C.R. Dolan, C.T. Fong, R.J.H. Smith, and K. Stephens (Eds.), *GeneReviews(R)*. Seattle, Washington.

41. Mahadeo, K.M., N. Diop-Bove, S.I. Ramirez, C.L. Cadilla, E. Rivera, M. Martin, . . . I.D. Goldman. (2011). Prevalence of a loss-of-function mutation in the proton-coupled folate transporter gene (PCFT-SLC46A1) causing hereditary folate malabsorption in Puerto Rico. *J Pediatr* **159**(4): 623–627, e621. doi:10.1016/j.jpeds.2011.03.005

42. Wang, Q., X. Li, Y. Ding, Y. Liu, Y. Qin, and Y. Yang. (2015). The first Chinese case report of hereditary folate malabsorption with a novel mutation on SLC46A1. *Brain Dev* **37**(1): 163–167. doi:10.1016/j.braindev.2014.01.010

43. Setchell, K.D., J.E. Heubi, S. Shah, J.E. Lavine, D. Suskind, M. Al-Edreesi,. . . L.N. Bull. (2013). Genetic defects in bile acid conjugation cause fat-soluble vitamin deficiency. *Gastroenterology* **144**(5): 945–955, e946; quiz e914–945. doi:10.1053/j.gastro.2013.02.004

44. Levy, H.L., P.M. Madigan, and V.E. Shih. (1972). Massachusetts metabolic disorders screening program. I. Technics and results of urine screening. *Pediatrics* **49**(6): 825–836. Online www.ncbi.nlm.nih.gov/pubmed/5041315

45. Brouwer-Brolsma, E.M., A.M. Vaes, N.L. van der Zwaluw, J.P. van Wijngaarden, K.M. Swart, A.C. Ham,. . . L.C. de Groot. (2015). Relative importance of summer sun exposure, vitamin D intake, and genes to vitamin D status in Dutch older adults: The B-PROOF study. *J Steroid Biochem Mol Biol*. doi:10.1016/j.jsbmb.2015.08.008

46. Rossi, M., G. Federico, G. Corso, G. Parenti, A. Battagliese, A.R. Frascogna,. . . G. Andria. (2005). Vitamin D status in patients affected by Smith-Lemli-Opitz syndrome. *J Inherit Metab Dis* **28**(1): 69–80. doi:10.1007/s10545-005-3676-8

Digestion!

Unscramble the words and then put the letters above the numbers in the puzzle below to discover the phrase related to Chapter 3 materials. All of the words are found in Chapter 3.

1. NOETEYTSCER

☐☐☐☐☐☐☐☐☐☐
       8

2. SEVPASI FUIDOINFS

☐☐☐☐☐☐☐ ☐☐☐☐☐☐☐☐☐
23 4   37

3. VACTIE TTNSPARRO

☐☐☐☐☐☐ ☐☐☐☐☐☐☐☐
20 21 33 12

4. LIMCESEL

☐☐☐☐☐☐☐
    5

5. CYHLMRIONOSC

☐☐☐☐☐☐☐☐☐☐☐
 2   48 36

6. TORNOP-ULPODEC EOLAFT NASROTRTREP

☐☐☐☐☐☐ ☐☐☐☐☐ ☐☐☐☐ ☐☐☐☐☐☐☐☐☐
           9   18 50   49

7. MUDSOI MUINATVILITM TOASENRRRTP

☐☐☐☐☐ ☐☐☐☐☐☐☐☐☐☐ ☐☐☐☐☐☐☐☐☐
         14 16 26 42   46 47 43 29

8. CINTOAPORHR

☐☐☐☐☐☐☐☐☐
7   28   24 32

9. BUNCI

☐☐☐☐☐
45 10

10. DENMUDOU

☐☐☐☐☐☐☐
25 17   31

11. RITSNNETA TEPRERCO AOPENITTL MALTANTEST

☐☐☐☐☐☐☐☐ ☐☐☐☐☐☐ ☐☐☐☐☐☐☐ ☐☐☐☐☐☐☐
34 1   51   39 33   27   52 22 44

12. VIDNIA

☐☐☐☐☐
  15

13. SEMTAIHASNI

☐☐☐☐☐☐☐☐☐
  43   30 3

14. TOGEIGONRS

☐☐☐☐☐☐☐☐
  6 19 35 11 41

15. NIPSVOITH

☐☐☐☐☐☐☐☐
  13   53

☐ ☐☐☐☐☐☐☐ ☐☐☐☐☐☐☐☐☐ ☐☐☐☐☐ ☐☐☐☐☐☐☐
1 2 3 4 5 6 7 8 9 10 11 12 13 14 15 16 17 18 19 20 21 22 23 24 25 26 27 28 29 30

☐☐☐☐☐☐☐☐☐☐☐☐☐ ☐☐☐☐☐☐☐☐☐☐
31 32 33 34 35 36 37 38 39 40 41 42 43 44 45 46 47 48 49 50 51 52 53

NOTES

_____

_____

_____

_____

_____

_____

_____

_____

_____

_____

_____

_____

_____

_____

_____

_____

_____

_____

_____

_____

_____

_____

_____

_____

_____

_____

_____

_____

CHAPTER 4

Got Energy?

Table of Contents

The most fundamental role for micronutrients—especially for the B vitamins but also for some minerals—is ATP synthesis. Every cell does it, and the cell needs vitamins and minerals to keep the process going. I'm always startled by the fact that most people learn about the Krebs or tricarboxylic acid (TCA) cycle and oxidative phosphorylation (A.K.A. the electron transport chain or ETC) in high school, but are not taught that the coenzymes and cofactors in most of the reactions are micronutrients—our vitamins and minerals. We've all heard our parents or other adults say to their children "Eat your veggies. They are full of vitamins," and yet some people don't realize that every living cell needs these vitamins (and minerals) to continue living. I've had students come up to me in class and tell me that all along they've learned

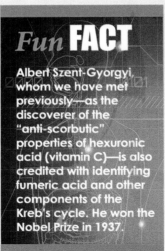

Fun FACT

Albert Szent-Gyorgyi, whom we have met previously—as the discoverer of the "anti-scorbutic" properties of hexuronic acid (vitamin C)—is also credited with identifying fumeric acid and other components of the Kreb's cycle. He won the Nobel Prize in 1937.

about the TCA and ETC, but no one mentioned that NADH was a form of niacin (and so on with the other B vitamins). As we'll see, niacin plays a HUGE role in ATP generation.

ATP is the energy currency that the cell uses to provide the "cash" for many enzymatic reactions to occur. It contains the mineral phosphorus, in the form of a phosphate group (adenosine tri-*phosphate)*. Multiple intracellular signaling reactions use ATP to phosphorylate proteins and lipids, transmitting signals from the cell membrane and other cellular organelles. One reference states that >160 kg of ATP is made collectively by our cells daily [2]. WOW! Because ATP is made, and then used and converted into ADP or AMP, and then recycled back to ATP again continuously, only about 250 g is estimated to be in the body at any given time—but this is the amount of energy equivalent to a AA battery [2]. Who knew that our bodies have enough available energy at any one time to fuel the trademarked pink bunny?

In this chapter, we are going to start with the end reactions—those which generate ATP, but then also talk about the breakdown of sugars, proteins, and fats in reactions that can funnel into the ATP generating processes. The body, it turns out, is a great recycler of things, so in addition to ATP/ADP/AMP recycling, proteins are broken into amino acids and recycled back into proteins or neurotransmitters, large fats are broken down into smaller ones, and sugars are converted into forms for storage and forms for ATP synthesis. Let's start with the end processes that happen inside the mitochrondria, including the pyruvate dehydrogenase complex reaction, the TCA cycle, and oxidative phosphorylation.

THE PATH TO ATP GENERATION

All paths can lead to ATP generation within the cell, and for this chapter, they will. Pyruvate is the output product from glycolysis, but can also be converted back into carbohydrates during gluconeogenesis, into fats when acetyl-CoA is not needed by the Krebs cycle, into the amino acid alanine, or into lactate and ethanol—and many vitamins serve as coenzymes in these reactions (Figure 4.1). We'll talk about each of these processes in this chapter, starting with the pyruvate dehydrogenase complex (PDH), which you should remember from chapter 1 and Figure 1.3. Pyruvate, via PDH and the TCA cycle, is generation of 15 ATP equivalents, so lots of energy for the cell!

Pyruvate dehydrogenase complex

Pyruvate, once transported into the mitochondrion, is trapped there and nearly immediately converted to acetyl-CoA, NADH, and CO_2 by the action of the pyruvate dehydrogenase complex (which we will refer to as PDH complex). As we previously discussed in chapter 1, the PDH complex requires three different subunits (see Figure 1.3), each with its own enzymatic activity, working together to convert pyruvate to acetyl-CoA, NADH, and CO_2. First, the E1 subunit of PDH complex performs the rate-limiting step in the reaction, and also is the subunit where there is

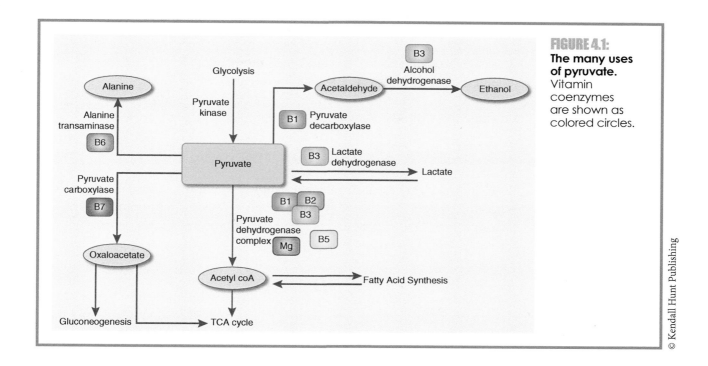

FIGURE 4.1:
The many uses of pyruvate. Vitamin coenzymes are shown as colored circles.

© Kendall Hunt Publishing

substrate specificity for pyruvate. This is important because the other two subunits can be shared with other complexes (which we'll learn about later in this chapter), and thus, E1 specifies that the complex breaks down pyruvate. As you might recall from chapter 1, the E1 subunit requires thiamine in its vitamer form, TPP as part of a substrate binding pocket for pyruvate. What we didn't talk about in chapter 1 was the requirement for magnesium in this pocket as well. The metal ion and TPP are held in place in the E1 subunit by hydrogen boding between amino acids in the binding pocket, hydrogens in TPP, and the magnesium ion. Together, these form a pocket for pyruvate to bind and be catabolized. The E1 subunit is regulated by phosphorylation (here comes nutritional phosphate!) with the phosphorylated subunit being the active form. When there is too much ATP, acetyl CoA or NADH builds up, and the E1 subunit is dephosphorylated, rendering it inactive.

Step two for the PDH complex involves the formation of acetyl CoA by subunit E2. The acetyl CoA is then immediately shuttled off to the TCA cycle, which we'll talk about below. The final step involves an oxidation reaction by FAD, transforming it to $FADH_2$, followed by oxidation of $FADH_2$ back to FAD by NAD+, forming NADH. Thus, we have riboflavin vitamers and niacin vitamers all participating in the PDH complex with thiamine, phosphate, and magnesium. That makes PDH complex quite a micronutrient dense set of enzymes!

Things can go very wrong if the gene coding for the E1 alpha subunit is altered or mutated in any way. This condition is very rare, and was first described in 1970 [3]. As the alpha subunit of the E1 enzyme is encoded by a gene on the X chromosome, the condition is considered to be X linked. However, females and males can both show signs of the condition, which is often lethal in the neonatal period due to lactic acidosis, and both neurological and muscular degeneration. In some cases, especially if the mutation in the gene affects the thiamine-binding portion of the E1 subunit, supplement with excess thiamine has been therapeutic [3].

Let's move on to the TCA cycle!

TCA cycle, or Krebs cycle, and the citric acid cycle

Take a look at Figure 4.2 and familiarize yourself with it before we delve any deeper. What do you see? What is the starting material? What is the ending material for each reaction? What vitamins and minerals do you see playing coenzyme and cofactor roles in these reactions?

First you should notice that the TCA cycle is indeed a cycle or circular. The starting material, citrate, is formed again in a circular fashion. There are three NAD+ vitamers (remember this is the niacin vitamer) which are converted to NADH and these will be funneled off into oxidative phosphorylation for the production of ATP. There are technically two FAD vitamers in the cycle—only one of these is converted and kept as FADH$_2$ of oxidative phosphorylation. The other one is using by alpha keto-glutarate dehydrogenase—and we'll talk about its fate a little later on, along with the TPP and CoA vitamers. The cofactors iron, magnesium, and calcium serve structural functions for their enzymes. The first step in the TCA cycle is the one catalyzed by citrate synthase—taking acetyl coA from the PDH complex reaction, and oxaloacetate from the last step in the TCA cycle and producing citrate to start off the cycle.

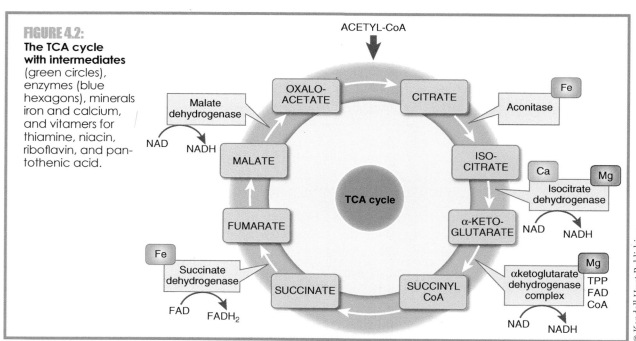

FIGURE 4.2:
The TCA cycle with intermediates (green circles), enzymes (blue hexagons), minerals iron and calcium, and vitamers for thiamine, niacin, riboflavin, and pantothenic acid.

© Kendall Hunt Publishing

So, let's talk about the first step in which we have a micronutrient need, that for aconitase, and as you will see, it is an unusual component of the TCA cycle, compared to the other "regular" enzymes. Aconitase within the TCA cycle converts citrate to isocitrate, and as shown in Figure 4.2 requires one iron cofactor. The iron is actually part of an iron-sulfur complex, which is one of the first reasons why aconitase is a little different: Iron-sulfur complexes (such as we'll see in oxidative phosphorylation) usually function as electron carriers, but in the case of aconitase, this iron-sulfur cluster is in the active site of the enzyme itself, directly involved in the "flipping" of citrate to form isocitrate. But that's not the only unique thing about aconitase. This enzyme links directly to iron sensing by the body. When iron is high, there are 4 Fe molecules in the iron-sulfur cluster, and aconitase is active in the TCA cycle. However, when iron is low, the iron-sulfur cluster contains just 3 Fe molecules, and aconitase leaves the TCA cycle [4]. This regulation is thought to slow down the TCA cycle, and the generation of NADH and $FADH_2$ when iron stores are low. There will be lots more about this specific topic when we talk about blood and iron storage. Hopefully though, for now you can see how iron sensing and specifically low iron stores could result in a slowing or stopping of the TCA cycle.

Moving along, the next enzyme in the pathway is isocitrate dehydrogenase, which converts isocitrate to alpha ketoglutarate (αKG). This is also one of the steps where NAD+ is converted to NADH, which is funneled to oxidative phosphorylation. Studies from the 1980s and one from 2008 have concluded that isocitrate dehydrogenase requires both magnesium and calcium ions for activity [5, 6]. In some cases, manganese can substitute for magnesium, but magnesium is the usual metal ion. What isn't clear at this writing is whether there is an enzymatic function for either of these metals within isocitrate dehydrogenase, or whether they play a structural role. There is a cytoplasmic form of isocitrate dehydrogenase in which Mg^{+2} is needed for the enzymatic conversion, but this is thought to be due to the requirement of NADP in the cytoplasmic form, rather than NAD for the mitochrondrial form—thus, more work needs to be done to sort this out. For our purposes, we will say that both calcium and magnesium are required, likely in structural cofactor roles, and low levels of either ion would impair enzymatic activity.

Alpha ketoglutarate dehydrogenase (αKGDH) complex is next in line, catalyzing the conversion of αKG to succinyl coA. Note that the name contains the word *complex* and also note the vitamers that are needed in this complex (see Figure 4.2). Do you notice any similarities with other enzymes we've talked about? Hopefully you just thought "PDH complex" to yourself, and if so—you're right! PDH and αKGDH complexes share the E2 and E3 subunits, and thus, share those vitamers— coA, NAD, and FAD—which are all needed by those shared parts of the complex. Review the section on the PDH complex to review those subunits. Specificity for αKG is conferred through the E1 subunit, which is unique for this complex. The E1 subunit is the αKGDH enzyme, with the αKG binding site containing TPP and the co-factor Mg^{+2}. Some very complex chemical and physical analysis has revealed the conformational jumping jacks that TPP undergoes during substrate interaction and conversion [7], and this appears to be the case for TPP in all of the E1 subunits it interacts with. We'll see another one later in this chapter in fact. We'll move on from αKGDH complex now, with the reminder that NAD is converted to NADH in the final step of its enzymatic reaction, and again, that NADH is shuttled over to oxidative phosphorylation to participate in ATP formation.

We are going to just briefly mention that the succinyl CoA synthetase reaction removes the CoA from succinyl CoA, *and* in a unique step for those of you interested in trivia, is the only step where either ATP or GTP (depending on the tissue) is formed via substrate phosphorylation—of course, involving the micronutrient phosphorus. However, while the CoA moiety is removed, and goes on to other pathways, no other micronutrients are needed for this step.

The next step in the cycle is a big one—succinate is converted to fumarate, and this part of the TCA cycle links directly to oxidative phosphorylation. Succinate dehydrogenase is the enzyme here, and it is also referred to as succinate coenzyme Q reductase, or oxidative phosphorylation complex II. The enzyme has four functional subunits, two that are functionally within the TCA and two that are functionally within oxidative phosphorylation. On the TCA side of things, the riboflavin vitamers FAD plays an important role in picking up two electrons and becoming $FADH_2$, and then transferring these electrons to an iron-sulfur cluster before transferring down into the electron transport cycle for ATP generation. We'll see this enzyme complex again in oxidative phosphorylation, so we'll move on to our last enzyme now.

Malate dehydrogenase catalyzes the conversion of malate to oxaloacetate in the last (but reversible) step in the TCA cycle. Interestingly, for this enzyme NAD binds first to the active site of the enzyme, and then malate binds, and the reaction progresses producing NADH which is shuttled off to oxidative phosphorylation as the last of three NADH molecules produced with each turn of the cycle [8]. It turns out that for malate dehydrogenase, NAD binding results in a structural or conformational change in the enzyme that allows for malate binding. This is interesting in that NAD is playing both a structural and coenzymatic role.

At this point we move into oxidative phosphorylation, just like many of the products would be doing. Keep in mind though that deficiency in these micronutrients can directly affect the enzyme where the vitamers or cofactor is needed, and in doing so, affect the overall TCA cycle.

Oxidative phosphorylation—making the ATP

You have likely learned about the electron transport chain and the coupling of electron transfer (donators and acceptors) in other classes, so in this section we will really focus on the vitamins and minerals needed as coenzymes and cofactors in the process.

The first step in the process is the enzyme, NADH dehydrogenase, which collects all of the NADH that was made during the TCA cycle (Figure 4.3). NADH dehydrogenase is a HUGE protein complex, consisting of 46 different subunits, some of which are encoded by nuclear genes and some by mitochondrial genes [9]. Luckily, we are not going to go through each of these subunits in detail. Recall that during the TCA cycle, NAD+ was an electron acceptor, creating NADH, the electron donor. Once NADH is shuttled into the oxidative phosphorylation process, the electrons are transferred to FMN, generating $FMNH_2$. Then starts a series of transfers of electrons to iron-sulfate clusters, with a final transfer to coenzyme Q10, or ubiquinone, converting it to QH_2 or ubiquinol. As you might imagine, with so many different subunits, and such a complex mechanism, things can go wrong, and mutations leading to mitochondrial pathologies have been characterized [9]. There is still much to be done though to understand how some of the more subtle mutations might have effects on oxidative phosphorylation.

We have already discussed succinate dehydrogenase, as two of its four subunits are directly involved in the TCA cycle. Reduction of succinate directly provides electrons, which feed into oxidative phosphorylation at this point, and are captured and transferred via FAD, which is converted to FADH2. Iron-sulfur clusters in the B subunit of the protein complex transfer the electrons eventually to ubiquinone, forming QH2/ubiquinol. Complex II also has an iron-containing heme molecule, which is thought to either be a structural component or may participate in reduction of reactive oxygen species—but as late as 2012, its exact function was still unknown [10]. We'll talk about complex III here, too, because as far as micronutrients go, this one (also known as cytochrome bc1) only needs iron, in iron

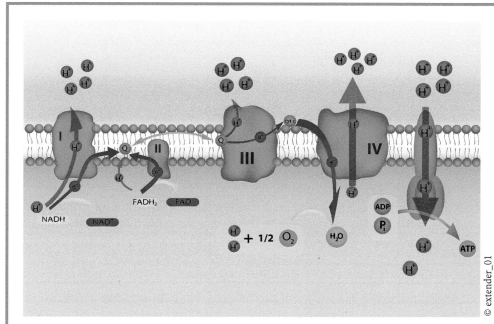

© extender_01

FIGURE 4.3:

The electron transport cycle or oxidative phosphorylation. Complex I is NADH dehydrogenase, complex II is succinate dehydrogenase, and is linked to the TCA cycle, complex III is cytochrome bc_1, and complex IV is cytochrome c oxidase. Finally, ATP synthase, which is sometimes called complex V is responsible for converting all of the electron energy into ATP. A more detailed structure of complex IV was shown in Figure 1.5B.

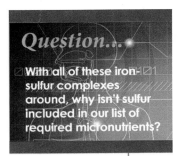

Question...

With all of these iron-
sulfur complexes
around, why isn't sulfur
included in our list of
required micronutrients?

sulfur complexes for electron transfer, and in three heme molecules, which in this case do participate in electron transfer [10]. The electrons are transferred to a heme moiety in cytochrome C, which sits in the membrane between complex III and complex VI.

A whole slew of minerals then come into play for complex. There are not vitamins at work here, but the complex, consisting of 13 different protein subunits using zinc and magnesium as structural cofactors, and iron and copper as enzymatic cofactors. Cytochrome C docks at complex IV first and transfers its electron load to copper, which then transfers to the first of two heme molecules (this one containing only iron). Next the electrons are transferred to a second heme molecule, which contains both iron and a second copper ion. As the electrons move, the H+ ions move in the opposite direction, forming a proton gradient, with the final electron acceptor being oxygen, and forming water. ATP synthase then steps in and performs the final and perhaps most important step in generating ATP. This requires the proton gradient, which was formed during oxidative phosphorylation, and also additional phosphorus to add to ADP, forming ATP. In the end, 10 NADH and 2 succinates made in the TCA cycle can generate up to 36 ATP molecules. That's quite a nice return on investment!

As we end this part of the chapter, think about how deficiency (or even toxicity) of any of the vitamins and minerals needed by PDH complex or TCA and oxidative phosphorylation pathways might impair these pathways. What tissues do you think would be most affected?

CREATINE PHOSPHATE, STORING ENERGY

Imagine this…you are in the gym and going for that 250 lb weight (ok, for me, more like 50 lb weight), and you ate about an hour ago, and had a good mix of macro- and micronutrients. Within 2 to 7 seconds, you can have that energy burst as excess ATP that was created when need was low (i.e., when you were sitting down and eating) was transferred, via the creatine phosphate shuttle from mitochondria to the myofibril. How does this molecule store ATP? Well, it isn't really storing the ATP, but the extra phosphate group, which can be removed from creatine phosphate and put back on to ADP, quickly forming ATP. The enzyme that performs this reaction in both directions is creatine kinase, and this enzyme uses magnesium as a metal cofactor bridge to hold on to the ADP/ATP molecule during the enzymatic reaction. So does taking creatine as a nutritional supplement aid in weight lifting exercise? Some studies say yes, while others say no, with the majority suggestive that there may be some benefit (examples [11-13]). One review states that creatine is not degraded during digestion, and rather up to 99% of it is taken up by muscle, or excreted [14]. However, is it effective if there is not enough magnesium around, or if the overall diet is not sufficient to produce ATP in the first place? Probably not. So, with that in mind, let's move on to other metabolic pathways that yield ATP or products that can produce ATP.

CARBOHYDRATE METABOLISM

Glycolysis

The process of glycolysis generates 2 ATPs by substrate-specific phosphorylation and 1 NADH, which can go directly into oxidative phosphorylation for generation of more ATP. The process needs the micronutrients magnesium, phosphorus, potassium, and niacin to complete its process. Let's look at the enzymes in the process and what they need.

Fun FACT

You might think bananas are your best sources for potassium, but gram for gram, dried prunes are, with nearly double the amount of K+ per 100 g.

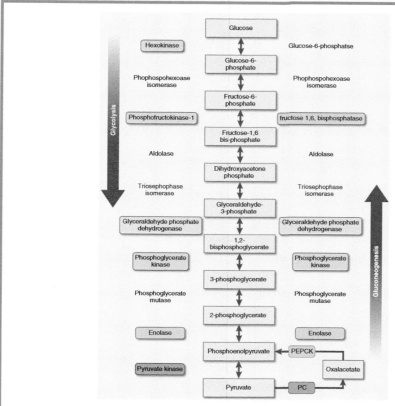

FIGURE 4.4: Glycolysis and gluconeogenesis. The enzymes hexokinase, phosphofructo kinase and phosphoglycerate kinase for glycolysis are boxed in blue-they all require both Mg^{+2} to serve as an ATP/ADP bridge, and phosphorus, which is being transfer from and to APT. The pink shaded box shows the formation of NADH from NAD (or the opposite reaction in gluconeogenesis) by glyceraldehyde-3-phosphate dehydrogenase, while the orange shaded box shows pyruvate kinase which needs Mg^{+2} to serve as an ATP/ADP bridge, phosphate for formation of ATP, and K as a structural co-factor. The purple shaded box shows enolase which uses Mg^{+2} not as an ATP/ADP bridge, but as a structural co-factor, and works in both glycolysis and gluconeogenesis. Fructose 1,6,-bisphosphate for gluconeogenesis also utilizes Mg^{+2} as a structural co-factor and so is boxed in purple. In gluconeogenesis, the green shaded box shows pyruvate carboxylase (PC), which requires biotin and Mg^{+2}. Phophoenyolpyruvate carboxykinase (PEPCK) requires an Mn+ molecule in its catalytic site, and this enzyme (in a tan shaded box) represents a rate-limited step in glycolysis. Those enzymes not boxed do not require micronutrients.

© Kendall Hunt Publishing

As shown in Figure 4.4, four enzymes in the process utilize Mg^{+2} as an ADP/ATP bridge. These enzymes also utilize phosphorus in ADP/ATP. Of the four, pyruvate kinase is unique in also using potassium as a structural cofactor. In a similar fashion, enolase does not use Mg^{+2} as an ATP/ADP bridge, but rather as a structural cofactor. All of these enzymes using Mg^{+2} belong to a class of enzymes called "metallo-enzymes" or "metal" enzymes, because they have a metal core, in this case Mg^{+2}. For enolase, the interaction of Mg^{+2} is still with a phosphate group, but instead of ADP/ATP, the Mg^{+2} forms part of the substrate binding pocket of enolase, holding 2-phosphoglycerate in place during the reaction. Also during glycolysis, glyceraldehyde-3-phosphate dehydrogenase (GAPDH) utilizes the niacin vitamers, NAD, to enzymatically produce NADH for use in oxidative phosphorylation. While GAPDH's function in glycolysis has been known for quite some time, only recently its other roles have come to light—it appears that GAPDH "moonlights" to borrow a term from protein biologists, to serve vastly different roles for the cell, depending on its environment. It can serve as a metabolic sensor for iron metabolism, a signaling protein for apoptosis, bind to actin filaments and microtubules in the cell, where it may be involved in vesicle trafficking, and in a surprising feat, at least from a molecular biology perspective, may bind to and regulate RNA expression [15]. This RNA regulation is thought to involve directed RNA binding to the NAD/substrate binding pocket within GAPDH [16]. Overall these different functions of GAPDH suggest that it serves as a metabolic sensor overall and inform the cell whether to keep glycolysis going or to switch to the pentose phosphate pathway and produce NADPH instead [17]. This switch might occur if a need for antioxidants arises, but the way that GAPDH can sense this need is still unclear, and more work is needed in this area. Before moving on the pentose phosphate pathway though, let's discuss the reverse direction for glycolysis, gluconeogenesis, which occurs mainly in the liver, serving as an alternative pathway for forming glucose from noncarbohydrate metabolic products.

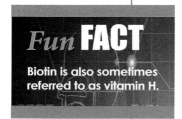

Fun **FACT**

Biotin is also sometimes referred to as vitamin H.

Gluconeogenesis

As shown in Figure 4.4 several of the glycolysis enzymes are shared with the reverse pathway of gluconeogenesis, but there are also unique enzymes. Keeping in mind what they share, and the vitamins and minerals needed for those processes, let's look at the unique gluconeogenesis enzymes and explore the additional requirements for the reverse reaction. This reverse reaction takes place mainly in the liver, where glucose synthesis is initiated to avoid hypoglycemia. The pyruvate that feeds into this pathway is usually generated by lactate, and through the enzyme lactate dehydrogenase, which requires NADH for conversion of lactate to pyruvate. There is also a requirement of NADH for GAPDH when it is working in the reverse direction in gluconeogenesis. Likewise, fructose 1,6-bisphosphase requires Mg^{+2}, but as a structural cofactor rather than an ATP/ADP bridge. Phosphoenolpyruvate carboxykinase (better known as PEPCK) tends to use a Mn^{+2+}, rather than a Mg^{+2}, and the manganese sits in its active site, likely participating in the enzymatic reaction and formation of GDP from GTP [18]. Finally, and perhaps most unique in the pathway, is pyruvate carboxylase. The very name carboxylase should eventually clue you in to the fact that many carboxylases utilize biotin. We'll see this for several other enzymes in this chapter. For pyruvate carboxylase, biotinylation of pyruvate carboxylase holoenzyme (the inactive form) activates it, as the biotin moiety is required in the active site area of the enzyme [19]. The enzyme that biotinylates pyruvate carboxylase is holocarboxylase synthetase—get it? The name tells you what this enzyme does—it adds something (in this case biotin) to the holo (inactive) carboxylases. While there are few instances of biotin nutritional deficiency, genetic conditions affecting holocarboxylase synthetase can affect how much biotin is needed by an individual to biotinylate their enzymes. This is because some of the mutations in holocarboxylase synthetase actually affect the ability of biotin to bind to the enzyme, and be ligated to the carboxylase. In an interesting set of experiments, researchers from the University of Nebraska showed that some mutations in holocarboxylase synthetase, such as the Q699R mutation, could be completely reversed (at least in a petri dish) by adding more biotin. Others, such as the L216R, were "dead" enzymes no matter how much biotin was added [20]. These in vitro findings are very consistent with treatment of individuals with holocarboxylase synthetase deficiency—in some cases high-dose biotin [21]. Taken together, deficiencies in two vitamins, or the minerals magnesium, manganese, potassium, or phosphorus (through GTP/ATP needs) all could affect gluconeogenesis and effectively blood glucose regulation in the body.

Before leaving carbohydrates we must address the pentose phosphate pathway, which can pull a glucose-6-phosphate away from glycolysis in order to create NADPH. I like to think of this as a protective pathway, as the NADPH which is generated can be used directly in producing reduced glutathione for free radical protection (Figure 4.5). Since both the TCA and especially electron transport/oxidative phosphorylation produce free radicals, this is an important parallel pathway.

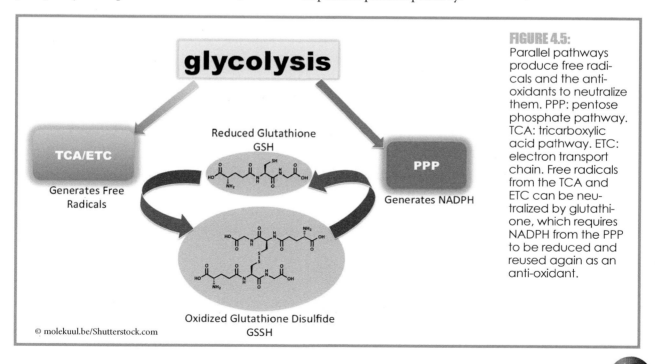

© molekuul.be/Shutterstock.com

FIGURE 4.5: Parallel pathways produce free radicals and the antioxidants to neutralize them. PPP: pentose phosphate pathway. TCA: tricarboxylic acid pathway. ETC: electron transport chain. Free radicals from the TCA and ETC can be neutralized by glutathione, which requires NADPH from the PPP to be reduced and reused again as an anti-oxidant.

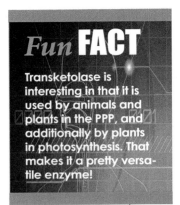

Fun **FACT**

Transketolase is interesting in that it is used by animals and plants in the PPP, and additionally by plants in photosynthesis. That makes it a pretty versatile enzyme!

Pentose phosphate pathway

As stated, the pentose phosphate pathway (also referred to as the hexose monophosphate shunt, but we'll abbreviate it PPP) pulls glucose-6-phosphate out of glycolysis and shuttles it into this pathway. This switch happens when glucose-6-phosphate dehydrogenase (G6PD) is activated by high levels of $NADP^+$ and oxidative stress. Thus, PPP requires niacin, and its vitamer $NADP^+$, and as we progress through this pathway, two equivalents of NADPH are made from the glucose-6-phosphate starting material, as well as ribulose-6-phosphate, which can be used in nucleotide synthesis. If nucleotide synthesis is not required, then the ribulose-6-phosphate molecule is eventually converted back into glucose-6-phosphate to start the process over again. In this second phase, which is also called the nonoxidative phase, the enzyme transketolase is required. Transketolase is one of just four TPP-requiring enzymes—two of which we have already talked about (alpha ketoglutarate dehydrogenase and pyruvate dehydrogenase E1 subunits). We'll talk about the fourth TPP-requiring enzyme before this chapter is over—so look out for it. In addition to TPP, transketolase has a calcium in its active site, which also interacts with the TPP coenzyme. Both are needed for full function of transketolase [22]. As in the E1 subunit for alpha ketoglutarate and pyruvate dehydrogenases, TPP is part of the substrate binding area of the enzyme and as such forms the closed active site for catabolism.

So far we have found a lot of vitamins and minerals that are involved in carbohydrate metabolism—can you name them all, and the enzymes that require them as coenzymes and cofactors? Can you name the role they play in those enzymes—as structural components, parts of the active site, or as enzymatic components? Before moving on to the section on lipid metabolism, it might be a good idea to generate a table or diagram for yourself to keep all of these straight—as we are going to add more to the "pile."

LIPID METABOLISM

There are two main substrates for energy generation, and although you will see in the last section of this chapter that protein catabolism can contribute to energy generating pathways, those two substrates are fats and carbs. In this section we are going to talk about fats—that is, how they get into the pathway and what they can contribute.

Beta oxidation

Free fatty acids bound to serum albumin travel through the bloodstream to cells that need them. Once inside the bloodstream, fatty acids must be transported into the mitochondria, and this is the first step we will discuss. Fatty acids in the cytoplasm are linked to coenzyme A (vitamin B5 vitamer) by a group of enzymes called fatty acyl CoA synthetases. These enzymes grab short, medium, and long chain fatty acids, and with the help of ATP, add on a CoA moiety. Remember—the word *synthetase* (rather than *synthase*) means "two things are ligated together," and this is exactly what happens. Next comes transfer of a carnitine molecule using carnitine acyl transferase I (also called CAT1, or carnitine palmitoyltransferase, CPT1), and this step allows transfer of the fatty acyl-CoA (especially the long ones, which can't diffuse on their own) into the inner membrane of the mitochondria. The structure of this enzyme has not yet been solved, and thus at this time we do not know if any mineral cofactors or vitamin coenzymes are needed—none have been reported to date.

While CAT1 does not appear to require micronutrients for function, synthesis of carnitine, which is needed for this process, and the transfer of fatty acids into the mitochondria does require them (Figure 4.6). The overall process requires 2 Fe^{+2} molecules, 2 ascorbate vitamin coenzymes, 1 PLP (B6), and an NAD [23]. Lets talk about each of these enzymes, step by step. 6-N-trimethyllysine hydroxylase enzyme requires both Fe^{+2} and vitamin C in the form of ascorbate. Studies have shown that Fe^{+2} is required to "hold on to oxygen" in the active site of the enzyme, which yields the hydroxylated product. Ascorbate performs its reducing action, maintaining Fe^{+2} in its reduced form following the reaction. The next enzyme in the process, 3-OH-6-N-trimethyllysine adolase, is a B6-requiring enzyme, which utilizes PLP as a coenzyme in the reaction process [24]. Deoxycarnitine aldehyde dehydrogenase has an absolute requirement for NAD+, although the structure–coenzyme function relationship has not been described [24]. A final hydroxylation

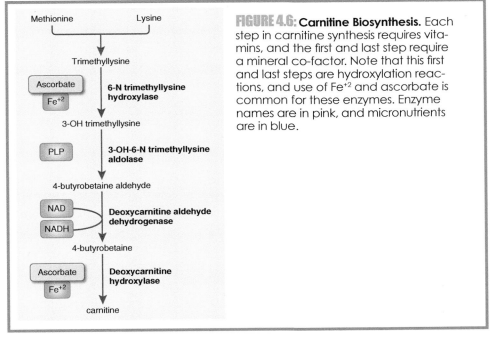

FIGURE 4.6: **Carnitine Biosynthesis.** Each step in carnitine synthesis requires vitamins, and the first and last step require a mineral co-factor. Note that this first and last steps are hydroxylation reactions, and use of Fe^{+2} and ascorbate is common for these enzymes. Enzyme names are in pink, and micronutrients are in blue.

© Kendall Hunt Publishing

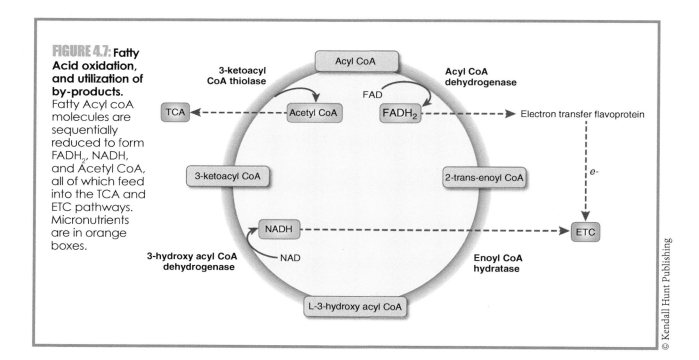

FIGURE 4.7: Fatty Acid oxidation, and utilization of by-products. Fatty Acyl coA molecules are sequentially reduced to form FADH$_2$, NADH, and Acetyl CoA, all of which feed into the TCA and ETC pathways. Micronutrients are in orange boxes.

© Kendall Hunt Publishing

step by deoxycarnitine hydroxylase results in the formation of carnitine. Again, this hydroxylation reaction utilizes Fe^{+2} and ascorbate much as described for the first reaction. Carnitine synthesis occurs mainly in the liver (rat) and in the liver, kidney, and brain (humans). However, since humans are omnivores, they can ingest up to 75% of their carnitine in their diet—the exception being strict vegetarians who likely use de novo synthesis of carnitine to meet all of their needs [24].

Once attached to carnitine, the fatty-acyl carnitine molecule utilizes a carnitine transporter to shuttle into the mitochondrial matrix where the real energy generation work can begin. It is inside the mitochrondrial matrix that carnitine acetyltransferase II (CAT2, or carnitine palmytoyltransferase II, CPT2) catalyzes breakdown of the fatty-acyl carnitine, releasing carnitine (which can be recycled back to pick up another fatty-acyl) and a fatty acyl CoA molecule. This fatty acyl CoA molecule can now enter beta-oxidation, where more micronutrients are needed to make the system work.

Beta-oxidation of fatty acyl CoAs yields acetyl CoA, which feeds into the TCA cycle, NADH and FADH$_2$—both of which feed directly into oxidative phosphorylation. Let's look at this more closely. As shown in Figure 4.7, the first step in breakdown occurs via acyl CoA dehydrogenase. This enzyme is a flavoprotein, requiring FAD and produces FADH$_2$ during the reaction. While not shown in the figure, the type of acyl CoA dehydrogenase that reacts with the fatty acyl CoA is dependent on what type it is—long, short, or medium chain. In humans there are at least three main enzymes in this family of dehydrogenases, and eleven total encoded by the genome [25]. The $FADH_2$ which once produced is transferred to electron transport flavoprotein ("ETF"), and, along with a dehydrogenase, can donate electrons to coenzyme Q, feeding them into the electron transport chain. The 3-hydroxy-acyl CoA dehydrogenase enzyme, in the third step of beta-oxidation, utilizes the niacin vitamer NAD to produce NADH, which is also funneled off to the electron transport chain through complex I. Finally, the last step in the cycle by the enzyme 3-keto-acyl CoA thiolase cleaves off the acetyl CoA molecule from the end of the fatty acid chain, leaving the fatty acid to start the process over again, and the acetyl CoA to enter the TCA cycle. Whew—that's a lot of energy from one turn of the beta-oxidation cycle.

One other vitamin is important in beta-oxidation and should be discussed here, and that's vitamin D. We'll go into more detail in Chapter 5 about this vitamin's function as a transcriptional regulator of genes, but for now, let's discuss the fact that in obese animals and obese humans beta-oxidation levels are lower than in their normal weight counterparts [26]. This seems a little counterintuitive. If there is more fat in an obese individual, shouldn't they use fat more as an energy source? I guess not, but could it be due to levels of a fat-soluble vitamin, namely vitamin D, in obese versus normal weight people? In a study of over 42,000 individuals, BMI was inversely correlated with 25-hydroxy–vitamin D levels (the lower the vitamin D, the higher the BMI). The authors argue though that obesity per se may lead to lower vitamin D levels, rather than the other way around (that low vitamin D is causative) [27]. Interestingly, another article published after the one above showed that a number of enzymes of beta-oxidation can be enhanced with vitamin D supplementation [28], but as this study was done in obese mice, it is not yet clear if the results translate to humans.

FAT AND CARBOHYDRATE METABOLISM, AND MICRONUTRIENT DEFICIENCY

Each of the enzymes discussed in the last two major sections of this chapter can be categorized as to which micronutrient deficiency would lead to low activity. However, in examining these enzymes and reviewing the material, one should consider the impact of B1, B2, B3, and B5 deficiency on energy metabolism through carbohydrate or lipid sources. These vitamins play the largest roles in the process, and deficiency of any one of them is likely to affect multiple enzymes and steps in the processes. This fact is reflected in the fact that deficiency of each of them has effects that manifest in fast-growing tissues and tissues with high-energy needs. Let's look at this in more detail in Table 4.1. What you should be able to appreciate is the similarity in symptoms for each of the deficiencies—affecting skin, nervous system, and the digestive system for the most part. This pattern reflects the fast-growing nature of skin and the epithelium of the digestive system, as well as the high-energy needs for neurons (and as we will see, the synthesis of some neurotransmitters

TABLE 4.1: Comparison of B1, B2, B3, and B5 deficiency symptoms

Beri-Beri (B1)	Ariboflavinosis (B2)	Pellagra (B3)	Pantothenic acid deficiency (rare) (B5)
Slowed Growth Mental Confusion Fluid Retention Vomiting	Slow growth Mouth sores Migraines	Dermatitis Tongue inflammation Dementia Diarrhea	Numbness Irritability Nausea

Can you generate a similar table for the mineral deficiencies — try this for iron, magnesium, manganese and phosphorus.

require these vitamins, too). Thus, micronutrient deficiency, and specifically B-vitamin deficiency, can directly impact these tissues due to effects on energy metabolism. As we'll see in the next section on protein metabolism, some of the same and some new vitamins and minerals are needed in these pathways. While this topic might not seem to belong in the "energy" chapter, protein metabolism pathways intersect with the other metabolism pathways ongoing in the cell, so we include them here.

PROTEIN METABOLISM

Cells are very "environmentally friendly" individuals, and do a lot of recycling of materials between processes. A good example of this is protein synthesis and breakdown. Many of our 20 amino acids are constructed from the carbon backbones of products of glycolysis and the TCA cycle (Figure 4.8). Many of these reactions require the PLP vitamer of vitamin B6, which is why vitamin B6 could be known as the "protein vitamin." Let's look at vitamin B6 in action.

Amino acid metabolism

Amino acids can be synthesized and broken down to other metabolites, or eventually made into waste via the urea cycle. We won't talk about the urea cycle here as we don't have interesting (i.e., major micronutrient-requiring) enzymes in this pathway. We will talk about some important vitamin B6–dependent enzymes in several categories—so let's get started!

Transaminases are enzymes that can move amine groups from one molecule to another—and always require PLP as a coenzyme in the reaction. This reaction is important for both amino acid synthesis and degradation. There are 54 known aminotransferases, all utilizing PLP, and found in all plant, animal, and bacterial species to date [29]. Let's look at aspartate transaminase enzyme (also called aspartate aminotransferase) as an example of an animal aminotransferase. The PLP

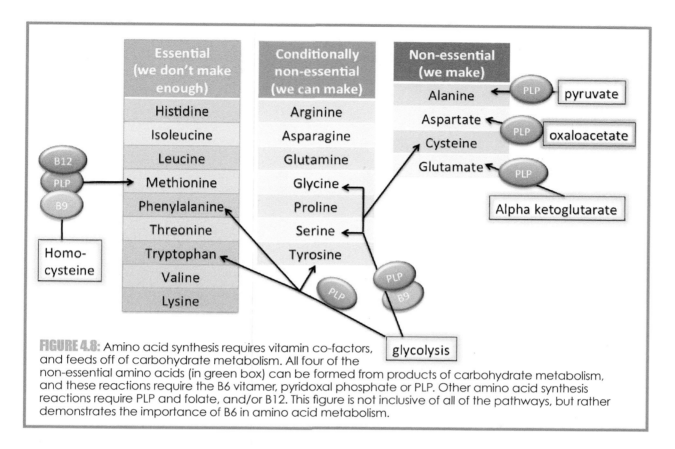

FIGURE 4.8: Amino acid synthesis requires vitamin co-factors, and feeds off of carbohydrate metabolism. All four of the non-essential amino acids (in green box) can be formed from products of carbohydrate metabolism, and these reactions require the B6 vitamer, pyridoxal phosphate or PLP. Other amino acid synthesis reactions require PLP and folate, and/or B12. This figure is not inclusive of all of the pathways, but rather demonstrates the importance of B6 in amino acid metabolism.

coenzyme sites are in the center of the enzyme, within its active site. The reaction itself can go in the forward direction (synthesizing aspartate) or in reverse direction (breaking down aspartate) (Figure 4.9A). Likewise, alanine aminotransferase performs a very similar reaction, but with pyruvate and alanine as products on alternate sides (Figure 4.9B). The alpha-ketoglutarate to glutamate reaction occurs for both of these processes. Alanine and aspartate aminotransferases are the most important aminotransferases for our discussion on protein metabolism, but as stated above, other aminotransferases exist, utilizing products of carbohydrate metabolism to transfer amino groups between products.

The next set of reactions important to amino acid metabolism is the transfer of methyl groups between coenzymes and amino acids. Serine and glycine amino acids have a very similar backbone structure, except that serine has a hydroxymethyl group added. The two amino acids can be interconverted using the enzyme serine hydroxymethyltransferase (SHMT) (also referred to as glycine hydroxymethyltransferase by some groups, but it's the same enzyme). This enzyme family requires PLP as a coenzyme, and folate vitamers as cosubstrates in the reaction (Figure 4.10). In an elegant set of experiments designed to see how PLP functions in the SHMT enzyme, Giardina and colleagues were able to show that PLP can play two distinct roles, depending on the "type" of SHMT enzyme [30]. The cytoplasmic

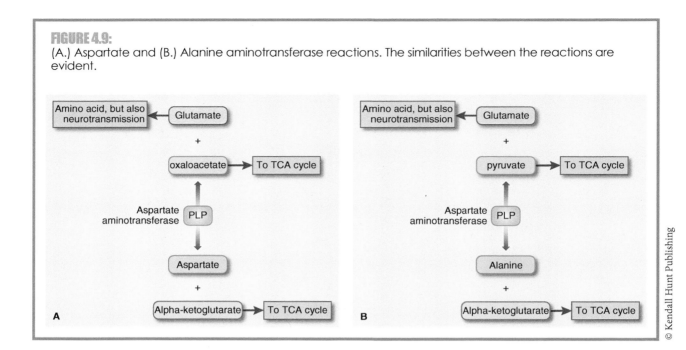

FIGURE 4.9:
(A.) Aspartate and (B.) Alanine aminotransferase reactions. The similarities between the reactions are evident.

FIGURE 4.10:
Serine hydroxymethyltransferase reaction

Serine hydroxymethyltransferase

Glycine + H_2O ⟷ PLP ⟷ Serine

5,10 methylene THF   THF

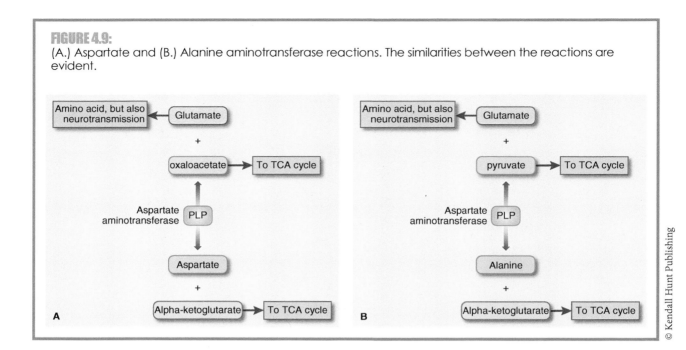

© Kendall Hunt Publishing

form of SHMT (SHMT1) exists as a tetramer in the cytoplasm, and when bound to PLP, forms its active site for the reaction, which PLP also takes part in. The mitochondrial form of SHMT (SHMT2) is found as a dimer, and only forms the tetramer when PLP interacts—and then again, PLP forms the active site for the enzymatic reaction. Thus, for SHMT enzyme, PLP can act both as a structural coenzyme and as an enzymatic coenzyme.

Another type of PLP-dependent enzyme, which is important in amino acid metabolism, is the racemase. This type of enzyme interconverts the D- and L- forms of an amino acid. Although there are seven known racemase enzymes, the majority of these are in bacteria, and only two are active in the animal kingdom [29], alanine and aspartate racemase. However, alanine racemase is only found in invertebrates, leaving us, for the purpose of this discussion, with aspartate racemase. This enzyme was only recently characterized in mammalian cells, where it appears to play an important role in brain neurotransmission, as well as amino acid metabolism. [31]. Whereas the "L" form of an amino acid is used for protein synthesis, it is the "D" form that is used in neurotransmission [31]. Look closely at the box to the right and you should see the difference between the two forms of asparate.

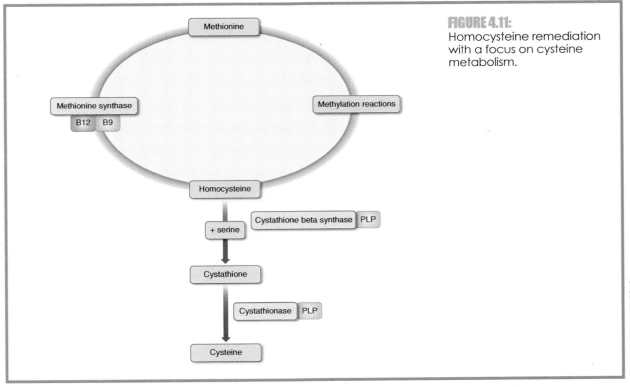

We next need to briefly discuss folate metabolism and the homocysteine pathway, as it relates to amino acid metabolism. We'll of course bring up this pathway later in the book when developmental biology is discussed. Homocysteine is a form of the amino acid cysteine, and is formed and then usually quickly metabolized through several pathways. The one we are going to focus on for the purpose of this chapter is the transulfuration pathway. In this pathway, homocysteine is removed via two PLP-dependent enzymes, crystathione beta synthase and crytathionase. For both of these enzymes, PLP plays a coenzymatic role, and structural research has indicated PLP sites in the active site of the enzymes [32]. While the other parts of the homocysteine remediation pathway require folate and other coenzymes, only PLP is needed in these reactions.

FIGURE 4.11:
Homocysteine remediation with a focus on cysteine metabolism.

© Kendall Hunt Publishing

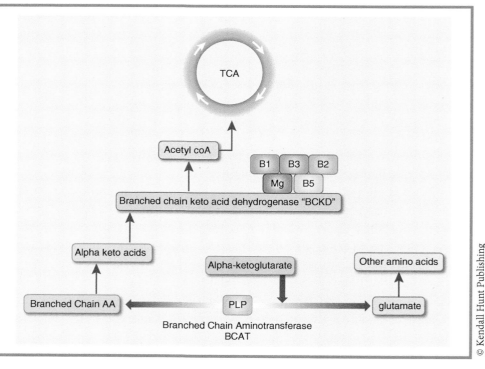

Lastly, we will discuss one very unique group of amino acids. The branched chain amino acids have (hmmm…as you might suspect from their name) a branched side chain—and these three amino acids (valine, leucine, and isoleucine) require a special aminotransferase, which does not so much form them but starts the process of breaking them down. As shown in Figure 4.12, the branched chain aminotransferase of which there are two—a mitochrondrial form and a cytoplasmic form, but for our purposes these work the same—breaks down the branched chain amino acids, forming alpha keto acids, and, in a second step of the reaction which includes an additional substrate alpha-ketoglutarate, forms glutamate. Glutamate is a neurotransmitter, so you can see the importance this breakdown may have in the brain, but interestingly, the products of this pathway can also feed into pathways that produce glutamine and alanine amino acids. Namely, and as shown in Figure 4.12, alpha keto acids are the main substrate for the branched chain keto-acid dehydrogenase (BCKD) enzyme complex. This enzyme is a complex of three subunits, and doesn't use PLP, but does use some vitamers and a mineral that we've seen before in this chapter. Namely, TPP, NAD, FAD, CoA, and Mg are required in one of the three subunits of this enzymes. TPP is part of the enzyme-binding pocket in subunit 1, while NAD and FAD are coenzymes, being converted to NADH and FADH2, which can feed into oxidative phosphorylation. Anyone recognize this enzyme? Do you remember any other enzymes with a similar structure and coenzyme requirement? You guessed right if you said that BCKD seems pretty similar to pyruvate dehydrogenase and alpha-ketoglutarate dehydrogenase

Maple syrup urine disease results when the E1 subunit of BCKD is nonfunctional due to an inherited mutation. Interestingly, mutations in E3, found in all three enzymes, as expected, affects all three enzymes, and results in a condition called "dighydroliopamine dehydrogenase deficiency" or DLD deficiency.

© Kendall Hunt Publishing

complexes. In fact, BCKD shares subunit E2 and E3 with pyruvate dehydrogenase, and alpha-ketoglutarate dehydrogase, and has a unique E1 subunit for its substrate binding domain.

We have covered four different types of PLP-dependent enzymes—amino-transferases, hydroxymethyltransferases, racemases, and synthases. In some cases we know exactly what PLP is doing in its role as a coenzymes (i.e., SHMT), but in other cases more work needs to be done to know if PLP's role is similar or different. PLP is actually a coenzyme for up to 4% of all known enzymes [29], and it is likely that not all of them have been studied in enough detail to discern PLP's exact mechanism. However, since most of PLP's function is in amino acid metabolism, and it is known that PLP can attach to amino groups in these substrates during the enzymatic action, it is likely that when amino groups need to be moved, a PLP-dependent enzyme will be involved.

CHAPTER SUMMARY

In general, substrate metabolism pathways for carbohydrates, fats, and proteins feed back into the general energy generation pathway—TCA cycle and electron transport.

- Carbohydrate metabolism utilizes many of the B vitamins and some minerals. Can you pair up the enzymes with their vitamins and minerals?
- Pyruvate dehydrogenase, alpha-keto-glutarate dehydrogenase, and branched chain keto acid dehydrogenase share two of their three subunits. How would deficiency of TPP affect all three? What about ariboflavinosis? Pellagra?
- Antioxidant production should balance free radical producing pathways in a healthy individual. Which pathways produce antioxidants and which produce free radicals?
- Vitamin D is the only fat-soluble vitamin that we talked about for these pathways—in the case of fat metabolism some of the beta-oxidation pathway genes are regulated by the vitamin D receptor.
- PLP functions in many amino acid metabolism pathways, and in some cases, works alongside folate vitamers.

POINTS TO PONDER

- Many of our metabolic pathways appear to be intertwined. If you mutate an enzyme in one part of the pathway, or have a vitamin or mineral deficiency affecting an enzyme in one part of the pathway, what happens in the other parts?
- What is the difference between a synthase and a synthetase? Just a few letters, but the names refer to the fact that they do different things. There is a committee for that...the Joint Commission on Biochemical Nomenclature [1] says that synthase is an enzyme that catalyzes synthesis, while a synthetase ligates two molecules. How many synthetases and synthases use vitamins and minerals (from this chapter)?
- Are there other fat-soluble vitamins that are affected by obesity? What about any minerals?
- What is the evidence that supplementation with B vitamins or required minerals will help in exercise performance?
- Is there any evidence in the literature for vitamin A to be involved in carbohydrate, protein, or fat metabolism?

References

1. Online www.chem.qmul.ac.uk/iubmb/newsletter/misc/synthase.html
2. Karp, G. (2009). *Cell and molecular biology: Concepts and experiments* (6th ed.). Hoboken, NJ: Wiley.
3. Patel, K.P., et al. (2012). The spectrum of pyruvate dehydrogenase complex deficiency: clinical, biochemical and genetic features in 371 patients. *Mol Genet Metab* **106**(3): 385–394.
4. Lushchak, O.V., et al. (2014). Aconitase post-translational modification as a key in linkage between Krebs cycle, iron homeostasis, redox signaling, and metabolism of reactive oxygen species. *Redox Rep* **19**(1): 8–15.
5. Qi, F., X. Chen, and D.A. Beard. (2008). Detailed kinetics and regulation of mammalian NAD-linked isocitrate dehydrogenase. *Biochim Biophys Acta* **1784**(11): 1641–1651.
6. Rutter, G.A., and R.M. Denton. (1989). Rapid purification of pig heart NAD+-isocitrate dehydrogenase. Studies on the regulation of activity by Ca2+, adenine nucleotides, Mg2+ and other metal ions. *Biochem J* **263**(2): 445–452.
7. Kumaran, S., M.S. Patel, and F. Jordan. (2013). Nuclear magnetic resonance approaches in the study of 2-oxo acid dehydrogenase multienzyme complexes—a literature review. *Molecules* **18**(10): 11873–11903.
8. Dasika, S.K., K.C. Vinnakota, and D.A. Beard. 92015). Determination of the

catalytic mechanism for mitochondrial malate dehydrogenase. *Biophys J* **108**(2): 408–419.

9. Pagniez-Mammeri, H., et al. (2012). Mitochondrial complex I deficiency of nuclear origin I. Structural genes. *Mol Genet Metab* **105**(2): 163–172.

10. Kim, H.J., et al. (2012). Structure, function, and assembly of heme centers in mitochondrial respiratory complexes. *Biochim Biophys Acta* **1823**(9): 1604–1616.

11. Devries, M.C., and S.M. Phillips. (2014). Creatine supplementation during resistance training in older adults-a meta-analysis. *Med Sci Sports Exerc* **46**(6): 1194–1203.

12. Herda, T.J., et al. (2009). Effects of creatine monohydrate and polyethylene glycosylated creatine supplementation on muscular strength, endurance, and power output. *J Strength Cond Res* **23**(3): 818–826.

13. Kilduff, L.P., et al. (2003). Effects of creatine on body composition and strength gains after 4 weeks of resistance training in previously nonresistance-trained humans. *Int J Sport Nutr Exerc Metab* **13**(4): 504–520.

14. Jager, R., et al. (2011). Analysis of the efficacy, safety, and regulatory status of novel forms of creatine. *Amino Acids* **40**(5): 1369–1383.

15. Seidler, N.W. (2013). *GAPDH: Biological properties and diversity. Advances in experimental medicine and biology.* Dordrecht/New York: Springer, pp. xiv, 295.

16. Nagy, E., et al. (2000). Identification of the NAD(+)-binding fold of glyceraldehyde-3-phosphate dehydrogenase as a novel RNA-binding domain. *Biochem Biophys Res Commun* **275**(2): 253–260.

17. Seidler, N.W. (2013). GAPDH and intermediary metabolism. *Adv Exp Med Biol* **985**: 37–59.

18. Holyoak, T., S.M. Sullivan, and T. Nowak. (2006). Structural insights into the mechanism of PEPCK catalysis. *Biochemistry* **45**(27): 8254–8263.

19. Jitrapakdee, S., et al. (2008). Structure, mechanism and regulation of pyruvate carboxylase. *Biochem J* **413**(3): 369–387.

20. Esaki, S., S.A. Malkaram, and J. Zempleni. (2012). Effects of single-nucleotide polymorphisms in the human holocarboxylase synthetase gene on enzyme catalysis. *Eur J Hum Genet* **20**(4): 428–433.

21. Baumgartner, E.R., and T. Suormala. (1997). Multiple carboxylase deficiency: inherited and acquired disorders of biotin metabolism. *Int J Vitam Nutr Res* **67**(5): 377–384.

22. Kochetov, G.A., and O.N. Solovjeva. (2014). Structure and functioning mechanism of transketolase. *Biochim Biophys Acta* **1844**(9): 1608–1618.

23. Borum, P.R. (1983). Carnitine. *Annu Rev Nutr* **3**: 233–259.

24. Vaz, F.M., and R.J. Wanders. (2002). Carnitine biosynthesis in mammals. *Biochem J* **361**(Pt 3): 417–429.

25. Houten, S.M., et al. (2015). The biochemistry and physiology of mitochondrial fatty acid beta-oxidation and its genetic disorders. *Annu Rev Physiol.*

26. Hulver, M.W., et al. (2005). Elevated stearoyl-CoA desaturase-1 expression in

skeletal muscle contributes to abnormal fatty acid partitioning in obese humans. *Cell Metab* **2**(4): 251–261.

27. Vimaleswaran, K.S., et al. (2013). Causal relationship between obesity and vitamin D status: bi-directional Mendelian randomization analysis of multiple cohorts. *PLoS Med* **10**(2): e1001383.
28. Marcotorchino, J., et al. (2014). Vitamin D protects against diet-induced obesity by enhancing fatty acid oxidation. *J Nutr Biochem* **25**(10): 1077–1083.
29. Percudani, R., and A. Peracchi. (2003). A genomic overview of pyridoxal-phosphate-dependent enzymes. *EMBO Rep* **4**(9): 850–854.
30. Giardina, G., et al. (2015). How pyridoxal 5'-phosphate differentially regulates human cytosolic and mitochondrial serine hydroxymethyltransferase oligomeric state. *FEBS J* **282**(7): 1225–1241.
31. Ota, N., T. Shi, and J.V. Sweedler. (2012). D-Aspartate acts as a signaling molecule in nervous and neuroendocrine systems. *Amino Acids* **43**(5): 1873–1886.
32. Aitken, S.M., P.H. Lodha, and D.J. Morneau. (2011). The enzymes of the transsulfuration pathways: active-site characterizations. *Biochim Biophys Acta* **1814**(11): 1511–1517.

Energy!!

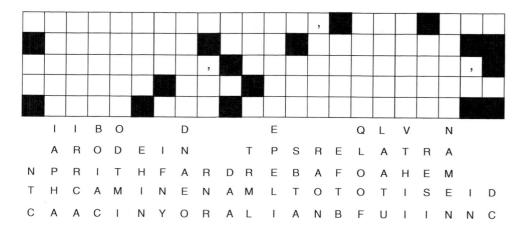

Instruction: Below each column of boxes are letters that will go into the boxes. For example, N, T, and C will go in one of the three boxes of the first column. Figure out the individual words by figuring out which letters go into each box, and you will solve a phrase relevant to energy metabolism. Commas are already included in the boxes.

NOTES

CHAPTER 5

Cellular Physiology
Signaling and Gene Regulation

Vitamins and minerals play key roles in cell signaling and gene regulation

Table of Contents

A cell is just a fatty bag of salty water with some protein and nucleic acid in it—or is it? What if we instead thought of all of the things each and every cell in our body is doing at this very moment, and considered how vitamins and minerals play a role in these processes—that is the journey we are about to embark on in this chapter. We will discover (I hope!) that the fatty bag of salty water is very busy indeed, and that the cell membrane, the salty water, the proteins, and the nucleic acids are responding to various signaling coming from the outside and inside of our cells—and all of this requires mineral and vitamin messengers to complete the job.

Just like cells, we send and receive messages every day—sometimes to the person next door, sometimes across town, to the other side of the country or even to a new country. The difference is that cells use vitamins and minerals in their signaling!

© Macrovector/Shutterstock.com

LIPID BYLAYERS AND RECEPTOR SIGNALING

Phospholipids

Let's start with the fatty bag that holds all of the parts of the cell inside. This bag is not just a passive bag, but a dynamic two-layered phospholipid structure (Figure 5.1), composed of phosphatidylcholine molecules generally on the outside, and phosphatidylinositol as well as phosphatidylenolamine on the inside of the bilayer. The position of phosphatidylinositol on the inside of the lipid bilayer becomes important in a minute—stay tuned. The layers can have different components, or different orientations depending on the

Lipid bilayers are composed of phospholipids, with phosphatidylinositol and phosphatidyleth-anolamine generally found on the inside of the membranes, and phosphatidylcholine. The molecules are arranged so that the hydrophilic parts (cho-line, inositol and the PO_4 group are on the outside of the cell, or facing the cytoplasm, while the glycerol and lipid parts are inside the lipid bilayer.

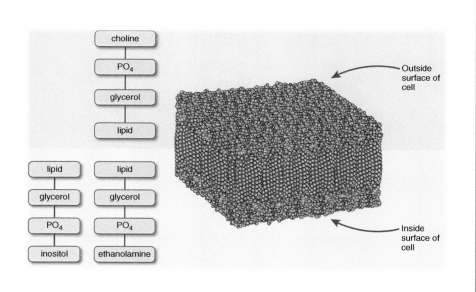

© molekuul.be/shutterstock.com

cell type, and depending on the lipid tail, can be either a loose bilayer or a tight one. When the bilayer is composed of phospholipids whose tails are made of sat-urated fats, such as palmitate, then the lipid bylayer is very structured and more rigid. On the other hand, when the lipid bilayer is composed of phospholipids made with unsaturated fats, such as oleate, then the lipid bylayer is more fluid. So what does this all have to do with vitamins or minerals? Well for minerals, we have phosphate as a necessary and prominent molecule in the lipid bilayer—the phospholipid bilayer. This is one of the reasons why phosphorus is a major mineral—in the group of minerals where the daily requirement is ~700 mg/day. And what about vitamins? There are no "real" (i.e., classified) vitamins present in the lipid bilayer, but choline is a "B-vitamin like" molecule, and was classified as an "essential nutrient" by the Food and Nutrition Board in 1998 [1]. Inositol on the other hand is not an essential nutrient at all, but is an important part of cell signaling from the lipid bilayer to the inside of the cell. Let's take a look.

Cell signaling and calcium waves

When a hormone or growth factor binds to its receptor, this primary messenger starts a signaling pathway that activates a number of different downstream path-ways. Think of it as gossip: one person tells another person, two people tell two others, and each of them tell three people, and so on until everyone in the neigh-borhood knows. In the cell, too, the initial primary message is amplified so that many different downstream second messages are made. As shown in Figure 5.2A,

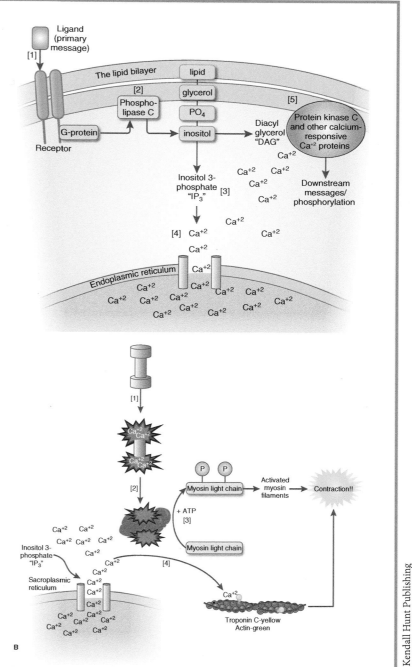

FIGURE 5.2A:
Cell signaling and calcium waves.
A. Cartoon of a cell showing the signaling that occurs when a signaling molecule, such as a hormone binds to its receptor. The messaging starts at the cell membrane with the primary messenger binding to its receptor [1]. This activates the g-protein which activates phospholipase C [2]. Activated phosphlipase C can cleave phosphoinositols in the lipid bilayer, forming IP_3 and DAG. IP_3 travels as a "second messenger" through the cell, and opens up calcium channels in the endoplasmic reticulum [4]. The calcium wave, along with DAG left in the membrane activates protein kinase C, which starts another set of messages traveling in the cell—resulting in phosphorylation of proteins. Other proteins are also activated by the calcium wave and start downstream signals as well.

FIGURE 5.2B:
Signaling downstream of the calcium wave in a myocyte. (1) Calmodulin is activated by calcium binding. (2) Activated calmodulin binds to and activates myosin light chain kinase (3) Myosin light chain kinase phosphorylates and activates the myosin light chain.
(4) At the same time, calcium is released from the sarcoplasmic reticulum by inositol-3- phosphate signaling and calcium binds troponin C, activating contraction.

© Kendall Hunt Publishing

a typical G-protein coupled receptor binding to its hormone message, the initial binding of the message leads to cleavage of phosphatidylinositol in the membrane, basically cleaving that phospholipid in half, generating inositol-3-phosphate (IP_3) and diacylglycerol (DAG)—both of which can signal other proteins in their pathways. IP3 and DAG are known as second messengers. IP_3, for example, can bind to intercellular calcium channels (in the endoplasmic reticulum of most cells, or the related sarcoplasmic reticulum of muscle cells), causing them to open and release calcium into the cytoplasm. Now we've got some mineral action, because that calcium wave travels throughout the cytoplasm, activating many new calcium-binding proteins, which we will talk more about in a moment. One quick example of these calcium-binding proteins, shown in Figure 5.2A, is protein kinase C or PKC. PKC is usually hanging around the cell membrane and is activated by *both* DAG and calcium. It then goes on to phosphorylate intracellular proteins, sending the message even father into the cell. So you can see that with a simple, hormonal message, bound to one (but usually more than one) receptor on the cell, many, many pathways can be activated, and these involve our macrominerals calcium and phosphorus.

Let's talk more about the calcium-regulated proteins, and also about some of the downstream intercellular proteins that are phosphorylated. For this, muscle cells or myocytes are a good system to study because the pathway is well characterized and ends up with an easy to see result, namely contraction. The pathway shown in Figure 5.2A would function in smooth muscle cells, through binding of a hormone such as angiotensin [2]. In skeletal muscle cells, a neurotransmitter would signal an action potential in the cell, which would rapidly result in calcium release and the next set of steps through contraction [3]. For the pathway shown in Figure 5.2B, which occurs after calcium has been released, smooth and skeletal muscles are similar. As stated, calcium signaling activates many proteins, but perhaps (by some people's opinion) one of the most important is calmodulin (calcium modulating protein). Calmodulin binds two calcium on each end of its dumbbell-shaped protein, and in doing this becomes active. Calcium binding to calmodulin causes a conformational change in the protein, such that it now seeks out calmodulin targets and wraps around them. Although not in Figure 5.2B, calmodulin can also phosphorylate itself (called "autophosphorylation") and in doing so activates itself even further (if that is possible, which it is!). One of the important calmodulin targets in muscle cells is the myosin light chain kinase (or MLCK) [4]. Kinases phosphorylate target proteins—or as a phosphate group, usually from ATP or GTP to the target amino acid chain. Myosin light chain kinase is responsible for phosphorylating the light chain of myosin and making it ready for contraction. Calcium-activated calmodulin wraps itself around MLCK, activating it, and in turn MLCK phosphorylates the light chain, leading to myosin fibril assembly. At approximately the same time, nearby, calcium waves have reached the actin bundles. These bundles have tropomysin and three types of troponin, one of which, troponin C, binds calcium (see Figure 5.2B). Binding of calcium to troponin C changes its structure, so that troponin C pulls tropomycin away from actin, exposing myosin-binding sites. When this occurs, the activated myosin can bind and contraction occurs. Throughout this process, multiple proteins are phosphorylated and some bind calcium. Both of these minerals cause structural changes to occur in the proteins, in some cases (as we have discussed) activating them. Thus, calcium and phosphorus are acting as structural cofactors in these processes.

Our muscles can't go on contracting forever, so something has to happen to stop the process. In the case of myosin light chains, a phosphatase—or protein that removes phosphorylation, comes in and removes the myosin light chain phosphorylation, rendering it inactive or at least ready for the next request to contract. There are many types of phosphatases and most leave us with free phosphate flowing in the cellular salt water. Likewise, calcium eventually falls off of its target proteins and is taken back up by the sarcomeric reticulum to be ready for the next wave of signaling to occur.

SECONDARY MODIFICATIONS AND GENE REGULATION

Vitamins and minerals play significant roles in gene regulation, both in affecting modification on genomic material and in regulating the actions of protein transcription factors and other proteins, as well as DNA, through secondary modification. In this chapter, we are going to look at vitamins and minerals that play a direct role in gene regulation—as part of transcription factor complexes—and those vitamins and minerals that play indirect roles—namely, as part of secondary modifications or required for the enzymes imparting secondary modifications (Figure 5.3) on proteins. Let's get started.

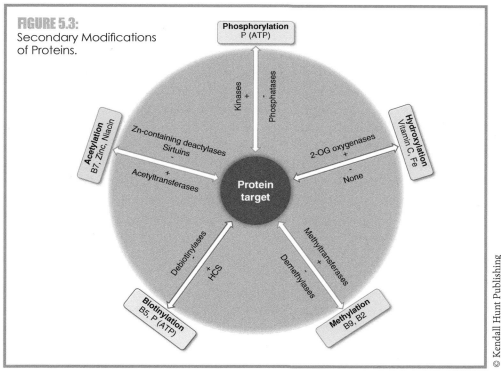

FIGURE 5.3:
Secondary Modifications of Proteins.

© Kendall Hunt Publishing

Modification of intracellular proteins

While many people should immediately associate phosphorylation with a need for phosphorus, can you think of other vitamins and minerals that might also be involved in secondary protein modifications? It turns out that proteins can be acetylated (requiring pantothenic acid), biotinyated (requiring B7), methylated (requiring folate), and hydroxylated (requiring vitamin C and iron). All of these are considered "post-translational modifications" or PTMs, which constitute a group of covalent additions of moieties to proteins, and usually result in a change of activity for that protein. There are actually many more types of PTMs and they have been compiled in several databases [5, 6]. For now, we focus on the types of PTMs listed above, but you should take a look at these online databases and see if you can find any other links to vitamins and minerals.

Let's talk about phosphorylation, which you already saw in the previous section. Phosphorylation of proteins occurs through kinases, and there are many different kinases (who themselves are sometimes the target of another kinase). Each of these utilizes ATP (containing our nutritional mineral phosphorus), and transfers a phosphate group from ATP to the target protein. This leaves a phosphorylated protein and ADP. Phosphorylation usually seems to activate a protein—a negative charge from the phosphate group is added, and this can expose an active site in an enzyme so that a metabolite can bind, change the position of the protein within the cell, change a protein's interactions with other proteins, and even change whether a protein "lives or dies"—whether it is targeted for degradation or allowed to continue functioning [7]. Proteins can be repeatedly phosphorylated and dephosphorylated. The dephosphorylation event is done by a phosphatase enzyme, leaving the phosphate group, which is usually recycled by the cell. Targets of kinases and phosphatases include other kinases, structural proteins (such as myosin light chain, as we saw previously), signaling proteins (such as calmodulin, which actually both binds calcium and autophosphorylates itself), receptors (which again often autophosphorylate, meaning they bind proteins, and then have a kinase region that phosphorylates another part of themselves), transcription factors, and histones (both of which we will discuss further below). For the cell, phosphorylation events are capable of fine-tuning events in response to signals from the cell environment, and can do so at the level of the cell membrane, the intracellular organelles, the cytoplasm, and in the nucleus. A nice review by Humphrey and colleagues summarizes the PTM phosphorylation well [7].

Proteins are also acetylated, and this also usually neutralizes the positive charge of a lysine amino acid within a protein, changing the activity of that protein. The acetylation process always requires acetyl-CoA as a cosubstrate in the reaction [8]. It can be added cotranslationally or post-translationally, depending on the enzyme (and there are many different acetyltransferases). To date, the known targets of these acetyltransferases include histones (discussed in detail below), transcription factors, and one structural protein, tubulin [8]. Deacetylation also requires vitamins and minerals (specifically niacin and zinc, which are required by the two classes of deacetylases), the sirtuin deacetylases (which require NAD+), and the Zn-containing deacetylases. NAD+ plays a coenzymatic role in the sirtuin family, while zinc plays a structural cofactor role in the Zn-containing deacetylases. A review on this subject was recently published by Menzies and colleagues [8].

While we saw in the previous chapter that holocarboxylase synthetase enzyme (HCS) biotinylates proteins such as carboxylases to activate those proteins for their roles in energy metabolism, did you know that HCS targets other cellular proteins as well? This finding is relatively new, but recent evidence indicates that HCS targets heat shock proteins (involved in the stress response) and histones (which will be discussed below in more detail). In each case, lysine amino acids are targeted, and the reaction requires ATP (so phosphorus again) as an energy source to covalently link biotin to the protein. The biotin moiety appears to provide activation in some cases (such as the carboxylases it targets in energy metabolism) and repression in others (such as in histone biotinylation). At this time, it appears that biotinylation can be actively removed, but the identification of these so-called "debiotinyase" enzymes has eluded scientists [9, 10].

Methylation is next on our list of vitamin-associated processes. This PTM requires the folate cycle, with S-adenosyl methionine as the methyl donor. Following transfer, S-adenosyl homocysteine forms, which needs the folate cycle for remediation. Thus, methylation of proteins (and as we'll see below, DNA) is part of, and required by, the folate cycle. There are two types of methyltransferases—arginomethyltransferases, which transfer a methyl group to an arginine amino acid within a protein, and lysine methyltransferases, which (as you might guess from the name), transfer a methyl group to a lysine amino acid within a protein. The position of the methylated amino acid, as well as the number of methylated amino acids within a protein, determines whether methylation has a positive or negative effect on the protein, with the majority of methylation sites leading to repression. Many different transcription factors and histone proteins cycle between methylation and demethylation, and a variety of lysine demethylase enzymes act to remove the methyl group. Some of these lysine demethylases required FAD (vitamin B2), while others utilize iron as a structural cofactor. However, at this time, an arginine demethylase enzyme has not been identified. A good review of protein methylation as it relates to transcription factors by Carr and colleagues should be read for more information on the subject [11].

Although there are many more types of protein PTMs, we'll lastly speak about hydroxylation of proteins by 2-oxoglutarate (2-OG) oxygenases. These oxygenases require iron as a structural cofactor, oxygen as a cosubstrate, and ascorbate as a coenzyme, needed to keep iron in a reduced state. Hydroxylation targets many different categories of proteins, including transcription factors and histones, structural proteins (such as collagen—very important for bone and skin matrix), signaling proteins, ribosomal proteins, and even splicing proteins [12]. For histones, hydroxylation is one way in which lysine methylation is relieved, with about 20 histone hydroxylases identified to date. The hydroxylation step appears to be an intermediate step in some processes, and a final step in others—thus, there are no known enzymes that specifically remove the hydroxylation; rather the hydroxyl PTM is either converted to another PTM or remains on the protein until it is degraded.

In summarizing these five PTMs that require vitamin and mineral coenzymes and cofactors, the importance of micronutrients in cellular regulation is evident. Conditions (genetic or through poor nutrition) that deprive an organism of micronutrients deprive the cell of important messengers that sense the microenvironment, nutrient, and protein needs. Without these the cell becomes like an uncharged iPhone™ unable to send or receive messages to and from the outside world.

MODIFICATIONS THAT AFFECT GENE EXPRESSION

Before we leave the topic of post-translational modifications, it is important to note the effect of modifications on gene expression. As noted above, transcription factors (including the TATA protein and its accessory proteins) and histones can undergo modifications that affect whether gene expression is up regulated or down regulated. This makes sense as transcription factors, by their very nature, are required to specifically activate and repress genes. Histones, which bind DNA and wrap chromatin, also play a role in gene regulation, and modification of histones by methylation, acetylation, and biotinylation (among other PTMs) can affect how tightly or loosely the DNA is wrapped around the histone. This configuration of histone-DNA wrapping determines how accessible the DNA is to transcriptional regulation. One interesting example of this is biotinylation of histones surrounding the gene for sodium dependent multivitamin transporter (SMVT). As you hopefully recall, this is the biotin and pantothenic acid receptor in the intestine. As biotin levels rise, HCS biotinylates histones—in particular, histone H4—including those histones surrounding the gene encoding SMVT. When biotin levels in the cell are high, biotinylation of histone H4 effectively shuts off the SMVT gene transcription by up to 85%, while the reverse is true when biotin levels are low [13].

DNA and RNA are also subject to modification by many of the same moieties as protein. One of the best studied examples of this is DNA methylation, which is responsible for epigenetic regulation of gene expression. Epigenetic regulation refers to changes in gene expression that are not due to changes in the base pair sequence of DNA, and in some cases can be inherited. Methylation of DNA occurs on cytosine residues and can be found both throughout the gene and localized to promoter regions, thus confirming gene regulation signals. DNA methylation usually occurs when a cytosine is followed by a guanosine residue, which is called a CpG dinucleotide, and these are further found in clusters, called "CpG islands." DNA methyltransferases use s-adenosyl methionine as part of the folate cycle, to transfer methyl groups to DNA and RNA. An excellent example of the importance of folate to methylation of DNA comes from a study that looked at folate regulation of its own receptor. When folate levels are low, the DNA in the CpG islands surrounding the genes for the reduced folate carrier and folate carrier 1 proteins are unmethylated, and thus, the folate receptors are expressed at a high level. Conversely, when folate levels are high and the cell does not need to take in more folate, the DNA in the CpG islands become highly methylated, effectively shutting off transcription of the gene.

Zinc finger transcription factors

Of all of the transcription factor families out there (and there are a lot—see the Animal Transcription Factor Database where 72 families are listed: http://www.bioguo.org/AnimalTFDB/family_index.php), we must discuss the zinc finger family of transcription factors, as this family executes vitamin A and vitamin D actions on gene expression. For both vitamin A (retinoic acid forms) and vitamin D (1, 25 hydroxy vitamin D3), zinc finger transcription factors serve as ligand-responsive receptors for the vitamers. That is to say that once either of these two vitamers bind to its receptor, the receptor translocates to the nucleus and mediates target gene expression. As noted in chapter 1 (see Figure 1.5), the name of the transcription factor family is derived from the fact that zinc serves as a structural cofactor for these proteins. Binding of zinc to cysteine amino acids in the protein results in the formation of "fingers" that can reach out and bind to the DNA. While the zinc-finger domain is found at the N-terminus of the protein, the ligand binding domain is found at the C-terminus. Let's look at the vitamin A, vitamin D, and thyroid hormone zinc finger transcription factors individually.

Vitamin A

There are actually six different forms of the vitamin A zinc finger transcription proteins: RAR subfamily (alpha, beta, and gamma) and RXR subfamily (alpha, beta, and gamma) (Table 5.1). While the RAR forms of the factor bind to all-trans retinoic acid, the RXR forms binds to the 9-cis form of retinoic acid, which makes sense as the two sub-amilies only share about 29% homology in their ligand binding domain [14]. All zinc finger transcription factors form dimers, or need to interact with another zinc finger family member to direct gene expression. This "other member" is usually RXR (at least for RAR, VDR, and THR), but other members use other dimerization partners or can homodimerize [15]. Interestingly, RXR is also capable of homodimerizing with itself, and it seems it is this combinatorial regulation of RXR (α, β, γ): RXR (α, β, γ) or RAR (α, β, γ): RXR (α, β, γ) is how gene regulation is fine tuned. In fact, and related to our discussion about histone modification, RAR:RXR heterodimer is known to recruit histone acetyltransferases to the region of the promoter where it is bound. Conversely, an RAR:RXR dimer that does not have retinoic acid can also bind to promoters and recruit deacetylases for gene repression [16]. We talk more about vitamin A and gene regulation targets

TABLE 5.1: Zinc Finger Transcription Factors important to micronutrient action

Zinc Finger Transcription Factor	Ligand	Major Function in Gene Regulation
Retinoic Acid Receptor (RAR-alpha, RAR-beta and RAR-gamma)	All trans retinoic acid	Developmental gene expression Skin gene expression
Retinoid X Receptor (RXR-alpha, RXR-beta, and RXR-gamma)	9-cis-retinoic acid	Dimerization partner for Zinc Finger Transcription factors Can also homodimerize
Vitamin D Receptor	1, 25 hydroxy Vitamin D_3	Gene expression related to bone metabolism
Thyroid Hormone Receptor (THR-alpha, THR-beta)	Triiodothyronine (T3) (iodine)	Thyroid axis/ metabolism

in several chapters of this book, so for our purposes here, keep in mind that for retinoic acid, vitamin A acts through gene regulation and utilizes zinc finger transcription factors of the RAR and RXR subfamilies.

VITAMIN D

The vitamin D receptor (VDR) is a single receptor protein, which binds to the active form of vitamin D, mediating vitamin D responsive signals. According to most reports, VDR usually heterodimerizes with RXR, but it can homodimerize [17]. Thus, in some situations, vitamin A sufficiency is required for vitamin D action. Like vitamin A zinc finger transcription factors, VDR binding to promoters recruits histone acetyltransferases and activates gene expression. We'll discuss some of these VDR target genes specifically in the skin and bone sections, as both of these tissues utilize vitamin D–specific gene regulation for differentiation and maintenance.

In an interesting twist though, VDR can act "nongenomically"—in other words, by not directly binding DNA [18]. This finding was also called "rapid response signaling" of VDR. The key is that these rapid responses occur within minutes, rather than hours, and are not inhibited by inhibitors of transcription or translation, thus indicating that the gene expression machinery is not (yet) in play for these responses. It appears that VDR bound to 1,25 hydroxy vitamin D_3 at the cell membrane does so in specialized membrane structures called "caveolae," or little wells, and from there can directly signal some of the cell signaling pathways that we discussed above, or can be transported through the cytoplasm and mediate traditional (but longer acting) gene expression changes. The rapid response always requires calcium, which gives us the clue to the types of signaling cascades that are activated—including phospholipase C, protein kinase C, among others. To date, none of the other zinc finger transcription factors have been found to mediate these rapid responses, making it a unique function for VDR.

THYROID HORMONE

Iodine is a component of thyroid hormone, and its receptors (thyroid hormone receptor, or THR) belong to the zinc finger transcription factor family. THR has both an alpha and a beta form, and like VDR, usually interact as a heterodimer with RXR—thus, like VDR require vitamin A for function [19]. Interestingly, T3 has both positive and negative effects on gene regulation, and these effects can both be mediated by THRs in conjunction with RXR. We talk more about THRs in our development section as thyroid hormone action is important for embryogenesis.

CHAPTER SUMMARY

The cell membrane is not a static bag around the cell. Rather it is an important first stop in cell signaling from the membrane to the nucleus or other organelle. This usually results in amplification of the initial signal such that a single hormone binding to its receptor can simultaneously activate multiple proteins and downstream pathways.

- Calcium waves, and calcium-responsive proteins such as calmodulin, mediate this amplification of cell signals.
- Proteins undergo post-translational modifications, which involve and require micronutrients such as phosphorus, pantothenic acid, B9, B7, and niacin. PTMs modify protein activity, either repressing or enhancing it.
- Modification of histones and DNA can modulate gene expression. Again micronutrients are key coenzymes and cosubstrates in these processes.
- Vitamin A, vitamin D, and iodine (thyroid hormone) utilize zinc finger transcription factors to mediate their genomic (gene regulation) actions.

POINTS TO PONDER

- Extracellular calcium levels are tightly regulated (as we will see when we talk about bone metabolism). What about intracellular calcium? How?
- What happens to PTM events when vitamin and mineral levels are low? How does the cell detect these and do something about it?
- Did you check out the PTM databases? Can you find other instances where PTMs require vitamins or minerals?
- Why does VDR, but not the other zinc finger transcription factors, have a rapid response system? What signals do you think are mediated by this system?

References

1. Institute of Medicine (U.S.). Standing Committee on the Scientific Evaluation of Dietary Reference Intakes. Panel on Folate, Other B Vitamins and Choline. Subcommittee on Upper Reference Levels of Nutrients. (1998). *Dietary reference intakes for thiamin, riboflavin, niacin, vitamin B_6, folate, vitamin B_{12}, pantothenic acid, biotin, and choline.* Washington, D.C.: National Academy Press, pp. xxii, 564.
2. Large, W.A., S.N. Saleh, and A.P. Albert. (2009). Role of phosphoinositol 4,5-bisphosphate and diacylglycerol in regulating native TRPC channel proteins in vascular smooth muscle. *Cell Calcium* **45**(6): 574–582.
3. Kuo, I.Y., and B.E. Ehrlich. (2015). Signaling in muscle contraction. *Cold Spring Harb Perspect Biol* **7**(2): a006023.
4. Tidow, H., and P. Nissen. (2013). Structural diversity of calmodulin binding to its target sites. *FEBS J* **280**(21): 5551–5565.
5. *PTM Statistics Curator: Automated Curation and Population of PTM Statistics from the Swiss-Prot Knowledgebase.* Online http://selene.princeton.edu/PTMCuration/
6. *dbPTM: An integrated database for protein post-translational modifications.* Online http://dbptm.mbc.nctu.edu.tw/index.php
7. Humphrey, S.J., D.E. James, and M. Mann. (2015). Protein phosphorylation: A major switch mechanism for metabolic regulation. *Trends Endocrinol Metab.*
8. Menzies, K.J., et al. (2015). Protein acetylation in metabolism-metabolites and cofactors. *Nat Rev Endocrinol.*
9. Hassan, Y.I., and J. Zempleni. (2006). Epigenetic regulation of chromatin structure and gene function by biotin. *J Nutr* **136**(7): 1763–1765.
10. Zempleni, J., et al. (2014). Novel roles of holocarboxylase synthetase in gene regulation and intermediary metabolism. *Nutr Rev* **72**(6): 369–376.
11. Carr, S.M., et al. (2015). Post-translational control of transcription factors: methylation ranks highly. *FEBS J.*
12. Ploumakis, A., and M.L. Coleman. (2015). OH, the Places You'll Go! Hydroxylation, Gene Expression, and Cancer. *Mol Cell* **58**(5): 729–741.

13. Zempleni, J., et al. (2009). Sodium-dependent multivitamin transporter gene is regulated at the chromatin level by histone biotinylation in human Jurkat lymphoblastoma cells. *J Nutr* **139**(1): 163–166.

14. Allenby, G., et al. (1993). Retinoic acid receptors and retinoid X receptors: interactions with endogenous retinoic acids. *Proc Natl Acad Sci USA* **90**(1): 30–34.

15. Zhang, R., et al. (2015). Transcriptional factors mediating retinoic acid signals in the control of energy metabolism. *Int J Mol Sci* **16**(6): 14210–14244.

16. le Maire, A., and W. Bourguet. (2014). Retinoic acid receptors: Structural basis for coregulator interaction and exchange. *Subcell Biochem* **70**: 37–54.

17. Wan, L.Y., et al. (2015). Relationship of structure and function of DNA-binding domain in vitamin D receptor. *Molecules* **20**(7): 12389–12399.

18. Haussler, M.R., et al. (2011). Vitamin D receptor (VDR)-mediated actions of 1alpha,25(OH)(2)vitamin D(3): genomic and non-genomic mechanisms. *Best Pract Res Clin Endocrinol Metab* **25**(4): 543–559.

19. Nagaya, T., et al. (1996). Second zinc finger mutants of thyroid hormone receptor selectively preserve DNA binding and heterodimerization but eliminate transcriptional activation. *Biochem Biophys Res Commun* **222**(2): 524–530.

Cell signaling

```
H O L O C A R B O X Y L A S E S Y N T H E T A S E
N I L U T R I S I P W M G Z T M J X Q P D B N J D
Z K Q B M Y G V J O T K D Q G T Y J H V Q X L Y B
G L L N V L X L G L T J R J K Y L O J B B L T Q T
E S A T A H P S O H P I X L T I S N J X J N Y D D
X L P D Y T T B T Z X T N N E P N Q N T Y D R P Q
Z B L G Y P Y Z Y D C X O Y H A L A J B K Y B D Z
B D L T X Q Q R G A I I Y A L P L J S L V B T W B
M T Z Y Z Y N M L D T C T X P A R O D E C B B G T
T G N J L L M C L A T I A P C Y T V E A Y Q T D X
E N I D O I I T L N D M T C N L B I L V R Q D G Y
X N L X V T W Y N Y G T W N I Q D M O X A K V T Q
V M D J R Y T K L D N N M D Z O O M Z N Q C L W M
T D R I P E Q I Y D X Y R V N D N G Y B N B Q G L
W Q O Y C N N V K J R X D T U Q K I R Z L L T D Z
X L Q A J O M M Q K B G T L B R R N T X B D D B Y
J Y J W S Y P X P J G B I Z W M B Z M E W B N P N
R B N I Y D D W R V N N L P Z N G G N M R N R K W
R J T Q Q L B D B M D Z T N Q W Z B Z T Y W J K R
V O M P R D D L Y Z M T L Z Y X J Q L Y M N P M D
L N D M Y W J M L Y T R B T M P V Q R N P Y M D B
```

Instructions: Each clue refers to a term from Chapter 5. Use the clues and then search for the term in the word search puzzle above.

	Clue	Answer
1.	Cell membrane component involved in signaling	_____
2.	Dumbbell-shaped calcium-binding protein	_____
3.	Phosphorylates proteins	_____
4.	Removes phosphate groups from proteins	_____
5.	Protein modification that requires B5	_____
6.	Protein modification that requires B7	_____
7.	Vitamin A vitamer involved in gene regulation	_____
8.	Vitamin D vitamer that binds to VDR	_____
9.	Protein deacetylases, which require NAD+	_____
10.	Needed by VDR and RXR as a structural cofactor	_____
11.	Enzyme that uses B7 as a coenzyme	_____
12.	Name of cellular structures involved in nongenomic vitamin D signaling	_____
13.	Thyroid hormone requires this micronutrient	_____

NOTES

CHAPTER 6

Free Radicals and the Micronutrients that Neutralize Them

Table of Contents

Let's get radical, and by this I don't mean to "depart markedly from the usual" as radical is defined in Webster's Free Dictionary [2]. What I mean is that we are going to talk about the molecules which contain unpaired electrons that are floating around in our body, what they do (the good and the bad), and how micronutrients help to neutralize them and keep our body and cells young, cancer free, and ready for the next attack. Autoxidation of the organic (carbon, oxygen, and hydrogen-containing) substances in our body generates free radicals and peroxides, namely $OH(\bullet)$, $O_2(\bullet-)$, $LO_2(\bullet)$, $HOOH$, and $LOOH$—the so-called reactive oxygen species (ROS). Oxidative stress is the so-called paradox of aerobic life. To survive in such an unfriendly oxygen environment, living organisms must obtain a variety of water- and lipid-soluble antioxidant compounds from food—antioxidant vitamins and minerals.

WHAT ARE FREE RADICALS? AND WHY DO WE HAVE THEM IN THE FIRST PLACE?

Simply, a free radical is a molecule with an unpaired electron. Without going into too much detail on nuclear physics, atoms are only stable, or nonreactive, when all charges are matched up and electrons are paired with an equal number of protons in the nucleus.

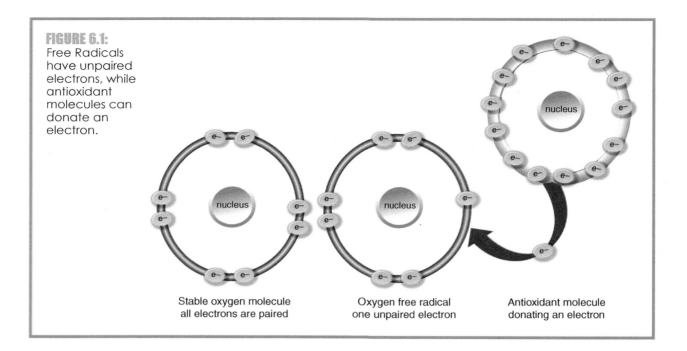

FIGURE 6.1:
Free Radicals
have unpaired
electrons, while
antioxidant
molecules can
donate an
electron.

Stable oxygen molecule
all electrons are paired

Oxygen free radical
one unpaired electron

Antioxidant molecule
donating an electron

Electrons must also be paired in the "electron cloud"; so, for oxygen, which has eight protons in its nucleus, the eight electrons would match (no charge) and would be paired (not a free radical oxygen) (Figure 6.1). However, when oxygen loses one electron (and we'll talk in a minute about how this might happen), it becomes a free radical, which is usually written O. That is because there is one less electron to balance the protons in the nucleus, and the seven remaining electrons cannot all be paired, leaving one unpaired (lonely) electron (indicated by the dot). However, just having an unpaired electron does not make an atom a free radical. Take, for example, fluorine, written as "F," having atomic number 9. It "sits" right next to oxygen "O" whose atomic number is 8. However, we don't talk much about fluorine; rather we talk about fluoride in biology. This is because with 9 electrons, 1 electron is left unpaired in the electron cloud, meaning F likes to naturally gain an electron and is usually found as F− ion, or fluoride, with 10 electrons and a negative charge. Gaining the electron makes F− an ion, but not a free radical. Another good example relevant to this class is the ferric and ferrous ions of iron. Iron, with abbreviation "Fe" and atomic number 26, has 26 protons in its nucleus and 26 electrons revolving around outside. As this is an even number, each proton can be nicely paired with an electron in the electron cloud. However, in biological systems, iron is highly reactive and can lose electrons making it either Fe^{2+} (ferrous iron ion, with 24 electrons) or Fe^{3+} (ferric iron ion with 23 electrons). These ions are floating around our body and incorporated into proteins that use iron as a structural or enzymatic cofactor. Ferric iron, Fe^{3+}, is an oxidant and if left on its own can create oxygen free radicals by stealing electrons—so we need antioxidants to intercede and donate electrons. We are getting a little ahead of ourselves here, but suffice to say, free radicals and oxidants have unpaired electrons and are quite reactive with

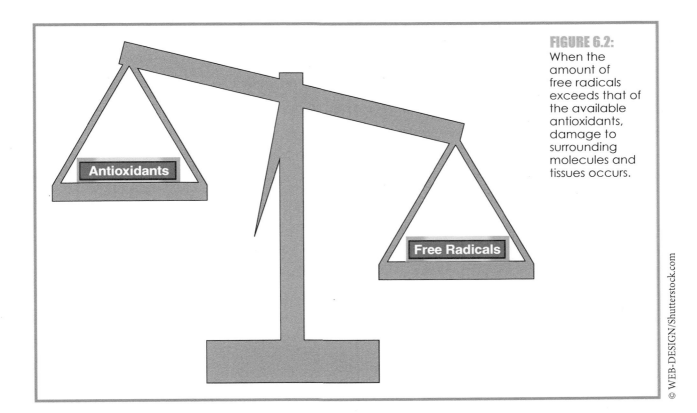

© WEB-DESIGN/Shutterstock.com

other molecules around them. With this information in hand, let's look at how free radicals are formed in our bodies.

Free radicals are formed during normal enzymatic reactions in our bodies, which include the electron transport chain (i.e., cytochrome *oxidase* C enzyme) and reaction by an enzyme called NADPH *oxidase*, which generates free radicals to fight infections. This is normal, and under normal circumstances our body has a good supply of antioxidants around to neutralize the free radicals once the infection is controlled and ATP is produced. However, if the balance between free radicals and antioxidants is tipped in favor of the reactive radicals (Figure 6.2), chaos ensues. Oxidants, such as ferric iron, will steal electrons from neighboring molecules and create reactive oxygen species (ROS) or oxygen free radicals. We then have a situation where the free radicals attack cell membranes, proteins, and even our DNA. The result is destructive—like rust on a car—and disruptive to normal cellular activities.

WHAT IS AN ANTIOXIDANT?

In the simplest sense, an antioxidant is a molecule that can neutralize oxidizers and free radicals. There are three conditions that must be met for an antioxidant to do its job: (1) it must be a molecule that can be easily oxidized (i.e., a "reducing" agent), but for which there are mechanisms in place to neutralize it back again; (2)

it must be a free radical scavenger, whose purpose is to roam around looking for molecules with lonely electrons to donate to; and (3) in the best-case scenario, it is found in the right place and at the right time to control and quench all newly generated oxidants and free radicals, keeping cellular activities functioning normally.

These are pretty important jobs, and thus there are several types of antioxidants to do these jobs—the water-soluble antioxidants, in which vitamin C takes the lead role, assisted by vitamin B3 in a supporting role; the fat-soluble antioxidants, with vitamin E in the lead role, with some vitamers of vitamin A playing supporting roles; and the mineral antioxidants, which include manganese and selenium as cofactors in proteins needed to produce and act as antioxidant enzymes. We'll go through each of these vitamin and mineral antioxidants in more detail in this chapter.

WATER-SOLUBLE ANTIOXIDANTS

The term water-soluble antioxidant means that the antioxidant activity of the molecule (and the molecule itself) resides in the aqueous part of the cell—the fluids, as opposed to the membranes and lipid portions of the cell. As the majority of a cell is actually aqueous (and we'll talk more about that in a later chapter), the water-soluble antioxidants have a lot of work to do in keeping aqueous free radicals neutralized. In this section, we'll discuss two major water-soluble antioxidants, vitamin C, which we get from our diet, and glutathione, which we can synthesize; so, while it is not a micronutrient, it is intimately involved in both vitamin C and, as we will see, vitamin E antioxidant functions.

Vitamin C keeps oxidation at bay

As discussed in Chapter 1 (Figure 1.1), humans cannot make vitamin C, because we have an inactive Gulo gene. While not making vitamin C might have been an evolutionary advantage (remember that making vitamin C also generates some oxidants), we now need to eat foods rich in vitamin C (or take a pill) to get our daily requirement (between 75 and 90 mg/day) [3]. Note that it is recommended that smokers take an additional 35–40 mg/day [3]. Why do you think that smokers are recommended to take in more vitamin C per day than nonsmokers? Hopefully you said because smokers take in carcinogenic and toxic compounds that can produce free radicals, and that is true [4]. What is also true is that on average, smokers have lower circulating levels of ascorbate, and there is some evidence, although modest, that increasing vitamin C intake can provide some reduction in oxidative stress levels if one does smoke [4].

So, what does vitamin C actually do to reduce oxidative stress? Vitamin C, in the vitamer form ascorbic acid (AA), can donate electrons and neutralize free radicals. In doing so, AA is converted first to semidehydroascorbate (SDA) and then to dehydroascorbate (DHA) or fully oxidized vitamin C.

Don't let *abbreviations* **confuse you...**

The "B5" in NADH-cytochrome B5 reductase is only the enzyme name/form and does not refer to Vitamin B5.

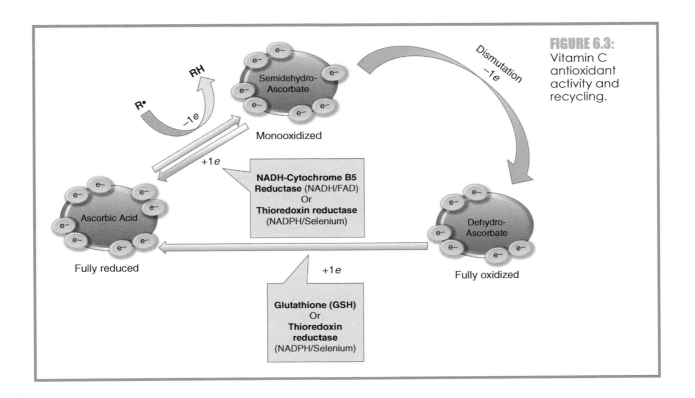

Remember that antioxidants basically give their life to neutralize free radicals, and by doing that, they become oxidized. However, one of the reasons that vitamin C, or AA, is an antioxidant is because there are mechanisms in place to help neutralize the oxidized forms.

As shown in Figure 6.3, AA reacts with free radicals, neutralizing them, and, in the process, forms the ascorbyl radical semidehydroascorbate (SDA). SDA is also a radical, but according to most sources [5], it is not as reactive as the free radicals that were neutralized. There are two different enzymes that can neutralize SDA, NADH-cytochrome B5 reductase, which requires NADH, and is a flavoprotein (requiring FAD), and thioredoxin reductase, a selenoprotein that utilizes NADPH. If not neutralized, then SDA is dismutated to DHA. Interestingly, DHA is also found in foods, and can be taken up by some cell types (such as liver). In all cases, DHA is degraded if it is not converted back to AA, by either glutathione (GSH) or thioredoxin reductase. However, this process is not as efficient in making AA (i.e., 100% is not converted back), and thus dietary AA is still needed [5].

As we will discuss in later chapters, AA also functions with oxygenase enzymes, where it is needed to convert Fe^{3+} back to Fe^{2+}. With these enzymes, DHA is formed and needs to be converted back (at least some of it) to AA, using mostly the GSH pathway. Thus, vitamin C recycling requires selenium with B3 (as thioredoxin reductase is a selenoprotein and uses NADPH) or B3 and B2 (for NADH-cytochrome B5 reductase).

Obviously we need vitamin C daily, as it is a water-soluble vitamin involved in many enzymatic reactions. Its antioxidant activities are a little more controversial, and the controversy surrounding these started with a study published by Ewan Cameron and Linus Pauling in 1976 [6], in which they showed that cancer patients treated orally with high-dose ascorbate (a whopping 10 g/day, started IV, and continued orally) had a significantly longer survival time (more than 200 days) than a control group without ascorbate treatment. The thought was that cancer has both inflammatory and pro-oxidant components, and antioxidants may block these and subsequently block cancer growth. In the Cameron and Pauling study, various cancer types were included, with matched controls, although treatment groups included only 100 patients, while the control group had 1000 patients. However, by 1982, controversy arose when Dr. William DeWys, Chief of Clinical Investigations at the National Cancer Institute, wrote an article concluding that there had been bias in the study—control cancer patients were labeled "untreatable" at a later cancer stage than the ascorbate-treated group *and* only Dr. Cameron monitored the ascorbate-treated group. Patients in the control group were monitored by many different physicians, all who could have had different criteria for deciding when a cancer was "untreatable" or terminal [7]. Two subsequent Mayo Clinic studies with high-dose ascorbate in more matched patients, both treated with and not previously treated with chemo, showed no effect of vitamin C in extending survival rates [8, 9]. What was the difference between these studies, in addition to the more rigorous evaluation of the patients for control and treatment groups? One additional difference was that Cameron and Pauling began with an intravenous (IV) treatment and followed with the oral dose [6]. Interestingly, subsequent trials with IV vitamin C have shown promise, especially in combination with chemotherapy [10].

So while vitamin C as an anti-cancer agent is still under intense investigation, there are some other studies suggesting that high-dose vitamin C may be useful to prevent disease or enhance quality of life. Aging research is one of these areas, likely due to the known "oxidative stress" that increases, with decreased glutathione levels, with aging. Multiple studies (reviewed in [11]) have been conducted in humans and animals with varying results. Others have examined vitamin C supplementation on various brain (learning, memory, neuronal survival) functions, since the brain is highly metabolic and therefore produces a lot of free radicals. As reviewed in a recent paper [12], animal studies support a role in memory and learning, as well as overall neuronal/brain structure, but human studies have not been able to confirm these findings. The good news is that even high doses of vitamin C are not harmful; so, more studies on the effectiveness of this antioxidant can be done, and perhaps fine-tuned to tease out the doses needed for optimal health, in both healthy individuals and those with disease. As discussed above, we already know that smokers need more vitamin C daily than nonsmokers due to the oxidants in cigarette smoke. We should, with more research, be able to discern other conditions where higher dose vitamin C intake may be needed.

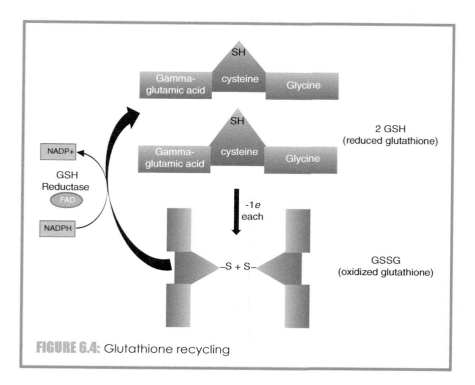

GSH synthesis and recycling

The synthesis of the thiol-tripeptide, GSH, is linked to homocysteine remediation through the alternate pathway where cysteine can be derived from homocysteine (Figure 4.11) and to amino acid synthesis namely for glutamate and glycine. The full structure of GSH (also known as L-γ-glutamyl-L-cysteinylglycine) is shown in Figure 6.4, and as one can see, the cysteine-derived portion of the molecule contains the thiol (SH) group, which is used in the reducing reactions. Two GSH molecules rapidly react to form GSSG, or oxidized glutathione. As a water-soluble antioxidant, GSH serves as an electron donor for the antioxidant enzyme (and selenium-containing) glutathione peroxidase. GSH itself is involved in vitamin C recycling, and in conjunction with vitamin C or E (as we'll see when we put it all together below) it participates in removing oxidizing toxins from cells [13].

Lucky for us, glutathione can be synthesized from amino acids we have on hand, and it can be recycled by the enzyme GSH reductase (Figure 6.4). GSH reductase is a flavoprotein, with the FAD vitamer at its reactive center, next to the substrate-binding area. It also requires NADPH for activity, as NADPH donates a proton (H+) for each molecule of regenerated GSH. However, aging has been strongly associated with lower overall glutathione levels. In some studies this is said to be due to a lower overall protein intake in elderly adults [14], and it is clear that cysteine levels, which can be modulated through diet or synthesis, are one of the rate-limiting factors in GSH synthesis [15]. However, it is also clear that synthesis (through the level of

Something to **CONSIDER**

reduced glutathione is sold as a general over-the-counter supplement. Would you recommend taking this? Why or why not?

GSH synthetase enzyme, which makes GSH from cysteine) can decline with aging, and multiple studies show that the overall circulating levels of GSH in the blood and other tissues are significantly lower in older adults than young ones [15]. But, as stated in this recent review [15], it is still not clear why GSH levels decline with aging, or if there is anything that can be done to prevent the decline. The author of this textbook would suggest that the best approach would be to maintain a healthy, vitamin C, B-vitamin, and protein-containing diet at all ages and stages of life, to at least ensure the nutrients are available for synthesis, and recycling of cellular antioxidants like glutathione.

In summary, the water-soluble antioxidants include vitamin C, which we need to ingest, and glutathione, which our bodies can make. These are the two that are either a vitamin (ascorbic acid) or needed by vitamins (glutathione) for regeneration pathways. There are other phytochemicals and food components with antioxidant activities that are also water soluble, but these are outside of the scope of this book and chapter.

FAT-SOLUBLE ANTIOXIDANTS

The lipid-soluble micronutrient antioxidants are vitamin E, otherwise known as the vitamer groups of the tocopherols and tocotrienols, and members of the carotenoid (vitamin A family), namely lycopene and beta (β) carotene. These fat-soluble antioxidants can be located within cellular membranes, providing onsite neutralization of peroxy-lipid free radicals arising from normal physiological processes, such as inflammation and mitochondrial respiration, as well as environmental and dietary pro-oxidants that can increase free radicals in our body [16]. An example showing how closely the structure of alpha-(α-)tocopherol, the bioactive vitamer of vitamin E, resembles the lipids found in cell or organelle membranes and how it can act to neutralize lipid radicals is shown in Figure 6.5.

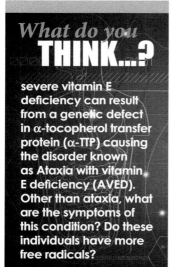

What do you
THINK...?

severe vitamin E deficiency can result from a genetic defect in α-tocopherol transfer protein (α-TTP) causing the disorder known as Ataxia with vitamin E deficiency (AVED). Other than ataxia, what are the symptoms of this condition? Do these individuals have more free radicals?

Vitamin E

Vitamin E is considered the powerhouse of the lipid-soluble antioxidants. As discussed in Chapter 1, there are eight naturally occurring vitamin E vitamers, namely alpha, beta, gamma, and delta (α, β, γ, and δ) tocopherols, and α, β, γ, and δ tocotrienols. Of these, α-tocopherol is the best studied and also considered to be the most bioavailable form of vitamin E, as the α-tocopherol transfer protein (α-TTP) binds most tightly and preferentially to this form—100% binding, compared to 50%, 30%, and 1% for the β, γ, and δ forms, respectively [17]. Does bioavailability correlate directly with bioactivity? Not necessarily. While α-tocopherol certainly has been well studied the most, and according to a recent paper, studies on tocotrienols only constitute about 3% of the literature on vitamin E [18], the α, β, and γ

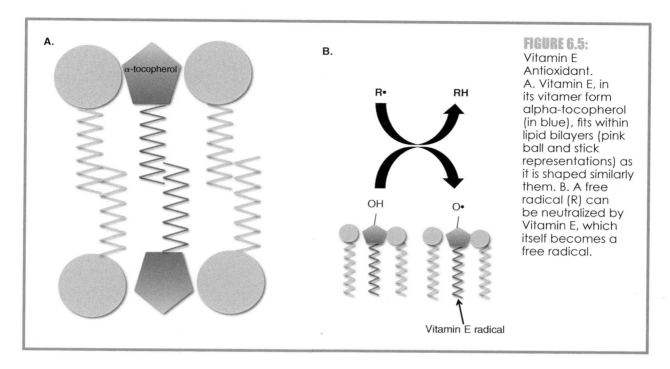

FIGURE 6.5:
Vitamin E Antioxidant.
A. Vitamin E, in its vitamer form alpha-tocopherol (in blue), fits within lipid bilayers (pink ball and stick representations) as it is shaped similarly them. B. A free radical (R) can be neutralized by Vitamin E, which itself becomes a free radical.

tocopherols *and* tocotrienols have similar antioxidant activities in some studies [18]. However, this is another area where we must say "more work is needed." In particular, how are tocotrienols transported throughout the body (if they even are) if they don't bind well to α-TTP? And then, what is their role in the body in the presence or absence of sufficient α-tocopherol? In one study, oral supplementation of α-tocotrienol, but not α-tocopherol, in α-TTP knockout female mice led to a restoration of fertility [19]. These data suggest that the tocotrienols have their own transport systems (or perhaps that there are more than one mode for transporting all vitamin E vitamers) and that they may either be converted into tocopherols or be independent activities. There is also evidence of seemingly nonantioxidant activities for vitamin E, such as modulation of certain enzymes and processes [18, 20], but these areas are even less well studied such that it is not always clear which form of vitamin E possesses those activities.

Since this chapter is on antioxidants, we will return now to vitamin E's known antioxidant activities and, in particular, the role vitamin E vitamers play in neutralizing lipid radicals. As shown in Figure 6.6A, vitamin E antioxidant activity is ultimately associated with both vitamin C and GSH antioxidant activity. Vitamin E radical is somewhat unstable, and so AA steps in to neutralize it, returning vitamin E to its nonoxidized state. Of course, this reaction results in the formation of DHA, which then is neutralized by GSH, as we have discussed before. In this way, one could say that both vitamin C and GSH participate in the cycle of lipid radical neutralization. GSH can also directly neutralize lipid radicals and does this as a cosubstrate for the selenoprotein glutathione peroxidase (GSH peroxidase, Figure 6.6B) [21], which we will discuss more in the section "Enzymatic antioxidants."

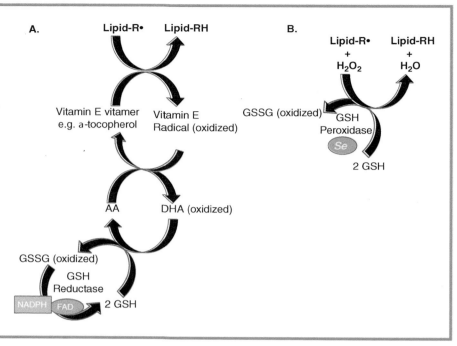

FIGURE 6.6: Putting it all together. (A) Vitamin E neutralization of lipids is linked directly to Vitamin C and glutathione pathways. (B) In addition, two glutathione molecules can directly neutralize lipid radicals with the help of GSH peroxidase and a selenium co-factor.

Intake versus **bioavailability**

there appears to be some discordance between how much Vitamin E is circulating, and how much dietary Vitamin E is consumed. What might cause this discordance?

So, what about vitamin E's role in neutralizing lipid free radicals associated with disease processes—does vitamin E supplementation over the RDA provide any protection against radical formation or damage? The current guidelines state that an intake of 22.4 IU per day is adequate for those 14 years of age and over. Yet, up to or perhaps even more than 90% of Americans do not consume the daily recommended levels [22]. Interestingly, this same study shows that circulating vitamin E values are normal for most individuals, with younger aged individuals showing slightly more deficiency than older individuals [22]. However, as stated in the study cited above, studies need to address the role of vitamin E supplementation in which vitamin E status is known. Also, bioavailable vitamin E may be low in certain disease processes, such as obesity [23] Additionally, total circulating vitamin E is low in some conditions, including Alzheimer's [23]and is reduced in elderly individuals with impaired lung function, compared to age-matched individuals with normal circulating levels [24]. Other examples exist, so take a look at the literature and make your own conclusions as to whether circulating levels of vitamin E might predict cause or effect of the disease.

So, what does this mean for the vitamin E supplementation studies? Many studies actually supplement at relatively high levels (i.e., 1000 IU), without noting what the circulating or dietary intake levels are in the patients, so we have to take some of this information with a grain of salt (or a teaspoon of oil, as it may be). For example, increased free radicals have been implicated in the liver conditions, nonalcoholic fatty liver disease (NAFLD), and the more severe form developing from NAFLD, nonalcoholic steatohepatitis (NASH). Treatment with vitamin E leads to minor histological improvements [25], and in a small study of just 45 patients, combination of vitamin E (1000 IU) with vitamin C (1000 mg) supplementation for just six months in half of those individuals appears to improve fibrosis associated with the disease, compared to placebo-treated patients [26]. Baseline or supplemented levels of vitamin E were not reported for either study, so we have no way of knowing how circulating levels might have been augmented (or not) by the treatment. In another study where both genotype and vitamin E levels were known, a positive interaction between functional HDL (nonoxidized) and vitamin E supplementation occurred only in individuals with a certain genotype, who also tended to have lower circulating vitamin E levels [27]. There are also lower levels of circulating vitamin E and higher levels of reactive oxygen species in patients with atopic dermatitis [28], and treatment with 400 IU/day for just four months reduced some of the systems in patients [29]. The downside of this information is that the first study did not assess vitamin E supplementation, while the second study did not assess vitamin E levels in the patients, so the information is all correlative at best.

The final nail in the coffin for vitamin E, at least until more studies are done using defined deficient individuals, comes from several studies, which were recently analyzed as part of one large meta-analysis. This analysis concludes that vitamin E supplementation, at doses above the RDA, is associated with an increase in "all-cause mortality," or simply, that the treatment groups succumbed to death at a higher rate than the control (placebo) groups. This does not rule out using vitamin E in specific treatments where circulating or dietary levels may be below the RDA or recommended levels, but does suggest that taking large supplemental doses of vitamin E over a long period of time may not be beneficial and may not improve overall health, especially if your levels are already within the normal range. Think about why this might be the case—and don't forget we generate and use oxidants in normal processes, and it may be the case that suppresses these normal oxidative processes is worse than just having a few free radicals around. As always, there is a balance (Figure 6.2) and one can have too much of a good thing.

Vitamin E supplements Over the counter supplements for vitamin E come in different IUs, and most have well over the RDA level, and nearing the upper limit for daily consumption. In addition, some formulations are "pure" α-tocopherol, while others are mixed. What should you recommend to a patient or yourself, especially if you are not getting sufficient levels of vitamin E from your diet?

Carotenoids

While vitamin A and the retinoids (preformed-vitamin A) are not antioxidants, some of the carotenoids, including those that can be converted to form retinoids (the pro-vitamin A carotenoids) and those that cannot (nonvitamin A carotenoids), are antioxidants (Figure 6.7). The most potent of the carotenoids are beta-carotene (β-carotene), which is a pro-vitamin A carotenoid, and lycopene, a nonvitamin A carotenoid. Let's look into the roles of these and other carotenoids and how they protect against free radicals.

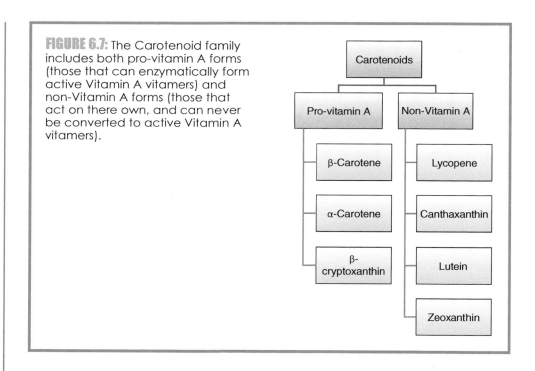

FIGURE 6.7: The Carotenoid family includes both pro-vitamin A forms (those that can enzymatically form active Vitamin A vitamers) and non-Vitamin A forms (those that act on there own, and can never be converted to active Vitamin A vitamers).

Of the more than 700 identified carotenes, β-carotene is the most abundant pro-vitamin A carotenoid in our diets and one of the most potent. The enzyme, β-carotene 15,15'-oxygenase (also called β-carotene monooxygenase 1, or BCMO1), converts β-carotene to retinaldehyde, which, as you might recall, is the substrate for both retinaldehyde dehydrogenase (RALDH—converts retinaldehyde to retinoic acid), and retinol dehydrogenese (RDH—converts retinaldehyde to retinol). However, it is β-carotene itself, in its nonconverted form is the functional antioxidant. β-carotene is highly lipophilic, and travels through the bloodstream in lipoproteins, such as LDL, where it can also integrate into cell and organelle membranes [30], quenching lipid free radicals and reactive oxygen species (O2Ÿ) that form within these membranes [30] (Figure 6.8).

It is the very location and lipophilic nature of carotenes, such as β-carotene, that lead to studies investigating β-carotene supplementation and supplementation or dietary levels of other carotenoids in association with various health conditions that were thought to be caused by high levels of reactive oxygen species. The most potent effects for β-carotene appear to be in cardiovascular and eye (photosensitive) diseases [30]. The most recent report on this, a meta-analysis of seven studies with 25,468 participants with 6,137 deaths, suggests that "all-cause mortality," that is, dying from anything, is inversely associated with serum β-carotene levels [31]. This is in complete contrast to studies examining all-cause mortality for high-dose supplementation, which show an increase in mortality with supplementation of either β-carotene or vitamin E (e.g., [32]). So, what does this mean? Should one supplement or not? This author feels that the data imply a dose–response, and perhaps a difference between natural, food-associated β-carotene, and synthetic

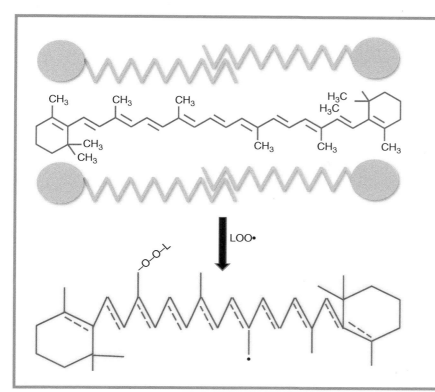

FIGURE 6.8: β-carotene (in blue) is located within lipid membranes (in pink), and there reacts with lipid free radicals (LOO•). It does this for radicals on the inside of the membranes, as compared to Vitamin E which works for radicals on the outside of membranes (see Figure 6.5). It becomes a free radical once it works to neutralize a lipid free radical.

© Leonid Andronov/Shutterstock.com

supplements taken with food or without foods that would naturally contain them. Therefore, try to get your vitamins from food and only supplement if you know you are deficient (as it relates to your current condition(s)).

For two other carotenes, lutein and zeaxanthin (nonvitamin A forming carotenes), the evidence suggests that both dietary and supplement forms of the vitamers can prevent age-associated macular degeneration (AMD). One of the causes of AMD is thought to be photodegeneration, simply due to the exposure of the eye to damaging light (UV). Both lutein and zeaxanthin can accumulate in the macula, a region of the retina needed for vision. In 2007, one of the first studies to look at macular degeneration and lutein/zeaxanthin found an inverse correlation between dietary intakes of lutein/zeaxanthin and AMD development and progression [33]. There was no effect of dietary β-carotene, vitamin C, vitamin A, or vitamin E. However, a follow-up study, this time using supplementation with a capsule containing either lutein and zeaxanthin or omega-3-fatty acids, along with vitamin C, zinc, vitamin E, and copper, was inconclusive as to the effects of lutein and zeaxanthin stating that there was no further decrease in AMD, compared to β-carotene [34]. A further analysis of the data (which one can find many comments on in the subsequent issues of *JAMA Ophthalmology* journal) reveals that when β-carotene is removed from the formulation, there is an 18% reduction in the risk for late-onset AMD [35]. Thus, we are again left with a bit of controversy on the subject, but the general

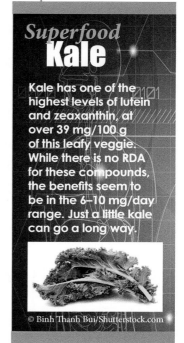

Superfood **Kale**

Kale has one of the highest levels of lutein and zeaxanthin, at over 39 mg/100 g of this leafy veggie. While there is no RDA for these compounds, the benefits seem to be in the 6–10 mg/day range. Just a little kale can go a long way.

© Binh Thanh Bui/Shutterstock.com

feeling from the ophthalmology community that inclusion of lutein and zeaxanthin in the diet or in the so-called eye vitamins might be warranted, especially in those with a family history of AMD [36].

While we will not speak about all 20+ carotenes that can act as antioxidants, it is necessary to mention one more carotene, lycopene. Lycopene is found in both fresh and canned tomatoes, and is thought to provide at least some of the health benefits from the tomato-rich Mediterranean Diet common to residents of Italy and Greece [37]. In fact, cooking of tomatoes converts the trans-form of lycopene into the more fat-soluble cis-form and may lead to the lower levels of some forms of cancer and for cardiovascular disease for people from these regions [37]. Interestingly, watermelon is a great source of the cis-form of lycopene [38]. One of the best health associations for lycopene is in the protection against prostate cancer. In one study, circulating levels of lycopene, but not of other carotenoids, were inversely associated with advanced stage or aggressive prostate cancer [39], while in another study, which was a meta-analysis of 34 studies, risk of developing prostate cancer was inversely correlated with higher lycopene levels [40]. *In vitro* studies suggest that lycopene levels may act directly on cancer cells, slowing growth, and blocking signaling pathways. The results in this study even showed that the effect on signaling may be direct—lycopene combined with a kinase in a cell free system still caused inhibition of signaling [41].

In sum, the carotenoids are an interesting group of molecules, having both vitamin A and nonvitamin A activities. We know that at least 20 of these carotenoids are present in human serum, and most of these have not been fully investigated as to requirements, roles, and possible health benefits. More work is needed in this area to fully realize their potential.

ENZYMATIC ANTIOXIDANTS

We cannot leave the topic of antioxidants without including a section on enzymatic antioxidants—particularly those that require mineral cofactors for their activity. In this section, we will discuss the families of superoxide dismutases, and the enzyme catalase. We've already seen the importance of the mineral selenium in selenoproteins, glutathione peroxidase, and thioredoxin reductase. Minerals are important in oxidant–antioxidant pathways due directly to their ability to share, steal, or transfer electrons between molecules.

Superoxide dismutases (SOD) catalyze the "dismutation" of radical superoxide (O_2^-) to either O_2 or hydrogen peroxide (Figure 6.9), which can be further broken down by catalase—the other antioxidant enzyme we'll discuss in this section. In humans (and other mammals), there are three forms of superoxide dismutases—SOD1, SOD2, and SOD3. While these enzymes are structurally and functionally related, SOD1 and SOD3 contain copper and zinc cofactors, while SOD2 contains manganese as its cofactor. In addition, each SOD form has its own cellular/extracellular location,

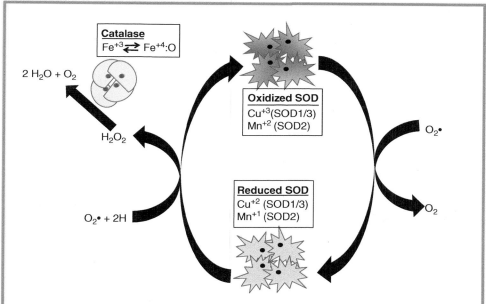

FIGURE 6.9: Mammalian superoxide dismutases are composed of either two (SOD1) or four (SOD2, and SOD3) identical subunits (blue), each with a mineral-containing active site (either copper or maganese, black dot). Superoxide is reduced to molecular oxygen in the first step of the reaction, leaving reduced SOD which can utilize another superoxide molecule with two protons to form hydrogen peroxide (H2O2) and return SOD to its oxidized and ready state. H2O2 can be further neutralized with catalase (green) using an iron cofactor (red dot). Iron binds to an oxygen molecule during the first step of the reaction, forming the first water molecule, and then extracts oxygen from a second hydrogen peroxide to make molecular oxygen (O2) and a second water molecule, regenerating the iron to start all over again.

with SOD1 found within the cytoplasm, SOD2 found within mitochondria, and SOD3 found in extracellular locations (for a review, see Fukai and Ushio-Fukai, 2011 [42]). However, each enzyme does essentially the same thing—neutralizes free radical oxygen species. The mineral cofactor sits within the active site (for SOD1 and SOD3, it's Cu and for SOD2, it's Mn) and directly donates, and then receives electrons in a reduction/oxidation reaction (Figure 6.9). For SOD1 and SOD3, Zn is a co-structural cofactor, rather than being involved in the antioxidant activity directly [42].

Mutations in SOD1 and, in particular, those mutations affecting the copper-binding area of SOD1 are responsible for the fatal, adult-onset neurodegenerative disease, amyotrophic lateral sclerosis (ALS), better known as Lou Gerhig's disease. While some studies have shown that Zn-binding capacity can contribute to the condition, the majority of studies of the human mutant proteins and engineered mouse mutant SOD1 demonstrate that altered copper binding by SOD1 leads to degeneration of motor neurons and contributes to disease phenotypes [43]. SOD proteins have a high affinity for copper ions, and in fact, the overall copper homeostasis in motor neurons appears to be disrupted in ALS mouse mod-

SOD pills for
sale!

Look online and you'll easily find companies selling SOD (not sure what form, as they don't specify) as a strong antioxidant and anti-aging drug. What do you think? Is there evidence that oral supplementation with SOD can improve health or reduce aging?

els, to the point where one of the proposed treatments for ALS is copper chelators to sop up the excess copper present [43]. The other two isoforms of SOD have not been strongly linked to causing human disease when mutated. Researchers have shown that polymorphisms in the human SOD2 gene are linked to impaired response to the drug cyclophosphamide in breast cancer patients [44] and a slightly increased risk of type I diabetes, especially in individuals of Japanese descent [45]. Polymorphisms and elevated expression of SOD3 (the extracellular SOD) appear to be associated with abnormal inflammatory states in the lung, including emphysema, chronic obstructive pulmonary disease, asbestosis, and acute lung injury [42]. Bringing this back to mineral deficiencies, low copper intake, while rare, can lead to neurological dysfunction [46] which could correlate with the connection of SOD1 to ALS, while reduced dietary intake of manganese has been associated with increased breast cancer, and in type II diabetes [47], again, correlative to the genetic polymorphisms in SOD2 discussed above.

Fun **FACT**

In vitro, human catalase has an optimal enzymatic temperature of 45°C, rather than our body's internal temperature of 37°C.

While SOD enzymes generally do good deeds in the cellular and extracellular environments where they work, they also leave us with hydrogen peroxide, which is not good. That's where the iron-containing catalase enzyme steps in to save the day. As shown in Figure 6.9, catalase can produce water and molecular oxygen from the product of the SOD reaction. To do this, catalase (which has four identical subunits) uses a heme core, and the iron at the core grabs one oxygen molecule from H_2O_2 in the first step of the reaction, forming the first water, and then a second oxygen from a second H_2O_2, forming a second water, and this time releasing molecular oxygen (O_2), returning iron to its reduced Fe^{3+} state. Catalase enzyme also is tightly bound to a single molecule of NADPH, although NADPH does not participate enzymatically in the reaction, and there is still discussion among researchers as to its role in the enzyme [48]. There are several studies suggesting a genetic link between a catalase gene polymorphisms and cancer [40, 49]. Individuals with acatalasemia (a lack of a functional catalase gene) were originally thought to have few associated phenotypes, except for low red blood cell catalase activity; however, of the 114 cases reported worldwide as of 2013, 97 of these patients have what the authors Goth and Nagy call, "age and oxidative distress disorders" [50]. With so few patients, it is difficult to make a clear assessment of which parts of these disorders are due directly to lack of catalase and which might be due to environmental or other genetic causes. A more recent paper by the same authors postulates and provides evidence for low catalase activity and associated polymorphism in the catalase gene in Hungarian patients with type II diabetes or microcytic anemia [51].

To conclude, minerals play a key role as cofactors in several of our antioxidant enzymes. Considering the fact that there are many populations with inadequate iron dietary intake [52] and a growing number of individuals getting manganese only from supplemented cereals rather than plant-based sources [47], antioxidant activity of enzymes requiring iron and manganese as cofactors could be impaired. It is clear that individuals with overall higher plant-based diets also have overall better health and lower susceptibility to some diseases [53]. Is this due to the higher bioavailability of vitamin and mineral antioxidants in those foods, or some other factor? Research furthering this area is ongoing with over 2000 articles found in a PubMed search with the terms "antioxidant" and "mineral" from 2014 to 2016.

CHAPTER SUMMARY

As we finish up this chapter, keep in mind that it is the balance of oxidants to antioxidants that seems to matter the most. It also seems that if you are getting the recommended amount of antioxidants from your diet, don't supplement unless you have a condition or activity (i.e., smoking), which calls for doses over the RDA.

- Water-soluble vitamin C and fat-soluble vitamin E are the main vitamin antioxidants.
- Don't forget about the carotenoids, a potent group of fat-soluble antioxidants, some of which can be directly converted into vitamin A. (Although vitamin A itself cannot function as an antioxidant.)
- Minerals play a key role in transferring electrons to and from antioxidant enzymes, including glutathione peroxidase, the SODs, and catalase.

POINTS TO PONDER

- Is vitamin C a viable treatment for cancer? Review the evidence for and against this treatment.
- One of the earliest findings on vitamin E demonstrated that deficient female rats spontaneously aborted their fetuses [1]. What is the mechanism behind this early finding—a lack of antioxidant activity or some other role for vitamin E vitamers in embryogenesis?
- What is the evidence for carotenoid protection against cardiovascular disease, and especially atherosclerosis?
- Can dietary interventions with minerals improve antioxidant status?

References

1. Evans, H.M. and K.S. Bishop, *On the existance of a hitherto unrecognized dietary factor essential for reproduction.* . Science, 1922. **56**(1458): p. 650–651.
2. Merriam-Webster Inc., *Merriam-Webster's medical dictionary*. Enl. print ed. 2007, Springfield, Mass.: Merriam-Webster.
3. Institute of Medicine (U.S.). Panel on Dietary Antioxidants and Related Compounds., *Dietary reference intakes for vitamin C, vitamin E, selenium, and carotenoids : a report of the Panel on Dietary Antioxidants and Related Compounds,*

Subcommittees on Upper Reference Levels of Nutrients and of Interpretation and Use of Dietary Reference Intakes, and the Standing Committee on the Scientific Evaluation of Dietary Reference Intakes, Food and Nutrition Board, Institute of Medicine. 2000, Washington, D.C.: National Academy Press. xx, 506 p.

4. Kelly, G., *The interaction of cigarette smoking and antioxidants. Part III: ascorbic acid.* Altern Med Rev, 2003. **8**(1): p. 43-54.

5. Linster, C.L. and E. Van Schaftingen, *Vitamin C. Biosynthesis, recycling and degradation in mammals.* FEBS J, 2007. **274**(1): p. 1-22.

6. Cameron, E. and L. Pauling, *Supplemental ascorbate in the supportive treatment of cancer: Prolongation of survival times in terminal human cancer.* Proc Natl Acad Sci U S A, 1976. **73**(10): p. 3685-9.

7. DeWys, W., *How to evaluate a new treatment for cancer.* Your Patient and Cancer 1982. **2**: p. 31-36.

8. Creagan, E.T., et al., *Failure of high-dose vitamin C (ascorbic acid) therapy to benefit patients with advanced cancer. A controlled trial.* N Engl J Med, 1979. **301**(13): p. 687-90.

9. Moertel, C.G., et al., *High-dose vitamin C versus placebo in the treatment of patients with advanced cancer who have had no prior chemotherapy. A randomized double-blind comparison.* N Engl J Med, 1985. **312**(3): p. 137-41.

10. Wilson, M.K., et al., *Review of high-dose intravenous vitamin C as an anticancer agent.* Asia Pac J Clin Oncol, 2014. **10**(1): p. 22-37.

11. Conti, V., et al., *Antioxidant Supplementation in the Treatment of Aging-Associated Diseases.* Front Pharmacol, 2016. **7**: p. 24.

12. Figueroa-Mendez, R. and S. Rivas-Arancibia, *Vitamin C in Health and Disease: Its Role in the Metabolism of Cells and Redox State in the Brain.* Front Physiol, 2015. **6**: p. 397.

13. Couto, N., J. Wood, and J. Barber, *The role of glutathione reductase and related enzymes on cellular redox homoeostasis network.* Free Radic Biol Med, 2016. **95**: p. 27-42.

14. McCarty, M.F. and J.J. DiNicolantonio, *An increased need for dietary cysteine in support of glutathione synthesis may underlie the increased risk for mortality associated with low protein intake in the elderly.* Age (Dordr), 2015. **37**(5): p. 96.

15. Ferguson, G. and W. Bridge, *Glutamate cysteine ligase and the age-related decline in cellular glutathione: The therapeutic potential of gamma-glutamylcysteine.* Arch Biochem Biophys, 2016. **593**: p. 12-23.

16. Halliwell, B., *Free radicals and antioxidants—quo vadis?* Trends Pharmacol Sci, 2011. **32**(3): p. 125-30.

17. Hosomi, A., et al., *Affinity for alpha-tocopherol transfer protein as a determinant of the biological activities of vitamin E analogs.* FEBS Lett, 1997. **409**(1): p. 105-8.

18. Peh, H.Y., et al., *Vitamin E therapy beyond cancer: Tocopherol versus tocotrienol.* Pharmacol Ther, 2016. **162**: p. 152-69.

19. Khanna, S., et al., *Delivery of orally supplemented alpha-tocotrienol to vital organs of rats and tocopherol-transport protein deficient mice.* Free Radic Biol Med, 2005. **39**(10): p. 1310-9.

20. Zingg, J.M., *Vitamin E: A Role in Signal Transduction.* Annu Rev Nutr, 2015. **35:** p. 135-73.

21. Aquilano, K., S. Baldelli, and M.R. Ciriolo, *Glutathione: new roles in redox signaling for an old antioxidant.* Front Pharmacol, 2014. **5:** p. 196.

22. McBurney, M.I., et al., *Suboptimal Serum alpha-Tocopherol Concentrations Observed among Younger Adults and Those Depending Exclusively upon Food Sources, NHANES 2003-20061-3.* PLoS One, 2015. **10**(8): p. e0135510.

23. Traber, M.G., *Vitamin E inadequacy in humans: causes and consequences.* Adv Nutr, 2014. **5**(5): p. 503-14.

24. Hanson, C., et al., *Serum tocopherol levels and vitamin E intake are associated with lung function in the normative aging study.* Clin Nutr, 2016. **35**(1): p. 169-74.

25. Sumida, Y., et al., *Involvement of free radicals and oxidative stress in NAFLD/ NASH.* Free Radic Res, 2013. **47**(11): p. 869-80.

26. Harrison, S.A., et al., *Vitamin E and vitamin C treatment improves fibrosis in patients with nonalcoholic steatohepatitis.* Am J Gastroenterol, 2003. **98**(11): p. 2485-90.

27. Costacou, T., et al., *Effect of vitamin E supplementation on HDL function by haptoglobin genotype in type 1 diabetes: results from the HapE randomized crossover pilot trial.* Acta Diabetol, 2016. **53**(2): p. 243-50.

28. Sivaranjani, N., S.V. Rao, and G. Rajeev, *Role of reactive oxygen species and antioxidants in atopic dermatitis.* J Clin Diagn Res, 2013. **7**(12): p. 2683-5.

29. Jaffary, F., et al., *Effects of oral vitamin E on treatment of atopic dermatitis: A randomized controlled trial.* J Res Med Sci, 2015. **20**(11): p. 1053-7.

30. Fiedor, J. and K. Burda, *Potential role of carotenoids as antioxidants in human health and disease.* Nutrients, 2014. **6**(2): p. 466-88.

31. Zhao, L.G., et al., *Dietary, circulating beta-carotene and risk of all-cause mortality: a meta-analysis from prospective studies.* Sci Rep, 2016. **6:** p. 26983.

32. Bjelakovic, G., et al., *Antioxidant supplements for prevention of mortality in healthy participants and patients with various diseases.* Cochrane Database Syst Rev, 2012(3): p. CD007176.

33. Age-Related Eye Disease Study Research, G., et al., *The relationship of dietary carotenoid and vitamin A, E, and C intake with age-related macular degeneration in a case-control study: AREDS Report No. 22.* Arch Ophthalmol, 2007. **125**(9): p. 1225-32.

34. Age-Related Eye Disease Study 2 Research, G., *Lutein + zeaxanthin and omega-3 fatty acids for age-related macular degeneration: the Age-Related Eye Disease Study 2 (AREDS2) randomized clinical trial.* JAMA, 2013. **309**(19): p. 2005-15.

35. Musch, D.C., *Evidence for including lutein and zeaxanthin in oral supplements for age-related macular degeneration.* JAMA Ophthalmol, 2014. **132**(2): p. 139-41.

36. Chew, E.Y. and T.E. Clemons, *Making sense of the evidence from the age-related eye disease study 2 randomized clinical trial-reply.* JAMA Ophthalmol, 2014. **132**(8): p. 1031-2.

37. Weisburger, J.H., *Lycopene and tomato products in health promotion.* Exp Biol Med (Maywood), 2002. **227**(10): p. 924-7.

38. Naz, A., et al., *Watermelon lycopene and allied health claims.* EXCLI J, 2014. **13**: p. 650-60.

39. Key, T.J., et al., *Carotenoids, retinol, tocopherols, and prostate cancer risk: pooled analysis of 15 studies.* Am J Clin Nutr, 2015. **102**(5): p. 1142-57.

40. Wang, Y., et al., *Effect of Carotene and Lycopene on the Risk of Prostate Cancer: A Systematic Review and Dose-Response Meta-Analysis of Observational Studies.* PLoS One, 2015. **10**(9): p. e0137427.

41. Assar, E.A., et al., *Lycopene acts through inhibition of IkappaB kinase to suppress NF-kappaB signaling in human prostate and breast cancer cells.* Tumour Biol, 2016.

42. Fukai, T. and M. Ushio-Fukai, *Superoxide dismutases: role in redox signaling, vascular function, and diseases.* Antioxid Redox Signal, 2011. **15**(6): p. 1583-606.

43. Hilton, J.B., A.R. White, and P.J. Crouch, *Metal-deficient SOD1 in amyotrophic lateral sclerosis.* J Mol Med (Berl), 2015. **93**(5): p. 481-7.

44. Glynn, S.A., et al., *A mitochondrial target sequence polymorphism in manganese superoxide dismutase predicts inferior survival in breast cancer patients treated with cyclophosphamide.* Clin Cancer Res, 2009. **15**(12): p. 4165-73.

45. Pourvali, K., M. Abbasi, and A. Mottaghi, *Role of Superoxide Dismutase 2 Gene Ala16Val Polymorphism and Total Antioxidant Capacity in Diabetes and its Complications.* Avicenna J Med Biotechnol, 2016. **8**(2): p. 48-56.

46. Institute of Medicine (U.S.). Panel on Micronutrients., *DRI : dietary reference intakes for vitamin A, vitamin K, arsenic, boron, chromium, copper, iodine, iron, manganese, molybdenum, nickel, silicon, vanadium, and zinc : a report of the Panel on Micronutrients ... and the Standing Committee on the Scientific Evaluation of Dietary Reference Intakes, Food and Nutrition Board, Institute of Medicine.* 2001, Washington, D.C.: National Academy Press. xxii, 773 p.

47. Freeland-Graves, J.H., T.Y. Mousa, and S. Kim, *International variability in diet and requirements of manganese: Causes and consequences.* J Trace Elem Med Biol, 2016.

48. Fita, I. and M.G. Rossmann, *The NADPH binding site on beef liver catalase.* Proc Natl Acad Sci U S A, 1985. **82**(6): p. 1604-8.

49. Crawford, A., et al., *Relationships between single nucleotide polymorphisms of antioxidant enzymes and disease.* Gene, 2012. **501**(2): p. 89-103.

50. Goth, L. and T. Nagy, *Inherited catalase deficiency: is it benign or a factor in various age related disorders?* Mutat Res, 2013. **753**(2): p. 147-54.

51. Nagy, T., et al., *Further acatalasemia mutations in human patients from Hungary with diabetes and microcytic anemia.* Mutat Res, 2015. **772**: p. 10-4.

52. Tussing-Humphreys, L., et al., *Rethinking iron regulation and assessment in iron deficiency, anemia of chronic disease, and obesity: introducing hepcidin.* J Acad Nutr Diet, 2012. **112**(3): p. 391-400.

53. Benzie, I.F. and S.W. Choi, *Antioxidants in food: content, measurement, significance, action, cautions, caveats, and research needs.* Adv Food Nutr Res, 2014. **71**: p. 1-53.

Free Radicals and Antioxidants

Solve the anagrams for the terms in your textbook. Anagrams are words or phrases, which when scrambled make other words or phrases. The spacing of the anagram and the original word or phrase does not have to match. For example, the author's name, DEBORAH GOOD, can be anagrammed as BREAD DOH GOO.

ANAGRAM	**TERM or PHRASE**
TOAD SAINT NIX	_____
COBRA TEAS	_____
MACE GLAMOR PHOTO	_____
ISLE MENU	_____
A DRENCHED EXIT RIOTUS	_____
TOENAIL THUG	_____
A DISCO INTRO	_____
HENNA AX ZIT	_____
ARCADE FLIERS	_____
A CIRCA HYDRID DISCO DO	_____
A DIMERIZED SPOUSE TUX	_____
AS CAT ALE	_____

CHAPTER 7

Fertilization, Development, and Growth

Table of Contents

IT'S ALL ABOUT CELL DIVISION AND DIFFERENTIATION

Before we go too far into the role of micronutrients in body systems, we must talk about the very start of things—fertilization, development, and growth of the organism. As you will see, we need both vitamins and minerals to start things off. At fertilization, for example, there are multiple waves of calcium (called calcium oscillations) that travel throughout the oocyte when the sperm penetrates the egg's cell membrane, leading to a block to polyspermy (meaning other sperm can't get in) and stimulation of both protein and DNA synthesis—as these are needed for the fertilized egg to start development[1, 2]. All of this involves many of the cellular signaling processes that we discussed in Chapter 5, including kinases utilizing phosphate to phosphorylate proteins, calmodulin mediating calcium binding to other proteins, and phosphatases removing phosphate from proteins [1, 2]. At the start of development, you can likely see that we already have a great need for minerals, and as you will see below, vitamins start to play a role in the process very quickly.

THE FOLATE CYCLE AND ONE CARBON METABOLISM

Almost as soon as fertilization takes place, the newly fertilized egg gets signals to begin synthesizing DNA in preparation for division. This process also requires the synthesis of new proteins, and that requires amino acids. As division takes off, differentiation will occur and requires DNA methylation and histone modifications to turn on and off various genes in the different cell lineages. Each of the processes mentioned above, at some level, requires the activity of the folate cycle and the vitamins B9, B12, B2, and B3, as well as zinc. Keep in mind that B12 contains the nutritional mineral cobalt, so that is a required micronutrient in these processes as well.

The placenta and yolk sac, as well as the uterine lining, contain receptors for folic acid and 5' tetrahydrofolate (THF) [5, 6], and you know these receptors from Chapter 3 (Table 3.2). At the histological level, folate receptors can be detected in the 8.5 day mouse embryo (a little over one-third of the way through pregnancy) [7], but likely are there even earlier in development. As both the reduced folate carrier, which binds to 5-methyl THF, and the proton-coupled folic acid transporter, which binds to folic acid, are present, it is also likely that the embryo and/or endometrial lining have the enzymes necessary to process folic acid and THF for further use. Thus, as shown in Figure 7.1, the first step following absorption of folic acid (synthetic) or dihydrofolate (DHF) (dietary) is the conversion of these forms to THF. For folic acid, this involves two steps with the same enzyme, dihydrofolate reductase—a niacin requiring enzyme. As you should also be able to see in Figure 7.1, molecules of NADPH are utilized in the reaction, which removes the two protons (H+) and puts them on B9, ultimately converting it to THF. THF is one of the active vitamers of B9 and can be used in the folate cycle, which is part of

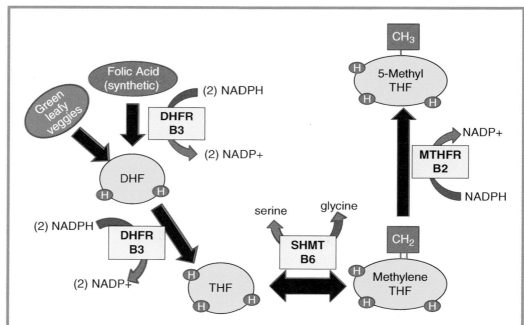

FIGURE 7.1: Processing of dietary dihydrofolate (DHF) or synthetic folic acid for use in the folate cycle. As B9 in any form is absorbed, it must be converted to THF and this requires dihydrofolate reductase (DHFR) as well as NADPH as a H donor. Note the increase in hydrogens on the B9 vitamers as they become THF. THF is then utilized in the folate cycle by serine hydroxymethyltransferase (SHMT), to make 5, 10, methyl THF (or methylene THF), which is further utilizes by methylene tetrahydrofolate reductase (MTHFR) to make 5-methyl THF. This product can then be used by the methionine cycle. Of import, B9 acts as a co-substrate in these reactions, whereas B3 acts as a co-enzyme, and proton donor.

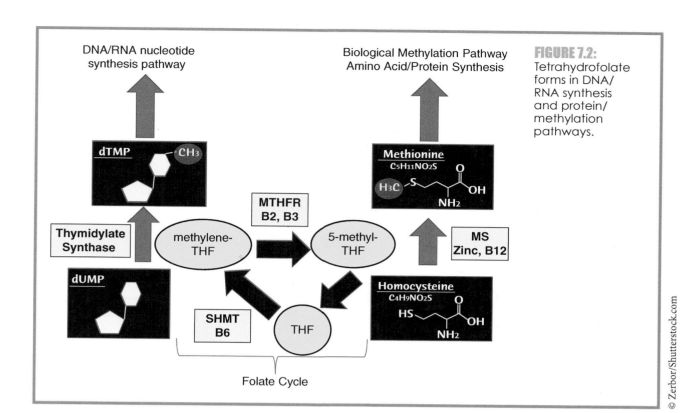

© Zerbor/Shutterstock.com

FIGURE 7.2:
Tetrahydrofolate forms in DNA/ RNA synthesis and protein/ methylation pathways.

one carbon metabolism process (Figures 7.1 and 7.4). As shown in Figure 7.1, B9 vitamers act as cosubstrates for enzymatic reactions which lead to the conversion of serine and glycine (serine hydroxymethyltransferase, SHMT), forming methylene THF (or 5,10-methylene THF). This product can either stay in the folate cycle or be utilized by thymidylate synthase for purine/DNA synthesis (Figure 7.2). If methylene THF stays in the folate cycle, then it is processed to 5-methyl THF by methyltetrahydrofolate reductase (MTHFR), a flavoprotein which also requires B3 in the form NADPH as a proton donor (Figure 7.1). 5-Methyl THF also either remains in the folate cycle or is utilized by methionine synthase (MS) leading to the methionine cycle (Figure 7.2). MS uses 5-methyl THF as a substrate to methylate homocysteine, rendering it not only nontoxic but also useful as the amino acid methionine. MS requires B12 as a coenzyme and zinc as a cofactor. Methionine, within the methionine cycle, can be shuttled out for protein synthesis or further adenylated to S-adenosyl methionine (SAM), which is now a substrate for DNA and protein methylation enzymes (Figures 7.2 and 7.3). Whew! I know that's a lot of utilization and shuttling, but hopefully by the end of this paragraph you will really appreciate how crucial folate metabolism is. One carbon metabolism and all of its implications for health and disease are very thoroughly summarized in a newly published review by Ducker and Rabinowitz [3].

However, we are not yet at the end of B9's importance in the body. Did you notice a product in Figure 7.2 called homocysteine? This product is normally

Homocysteine

High homocysteine levels are found in Alzheimer's disease, as well as cardiovascular disease, and several other conditions [3]. As you might have suspected, supplementation with B9, B12, and B6 can reduce homocysteine levels in the serum. However (and interestingly), vitamin supplementation per se does not reduce mortality in several studies (see this meta-analysis as an example) [4]. What do you think is going on?

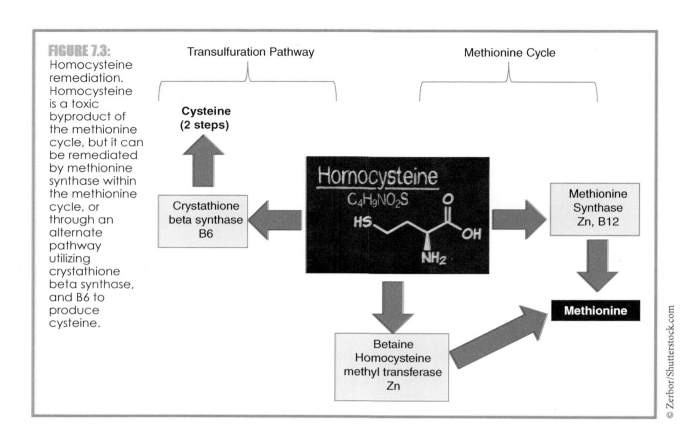

FIGURE 7.3: Homocysteine remediation. Homocysteine is a toxic byproduct of the methionine cycle, but it can be remediated by methionine synthase within the methionine cycle, or through an alternate pathway utilizing crystathione beta synthase, and B6 to produce cysteine.

Transulfuration Pathway

Methionine Cycle

Cysteine
(2 steps)

Crystathione
beta synthase
B6

Homocysteine
C₄H₉NO₂S

Methionine
Synthase
Zn, B12

Methionine

Betaine
Homocysteine
methyl transferase
Zn

© Zerbor/Shutterstock.com

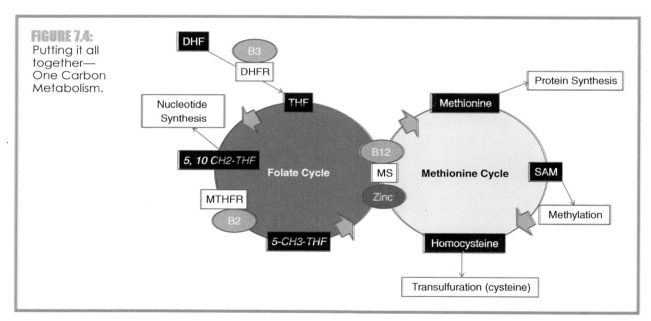

FIGURE 7.4: Putting it all together— One Carbon Metabolism.

DHF

B3

DHFR

THF

Nucleotide
Synthesis

5, 10 CH2-THF

Folate Cycle

B12

MS

MTHFR

Zinc

B2

5-CH3-THF

Methionine

Protein Synthesis

Methionine Cycle

SAM

Methylation

Homocysteine

Transulfuration (cysteine)

produced during the methionine cycle, but it *must* be remediated either by use in the methionine cycle (through MS) or through an alternate pathway called the transsulfuration pathway (Figures 7.3 and 7.4). In this alternate pathway, the enzyme crystathione beta-synthase (which requires B6) performs the first step in transforming homocysteine into cysteine (Figure 7.3).

Dietary and genetic consequences of deficiency

Metabolism of Vitamin B9 intersects homocysteine remediation, amino acid synthesis (and protein synthesis), DNA and RNA synthesis, and methylation of proteins and DNA (which results in gene and protein regulation). With so much involved, you have probably already guessed that dietary deficiencies of any of the vitamins or minerals involved in one-carbon metabolism, as well as genetic variants that affect functioning of any of the enzymes of one-carbon metabolism, will have effects on the organism from embryogenesis through old age. Indeed, most of you already know that pregnant women are given a vitamin and mineral supplement. This multivitamin is given to supply these and other micronutrients to a pregnant woman and her developing child, as the demands for micronutrients rise exponentially during pregnancy. So what happens when there is a dietary deficiency of B9, B12, B6, or zinc? We'll leave riboflavin and niacin out at this point as deficiencies of these micronutrients will affect the health of a woman so much that she likely would not get pregnant. But let's talk about B9, B12, B6, and zinc nutritional deficiencies as they relate to pregnancy, embryogenesis, and development of tissues.

Here we will move to the topic of developmental neural tube defects (NTD), as these are the most common outcome of deficiency in vitamin B9, B12, and B6 during pregnancy. An NTD occurs when there is incomplete closing of the developing neural tube leaving exposed spinal cord or brain, or a bulging of the spinal cord or brain out of the head or spinal areas. The Center for Disease Control (CDC) has vital statistics on the number of two NTDs, spina bifida (affecting the spine), and anencephaly (affecting the head) in the United States from 1991, prior to folate fortification of grains, through 2006 [8]. And a recent peer reviewed journal article provides worldwide data on NTD rates in the year 2015 [9]. What we know from the US data is that, in 1995, prior to the 1996 policy by the US Food and Drug administration authorizing folate fortification of grains (it was mandated in 1998), the rate of NTDs peaked (per 100,000 live births) at 27.98 for spina bifida and 11.71 for anencephaly [8]. By 2006, following approximately 10 years of folate fortification in the United States, the rates were 17.99 and 11.21, respectively [8]. In 2015, US rates for overall protection from NTD (grouping spina bifida and anencephaly rates together) showed an overall protection of 90% of possible estimated cases that would have arisen in the absence of fortification [9]. Worldwide, the rates are even worse, with only 13% of the cases being prevented, mainly because a lot of countries, including those in Europe and Asia, still do not fortify their grains [9, 10]. Hmmmm, did you think the rates would go to zero, especially in countries with folate fortification of grains? Let's think about why this hasn't occurred. I'll propose several reasons, based on evidence for why we might still see NTDs in populations with fortification.

First, only folate, niacin, and thiamine are currently being fortified in cereal grains. In 2000, a study of red blood cell folate status in adults, including women

TABLE 7.1: Micronutrients, divided into the essential vitamins and minerals for humans.

Vitamin Deficiency	Symptoms	
B9/Folate	Neural Tube Defects Megaloblastic anemia Elevated homocysteine (cardiovascular and neural issues) Weakness Low Weight Birth	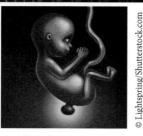
B12/cobalamin	Neural Tube Defects Megaloblastic anemia Elevated homocysteine (cardiovascular and neural issues)	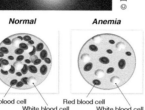
B6	Sideroblastic anemia Pellagra-like symptoms	

© Lightspring/Shutterstock.com

© Designua/Shutterstock.com

Normal | Anemia

Red blood cell | Red blood cell
White blood cell | White blood cell

of childbearing age, shows that only 0.5% of the population was B9 deficient [11]. This is great news! But to explain the persistence of NTDs in the US population postfortification, we have to possibly look at other micronutrients and genetic conditions that might require individuals to have even higher B9 intake than the general population. A 2016 study which examined folate and B12 levels in women who gave birth to babies with and without NTDs showed that those babies with NTDs had mothers with marginally low (still significantly different) folate levels but highly significantly lower B12 levels [12]. Since vitamin B12 is needed by methionine synthase, might we need to consider B12 supplementation as a preventative measure as well? Of course, many women take prenatal vitamins, but this study in particular indicated that those women in rural areas may not get these additional supplements, and this may account for the steady NTD rate in the United States and worldwide (the study was done in Turkey) [12]. And consider as well that we also need vitamin B6 and the minerals zinc and cobalt for full functioning of one carbon metabolism. Take a look at Table 7.1 for a full listing of symptoms for B9, B6, and B12 deficiencies, as they relate to pregnancy, as well as blood cells, which require constant proliferation and differentiation. We'll talk more about the anemias in Chapter 10. In finishing up this section on dietary deficiency of B9, please note that current recommendations are based on both a systematic review of data and an epidemiological study that US women get sufficient folate in their diets, concluding that no additional B9 supplementation is required, except in specialized cases [13, 14].

See for yourself...

Can you find peer-reviewed papers describing on whether B6 or zinc status might affect NTD rates?

In addition to dietary deficiency, as always, we need to consider genetic conditions which might require an individual to have a higher need for micronutrients (Table 7.2). Consider single nucleotide polymorphisms in MTHFR. To date, two major variants in MTHFR, A1298C, which is found in 7–12% of North American, European, and Australian populations, and C677T, where approximately

TABLE 7.2: Genetic conditions affecting one-carbon metabolism. Most of the information in this table can be found in the review paper by Doudney et al., 2009. Increases in cleft palate with DHFR variants were reported by Martinelli et al., 2014. Cubilin variants were reported by Franke et al., 2009. SHMT1 variants were reported by Wernimont et al., 2011.

Condition	Gene	Consequences
methylenetetrahydrofolate reductase deficiency	MTHFR	• Developmental delays • Increased neural tube defects • Fetal loss/death • Hyperhomocysteinemia
Methionine Synthase Deficiency	MS	• Fetal death • Increased neural tube defects • Hyperhomocysteinemia • Megaloblastic anemia
Dihydrofolate reductase deficiency	DHFR	• Increased neural tube defects • Cleft palate (?) • Megaloblastic anemia
Cystathionine-beta-synthase variants	CBR	• Hyperhomocysteinemia
Reduced folate carrier deficiency	RCF	• Increased neural tube defects • Hyperhomocysteinemia
Cubilin variant	CUBN	• Neural Tube defects (due to reduced B12 uptake)
serine hydroxymethyltransferase variant	SHMT1	• Hyperhomocysteinemia (only in association with MTHFR variants)

20–40% of Caucasian or Hispanic individuals are heterozygous for the variant, have been linked to higher than normal homocysteine levels in carriers [15]. In these individuals, supplementation with folic acid can reduce circulating homocysteine levels [15]. Currently, genetic testing for MTHFR variants is neither required nor recommended by national genetic counseling organizations, even though carriers may be some increased risk of both fetal death and NTDs [15]. As shown in Table 7.2 [16–19], other genetic conditions could also increase spontaneous fetal death and/or NTD, and in adults they are associated with defects in one carbon metabolism, most notably, hyperhomocysteinemia.

As we wrap up this section on folate and one carbon metabolism, keep in mind that, as said in the beginning paragraphs, "it's all about cell division and metabolism"—such that any tissue, embryonic or adult, that requires DNA, RNA, proteins, and methyl groups for metabolism can be affected by a B9 dietary deficiency or other micronutrient deficiency. However, those tissues that are rapidly dividing and/or differentiating are going to show the greatest impairment, which is why we discuss one carbon metabolism in this chapter.

RETINOIC ACID

Pimple treatment and pregnancy don't mix...

Isotretinoin is an antiacne drug which comes with both a warning (do not become pregnant while taking this medication) and a requirement (to take birth control medicines while on it). Isotretinoin is a form of retinoic acid, and while it does appear to help with acne, it can cause birth defects, including hearing and vision impairment and facial deformities.

All chordates—those animals with spinal cords—need vitamin A, which is converted to retinoic acid using two sequential oxidation steps (and NAD+) and two dehydrogenase enzymes (Figure 7.5). As we learned in Chapter 5, retinoic acid is a ligand for the RAR and RXR zinc finger transcription factors. Thus, in developmental processes that require vitamin A, zinc is required as well as B3.

Developmental patterning of the body plan relies on vitamin A signals that start very early in embryogenesis to form the anterior–posterior planes of the body, and as shown in Figure 7.6, these are somewhat easy to see in humans when the regions of spinal cord innervation are visualized. Most of the work was actually done using zebrafish or mouse embryos (for example, [20, 21]), but we can apply the principles to human spinal cord and cranial/caudal development. In general, a retinoic acid gradient is produced due to the expression of RALDH, to synthesize RA within cells, and CYP26, to degrade RA in cells in other regions of the embryo. That is to say, when RALDH is present and expressed in a tissue, RA is synthesized and quickly can diffuse if not for the expression of CYP26 to restrict RA regionally [22]. So why does this result in regional patterning? Because RA, along with other factors, regulates the expression of HOX genes (homeobox transcription factors), which then turn on and off other genes that pattern the developing embryo, vitamin A and each of the vitamin A metabolizing enzymes are needed for complete embryogenesis. This was clearly shown by a number

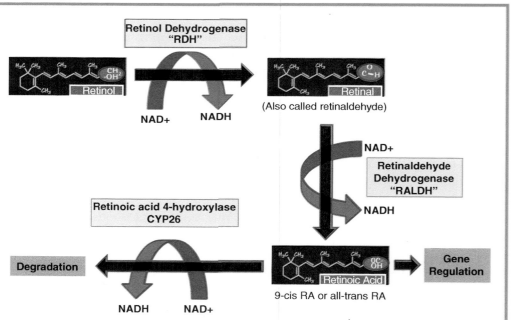

FIGURE 7.5: Biosynthesis and degradation of retinoic acid from retinol. Circulating retinol undergoes two B3-depedent steps to produce retinoic acid, with the 9-cis or all –trans forms made from different RALDH isoforms.

© Zerbor/Shutterstock.com

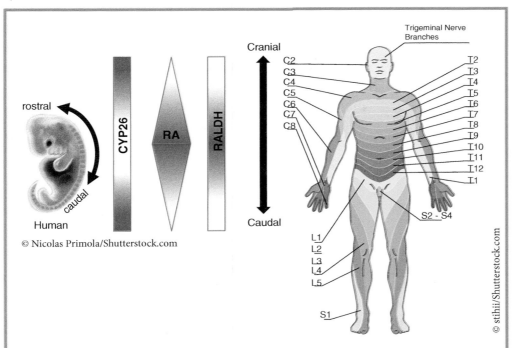

© Nicolas Primola/Shutterstock.com

© stihii/Shutterstock.com

FIGURE 7.6: Spinal cord innervation demonstrates human body plan organization by retinoic acid. Retinoic acid is synthesized where there is the highest amount of RALDH enzyme, but levels of CYP26, which degrades RA, ultimately determine how much RA is around. Combined with other factors, such as the level of the growth factor FGF, embryonic patterning occurs. While much of the information has come from zebrafish and mouse embryos, it applies to human development as well (Samarut et al., 2014).

of mouse knockouts of RA synthesis and metabolizing enzymes, which display disrupted body plans and embryonic or neonatal death [23]. For example, a deletion of RALDH2 leads to embryonic lethality at midgestation (day 9.5) with a lack of forearms, abnormal axis patterning, and missing hindbrain [24]. Meanwhile, whole body deletion of the CYP26 gene using mouse knockout technology results in too much RA in the wrong places leading to a lack of a posterior, or so-called "caudal agenesis" [25].

Vitamin A deficiency worldwide is the leading causes of childhood blindness (World Health Organization, http://www.who.int/nutrition/topics/vad/en/), and this is due to the continuing need for retinal in vision. However, given RA's requirement during development, do we see more developmental problems with vitamin A deficiency in pregnant women? Maybe, but with a caveat. First, males with vitamin A deficiency have very poor spermatogenesis [26]. Females with vitamin A deficiency prior to conception fail to show gestational stages past implantation, with reabsorption of the fetuses [26]. If vitamin A is supplied in early gestation and then depleted mid- or later in gestation, tissues that are developing later are affected, including intestinal villi, skeleton, and some glands [26]. In this situation, one might see postnatal rather than embryonic or developmental problems because vitamin A (retinol) can be stored in the liver for months at a time. To summarize, depleting vitamin A early in embryogenesis will result in lethality, while later depletion can be compensated for by fetal-placental transfer, or by feeding breast milk after birth. Currently, neonatal or prenatal high-dose vitamin A supplementation (prior to six months of age) is not recommended, while supplementation to infants aged six months to five years in areas of low vitamin A status does occur to prevent blindness and mortality [27].

IODINE'S SINGLE FUNCTION

Speaking of micronutrient deficiencies, did you know that thyroid disease is the most common non-communicable disease worldwide, with the burden affecting mainly developing world populations in Africa and Asia [28]? Untreated congenital (during development) thyroid disease leads to cretinism, which manifests with mental retardation and short stature. However, according to the World Health Organization, they are on the verge of treating the most preventable form of brain damage—with iodized salt.

Most people recognize the familiar girl in her rain gear, which was the trademark for Morton's Salt. Only the version on the right is iodized.

© LunaseeStudios/ Shutterstock.com

Let's look at the situation in the United States prior to the introduction of iodized salt. Prior to World War I, 30% of recruits were rejected due to goiter. Many of these individuals were in the so-called goiter-belt of the United States, which extended coast to coast and from the Canadian border to as far south as Virginia in the east, and Nevada and Northern California in the west. Based on a series of papers by Dr. David Marine and his assistant O.P. Kimball, which describes a single experiment documenting the incidence of goiter in Akron, Ohio, and response to sodium iodide treatment [29], Dr. David Cower, a Michigan pediatrician, proposed that "everyone uses salt on a daily basis. Iodized salt, therefore, would be the most uniform, efficient, and cheapest means of supplementing iodine into the diets of Michiganders regardless of social circumstances or where they lived" [30]. On May 1, 1924, Morton's iodized salt first appeared in grocery stores in Michigan, and by the end of the year, the commercialized versions of Morton's iodized salt were being sold throughout the United States [30]. A later report documented a one standard deviation rise in IQ in Michigan following supplementation [31].

Ok, so if iodine is so important to the thyroid, and the brain—what's its role? Iodine's single function is as a cofactor in the thyroid hormones, thyroxine (T4) and triiodothyronine (T3). To simplify this even further, T4 is thus called because it has 4 iodine molecules, while T3 has three of them (Figure 7.7). T3 is the active form and the one that binds the thyroid hormone receptor (remember from Chapter 5, this requires vitamin A and RXR). The conversion of T4 to T3 is performed by an enzyme called 5' deiodinase, and here we introduce the cofactor selenium, which 5' deiodinase

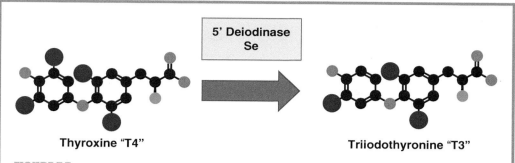

FIGURE 7.7: Deiodinazation of T4 by 5' deiodinase forms active thyroid hormone, T3. The 5' deiodinase enzyme requires selenium as an enzymatic co-factor. Selenium is actually part of a modified amino acid, selenocysteine, which is incorporated into the enzyme during translation. Note that the number of iodine molecules (in purple) goes from four in T4 to three in T3.

© molekuul_be/Shutterstock.com

needs to function. There are actually three different forms of deiodinase (D1, D2, and D3) [32], and here's where things get interesting. While D2 converts T4 to T3, forming active thyroid hormone, D3 can either convert T4 to an inactive form of T3 (called reverse T3) or convert active T3 to inactive T2—all while removing iodine [32]. D1 on the other hand is a bit more controversial because it appears to both activate and deactivate T4, but a knockout mouse model generated in 2006 appears to suggest that it may play a protective role in preventing hyperthyroidism [33].

So why is thyroid hormone so important to the developing brain during embryogenesis and in the postnatal period? First, let's point out that initially and until about midgestation, the developing organism obtains all of its thyroid hormone from the mother. By about midgestation, the thyroid has formed sufficiently to begin producing T4 within the colloid, using tyrosine as the starting material. Thus, iodine is needed both by the mother and the developing fetus during pregnancy. All low birth weight humans also have low serum T3 levels [34]. Thyroid hormone is known to be important to the developmental growth of nearly every tissue—but is particularly required in the development of the skeleton, lungs, and adipose tissues [34]. In addition, the developing brain utilizes T3 to activate many genes required for neurogenesis, neuronal differentiation, neuronal migration, and axon myelination [35]. Thus, iodine deficiency which would lower available T3 for THR activity would impair overall growth of the fetus, as well as brain development. One researcher even suggests that extended exposure to thyroid hormones in primates, and in particular humans, was responsible for the evolutionary gains in intellect by our species [35].

The thyroid axis is tightly regulated, with low T3 and T4 levels sensed by hypothalamic neurons in the paraventricular nucleus, which release thyrotropin releasing hormone (TRH) within the median eminence, just above the pituitary signaling the pituitary to release thyroid stimulating hormone (TSH) (Figure 7.8). TSH

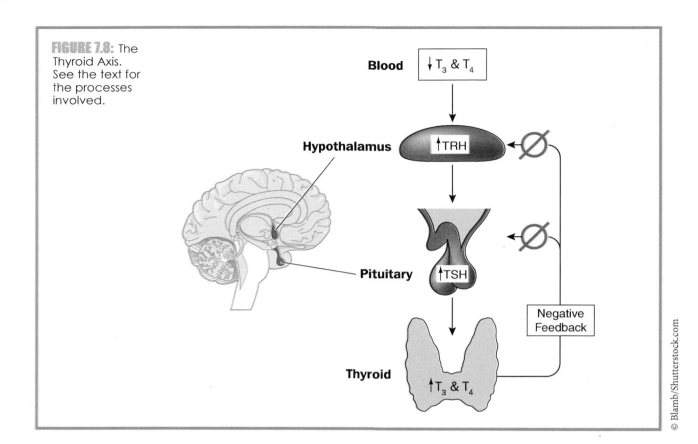

© Blamb/Shutterstock.com

FIGURE 7.8: The Thyroid Axis. See the text for the processes involved.

then stimulates the thyroid to produce more T4, which subsequently, and in a tissue-specific manner, is converted to T3 by the deiodinases. High levels of T3 or T4 are also sensed by both the hypothalamus and the pituitary to complete a negative feedback loop (Figure 7.8). Thus, local activation of T4 by deiodinases, along with a tightly regulated thyroid axis, maintains prenatal developmental programs and continues throughout adulthood.

When things go wrong

As you might have already guessed, because of the tight regulation of thyroid hormones, too much or too little TH is detrimental to health. In the case of too little, we've discussed the effects of iodine deficiency. But what about other factors that can impair a tissue's ability to make, transport, or activate thyroid hormones? First, in chapter 3, we discussed many transporters for minerals, but one that was left out was the sodium-iodide symporter (NIS) [36] (since I knew we'd be discussing it here). Interesting isn't it that both sodium and iodine are cotransported in tissues such as the small intestine, and the thyroid, which might be one of the reasons why iodination of salt was a brilliant move. But getting back to issue at hand, Table 7.3 shows some genetic causes of hypo- and hyperthyroidism. For example,

TABLE 7.3: Some unique genetic conditions leading to hypo- and hyperthyroidism

Condition	Cause	Symptoms
I- Transport Defect (ITD)	NIS Deficiency	Congenital hypothyroidism
Allan-Herndon-Dudley Syndrome	MCT8 Deficiency	• X-linked • Motor developmental delay • Elevated serum T3
Unnamed	Selenocysteine insertion sequence binding protein 2 (SBP2) Deficiency	• Reduced growth • Low T3/T4 levels
Familial non-autoimmune Hyperthyroidism	TSHR genetic activation	• Increased metabolism • Weight loss • Heart palpitations

researchers have recently shown that some individuals, despite getting sufficient dietary iodine, develop congenital hypothyroidism due to genetic variations in NIS, as the ability of the thyroid (and likely the small intestine) to take up iodine is impaired in this condition [36]. There are at least 13 different variants that can affect the function of NIS, and likely more will be found and characterized [36]. Variants affecting the TSH receptor, on the other hand, tend to be activating, and carriers of these genetic variants show familial hyperthyroidism [37]. The variants lead to increased signals downstream of the receptor, including increased expression of NIS, increased iodine uptake by the thyroid, increased synthesis and secretion of T3, and increased thyroid growth [37]. The condition is symptomatically similar to autoimmune Graves' disease, where the body makes antibodies that actually mimic TSH, causing persistent stimulation of the TSH receptor and hyperthyroidism.

Iodine may be a single function micronutrient—its only role is as a cofactor in all forms of thyroid hormone, but as this section points out, there are "Grave" consequences of having too much or too little of it. Think about this concept the next time you shake salt on your french fries.

CHAPTER SUMMARY

According to some, the definition of a living entity is that it can reproduce. As we've seen in this chapter, reproduction, development, and growth require one carbon metabolism, vitamin A, and thyroid hormone. Of course, at some point all of the vitamins and minerals come into play, but the micronutrients discussed in this chapter are the most important to consider for these processes.

- The folate cycle and the methionine cycle together are called "one carbon metabolism. These processes connect B9 and its vitamers to homocysteine remediation (formation of methionine or cysteine), amino acid synthesis (serine/glycine), and nucleotide synthesis, requiring B2, B3, B6, B12 (cobalt), and zinc.
- Too much or too little vitamin A can wreck embryogenesis—with a retinoic acid gradient being established in the embryo with the opposing effects of RALDH and CYP26 enzymes. Remember that both niacin and zinc are needed for full vitamin A activity.
- While this chapter focused mainly on embryonic needs for iodine and thyroid hormone, the thyroid continues to need iodine to synthesize thyroid hormone daily.

POINTS TO PONDER

- Think about the processes that B9 is involved in. Do you think supplementing with B9 would be beneficial or detrimental to someone with cancer (or even with a predisposition to cancer)?
- What are the physiological consequences of hyperhomocysteinemia in adults? Is there a need to supplement individuals at times other than pregnancy?
- Are there genetic lesions in vitamin A metabolism genes, such as RDH, RALDH, CYP26, or the receptors that might affect human fertility and embryonic development?
- What adult tissues most require thyroid hormone (hint—What tissues or systems are affected in hypo- and hyperthyroidism?)
- With the increases in sodium intake, worldwide, but especially in the United States, are there increases in iodine intake as well? Do processed foods contain iodized or non-iodized salt? Should individuals on low sodium diets worry about their iodine intake?

References

1. Nomikos, M., K. Swann, and F.A. Lai. (2012). Starting a new life: sperm PLC-zeta mobilizes the Ca2+ signal that induces egg activation and embryo development: an essential phospholipase C with implications for male infertility. *Bioessays*, **34**(2): 126–34.

2. Shirakawa, H., T. Kikuchi, and M. Ito. (2016). Calcium signaling in mammalian eggs at fertilization. *Curr Top Med Chem*, **16**(24): 2664–76.

3. Ducker, G.S. and J.D. Rabinowitz. (2016). One-carbon metabolism in health and disease. *Cell Metab*.

4. Huang, T., et al. (2012). Meta-analysis of B vitamin supplementation on plasma homocysteine, cardiovascular and all-cause mortality. *Clinical Nutrition*, **31**(4): 448–454.

5. Maddox, D.M., et al. (2003). Reduced-folate carrier (RFC) is expressed in placenta and yolk sac, as well as in cells of the developing forebrain, hindbrain, neural tube, craniofacial region, eye, limb buds and heart. *BMC Dev Biol*, **3**: 6.

6. Yasuda, S., et al. (2008). Placental folate transport during pregnancy. *Biosci Biotechnol Biochem*, **72**(9): 2277–84.

7. Cherukad, J., V. Wainwright, and E.D. Watson. (2012). Spatial and temporal expression of folate-related transporters and metabolic enzymes during mouse placental development. *Placenta*, **33**(5): 440–8.

8. Matthews, T.J., *Trends in Spina Bifida and Anencephalus in the United States, 1991-2006*, N.V.S.S. CDC/NCHS, Division of Vital Statistics, Editor. 2015, U.S. Department of Health & Human Services

9. Arth, A., et al. (2016). A 2015 global update on folic acid-preventable spina bifida and anencephaly. *Birth Defects Res A Clin Mol Teratol*, **106**(7): 520–9.

10. Atta, C.A., et al. (2016). Global Birth Prevalence of Spina Bifida by Folic Acid Fortification Status: A Systematic Review and Meta-Analysis. *Am J Public Health*, **106**(1): e24–34.

11. Pfeiffer, C.M., et al. (2005). Biochemical indicators of B vitamin status in the US population after folic acid fortification: results from the National Health and Nutrition Examination Survey 1999–2000. *Am J Clin Nutr*, **82**(2): 442–50.

12. Peker, E., et al. (2016). The levels of vitamin B12, folate and homocysteine in mothers and their babies with neural tube defects. *J Matern Fetal Neonatal Med*, **29**(18): 2944–8.

13. Lassi, Z.S., et al. (2013). Folic acid supplementation during pregnancy for maternal health and pregnancy outcomes. *Cochrane Database Syst Rev*, (3): CD006896.

14. Mosley, B.S., et al. (2009). Neural tube defects and maternal folate intake among pregnancies conceived after folic acid fortification in the United States. *Am J Epidemiol*, **169**(1): 9–17.

15. Levin, B.L. and E. Varga. (2016). MTHFR: Addressing genetic counseling dilemmas using evidence-based literature. *J Genet Couns*, **25**(5): 901–11.

16. Doudney, K., et al. (2009). Evaluation of folate metabolism gene polymorphisms as risk factors for open and closed neural tube defects. *Am J Med Genet A*, **149A**(7): 1585–9.

17. Franke, B., et al. (2009). An association study of 45 folate-related genes in spina bifida: Involvement of cubilin (CUBN) and tRNA aspartic acid methyltransferase 1 (TRDMT1). *Birth Defects Res A Clin Mol Teratol*, **85**(3): 216–26.

18. Martinelli, M., et al. (2014). Evidence of the involvement of the DHFR gene in nonsyndromic cleft lip with or without cleft palate. *Eur J Med Genet*, **57**(1): 1–4.

19. Wernimont, S.M., et al. (2011). Polymorphisms in serine hydroxymethyltransferase 1 and methylenetetrahydrofolate reductase interact to increase cardiovascular disease risk in humans. *J Nutr*, **141**(2):. 255–60.

20. Marshall, H., et al. (1996). Retinoids and Hox genes. *FASEB J*, **10**(9): 969–78.

21. Samarut, E., et al. (2015). ZebRA: An overview of retinoic acid signaling during zebrafish development. *Biochim Biophys Acta*, **1849**(2): 73–83.

22. Lara-Ramirez, R., E. Zieger, and M. Schubert. (2013). Retinoic acid signaling in spinal cord development. *Int J Biochem Cell Biol*, **45**(7): 1302–13.

23. Kumar, S., et al. (2012). Alcohol and aldehyde dehydrogenases: retinoid metabolic effects in mouse knockout models. *Biochim Biophys Acta*, **1821**(1): 198–205.

24. Niederreither, K., et al. (1999). Embryonic retinoic acid synthesis is essential for early mouse post-implantation development. *Nat Genet*, **21**(4): 444–8.

25. Sakai, Y., et al. (2001). The retinoic acid-inactivating enzyme CYP26 is essential for establishing an uneven distribution of retinoic acid along the anterio-posterior axis within the mouse embryo. *Genes Dev*, **15**(2): 213–25.

26. Clagett-Dame, M. and D. Knutson. (2011). Vitamin A in reproduction and development. *Nutrients*, **3**(4): 385–428.

27. Rogers, L. and R.-R.-J. P. (2011). Neonatal vitamin A supplementation. *World Health Organization*.

28. Fualal, J. and J. Ehrenkranz. (2016). Access, availability, and infrastructure deficiency: The current management of thyroid disease in the developing world. *Rev Endocr Metab Disord*.

29. Carpenter, K.J. (2005). David Marine and the problem of goiter. *J Nutr*, **135**(4): 675–80.

30. Markel, H. (1987). "When it rains it pours": endemic goiter, iodized salt, and David Murray Cowie, MD. *Am J Public Health*, **77**(2): 219–29.

31. Feyrer, J., D. Politi, and D.N. Weil. (2013). The Cognitive Effects of Micronutrient Deficiency: Evidence from Salt Iodization in the United States. *NATIONAL BUREAU OF ECONOMIC RESEARCH*.

32. Bianco, A.C. and B.W. Kim. (2006). Deiodinases: implications of the local control of thyroid hormone action. *J Clin Invest*, **116**(10): 2571–9.

33. Schneider, M.J., et al. (2006). Targeted disruption of the type 1 selenodeiodinase gene (Dio1) results in marked changes in thyroid hormone economy in mice. *Endocrinology*, **147**(1): 580–9.

34. Forhead, A.J. and A.L. Fowden. (2014). Thyroid hormones in fetal growth and prepartum maturation. *J Endocrinol*, **221**(3): R87–R103.

35. Stenzel, D. and W.B. Huttner. (2013). Role of maternal thyroid hormones in the developing neocortex and during human evolution. *Front Neuroanat*, **7**: 19.

36. Portulano, C., M. Paroder-Belenitsky, and N. Carrasco. (2014). The Na+/I-symporter (NIS): mechanism and medical impact. *Endocr Rev*, **35**(1): 106–49.
37. Hebrant, A., et al. (2011). Genetic hyperthyroidism: hyperthyroidism due to activating TSHR mutations. *Eur J Endocrinol*, **164**(1): 1–9.

Crossword

Reproduction and Development

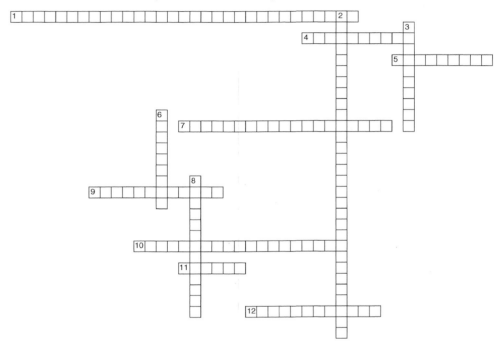

ACROSS
1 A flavoprotein in the folate cycle
4 A consequence of B9 deficiency
5 Full name of vitamin B12
7 The alternate name of the folate cycle
9 Toxic metabolite that is generated by the methionine cycle
10 Consequence of B6 deficiency
11 Caused by hyperthyroidism
12 At fertilization, this occurs, involving a micronutrient, and blocking polyspermy
DOWN
2 Enzyme needed for conversion of serine and glycine
3 Selenium-containing enzyme in the thyroid axis
6 Leading consequence of vitamin A deficiency in children
8 Dietary form of B9

NOTES

CHAPTER 8

The Skeletal System— Not Just Structural!

Table of Contents

Our skeletal system is a highly dynamic system composed of 206 bones in adults. Overall, this system is responsible for supporting us and helping us move, protecting internal organs such as the brain and lungs, producing blood and immune cells, as we will see in a later chapter, and most importantly for the purpose of this chapter, serving as a storage reservoir for calcium and phosphorus. Calcium is the most abundant mineral in our body, due in part to its storage in bone, and also, as we saw in Chapter 5, its role in cell signaling. Phosphorus, the second most abundant mineral in our bodies is also involved in both cell signaling, and as a component of bone.

Hydroxyapatite makes up approximately 70% of the dry weight of bone, and both calcium and phosphorus serve as structural cofactors within the hydroxyapatite molecule. Hydroxyapatite is composed of 39.8% calcium, and 18.5% phosphorus, with hydrogen and oxygen making up the remainder of the molecule, which has a chemical formula of $Ca_{10}(PO_4)_6(OH)$ [1]. In addition, a modified form of hydroxyapatite, where the –OH group is replaced with a fluoride molecule (written $Ca_5(PO_4)_3F$) is a major component of tooth enamel. Calcium is also bound to osteocalcin (also called "bone gla protein," BGP) and matrix gla protein (MGP), and as a structural cofactor within the bone matrix, facilitates protein:protein, and protein:phospholipid interactions. However, calcium and phosphorus storage and structural function in bone is only part of the skeletal systems role in our bodies' metabolism—as we will see, metabolism of these inorganic minerals actually favors plasma/serum, not bone, homeostasis of calcium and phosphorus, which is why dietary deficiencies in calcium, phosphorus, and vitamin D lead to reduced mineralization of our bone. Let's see how and why calcium and phosphorus concentrations in plasma are regulated and why this is so important to our health.

VITAMIN D METABOLISM

A discussion of bone is not complete without specifically talking about the metabolism of vitamin D. As we know from the previous chapters, vitamin D is a fat-soluble vitamin, and enters the body through the digestive tract within micelles, and through the bloodstream within chyllomicrons. What we haven't talked about yet is where the "first stop" is for dietary vitamin D (cholecaciferol) and the fact that we can make at least some of the vitamin D that we need within our own bodies. So, let's start there.

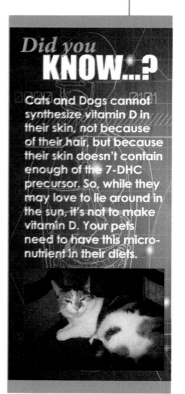

Did you KNOW...?

Cats and Dogs cannot synthesize vitamin D in their skin, not because of their hair, but because their skin doesn't contain enough of the 7-DHC precursor. So, while they may love to lie around in the sun, it's not to make vitamin D. Your pets need to have this micronutrient in their diets.

Vitamin D is unique among the fat-soluble vitamins in that we can synthesize the precursor molecule, cholecaciferol, from the cholesterol precursor, 7-dehydrocholesterol (7-DHC) (Figure 8.1). Interestingly, this initial process does not require any fancy enzymes—just ultraviolet (UV) (type B) rays, and a warm skin temperature. Exposure of 7-DHC to UVB rays (basically when you go out into bright sunlight), causes conversion of 7-DHC to previtamin D_3 (also called precalciferol). Then the warmth of our skin causes isomerization of precalciferol to cholecalciferol. As you might imagine, this whole process is influenced by how much exposure to sunlight occurs for each individual, with people in the Northern hemisphere receiving less UVB radiation during winter [2]. The cholecalciferol formed in the skin is transported exclusively bound to vitamin D binding protein (as compared to dietary vitamin D_3, which as we noted above, is transported within chylomicrons) [1].

The first stop for both is the liver where vitamin D is converted into 25-(OH) vitamin D_3 (calcidiol) by the action of the enzyme, 25-hydroxylase [3]. For full activity, 25-hydroxylase enzyme requires NADPH as a coenzyme, which is involved in an electron-transferring reaction leading to hydroxylation of vitamin D_3 and producing calcidiol[4]. It is calcidiol or 25-hydroxy-vitamin D_3 that is used in tests to determine circulating vitamin D levels. Why is that? As we will see below, the next enzyme in the process, 1-alpha hydroxylase in

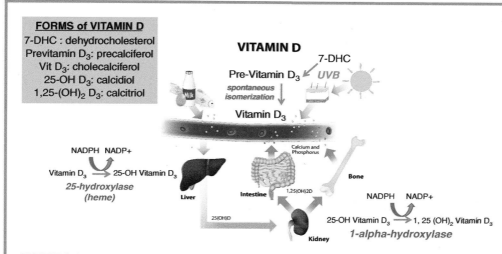

FORMS of VITAMIN D
7-DHC : dehydrocholesterol
Previtamin D_3: precalciferol
Vit D_3: cholecalciferol
25-OH D_3: calcidiol
1,25-$(OH)_2$ D_3: calcitriol

VITAMIN D

7-DHC
Pre-Vitamin D_3 — UVB
spontaneous isomerization
Vitamin D_3

NADPH NADP+
Vitamin D_3 → 25-OH Vitamin D_3
25-hydroxylase (heme)
Liver

Calcium and Phosphorus
Bone
Intestine
1,25(OH)2D
25(OH)D
Kidney

NADPH NADP+
25-OH Vitamin D_3 → 1, 25 $(OH)_2$ Vitamin D_3
1-alpha-hydroxylase

FIGURE 8.1: Metabolism and action of vitamin D. Pre-vitamin D3 can be formed from 7-dehydrocholesterol when the skin is exposed to UVB rays. It then spontaneously isomerizes to Vitamin D3 which is transported to the bloodstream bound to Vitamin D binding protein. Dietary Vitamin D3 is also absorbed from the intestine and transported in the bloodstream, usually within chylomicrons before being delivered to the liver. Within the liver Vitamin D3 is converted to calcidiol by B3-requiring 25-hydroxylase enzyme. Calcidiol, bound to Vitamin D binding protein travels to kidney to finally be converted to active calcitriol by the 1-alpha hydroxylase enzyme, which also requires Vitamin B3. Active Vitamin D (calcitriol) now travels to target tissues (bound by Vitamin D binding protein) to mediate calcium and phosphorus regulation, as well as other genomic/gene regulatory actions. Vitamin D2 can follow a similar pathway following ingestion, but is not as potent as Vitamin D3.

© Designua/Shutterstock.com

the kidney, appears to be more tightly regulated by calcium levels. By controlling this second enzyme, one controls active vitamin D, but not the availability of vitamin D. Thus, calcidiol is a measure of available vitamin D, with low levels indicating a vitamin D deficiency either through diet or skin production.

Calcidiol travels through the blood bound to vitamin D binding protein (sometimes abbreviated DBP). DBP is an albumin-like or globulin-like protein, which a very high affinity for all types of vitamin D. According to one article, up to 85% of all calcidiol is bound to DBP [5]. When it reaches the kidney, the DBP is taken up by an endocytic process occuring via normal filtering within the proximal tubules of the kidney. Here's where it gets interesting though (at least from a vitamin perspective . . .). A protein called megalin grabs the vitamin D-DBP complex for endocytosis, but this protein also requires another protein, cubilin as a coreceptor [4]. You should remember cubilin as a protein involved in intrinsic factor-B12 uptake in the intestine—yup, this is the same protein, now in the kidney and also taking up vitamin D. Once taken up by this process, if 1-alpha-hydroxylase enzyme is present, calcidiol will be converted to calcitriol (1, 25(OH)-vitamin D3) and pushed back out into circulation (bound to DBP) to travel to its target tissues, including bone.

Again, 1-alpha-hydroxylase enzyme requires NADPH for that second hydroxylation reaction [5].

As we've discussed previously calcitriol binds to the vitamin D receptor (VDR), which is found on nearly all cell types of the body. In other chapters we will talk about the vitamin D effects on immunity, nervous system, and skin. For now, let's focus on its major role in calcium and phosphorus homeostasis.

CALCIUM AND PHOSPHORUS HOMEOSTASIS—I HAVE A BONE TO PICK WITH YOU!

As the title of this section (hopefully) suggests, calcium and phosphorous homeostasis in our body fluids comes about through "picking" of our bones—such that when calcium or phosphorus levels are low in plasma or serum, our bones are remodeled to release calcium. For our body's metabolism, the goal is to maintain calcium and phosphorus levels within a very narrow range in the plasma. When the levels of these minerals in plasma drop below physiological levels, the body recruits more minerals out of its storage vessel, the bone. The normal concentration of calcium within the plasma is between 8 and 10 mg/dl [6]. Over a 24-hour period, approximately 10 mmol of calcium is exchanged between plasma and bone [7] meaning that bone remodeling, bone building, and calcium homeostasis are all very dynamic processes. Let's now see how vitamin D is involved in this process, and how the parathyroid and thyroid organs, and our digestive and excretory systems sense and maintain homeostasis in the body.

Calcium and phosphorus absorption

In Chapter 3, we briefly discussed the uptake of inorganic minerals, listing the receptors for calcium and phosphorus in Table 3.3. I didn't spend much time on these receptors in Chapter 3 because I knew we would discuss these two receptors in more detail here, in our skeletal system chapter.

Both calcium and phosphorus use ion channels for uptake of their respective minerals. For calcium, the transient receptor potential (TRP) family member, V6 is responsible for active calcium transport from the duodenum portion of the small intestine. The gene for TRPV6 is vitamin D responsive, meaning that its promoter region has a vitamin D-responsive element and increased mRNA is expressed in the presence of vitamin D [8]. This is one of the main ways in which vitamin D regulates calcium levels in the body. The importance of the vitamin D receptor (VDR) in regulating active calcium uptake through TRPV6 was shown using mice containing a targeted deletion of VDR [9]. The VDR-knockout mice showed hypocalcemia, hyperparathyroidism, elevated serum $1,25\text{-}(OH)_2D_3$ levels, and decreased calcium content in bone, along with reduced expression of TRPV6 protein and mRNA [9].

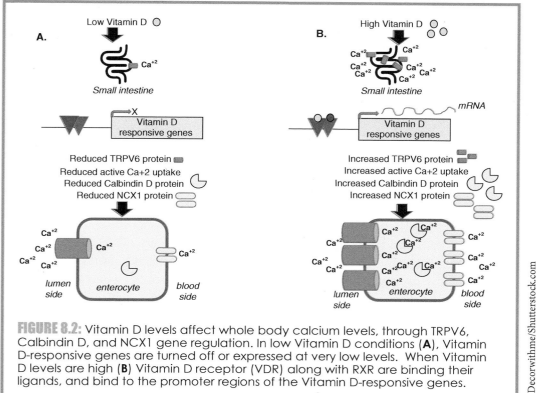

FIGURE 8.2: Vitamin D levels affect whole body calcium levels, through TRPV6, Calbindin D, and NCX1 gene regulation. In low Vitamin D conditions (**A**), Vitamin D-responsive genes are turned off or expressed at very low levels. When Vitamin D levels are high (**B**) Vitamin D receptor (VDR) along with RXR are binding their ligands, and bind to the promoter regions of the Vitamin D-responsive genes.

© Decorwithme/Shutterstock.com

As calcium influx was particularly impaired when mice were on a low calcium diet, but not on a high calcium diet, this was the first indication that TRPV6 was responsible for active, vitamin-D mediated uptake of calcium, and that calcium absorption could occur passively when intake levels were high. Later, studies showed that the vitamin D receptor, in a heterodimer with the retinoid X receptor RXR, mediate gene expression of TRPV6, via up to six different VDR elements in the promoter region [10]. Upon vitamin D activation, transcriptional coactivators were recruited to the promoter, and histones wrapping the DNA within the TRPV6 promoter become acetylated. Thus, as shown on Figure 8.2, vitamin D levels positively regulate calcium uptake by the intestine (especially when overall calcium intake is low), via VDR-mediated transcription of TRPV6. Once in the enterocytes, calcium is complexed with calbindin, and finally excreted into the bloodstream via the NaCa pump, NCX1. Both calbindin, and NCX1 are positively increased by vitamin D_3 in a complex with VDR and RXR. Once calcium is secreted into the bloodstream, about 50% of it is free, and most of the rest is bound to proteins, such as albumin and immunoglobulin[8].

For phosphorus, the type IIb sodium-phosphate (Na(+)−P(i)) cotransporter does the job in the small intestinal lumen [11] (note that the type IIa transporter works in the kidney—we'll talk about that momentarily).

The Werner and Kinne (2001) [11] paper also describes the evolution and comparison of phosphate channels from bacteria to humans.

When vitamin D is depleted from weanling rats by giving them a nonvitamin D-containing diet, and holding them in a room without UV light (remember rats, like us can synthesize vitamin D), phosphate uptake is significantly reduced. Adding back vitamin D_3 or the fully active 1,25(OH) vitamin D_3 leads to increased phosphate fluxes in the jejunum [12]. Here's the catch though . . . We know vitamin D acts through its steroid hormone receptor, vitamin D receptor (VDR), and transcriptionally-regulates expression of genes—right? But in a later study done in mice, vitamin D treatment increased phosphate absorption by enterocytes, but through increased protein, not mRNA levels of NaPi-IIb receptor [13]. A vitamin D analog, which was developed in Japan for the treatment of osteoporosis, ED-71 [1α,25-dihydroxy-2β-(3-hydroxypropyloxy), however, can induce NaPiIIb mRNA in small intestine [14]. This induction of NaPiIIb requires VDR as VDR knockout mice no longer show the mRNA induction [14]. What can we conclude from these two studies? The authors of the later study [14] suggest that because ED-71 is a more potent analog of vitamin D, which is not readily broken down, the results may reflect a difference in concentration or timing between the two studies—in other words, it is likely that vitamin D (namely 1,25(OH) vitamin D3) does induce NaPiIIb mRNA transcription through VDR, but may also work nontranscriptionally to regulate NaPiIIb translocation to the enterocyte luminal surface. This "nongenomic" mechanism, which involves intracellular signaling, was discussed in Chapter 5.

Calcium blood concentration determines PTH secretion

Once absorbed by the intestine, calcium and phosphate are released into the bloodstream. Calcium, and not phosphate, is the mineral that is sensed by multiple tissues, and most importantly the parathyroid and thyroid glands (Figure 8.3). Let's examine how calcium levels are sensed, and what happens to maintain Ca^{+2} blood concentrations. As a reminder, our body's physiology is most interested in maintaining these blood concentrations and will do so at the expense of bone, which is the storage unit for calcium and phosphorus.

McGill University hosts an entire website dedicated to CaSR proteins and CaSR-related genetic conditions http://www.casrdb.mcgill.ca/

In the bloodstream, about 50% of the calcium is freely available in its ionic form, which means the amounts are able to be detected by calcium sensors located in the parathyroid gland, the thyroid, the kidney, and in bone (among other tissues—but for the purpose of this discussion, these are the most important). CaSRs (Calcium sensor receptors) are G-protein coupled receptors, which can bind to extracellular calcium. When this happens, phospholipase C (PLC) is activated, and a cascade of signaling occurs, which ultimately results in reduced protein expression of PTH or calcitonin (Figure 8.2).

Let's talk first about PTH secretion. Basically, calcium sensing does not change PTH mRNA expression, but rather, calcium sensing changes whether or not PTH mRNA will be degraded or translated into protein (Figure 8.4). When high calcium

CALCITONIN and PARATHORMONE
(hormonal regulation of blood calcium levels)

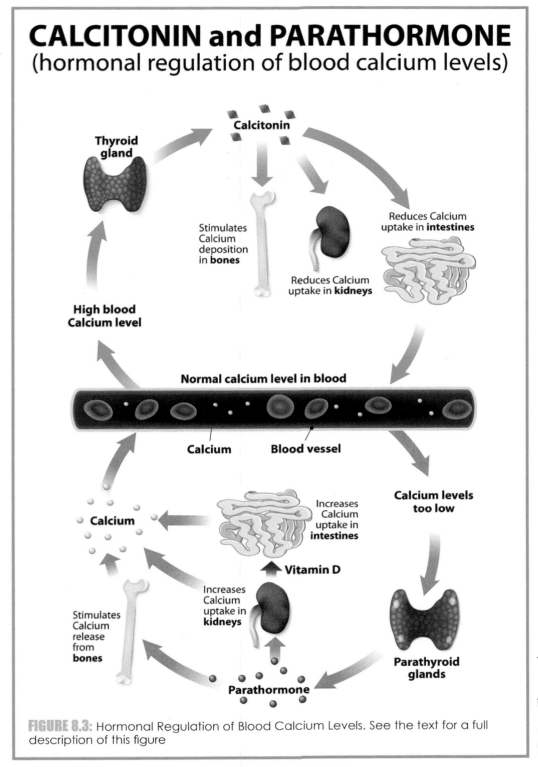

FIGURE 8.3: Hormonal Regulation of Blood Calcium Levels. See the text for a full description of this figure

© Designua/Shutterstock.com

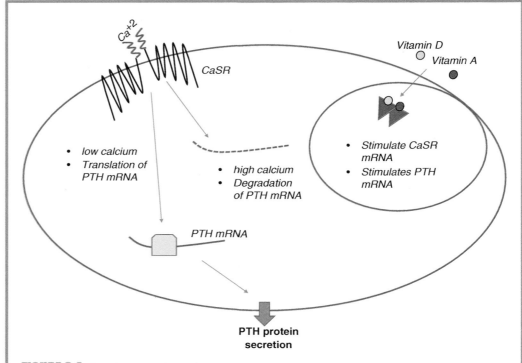

FIGURE 8.4: Calcium sensing within the parathyroid gland leads to changes in PTH secretion. While Vitamin D can stimulate PTH mRNA, it is the level of calcium in the blood that determines whether PTH is secreted. This occurs because in the presence of calcium, signaling cascades result in degradation of the PTH mRNA. With no mRNA, no PTH is secreted. On the other hand, when there is low calcium, the signaling does not occur, and PTH mRNA and protein is made. As one can see, Vitamin D (along with Vitamin A) ensures that CaSR and PTH mRNAs are expressed, but calcium levels determine if PTH protein is secreted.

levels are sensed, PTH is degraded and not secreted (meaning that bone resorption doesn't occur—bone building does, Table 8.1). Conversely, with low calcium levels, PTH mRNA is translated into protein and PTH is secreted [15]. PTH then directs bone resorption and degradation to release more calcium into the bloodstream. It also instructs kidney cells to stop secreting excess calcium. There is limited information on whether phosphorus is sensed by the parathyroid gland and whether phosphorus levels in serum regulate PTH protein expression. For now, calcium is the main player in homeostasis. One key point to keep in mind is that vitamin D stimulates PTH secretion, which can result in breakdown of bone if calcium levels are too low. Thus, while we often think of vitamin D as a bone-building hormone, it is really a calcium-regulating hormone, with its focus on maintaining blood serum calcium levels. Storage of calcium in bone only occurs when levels of circulating calcium are sufficient (and hopefully here vitamin D did its job to induce calcium dietary uptake!), and when calcium signaling within the parathyroid hormone results in degradation of PTH mRNA and no PTH secretion.

TABLE 8.1: Actions of Vitamin D3, PTH and Calcitonin on calcium and phosphate levels

	Effects on Ca^{+2}	Effects on Pi
Calcitriol (1,25 (OH) D$_3$)	↑ Intestinal absorption ↑ TRPV6 receptor protein and mRNA ↑ Calbindin and NCX1 mRNA	↑ Intestinal absorption ↑ NaPi IIb receptor protein and mRNA
PTH	↓ Urinary excretion ↓ Renal reabsorption ↓ Bone resorption/breakdown	↓ Urinary excretion ↓ Bone resorption/breakdown
Calcitonin	↑ Bone mineralization ↑ Renal reabsorption	↑ Bone mineralization

Thyroid sensing of calcium levels (yes, here's where calcitonin secretion is controlled)

Calcium levels also modulate gene regulation within the thyroid. This is a great thing, as calcium sensing can guard against hypercalcemia (thyroid sensing) as well as hypocalcemia (parathyroid sensing). So, as you might expect, the result of high calcium sensing by the CaSR in the thyroid leads to calcitonin secretion and bone building (Figure 8.3). This occurs through a signaling cascade, initiated calcium, which leads to transcription of the calcitonin gene [16]. As there is no similar mRNA degradation scenario for calcitonin in the thyroid, like we saw for PTH mRNA, high calcium simply leads to calcitonin hormone secretion. Calcitonin receptors are present on bone cells, and you may be surprised to find out that it acts most directly by inhibiting osteoclast from breaking down and remodeling bone, rather than acting on osteoblast to promote calcium deposition into bone, and bone growth [17]. Inhibition of bone remodeling tips the balance in favor of bone deposition, leading to calcium storage in bone and new bone cells. There is one report that calcitonin can directly inhibit osteoblast and osteocyte apoptosis, or cell death, but this finding is controversial according to some reports [17]. Suffice to say that calcitonin certainly prevents further bone loss in the face of high calcium levels, and leads to calcium storage in bone.

> Think about what happens to thyroid and parathyroid cells when an individual has Hashimoto's (an autoimmune destruction of the thyroid). Could this condition affect bone metabolism?

Kidney and bone responses to changing calcium and hormone levels

Both the kidney and bone tissues respond to changing calcium, PTH, and calcitonin levels to ultimately maintain calcium homeostasis. While Figure 8.3

shows the general mechanisms in kidney and bone, what is really going on at the molecular and cellular levels? In the kidney, PTH stimulates mRNA levels of 1-hydroxylase enzyme, leading to formation of active calcitriol, and reduces levels of the 24-hydroxylase enzyme, which can degrade vitamin D [18, 19]. The net result is an increase in active, circulating vitamin D levels, and ultimately increased calcium retention in the kidney. Likewise, as calcitonin acts in the opposite direction, calcitonin secreted from the thyroid reduces expression of the 1-hydroxylase enzyme, leading to lower levels of circulating active calcitriol (1,25-$(OH)_2$ vitamin D3), preventing hypercalcemia [3]. As shown in Figure 8.3 these hormones also have direct actions on bone. Specifically, calcitonin directly inhibits osteoclasts, leading to more bone formation [20]; however, there is not sufficient evidence of a direct action on bone osteoblasts (Figure 8.5). Conversely, PTH activates osteoclasts through complex cell signaling pathways [21] that are beyond what we need to know for the purpose of this chapter. While PTH does not appear to directly repress osteoblasts, at least one study suggests that there is a requirement for osteoblast signaling to ultimately lead to osteoclast activation [21].

Bone and renal tissue also directly responds to circulating calcium levels. This might come as a surprise to some, as these tissues seems to be "at the mercy" of calcitonin and PTH. However, the newest research shows that while CaSR is most

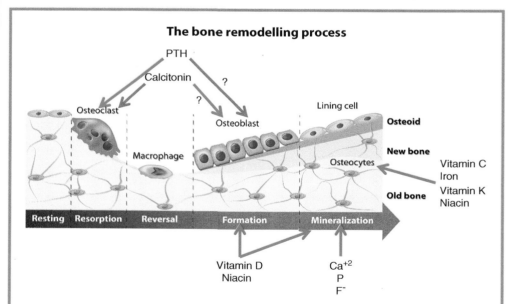

FIGURE 8.5: Bone remodeling is a normal processes. However, when there are vitamin or mineral deficiencies, bone remodeling does not occur properly, leading to formation of spongey, non-mineralized bone. Vitamin C and iron are needed to maintain the collagen extracellular matrix, along with Vitamin K (which requires niacin), to produce bone extracellular matrix proteins BGP and MGP. Vitamin D and niacin are needed so that the process of bone formation can occur. Calcium, phosphorus and fluoride are needed for strong mineralization.

© Designua/Shutterstock.com

highly expressed in parathyroid gland, it is also expressed in kidney and to a lesser extent in bone tissue, specifically osteoblasts and osteocytes, and less frequently in osteoclasts [22]. In bone, high calcium levels, sensed by osteoblast-expressed CaSR, stimulates osteoblast proliferation [22]. This is interesting, in that even in the presences of PTH, calcium sensing by osteoblasts can lead to bone formation, and is supported by the finding that mice with a deletion of CaSR in their osteoblasts have low bone mineral density [23]. Likewise, CaSR expression in the kidney results in calcium retention when calcium levels are low and calcium excretion when sensed levels are high, despite PTH or calcitonin levels [24].

In summary, calcium, PTH, and calcitonin coordinately work to maintain serum calcium levels. However, it seems that serum calcium levels ultimately are sensed and responded to in bone, kidney, and thyroid and parathyroid glands, making calcium ultimately in control of its own concentrations in the body. Consider this, as later on in the chapter we will discuss how genetic mutations in CaSR lead to problems with whole body calcium homeostasis.

OTHER MICRONUTRIENTS INVOLVED IN BONE

Our skeleton is dynamic, and not just a barren hydroxyapatite scaffold. It contains cells, such as the osteoblasts which build bone, osteoclasts which remodel and degrade bone, and osteocytes which maintain bone (Figure 8.5). As I hope you have now learned (and appreciated), bone's dynamic processes are meant to maintain calcium homeostasis in our body, as well as serve as our structural skeleton. However, calcium, phosphate, and vitamin D are not the only micronutrients needed for this dynamic structure—as we will see below, other fat and water soluble vitamins are involved, along with other minerals that are needed for healthy bone.

Collagen synthesis and triple helix formation

The osteoblasts are unique in that they synthesize both the hydroxyapatite molecule, and weave it together with type I collagen to form strong bone matrices. The synthesis of collagen is dependent on thyroid hormone, through the thyroid hormone receptor (THR) [25] in complex with RXR, meaning that collagen synthesis requires vitamin A (9-cis retinoic acid) for RXR, and selenium (for the deiodinase to form T4, which activates THR). Unlike a lot of proteins, which simply need to be synthesized and translated in order to be functional, collagen requires an extra step, hydroxylation. Hydroxylation of the proline and lysine residues with the amino acid chain of collagen results in aggregation and cross-linking of the individual collagen amino acid strands into the pro-collagen triple helix molecule (Figure 8.6). This process requires iron and ascorbate (vitamin C), as well as alpha-ketoglutarate from the TCA cycle. After transport to the extracellular matrix, pro-collagen is assembled into the collagen fibril, requiring lysyl oxidase enzyme to oxidize amino-groups of lysine in both collagen and elastin to produce a very

© molekuul_be/Shutterstock.com

FIGURE 8.6:

Hydroxylation of Collagen. The newly synthesize collagen protein strand undergoes hydroxylation reaction at proline and lysine residues, which allows for assembly of three collagen strands into the pro-collagen triple helix. Pro-collagen is then transported to the extracellular matrix where it is assembled into collagen fibrils.

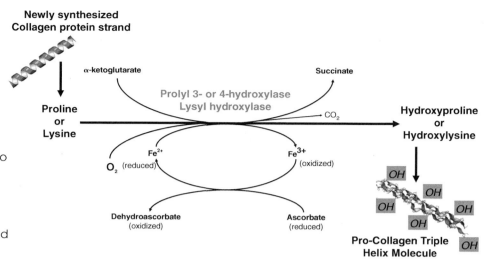

strong aldol cross-link between the two proteins [25]. Lysyl oxidase utilizes copper as a cofactor, and in the process forms hydrogen peroxides (which as we saw in the antioxidant chapter, need to be neutralized). Thus, collagen synthesis and fibril formation require two minerals—iron and copper—and vitamin C, adding these micronutrients to the growing list of vitamins and minerals needed for a healthy skeleton.

Vitamin K-dependent carboxylation

Also in the bone extracellular matrix are proteins that bind to and interact with calcium. In order to do so, they must undergo a carboxylation reaction, which is dependent upon the enzyme gamma-glutamyl carboxylase. This enzyme is vitamin K dependent, as shown in Figure 8.7. Specifically, the vitamin K-dependent gamma-glutamyl carboxylase reacts with glutamate residents in the amino acid chains of proteins, such as osteocalcin ("OC," also called bone gla protein or BGP) and matrix gla protein (MGP) [26]. The carboxylated proteins now have the ability to cross-link with calcium, either as a free ion or within hydroxyapatite, making for a mineralized extracellular bone matrix. Osteocalcin is one of the major proteins secreted by osteoblasts, and thus the importance of vitamin K-dependent carboxylation in bone-building processes cannot be underemphasized. Furthermore, gene expression for both OC and MGP are stimulated by calcitriol [26].

While vitamin D requires several steps to become active, vitamin K (especially menaquinone, K_2, which is more potent than phylloquinone, K_1) can be utilized following a single activation step, requiring NADPH and then recycled without any additional micronutrient requirement (Figure 8.7). Additionally, in relatively new findings, vitamin K can act as a ligand for steroid and xenobiotic receptor, SXR to

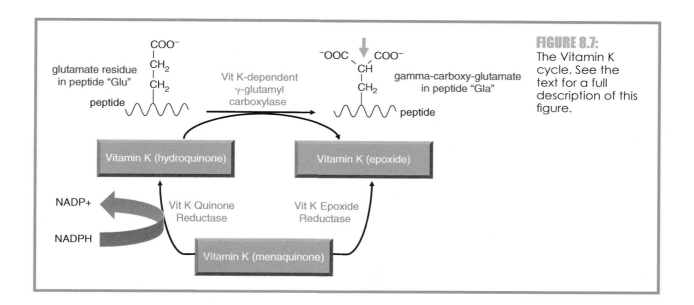

FIGURE 8.7: The Vitamin K cycle. See the text for a full description of this figure.

regulate genes, including collagen I and collagen IV within osteoblasts [27]. Consider this in light of that new fact . . . three of the four fat-soluble vitamins act as ligands for transcription factors.

Here's something to chew on—the role of fluoride

A chapter on the skeletal system would not be complete without talking about fluoride. As most people already know, fluoride is important to the health of our teeth—but do you know why? Fluoride is actually incorporated into the hydroxyapatite crystal of a developing tooth, and likewise can be incorporated into skeletal bones as well. Let's stick with teeth for now, and as you may recall from Chapter 2, the author was part of some of the original studies showing that incorporation of fluoride into drinking water could lead to lower incidences of cavities (Figure 2.3) [28]. However, there is some disagreement as to whether fluoride is a required nutrient (i.e., our bodies cannot live without it) or simply provides added protection from caries. For teeth, fluoride incorporates into hydroxyapatite with fluoride-containing hydroxyapatite being much more acid-resistant than regular hydroxyapatite [29]. Since hydroxyapatite is one of the main components of both the dentin and the tooth enamel, and dental caries are caused in a two-step processing involving acid dissolution of the enamel, followed by bacterial metabolism of carbohydrates in the dental plaque, it is clear that the more acid-resistant the teeth are, the less likely they are to develop cavities.

So how about bone—can fluoride incorporate into the hydroxyapatite of our skeletons as well? The answer is a resounding "YES" [29]. Is that good for our bones? Here the answer is a weaker "MAYBE." In one study using mice, there was no effect on bone mineral density with increasing levels of fluoride, although fluoride incorporation in bone increased significantly with increasing treatment levels [30]. In humans, fluoride also incorporates into bone, and some studies have shown severe incorporation (fluorosis, caused by years of high exposure) can lead to bone pain, and significantly elevated bone mineral density ([31]). However, the levels found in fluorinated drinking water have not been linked to bone mineral density issues in humans, and the most recent recommendations from government agencies is to continue water fluoridation practices in communities [32].

MICRONUTRIENT-ASSOCIATED CONDITIONS OF THE SKELETAL SYSTEM

Bone homeostasis consists of both bone growth and bone remodeling. As shown in Figure 8.5, bone remodeling is a normal process that is occurring in each of us right now. It requires many micronutrients throughout the cycle of remodeling, and if any are deficient, skeletal abnormalities can occur. During childhood and in adolescents, there is more bone growth than "withdrawal," especially if micronutrients are kept within normal range and the skeleton growth, attaining its most density (and overall amount/length) in the early 1920s. In this section, we will discuss how both bone growth and bone-remodeling processes can be disrupted when micronutrient intake or metabolism goes awry.

Calcium, phosphorus, and vitamin D associated conditions

The importance of calcium, phosphorus, and vitamin D to bone health cannot be understated, and their importance is particularly visible when one considers both the dietary and genetic factors that affect bone and involve these micronutrients. Table 8.2 shows the consequences of dietary deficiency and toxicity of calcium, vitamin D, and phosphorus (as well as other micronutrients which we will talk about later). A discussion of the skeleton would not be complete without talking about the most well-known deficiency conditions—osteoporosis, osteomalacia, and rickets (Figures 8.8 and 8.9).

Osteoporosis is a decrease in overall bone strength due to a lack of dietary calcium (Figure 8.8). This occurs most commonly in adults, and especially in the elderly, resulting in fractured or broken bones of the hip, forearm, or back vertebra. According to the International Osteoporosis Foundation (https://www.iofbonehealth.org/ epidemiology), worldwide, 200 million people suffer from osteoporosis, with one in three women, and one in five men experiencing an osteoporotic fracture during their lifetime. While there are other conditions and medications that can contribute to bone loss, intake of dietary calcium is the main dietary cause of osteoporosis. Preceding full osteoporosis is the condition, osteopenia, where bone mineral density is lower than recommended, but not low enough to be classified as osteoporosis.

TABLE 8.2: Causes and association of bone/skeletal conditions with dietary deficiency or toxicity of micronutrients

Skeletal System Micronutrients	Condition caused by Dietary Deficiency	Condition caused by Dietary Toxicity
Calcium	Osteoporesis	Kidney Stones Hypercalcemia
Phosphorus	Osteomalacia	Hyperphosphatemia
Iron	Reduced bone trabeculae	?
Fluoride	Dental caries	CaF insoluble precipitates Fluorosis
Copper	Reduced bone mineral density	?
Selenium	Osteoarthitis	?
Vitamin D	Osteomalcia, Rickets	Hypervitaminosis D Kidney Stones Hypercalcemia
Vitamin K	Weak bones	?
Vitamin C	Scurvy Weak bones/ECM	Likely none
Niacin	Pellagra Dental caries Osteoporosis	Likely none

In each condition, bone repair and new bone growth is slower compared to bone aging and demineralization, leading to less new bone and more old, fragile bone. What can one do to prevent osteopenia and osteoporosis? For both women (aged 51 and older) and men (aged 71 and older), recommended daily intake of calcium is increased, compared to younger adults [33]. Remember that calcium is regulated so that blood serum levels are normal, not so that bone is maintained. To the body, the bone is merely a storage site for calcium. Intake of sufficient dietary calcium ensures that the bone will not have to be robbed to maintain cellular processes that require calcium.

Vitamin D-deficient osteomalacia results when calcium and phosphate intake may be sufficient, but bone mineralization is still reduced (Figure 8.9A). Because as we found out, vitamin D stimulates calcium and phosphorus uptake from the small intestine, if active calcitriol levels are reduced (again, we are considering this to be a dietary reduction, but genetic conditions do occur, and will be discussed), the intestinal receptor for calcium TRPV6, and the receptor for phosphate NaPi-IIb will not be induced, nor will all of the other vitamin D-responsive genes needed for uptake be expressed properly

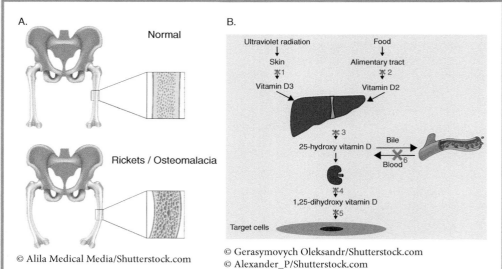

© Alila Medical Media/Shutterstock.com

© Gerasymovych Oleksandr/Shutterstock.com
© Alexander_P/Shutterstock.com

FIGURE 8.8: **A.** Bone softening and reduced bone mineral density with rickets (children) and osteomalacia (Adults). Osteomacia results from reduced deposition of minerals into bone—and reduced overall formation of new bone, meaning it can occur in both children and adults **B.** Vitamin D deficiency can be caused by genetic, dietary or environmental conditions at various steps in Vitamin D metabolism. **1.** Vitamin D formation in the skin is disrupted, either through low UVB exposure, skin conditions, or through genetic conditions affecting conversion of 7-dehydrocholesterol to vitamin D3. **2.** Low vitamin D dietary intake, or conditions that affect Vitamin D absorption can reduce whole body Vitamin D. **3.** Liver conditions, or genetic mutation of the 25-hydroxylase, or reduced niacin (which is needed by the enzyme) can affect Vitamin D3 conversion to 25-hydroxy vitamin D3. **4.** Kidney conditions, or genetic mutation of the 1-hydroxylase enzyme, or reduced niacin (which is needed by the enzyme) can affect conversion of 25-hydroxy Vitamin D3 to 1, 25-hydroxy Vitamin D3 or calcitriol, the active form. **5.** Mutations in the Vitamin D receptor can lead to insensitivity of the target cells to calcitriol. **6.** Mutations of the Vitamin D binding protein can lead to problems with transport in the blood of all forms of Vitamin D

(see Figure 8.2 and Table 8.1 as a reminder . . .). Since intake of calcium and phosphorus is the first step in the entire pathway of events leading to both calcium/phosphate regulation, lack of vitamin D messes up the entire process (Figure 8.9B). The result is that the bone is robbed of micronutrients to ensure serum levels are adequate, leading to soft bone (as compared to brittle old bone in osteoporosis) [34]. Of note, phosphate-deficient osteomalacia results when phosphorus/phosphate intake is low, or more commonly, when renal losses (mainly due to kidney conditions) are greater than intake. Rickets, caused by reduced vitamin D levels during childhood, when bone is growing (or should be), also presents with softened bones, curved spines and legs, and bone pain [34]. In addition, children can die from seizures, or cardiac arrest caused by low blood calcium levels. While one might think rickets is a disease of the past, a 2014 study has noted that in Britain, rickets is at a historical high [35]. Similarly, and perhaps not coincidently, there is a resurgence of vitamin D deficiency, worldwide [3]. With the

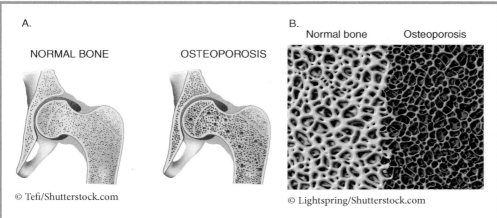

A.

NORMAL BONE   OSTEOPOROSIS

© Tefi/Shutterstock.com

B.

Normal bone   Osteoporosis

© Lightspring/Shutterstock.com

FIGURE 8.9: Normal (left) versus osteoporosis (right) in the hip (**A**) or as a close up (**B**) showing the thin, brittle bone areas which are prone to breakage. In osteoporosis, compared to osteomalcia, bone breakdown out paces bone formation due to low available calcium, and bones become brittle. This only occurs in adults where old bone is not replaced with new bone.

American Medical Association/NIH (adequacy at >50nmol/L [36]) and Endocrine Society (adequacy at < 75nmol/L [37]) differing on the sufficient serum range for 25-OH vitamin D₃ levels, more work is obviously needed to understand and correct this issue.

The Wintermeyer et al. paper (2016) [34] is an excellent view of "all things Vitamin D" in the skeletal (and muscular) systems.

Vitamin K, vitamin C, iron, copper, niacin associated conditions

Deficiency of most of other micronutrients that we've discussed can lead to skeletal- and bone-associated conditions, although most have effects on other more prominent systems. For example, a dietary deficiency of vitamin K will likely cause bleeding problems, due to vitamin K-mediated carboxylation of clotting proteins, before it shows in bone conditions. However, there are links to adequate dietary vitamin K intake (phylloquinone, usually from plant sources) and reduced fracture risk, and the opposite—reduced serum phylloquinone levels, and under-carboxylated osteocalcin, and reduced bone mineral density [38]. Likewise, one of the earliest studies on scurvy showed both bone and cartilage lesions in guinea pigs given a scorbutic diet (i.e., low vitamin C), for just one month [39]. Finally, as shown in Table 8.2, dietary deficiency of other trace minerals can directly affect bone health [25]. On the other hand, dietary toxicity of micronutrients oftentimes leads to formation of mineral precipitates in places where they shouldn't be—such as calcium deposits in arteries and kidneys, and fluorosis of the teeth and bones (Table 8.2) [31, 40, 41].

Genetic conditions affecting the skeleton

Regulation of calcium and phosphate levels in our bodies, and maintenance of the skeleton are complex processes, involving many more genes and associated proteins than we have the time (and space) to discuss. However, it is important to highlight some of the genetic conditions that affect the skeleton by way of disrupting micronutrient metabolism. Some of these conditions are shown in Table 8.3.

SNPing into
bone density

Many single nucleotide polymorphisms (SNPs), or the now more accepted phrase single nucleotide variants (SNVs), occur throughout our genomes. While some cause disease, others may predispose us to having a higher or lower need for a certain micronutrient—in this case the variant may result in a slightly less or more active enzyme than "normal."

The first group of disorders that we will discuss is those involving vitamin D metabolism and action. There are actually quite a few disorders in this category, but we are going to focus on two—hereditary vitamin D-dependent rickets, type I and type II. You will also see these two conditions abbreviated VDDR1 and VDDR2. In both of these conditions, regardless of dietary intake of vitamin D and sun exposure, the patient displays vitamin D deficiency, despite having high circulating 25-OH vitamin D_3. In type I, this is due to an inactivating mutation in the 1-alpha hydroxylase enzyme, resulting in the inability to convert 25-OH vitamin D_3 to fully active $1,25\text{-}(OH)_2$ vitamin D_3 or calcitriol [42, 43]. There are multiple places in the enzyme where inactivating mutations have been found [42, 43]. In type II, calcitriol is produced, but due to an inactivating mutation in the vitamin D receptor, calcitriol signaling is blunted [43, 44]. In each condition, serum calcium and phosphorus levels are low, and rickets (which is resistant to vitamin D treatment, as the name of the syndromes suggest) ensues. For both, supplementation with calcitriol, but not calcidiol, can alleviate symptoms [43].

TABLE 8.3: Genetic conditions associated with the skeletal system

Genetic Condition	Micronutrient affected	Affected gene/protein	Phenotype
pseudovitamin D deficiency rickets (Type I) VDDR1	Vitamin D	vitamin D 1α-hydroxylase	Rickets
hereditary vitamin D-resistant rickets (Type II) VDDR2	Vitamin D	VDR	Rickets
Dent's Diease	Phosphorus/Chloride	CLCN5 (chloride channel CIC5) X-linked	Calcium Kidney Stones Excess calcium in urine Hypercalciumuria Hyperphosphatemia
X-linked Hypophosphatemic rickets	Phosphorus	PHEX (zinc-dependent endopeptidase)	Hypophostatemia Osteomalacia/Rickets
		CaSR	
VKCFD type I (Vitamin K clotting factor deficiency)	Vitamin K	Gamma-glytamyl carboxylase	Skeletal deformities
VKCFD type II (Vitamin K clotting factor deficiency)	Vitamin K	Epoxide reductase	Skeletal deformities
Keutal Syndrome	Vitamin K/calcium	MGP	Diffuse cartilage calcification

The next group of genetic conditions to discuss are those causing hypo-phosphatemic rickets, or rickets symptoms affecting phosphate levels, but with (usually) normal to high calcium levels. Both of these genetic conditions are X-linked, which means that males are more frequently victims to the conditions, needing only to inherit one mutant allele to show symptoms. With X-linked diseases, females are carriers of the genetic condition who only sometimes show minimal symptoms. Dent's disease results from a nucletotide variation that affects a chloride transporter, ClC5 (gene name CLCN5). Chloride you say!! I thought we were talking about calcium and phosphorus!!! Well, only recently people have started to figure out why changes in a chloride transporter would result in hypercalcemia and the other phenotypes associated with Dent's. It turns out that this chloride channel is responsible for acidifying lysosomes that should gather and degrade low molecular weight proteins in urine—when there is a mutation this doesn't happen, and there is renal damage, which could lead to urine hypercalcenemia [45, 46]. However, these results are based on the analysis of two mutant proteins, and there are over 150 known mutants in CLCN5 that can cause Dent's—leading one to speculate that other mechanisms could also account for the calcium disregulation that is seen. In the other X-linked condition, X-linked hypophosphatemic rickets, the phenotype is rickets, but with only reduced phosphate levels and normal calcium levels. In addition, both males and females show this condition as some of the variations are inherited in a dominant X-linked fashion. The causative mutations have been found in a gene called "PHEX," which is a phosphate-regulating endopeptidase, or an enzyme that cleaves proteins [47]. However, researchers don't quite understand how phosphates are regulated by this protein-only that they are. One theory, which is supported by research findings using a mouse model of X-linked hypophospha-temic rickets [47], is that proteins rich in an amino acid motif (acidic serine- and aspartic-rich motif "ASARM") are "mineralization-inhibiting," leading to low bone mineralization when they accumulate. Since active PHEX is needed for protein degradation, some of the mineralization-inhibiting ASARM protein accumulate when PHEX is defective. One of these ASARM proteins, osteopontin has been shown to accumulate in the mineral-poor bone found in a mouse model of this condition [47].

Food for thought

Why do you think there are no calcium receptor (TRPV6) inactivating mutations shown in Table 8.3?

Finally we move to the third class of genetic conditions listed on Table 8.3—those involving vitamin K. Two related conditions, mainly known for their effects on clotting, especially in newborns, are the vitamin K clotting factor deficiency I and II (VKCFD type I and VKCFD type II), which result from inactivating mutations in gamma glutamyl carboxylase, or epoxide reductase enzymes respectively. For both, type I, the enzyme that directly carboxylates MGP and osteocalcin is affected, while for type II there is low levels of vitamin K recycling overall—and in both cases, vitamin K supplementation is the treatment. While the blood clotting consequences are the most life threatening at birth, the skeletal deformities that are present at birth, such as flat nose, mild hypoplasia of bone in the face, short neck, and

What about mutations in calcitonin, PTH, or the receptors for these hormones—check out Genetics Home Reference (https://ghr.nlm.nih.gov/) to find out if variations in any of these cause bone disease

underdeveloped ears can persist despite treatment [48]. Similarly, patients with Keutal syndrome, which is due to mutations in the MGP gene, display abnormal calcification of soft tissues, and hypophasia of the face. In this case, vitamin K treatment is usually not helpful, as it is the target protein, and not the vitamin K-dependent enzyme that is affected [49].

There are other genetic conditions that through altered micronutrient metabolism affect skeletal development or remodeling, but the ones listed in Table 8.3 are the major ones. By going through the pathways again and familiarizing yourself with the proteins (and their genes), you can probably guess at where mutations might be deleterious or even lethal to the organism.

CHAPTER SUMMARY

We often think of calcium and vitamin D as the key micronutrients for bone and skeletal health, but hopefully after reading this chapter, you will see that there are many other important and needed micronutrients for bones.

- While it may seem that the skeletal system was "built for structural support," it also serves as a reservoir of calcium (and phosphorus), one of its most important functions.
- Vitamin D regulates many of the genes needed to make the proteins responsible for calcium and phosphorus uptake and sensing.
- Disruption to calcium or phosphorus uptake, or vitamin D metabolism most frequently results in loss of calcium from the skeleton and resulting skeletal osteoporosis or osteomalacia.

POINTS TO PONDER ▢▢▢▢▢▢▢1111▢▢▢1▢1▢

- What can you find out about the proportion of vitamin D that is made in our skin versus that which we need to get from our diet? Would there be any situation where we could get it all from one or the other source?
- Does vitamin K toxicity affect calcium levels?
- What other genetic conditions affect calcium, vitamin D, vitamin K, or phosphorus regulation and have skeletal consequences?

References

1. Haddad, J.G., et al., *Human plasma transport of vitamin D after its endogenous synthesis.* The Journal of clinical investigation, 1993. **91**: p. 2552–5.

2. Chen, T.C., Z. Lu, and M.F. Holick, *Photobiology of Vitamin D*, in *Vitamin D*. 2010, Humana Press: Totowa, NJ. p. 35-60.

3. Christakos, S., et al., *Vitamin D: Metabolism, Molecular Mechanism of Action, and Pleiotropic Effects.* Physiological reviews, 2016. **96**: p. 365–408.

4. Nykjaer, A., et al., *Cubilin dysfunction causes abnormal metabolism of the steroid hormone 25(OH) vitamin D3.* Proceedings of the National Academy of Sciences, 2001. **98**: p. 13895–13900.

5. Prosser, D.E. and G. Jones, *Enzymes involved in the activation and inactivation of vitamin D.* Trends in Biochemical Sciences, 2004. **29**: p. 664–673.

6. *Calcium blood test: MedlinePlus Medical Encyclopedia.*

7. *Serum Calcium: Reference Range, Interpretation, Collection and Panels.*

8. Barley, N.F., et al., *Epithelial calcium transporter expression in human duodenum.* American journal of physiology. Gastrointestinal and liver physiology, 2001. **280**: p. G285–90.

9. Van Cromphaut, S.J., et al., *Duodenal calcium absorption in vitamin D receptor-knockout mice: functional and molecular aspects.* Proceedings of the National Academy of Sciences of the United States of America, 2001. **98**: p. 13324–9.

10. Meyer, M.B., et al., *The human transient receptor potential vanilloid type 6 distal promoter contains multiple vitamin D receptor binding sites that mediate activation by 1,25-dihydroxyvitamin D3 in intestinal cells.* Molecular endocrinology (Baltimore, Md.), 2006. **20**: p. 1447–61.

11. Werner, A. and R.K. Kinne, *Evolution of the Na-P(i) cotransport systems.* American journal of physiology. Regulatory, integrative and comparative physiology, 2001. **280**: p. R301–12.

12. Lee, D.B., M.W. Walling, and D.B. Corry, *Phosphate transport across rat jejunum: influence of sodium, pH, and 1,25-dihydroxyvitamin D3.* The American journal of physiology, 1986. **251**: p. G90–5.

13. Marks, J., et al., *Intestinal phosphate absorption and the effect of vitamin D: a comparison of rats with mice.* Experimental physiology, 2006. **91**: p. 531–7.

14. Brown, A.J., F. Zhang, and C.S. Ritter, *The vitamin D analog ED-71 is a potent regulator of intestinal phosphate absorption and NaPi-IIb.* Endocrinology, 2012. **153**: p. 5150–6.

15. Kumar, R. and J.R. Thompson, *The regulation of parathyroid hormone secretion and synthesis.* Journal of the American Society of Nephrology : JASN, 2011. **22**: p. 216–24.

16. Suzuki, K., et al., *Thyroid transcription factor 1 is calcium modulated and coordinately regulates genes involved in calcium homeostasis in C cells.* Molecular and cellular biology, 1998. **18**: p. 7410–22.

17. Zaidi, M., et al., *Forty years of calcitonin—where are we now? A tribute to the work of Iain Macintyre, FRS.* Bone, 2002. **30**: p. 655–663.

18. Rasmussen, H., et al., *Hormonal control of the renal conversion of 25-hydroxy-cholecalciferol to 1,25-dihydroxycholecalciferol.* Journal of Clinical Investigation, 1972. **51**: p. 2502–2504.

19. Zierold, C., J.A. Mings, and H.F. DeLuca, *Parathyroid hormone regulates 25-hydroxyvitamin D3-24-hydroxylase mRNA by altering its stability.* Proceedings of the National Academy of Sciences, 2001. **98**: p. 13572–13576.

20. Felsenfeld, A.J. and B.S. Levine, *Calcitonin, the forgotten hormone: does it deserve to be forgotten?* Clinical Kidney Journal, 2015. **8**: p. 180–187.

21. Silva, B.C. and J.P. Bilezikian, *Parathyroid hormone: anabolic and catabolic actions on the skeleton.* Curr Opin Pharmacol, 2015. **22**: p. 41–50.

22. Goltzman, D. and G.N. Hendy, *The calcium-sensing receptor in bone—mechanistic and therapeutic insights.* Nature Reviews Endocrinology, 2015. **11**: p. 298–307.

23. Chang, W., et al., *The extracellular calcium-sensing receptor (CaSR) is a critical modulator of skeletal development.* Science signaling, 2008. **1**: p. ra1.

24. Toka, H.R., et al., *Calcium Sensing in the Renal Tubule.* Physiology (Bethesda, Md.), 2015. **30**: p. 317–26.

25. Medeiros, D.M., *Copper, iron, and selenium dietary deficiencies negatively impact skeletal integrity: A review.* Experimental Biology and Medicine, 2016. **241**: p. 1316–1322.

26. Atkins, G.J., et al., *Vitamin K promotes mineralization, osteoblast-to-osteocyte transition, and an anticatabolic phenotype by {gamma}-carboxylation-dependent and -independent mechanisms.* American journal of physiology. Cell physiology, 2009. **297**: p. C1358–67.

27. Ichikawa, T., et al., *Steroid and Xenobiotic Receptor SXR Mediates Vitamin K2-activated Transcription of Extracellular Matrix-related Genes and Collagen Accumulation in Osteoblastic Cells.* Journal of Biological Chemistry, 2006. **281**: p. 16927–16934.

28. Miller, A.J. and J.A. Brunelle, *A summary of the NIDR community caries prevention demonstration program.* Journal of the American Dental Association, 1983. **107**: p. 265–9.

29. Everett, E.T., *Fluoride's Effects on the Formation of Teeth and Bones, and the Influence of Genetics.* Journal of Dental Research, 2011. **90**: p. 552–560.

30. Mousny, M., et al., *The genetic influence on bone susceptibility to fluoride.* Bone, 2006. **39**: p. 1283–1289.

31. Izuora, K., et al., *Skeletal fluorosis from brewed tea.* The Journal of clinical endocrinology and metabolism, 2011. **96**: p. 2318–24.

32. *NHMRC Public Statement: Efficacy and Safety of Fluoridation | National Health and Medical Research Council.*

33. *Dietary Reference Intakes for Calcium and Vitamin D.* 2011, Institute of Medicine, National Academies Press: Washington, DC.

34. Wintermeyer, E., et al., *Crucial Role of Vitamin D in the Musculoskeletal System.* Nutrients, 2016. **8**: p. 319.

35. Goldacre, M., N. Hall, and D.G.R. Yeates, *Hospitalisation for children with rickets in England: a historical perspective.* Lancet (London, England), 2014. **383**: p. 597–8.

36. *Vitamin D — Health Professional Fact Sheet.*

37. Holick, M.F., et al., *Evaluation, Treatment, and Prevention of Vitamin D Deficiency: an Endocrine Society Clinical Practice Guideline.* The Journal of Clinical Endocrinology & Metabolism, 2011. **96**: p. 1911–1930.

38. Sahni, S., et al., *Dietary Approaches for Bone Health: Lessons from the Framingham Osteoporosis Study.* Current Osteoporosis Reports, 2015. **13**: p. 245–255.

39. Ham, A.W. and H.C. Elliott, *The bone and cartilage lesions of protracted moderate scurvy.* The American journal of pathology, 1938. **14**: p. 323–336.5.

40. Calvo, M.S. and J. Uribarri, *Public health impact of dietary phosphorus excess on bone and cardiovascular health in the general population.* The American journal of clinical nutrition, 2013. **98**: p. 6–15.

41. Ronco, C. and M. Cozzolino, *Mineral metabolism abnormalities and vitamin D receptor activation in cardiorenal syndromes.* Heart failure reviews, 2012. **17**: p. 211–20.

42. Kato, S., *Genetic mutation in the human 25-hydroxyvitamin D3 1α-hydroxylase gene causes vitamin D-dependent rickets type I.* Molecular and Cellular Endocrinology, 1999. **156**: p. 7–12.

43. Kato, S., et al., *Molecular genetics of vitamin D- dependent hereditary rickets.* Hormone research, 2002. **57**: p. 73–8.

44. Malloy, P.J., et al., *Hereditary vitamin D resistant rickets caused by a novel mutation in the vitamin D receptor that results in decreased affinity for hormone and cellular hyporesponsiveness.* The Journal of clinical investigation, 1997. **99**: p. 297–304.

45. Alekov, A.K., *Mutations associated with Dent's disease affect gating and voltage dependence of the human anion/proton exchanger ClC-5.* Frontiers in Physiology, 2015. **6**.

46. Satoh, N., et al., *A pure chloride channel mutant of CLC-5 causes Dent's disease via insufficient V-ATPase activation.* Pflügers Archiv - European Journal of Physiology, 2016. **468**: p. 1183–1196.

47. Barros, N.M.T., et al., *Proteolytic processing of osteopontin by PHEX and accumulation of osteopontin fragments in Hyp mouse bone, the murine model of X-linked hypophosphatemia.* Journal of bone and mineral research : the official journal of the American Society for Bone and Mineral Research, 2013. **28**: p. 688–99.

48. Watzka, M., et al., *Bleeding and non-bleeding phenotypes in patients with GGCX gene mutations.* Thrombosis Research, 2014. **134**: p. 856–865.

49. Munroe, P.B., et al., *Mutations in the gene encoding the human matrix Gla protein cause Keutel syndrome.* Nature genetics, 1999. **21**: p. 142–4.

Cryptogram Puzzle

Calcium and Phosphorus Regulation

A W K A E P Z D E D   R O A T O P E Z D   Z A A F T R   G N O D

P N O T O   E R   N E L N   J K Z Z Y   A W K A E F M ,

G N E K O   X W T W P N U T Z E Y   R O A T O P E Z D   Z A A F T R

G N O D   A W K A E F M   K O V O K R   W T O   P Z Z   K Z G

Instructions: Solve the phrase that deals with calcium and phosphorus regulation by breaking the code. Each letter of the alphabet stands in for a different letter.

Hint: Z = O

NOTES

CHAPTER 9

Fluid-Electrolyte Balance, and the Excretory System

Table of Contents

GENERAL PRINCIPLES

Early in our K-12 training, we all learn about osmosis and diffusion, but do we ever really consider these processes in terms of micronutrients and how they are involved? Probably not until now! So, let's talk about fluid balance, specifically relating how micronutrients are involved in regulating water levels in our cells, tissues, and blood.

First we need to discuss the general principles, and get some terminology out of the way (Table 1). Diffusion refers to the process by which molecules (i.e., glucose) or ions (i.e., Na^+) move along a concentration gradient if there is nothing impeding their movement (note that this is not true in cells or for cell membranes, as we'll see later). The process always goes from high concentration to low concentration, and does not involve any energy—just movement of the molecules or ions from where they are most concentrated to where they are least concentrated until equilibrium is achieved. Osmosis on the other hand refers only to the movement of water. In general, water flows in the same direction as the ions or molecules (and this will become an important concept later in this chapter, when we talk about things that can affect water balance), going from where there is more water, to where there is less water, eventually coming to an equilibrium. Remember that both osmosis and diffusion happen if there are no other outside forces pushing

TERM	MOLECULES MOVING	CONDITION	ASSOCIATED WITH
Diffusion	Molecules or ions	From high concentration to low concentration	Along a concentration gradient
Osmosis	Water	From high concentration to low concentration	Along a concentration gradient, following molecules or ions
Tonicity	Non-permeable solutes	Stays on one side of the membrane	May cause water balance issues
Active Transport	Molecules or ions	From low concentration to high concentration	Occurs against a concentration gradient/requires energy

in the opposite direction-including pressure, nonpermeable membranes, or active transport processes, which not only usually pump against a gradient but also require energy (ATP) to do so. So, for diffusion and osmosis, water and molecules or ions move from a hyperosmotic environment (high ions and high water), to a hypo-osmotic environment (low ions, low water), eventually balancing everything out (iso-osmotic environment).

There is one other set of terms that we should deal with upfront—tonicity. Tonicity refers to concentrations of solutes (molecules and ions) that cannot readily pass through a membrane with hypertonic solutions having high nonpermeable solutes, and hypotonic solutions having low nonpermeable solutes—all measured relative to where they are going (i.e., plasma or cells). A good example is physiological saline, which is isotonic at 0.9% weight NaCl/volume water or 309 mOsm/L (milliosmol/liter). As sodium generally cannot diffuse through a cell membrane, we'll use this example in the next section when talking about cellular fluid balance and active transport.

In our bodies, the main ions that are at play in the blood serum/plasma and cellular compartments are sodium, chloride, potassium, calcium, and magnesium. In this chapter, we are going to focus on these minerals, as well as some molecules that are also in the slurry of body fluids, including proteins, fats, and carbs. As you will see, sodium (Na^+) is a major player in this

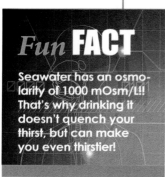

Fun **FACT**

Seawater has an osmolarity of 1000 mOsm/L!! That's why drinking it doesn't quench your thirst, but can make you even thirstier!

process, and although the cell uses sodium in signaling (especially in the nervous system), this mineral is the main one responsible for maintaining whole body fluid balance.

CELLULAR FLUID BALANCE

Before we talk about the excretory system, we must discuss cellular fluid balance, because it is at the cellular level that water and salt are regulated, and ultimately go into either the plasma or the urine. Many of you have already seen similar figures as that in Figure 9.1 showing what happens to cells in solutions with different osmolarities. Here the term "tonicity" also comes into play—as solutions that contain substances that cannot readily diffuse increase the tonicity of a solution. Examples

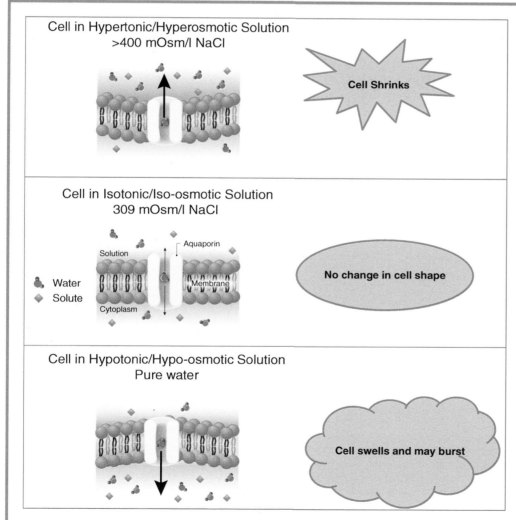

Cell in Hypertonic/Hyperosmotic Solution
>400 mOsm/l NaCl

Cell Shrinks

Cell in Isotonic/Iso-osmotic Solution
309 mOsm/l NaCl

Solution
Aquaporin
Water
Solute
Membrane
Cytoplasm

No change in cell shape

Cell in Hypotonic/Hypo-osmotic Solution
Pure water

Cell swells and may burst

FIGURE 9.1: Changes in cell shape as a result of their environment. Hypertonic/hyperosmolar solutions result in cell shrinkage as water rushes out. Hypo-tonic and hypo-osmolar solutions will cause cells to swell as water rushes in. The mechanisms in this chapter are meant to maintain cells in isotonic/iso-osmotic conditions.

© Designua/Shutterstock.com

of these include hormones, glucose, and other proteins. In effect, cells within a solution of high tonicity (hypertonic) will shrink as water rushes out, through aquaporin water channels. Conversely, in a solution of low tonicity (such as pure water—the lowest possible osmolarity and tonicity), water will enter the cell, causing cell swelling.

So why would a red blood cell, or any cell have this mechanism that would potentially cause it to burst or shrivel at the mercy of the external environment? This was a question for many years, and lead to the original discovery of aquaporin channels, and specifically aquaporin 1 in 1985 [2]. Aquaporins are found in many different cell types, but is very concentrated in red blood cells, endothelial lining cells, lung, and in the kidney. In red blood cells, the prevailing thought is that the high aquaporin density at the membrane aids in the ability of the red blood cell to respond to the environment and allows for fluctuation of water balance based on the cell's environment. The quick balance of water flowing into and out of the cell is thought to facilitate membrane oscillation and ease of transport through capillaries [2]. As we will see in other cell types, aquaporin density at the cell membrane is regulated by both membrane translocation, and by gene transcription.

In addition to aquaporins, cell membranes have channels and transporter molecules that can actively transport ions and other molecules (Figure 9.2). Each of these transporters requires energy, usually in the form of ATP, or sometimes GTP. While we will talk more about gated ion channels in our nervous system chapter, these proteins are a form of active ion transport for cells. Gated ion channels only let ions in (such as sodium or calcium) when bound by a chemical messenger, such as a neurotransmitter. As the neurotransmitter binds, the "gate" opens, allowing for the flow of ions into the cell. These channels often use GTP as an energy source

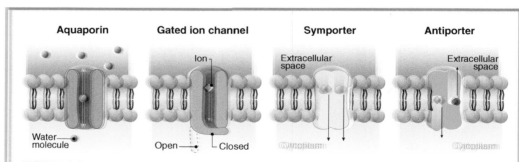

FIGURE 9.2: Types of transporters Aquaporins are water channels, which translocate to the membrane to let water flow in more rapidly than by simple diffusion alone. Gated ion channels only let ions in when they are bound by a chemical messenger, such as a neurotransmitter. These will be more thoroughly discussed in a later chapter. Symporters transport two ions in the same direction. An example is the Na/I transporter discussed in Chapter 7. Antiporters, such as the sodium-potassium pump, transport two ions in opposite directions.

© Designua/Shutterstock.com

with (e.g., [3]) to open that gate. ATP is the energy source for most of the cell transporters, which can be grouped into uniporters (transporting a single molecule), symporters (transporting two molecules in the same direction) and antiporters (transporting two molecules in opposite directions). We have already seen an example of uniporters at work with sodium uptake by the epithelial sodium transporter, ENaC. This so-called "non-voltage gated ion channel" is also important in the overall water balance in the body, and is expressed in places such as the kidney and the lungs, as well as the intestine, where it works to regulate cellular sodium ion flow [4]. Another uniporter that is of particular interest medically is the Cystic Fibrosis Transmembrane Receptor or CFTR. This transporter, which is expressed in kidney, intestine, and most importantly lung, transports chloride out of the cells, with water following through the channel passively. When the channel is not working (such as in the disease, cystic fibrosis), water and ions do not flow out of the epithelial cells, causing a thickened mucus [5]. Both sodium and iodide are transported into thyroid colloid by the Na^+/I^- symporter (NIS) discussed in Chapter 7. Again, this process requires ATP to drive sodium and iodide into the colloid of the thyroid [6]. Finally, we need to discuss antiporters, and there are many; in fact, some which we have already discussed, such as the reduced folate carrier (RFC). While both RFC and the Proton-coupled folate transporter (PCFT) transport B9 vitamers, and both use ion coupled transport as the mechanism. RFC is an antiporter, where phosphate is pumped out while folate is carried in, whereas PCFT is a symporter, pumping protons and folic acid into cells [7].

Did you KNOW...?

The sodium multivitamin transporter (SMVT) is a member of the same family of transporters as NIS.

However, probably the most well-known antiporter is the Na^+/K^+ ATPase pump, which pumps out three sodium ions, brings in three potassium ions, and hydrolyzes ATP in the process (Figure 9.3). This process not only allows cells, such as cardiac and nerve cells to maintain an electrochemical balance, but is also crucial in maintaining fluid balance in the surrounding interstitial fluid [8]. Potassium is the main intracellular cation, and without the action of the Na^+/K^+ pump, cells would not be able to maintain high levels of potassium inside them [9]. According to one source [9], only 2% of the total body potassium is found in any extracellular fluid including the plasma, and interstitial fluids of the body. Because of the inverse relationship between potassium and sodium in body fluids, the FDA allows diet claims stating that high potassium intake may lower risk for cardiovascular disease and more specifically hypertension. In fact, many (but not all) studies have shown that potassium supplements alone can lower systemic blood pressure in patients, due to the overall effect on sodium and water balance in the body [9].

What is the difference between osmolality and osmolarity?

The first measures osmoles of solute per kilogram of solvent, while the second (and the one we will use) measures osmoles per liter of solution.

Thus, cellular water balance, through simple diffusion, aquaporins, and various transporters that regulate ion balance is the basis for overall water and fluid balance in the body. As we will see in the next sections of this chapter,

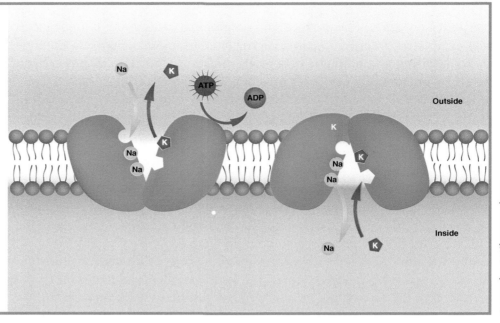

© extender_01/Shutterstock.com

FIGURE 9.3: The sodium-potassium pump. Sodium ions are brought into the cell, and potassium ions moved out. ATP is required for this active transport process.

whole body sensing of osmolarity and water involve the brain, and excretory system, and even minor perturbations of the system can be deadly.

WHOLE BODY FLUID BALANCE

So what about whole body fluid balance? First, let's discuss where water comes from. Of course, a lot of it comes from drinking water (and here we are talking about pure water, water containing foods, and any non-caffeinated, non-sugared drink). We also get some from metabolic processes—such as the metabolism of carbs, proteins, and fats. Together this accounts for about 1–2 liters per day of water intake, referred to as our preformed water intake (Figure 9.4). Then we have water that is lost each day, in the form of sweat, respiration, and excretion of urine and feces. This accounts for about 1.4 liters per day. So, given these numbers, you can see that while metabolic processes, respiration, sweat, and excretion will stay approximately constant, whether you are dehydrated or in normal hydration will depend on how much water you drink each day (balanced with any extra activity or exertion performed). So, how does your body know if you are dehydrated or not? It does so through specialized osmoreceptors in the brain, which can detect increases in osmolarity of the plasma above 300 mOsm/L, blood volume sensors in the blood vessels, which can detect decreased

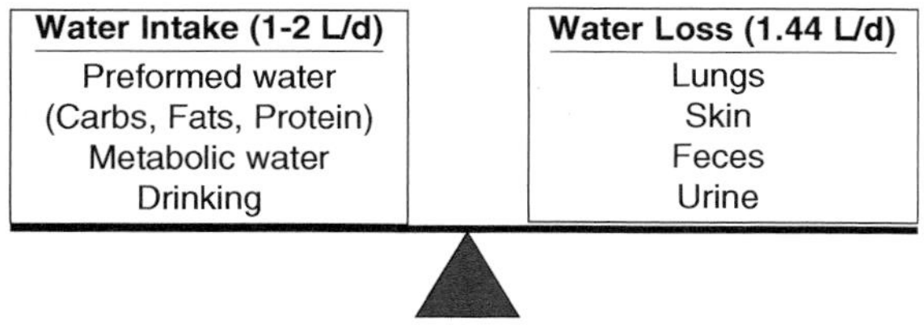

Water Intake (1-2 L/d)	Water Loss (1.44 L/d)
Preformed water (Carbs, Fats, Protein)	Lungs
Metabolic water	Skin
Drinking	Feces
	Urine

FIGURE 9.4: Water balance under normal conditionsv

blood pressure, and water ingestion sensors (i.e., oropharyngeal receptors) in the throat that can detect if you've had any water to drink lately [10]. With that background in mind, let's move on to talk about how these systems are activated when increased osmolarity, or decreased blood volume/pressure is detected.

Renin-angiotensin system

The rate-limiting and regulated step in the Renin-Angiotensin system is the secretion of renin from the kidney. Renin is a proteolytic enzyme that cleaves angiotensinogen to produce angiotensin, and starting the cascade of events that lead to sodium retention by the kidney (Figure 9.5) [11]. Baroreceptors, which are found in the juxtaglomerular cells of the arterioles in the kidney, actually sense changes in blood pressure as the blood passes through these regions. Increased arterial pressure blocks renin release, while decreased arterial pressure, and decreased "stretching" of the arteriole, stimulates renin release through a calcium and cAMP-mediated cellular signaling pathway [11]. When renin is secreted, it attacks circulating angiotensinogen to produce angiotensin (Figure 9.5). Angiotensin requires further cleavage by angiotensin converting enzyme (ACE), to become angiotensin II. It is angiotensin II that has two main actions as it relates to sodium regulation: (1) It stimulates the adrenal glands to produce aldosterone. Aldosterone regulates sodium reabsorption by increasing the activity and synthesis of the epithelial sodium channel (ENaC) in the distal tubules of the kidney, effectively increasing sodium uptake (retention) by the kidney and (2) Angiotensin II directly can increase EnAC translocation to cell membranes in the proximal tubes, increasing sodium retention from urine [12]. So far you should see and appreciate that there are back up systems to make sure that sodium levels are maintained—even if the adrenal/aldosterone system is defective, angiotensin II can still directly stimulate ENaC uptake of sodium. Likewise, as we'll

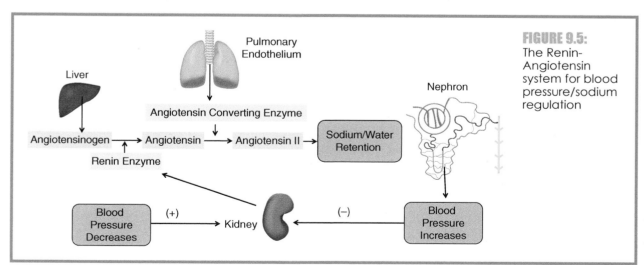

© joshya/Shutterstock.com

FIGURE 9.5: The Renin-Angiotensin system for blood pressure/sodium regulation

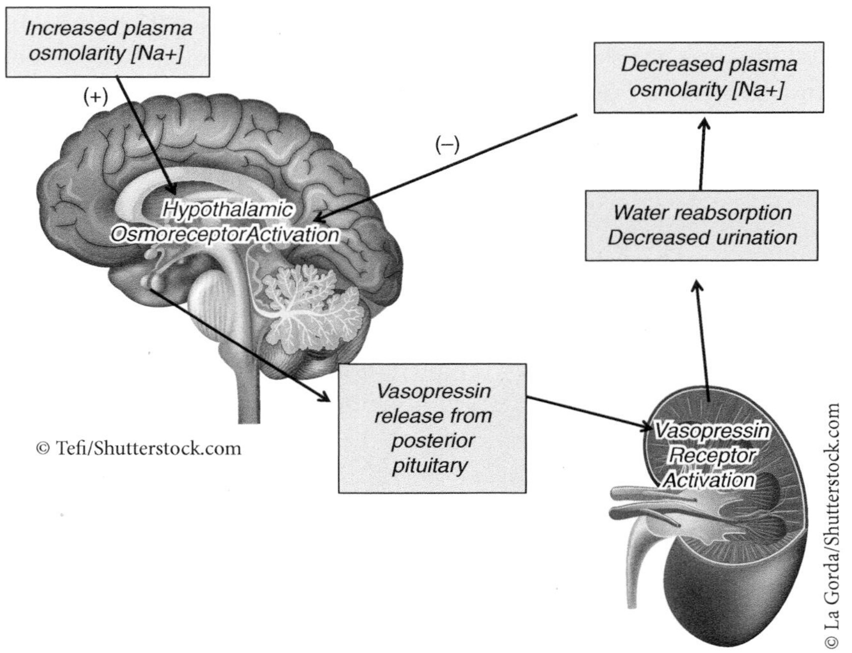

FIGURE 9.6: The hypothalamic-pituitary-kidney water balance regulatory system. Vasopressin release is modulated through osmo-receptors found on hypothalamic neurons. Vasopressin binds to its receptors in kidney (principal cells), and causes water reabsorption (the so-called "anti-diuretic hormone" and decreased urination.

Increased plasma osmolarity [Na+]

(+)

Decreased plasma osmolarity [Na+]

(−)

Hypothalamic OsmoreceptorActivation

Water reabsorption Decreased urination

© Tefi/Shutterstock.com

Vasopressin release from posterior pituitary

Vasopressin Receptor Activation

© La Gorda/Shutterstock.com

Fun FACT

While humans, rats, mice, and many mammals maintain fluid osmolarities around 300 mOsm/L, an organism that lives in a dry condition, such as the desert frog, has a plasma osmolarity of around 650 mOsm/L, and a shark (living in salt water) maintains an osmolarity of ~1100 mOsm/L. On the other end of the spectrum, animals living in fresh water maintain lower osmolarity, such as tadpoles (~200 mOsm/L) or clams (~50 mOsm/L) [1].

see in the next section, water will be stimulated to flow in the direction of sodium (i.e., retained) with stimulation of aquaporins by anti-diuretic hormone/vasopressin—another backup system to make sure that plasma osmolarity/water balance in the body is maintained.

Hypothalamic-pituitary-kidney vasopressin system

As we've seen in the previous sections, small perturbations in plasma osmolarity activate a kidney-mediated system that modulates sodium excretion or retention. However, central control of water balance occurs through hypothalamic osmoreceptors. Neurons, which are located near the third ventricle of the brain—an area which lies above the pituitary and is formed by the walls of the hypothalamus—sense the osmolarity of the cerebral spinal fluid by "feeling" the water conditions. How is this done? Well, transient receptor potential vanilloid (TRPV) family of cation channels appear to serve as potential "mechanic-stretch" receptors. Please note that this is the same family as the calcium channel (TRPV6) we talked about in Chapter 8. However, in the case of osmoregulation, it is TRPV1, TRPV2, and TRPV4 (neuronal) doing the job [13]. Basically, these channels, and TRPV4 in particular respond to neuronal swelling—when the outside environment is hypo-osmotic, and water flows into the cells through aquaporins (aquaporin 1 in the brain), increasing cell size. Aquaporin 1 even appears to colocalize with TRPV2 at the neuron cell membrane [14]. With more water/less sodium sensed, an inhibitory signal is sent, stopping release of vasopressin (i.e., anti-diuretic hormone), and resulting in water release from the kidney (Figure 9.6) [13, 14]. This seems a bit counterintuitive—shouldn't decreased water *stimulate* vasopressin release, rather than increased water stopping release? One review suggests that this method, although seemingly opposite of what one would expect means that vasopressin release stays on until slight swelling of osmoreceptor-containing neurons is detected [13]. In fact, changes of just 1–2 mOsm/L can effectively shut off vasopressin secretion [1]. However, whole cell voltage recording studies were able to show that changes of +/− 30 mOsm/L in surrounding fluid could increase and decrease (respectively) osmoreceptor neuron firing, suggesting that there may be both hypo- and hyperosmolar sensing [1].

What about sodium levels—are they detected by hypothalamic neurons as well? It does appear so. In 2011, mice with genetic lesions in a gene called Nalcn were shown to have constitutively hypernatremic plasma—that is, maintaining higher sodium levels, than normal mice [15]. This gene encodes a protein called the sodium (Na) leak channel, nonselective (Nalcn). It appears that this protein channel, expressed in neurons allows sodium to leak in, and the changes in sodium levels are relayed as neuronal signals. However, at this time, the link between Nalcn function and vasopressin levels has not been made, so it is not clear if any direct sodium detection leads to changes in vasopressin secretion. For now, we leave that to the kidney-renin-angiotensin system, and water balance/osmolarity to the hypothalamic-pituitary-kidney system.

We have established that hyperosmotic conditions result in continuous secretion of vasopressin (let's call it ADH for short) from the posterior pituitary (Figure 9.6). Once ADH is in circulating, it targets the vasopressin receptor, which is found on the kidney principal cells, signals through a cAMP-regulatory pathway that leads to protein kinase activation, phosphorylation of aquaporin proteins (specifically aquaporin 2), causing them to translocate to the luminal membrane-side of the cell—the urine side—resulting in reabsorption of water from the urine or anti-diuresis (Figure 9.7) [16]. When ADH signals cease, as water volume increases and plasma osmolarity decreases, then the phosphorylation of aquaporin 2 also ceases, and the protein is no longer translocated to the luminal membrane. In addition to protein trafficking to and from the cell membrane, vasopressin signaling also increases aquaporin 2 mRNA and protein levels [17], effectively increasing the amount of aquaporin 2 available to be translocated to the luminal membrane (Figure 9.7). Thus, the net effect is increased water retention by the principal cells, which is eliminated by flow of the water out through other aquaporins locating on the blood plasma side of the cell. As the water levels in blood increase, this will shut off signaling within the osmoreceptors, leading to an inhibition of vasopressin release with hydration and water balance restored (Figure 9.6).

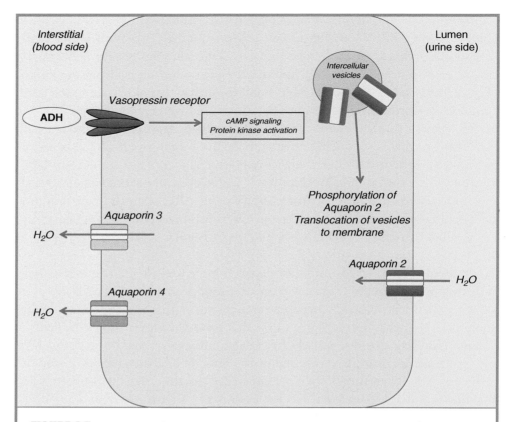

FIGURE 9.7: Cellular events of water balance regulation in the kidney. Vasopressin (ADH) binding to its receptor on the principal cell of the kidney causes aquaporin 2 to translocate to the apical membrane and take up water from the lumen. In addition, aquaporin-3 and -4 located on the basolateral side of the cell, release water into the blood/interstitial fluid. Aquaporin 4 is not regulated by vasopressin, while aquaporin 3 levels are regulated, but through mRNA levels only and not translocation.

Thus it might be easiest to think of the vasopressin system as that which modulates water levels, and the renin system as that which modules sodium levels. However, water follows the ions, and as you can see, these two systems are inextricably linked to one another—and perturbation of one will lead to the overall hydration problems, as we will see in the next section.

FLUID BALANCE DISRUPTION

Long-term disruption to water balance can result in systemic issues. For dehydration these include constipation, high blood pressure, and tissue damage-especially kidney, heart, arteries, and the nervous system, while for overhydration (water intoxication), these include diarrhea, muscle cramping, vomiting, dizziness, coma, and even death can occur. Let's look at some of the causes of both severe dehydration and sodium toxicity (hypernatremia), as well as over-hydration, water toxicity,

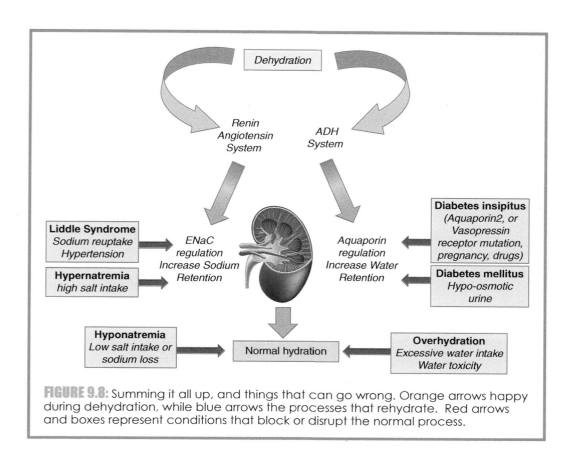

FIGURE 9.8: **FIGURE 9.8:** Summing it all up, and things that can go wrong. Orange arrows happy during dehydration, while blue arrows the processes that rehydrate. Red arrows and boxes represent conditions that block or disrupt the normal process.

and hyponatremia. Figure 9.8 provides an overview of water balance a look at places where it can be disrupted.

Diabetes

The term diabetes comes from the Greek word for "siphon"—most notably because large amounts of water (urine) are produced in patients with uncontrolled diabetes. There are two forms that need to be discussed in this section—Diabetes Insipidus and Diabetes Mellitus—both show water balance dysregulation, but for different reasons.

DIABETES MELLITUS

Most people are familiar with Diabetes Mellitus—usually referred to as type I and type II diabetes. According to CDC data compiled in 2015, from 2005 to 2014, the number of persons diagnosed with diabetes has increased from 5.5 million in 2005 to over 22 million in 2014 [18]. The intent of this section is not to talk about the causes of most cases of type I and type II diabetes mellitus (DM), or the treatment options, but rather, what happens in a diabetic person when their blood sugar goes uncontrolled (and for many people there is a period of time prior to diagnosis when this occurs . . .). In normal individuals, blood glucose is reabsorbed back into the kidney and blood, rather than excreted. However, in individuals with uncontrolled

DM, glucose in the blood is high, and oversaturates the recovery ability of the kidney—and therefore is not fully recovered from the urine. What happens then is due to the normal process of water flowing from a high water/low solute environment (hyper-osmotic) to a low water/high solute environment (hypo-osmotic). Water flows into the urine, diluting it.

The osmolarity of plasma and urine is calculated using the formula:

$$\text{Osmolarity in mOsm/L} = [\text{urea}] + [\text{glucose}] + 2([\text{Na}] + [\text{K}])$$

What you should see here is that glucose concentration in the compartment being measured, is additive to the total osmolarity of the fluid, in this case, urine. As glucose flows into the urine, water does too, as it will flow from the direction of "more" to "less." In the diabetic state, glucose does not get reabsorbed to capacity, meaning that the urine has more glucose than the plasma…and thus, more water as well. In the uncontrolled diabetic, urine is dilute, light in color, and full of glucose. If the person does not balance the water loss, a condition called "diabetic hyper-osmolar syndrome" ensues [19]. The patients with this condition show excessive thirst, even when excess fluids are consumed, lack of sweating, shortness of breath, high pulse rate, and may even show mental confusion. In addition, there may be alterations in other minerals, such as phosphorus, potassium, and calcium, along with either hypo- or hypernatremia, which can fluctuate due to water content of the serum, and the content of other proteins, and especially lipids [19]. This complex disorder results in systemic electrolyte and water balance irregularities, which are only "fixed" by regulating glucose levels in the diabetic patient. However, by that time, damage to kidneys (renal failure) or brain (cerebral edema, leading to at minimum, confusion) may be irreversible.

DIABETES INSIPIDUS

There are different forms of Diabetes Insipidus (DI)—X-linked, autosomal, pregnancy-associated, and acquired [20]. All result in very dilute urine (without the glucose—just water), and electrolyte balances, and most have high levels of serum vasopressin (i.e., a functioning hypothalamic-vasopressin response) (exceptions below). In the X-linked form, inactivating mutations in the vasopressin receptor result in little to no response to circulating vasopressin levels [21]. As female carriers usually have one normal vasopressin 2 receptor, and one mutated receptor, they may have polyuria to a lesser degree than males with only one X-chromosome carrying a mutant vasopressin 2-receptor allele. In the autosomal form, mutations in the aquaporin 2 gene can be either recessive (requiring the person to have two mutant copies to show a phenotype) or dominant (one mutant copy of the gene confers the condition) [21]. Mutant aquaporin proteins are not properly translocated to the urine-side of the principal cell, and thus, water is not reabsorbed from the urine. In both cases (X-linked and autosomal) patients show severe dehydration with dilute urine shortly after birth, and intervention with fluids and electrolytes must start immediately to prevent death [21]. In the acquired form of DI, the kidney is damaged by drugs [20]—most commonly chemotherapeutic or lithium for mental illness, resulting in reduced filtering capacity and polyuria, despite high vasopressin levels.

There are two forms in which vasopressin levels are low, and these the pregnancy-associated DI, and a pituitary form. In the pregnancy-associated form (also called gestational DI), there is excessive vasopressinase enzyme in the serum—and this results in degradation of circulating vasopressin in the mother's serum [22]. While all placenta trophoblast cells make the enzyme, it appears that females with liver disease (where the enzyme would normally be cleared) might be most susceptible to the condition [22]. The other form of DI with low or absent vasopressin levels occurs when there is a direct genetic mutation in the gene, which inactivates or reduces the activity of the vasopressin protein. This is also caused hypothalamic/autosomal DI [20].

Overall, both forms of diabetes—DM and DI result in dilute urine with electrolyte disturbances although due to different primary causes. While treatment and management of these conditions are beyond the scope of this section, they do involve monitoring of plasma and urine osmolarity as well as (if possible) direct treatment of the causes of the diabetes.

Hyponatremia

Hyponatremia is one of, if not *the* most common electrolyte condition that medical professionals encounter. For example, patients on sodium-limited diets (e.g., heart failure patients), have about a 20% frequency of hyponatremia when hospitalized, mostly due to low fluid intake accompanying the low sodium diets [23]. This results in water being retained by the kidney, in order to increase sodium levels in the plasma, leading to an overall edema (including cerebral edema). Another cause of hyponatremia occurs in extreme exercise when there appears to be increased secretion of vasopressin, accompanied by high fluid intake [23]. The overall effect is to lower plasma sodium levels, which in some marathon runners and solders has resulted in collapse and even death [23, 24]. Again, treatments are really outside of the scope of this section, and in some cases, it is still controversial as to what "best practices" should be used [23].

Hypernatremia

For many, low sodium levels are not the problem. In a recent review of sodium consumption levels for individuals, most were well above the suggested daily intake level of 1500 mg of sodium (3.8 grams of table salt) [25]. Are we all living in a state of hypernatremia? In addition to increased thirst, as the body systems for water try to modulate and excrete the excess sodium, high sodium concentrations can directly damage kidneys, and blood vessels due to high blood pressure [25]. Reducing sodium intake by even 1 gram per day can lower both systolic and diastolic blood pressure levels [25], suggesting that even modest reductions can be beneficial to the overall health. We should all likely consider this for ourselves—could you reduce your salt intake by 1–2 grams per day? What foods contain hidden sodium? Do you prefer salty foods?

This is a condition in which hypernatremia and hypertension occurs even with low sodium intake, due to a genetic variation in the ENaC receptor. The syndrome, called Liddle Syndrome, is caused by an *activating* (i.e., increased activity, or a "gain-of-function") mutation in ENaC, leading to ENaC-dependent reabsorption of sodium from the urine, despite all other regulatory systems trying to modulate electrolyte balance. High blood pressure and low overall renin levels are common symptoms of Liddle Syndrome.

CHAPTER SUMMARY

The excretory system is modulated by two major regulatory systems—the hypotalamic-pituitary-vasopressin, and the kidney-renin-angiotensin. Both of these further direct the kidney principal cells to either increase or decrease excretion of water and electrolytes (mainly sodium) through molecular signaling pathways that direct sodium channels and/or water channels to the apical (blood) and basal-lateral (urine) sides of the cell. Plasma osmolarity is fine-tuned by these systems, so perturbations that affect the regulatory pathways have profound effects on whole body water balance.

- Plasma and tissue fluid osmolarity is maintained within very tight concentrations by several body systems.
- Cellular fluid balance is also tightly regulated by sodium/potassium pumps, and aquaporin proteins.
- The renin-angiotensin system modulates water balance in response to changes in blood pressure, as measured by baroreceptors in the kidney
- The vasopressin system modules water balance in response to sodium and water concentrations, as measured by osmoreceptor neurons in the brain.
- Genetic and acquired conditions can perturb water and electrolyte balance in our bodies.

POINTS TO PONDER ☒☒☒☒☒☒☒1111☒☒☒☒☒☒☒

- Ouabain is a drug that is (or has been) used in cardiac patients. It competitively inhibits the Na/K-ATPase by binding in the K-binding site. How do you think taking it would affect plasma osmolarity?
- There are actually several other sodium channels/receptors/exchangers. Look up one or more of these and think about the role they might play in plasma or tissue osmolarity.
- Exercise and caffeine can both modulate hydration levels albeit by separate methods. What other environmental, food-based, or genetic conditions might also affect whole-body hydration?

References

1. Bourque, C.W. (2008). Central mechanisms of osmosensation and systemic osmoregulation. *Nat Rev Neurosci*, **9**(7): 519–531.
2. Benga, G. (2012). The first discovered water channel protein, later called aquaporin 1: molecular characteristics, functions and medical implications. *Mol Aspects Med*, **33**(5-6): 518–534.
3. Proft, J. and N. Weiss (2015). G protein regulation of neuronal calcium channels: back to the future. *Mol Pharmacol*, **87**(6): 890–906.
4. Hanukoglu, I. and A. Hanukoglu. (2016). Epithelial sodium channel (ENaC) family: Phylogeny, structure-function, tissue distribution, and associated inherited diseases. *Gene*, **579**(2): 95–132.
5. Schmidt, B.Z., et al. (2016). Cystic fibrosis transmembrane conductance regulator modulators in cystic fibrosis: current perspectives. *Clin Pharmacol*, **8**: 127–140.
6. Dohan, O., et al. (2003). The sodium/iodide Symporter (NIS): characterization, regulation, and medical significance. *Endocr Rev*, **24**(1): 48–77.
7. Zhao, R., S. Aluri, and I.D. Goldman. (2016). The proton-coupled folate transporter (PCFT-SLC46A1) and the syndrome of systemic and cerebral folate deficiency of infancy: Hereditary folate malabsorption. *Mol Aspects Med*.
8. Aperia, A., et al. (2016). Na+-K+-ATPase, a new class of plasma membrane receptors. *Am J Physiol Cell Physiol*, **310**(7): C491–C495.
9. Stone, M.S., L. Martyn, and C.M. Weaver (2016). Potassium Intake, Bioavailability, Hypertension, and Glucose Control. *Nutrients*, **8**(7).
10. Thornton, S.N. (2010). Thirst and hydration: physiology and consequences of dysfunction. *Physiol Behav*, **100**(1): 15–21.

11. Harrison-Bernard, L.M. (2009). The renal renin-angiotensin system. *Adv Physiol Educ*, **33**(4): 270–274.

12. Zaika, O., et al. (2013). Direct activation of ENaC by angiotensin II: recent advances and new insights. *Curr Hypertens Rep*, **15**(1): 17–24.

13. Sharif-Naeini, R., et al. (2008). Contribution of TRPV channels to osmosensory transduction, thirst, and vasopressin release. *Kidney Int*, **73**(7): 811–815.

14. Hill, A.E. and Y. Shachar-Hill (2015). Are Aquaporins the Missing Transmembrane Osmosensors? *J Membr Biol*, **248**(4): 753–765.

15. Aylor, D.L., et al. (2011). Genetic analysis of complex traits in the emerging Collaborative Cross. *Genome Res*, **21**(8): 1213–1222.

16. Juul, K.V., et al. (2014). The physiological and pathophysiological functions of renal and extrarenal vasopressin V2 receptors. *Am J Physiol Renal Physiol*, **306**(9): F931–F940.

17. Radin, M.J., et al. (2012). Aquaporin-2 regulation in health and disease. *Vet Clin Pathol*, **41**(4): 455–470.

18. *Number (in Millions) of Civilian, Non-Institutionalized Persons with Diagnosed Diabetes, United States, 1980–2014*, C.f.D.C.a. Prevention, Editor. 2015.

19. Liamis, G., et al. (2014). Diabetes mellitus and electrolyte disorders. *World J Clin Cases*, **2**(10): 488–496.

20. Robertson, G.L. (2016). Diabetes insipidus: Differential diagnosis and management. *Best Pract Res Clin Endocrinol Metab*, **30**(2): 205–218.

21. Bichet, D.G. and D. Bockenhauer. (2016). Genetic forms of nephrogenic diabetes insipidus (NDI): Vasopressin receptor defect (X-linked) and aquaporin defect (autosomal recessive and dominant). *Best Pract Res Clin Endocrinol Metab*, **30**(2): 263–276.

22. Marques, P., K. Gunawardana, and A. Grossman (2015). Transient diabetes insipidus in pregnancy. *Endocrinol Diabetes Metab Case Rep*, **2015**: 150078.

23. McGreal, K., et al. (2016). Current Challenges in the Evaluation and Management of Hyponatremia. *Kidney Dis (Basel)*, **2**(2): 56–63.

24. Nolte, H.W., et al. (2015). Exercise-associated hyponatremic encephalopathy and exertional heatstroke in a soldier: High rates of fluid intake during exercise caused rather than prevented a fatal outcome. *Phys Sportsmed*, **43**(1): 93–98.

25. Kotchen, T.A., A.W. Cowley, Jr., and E.D. Frohlich (2013). Salt in health and disease—a delicate balance. *N Engl J Med*, **368**(13): 1229–1237.

Conditions Affecting Water Balance

```
D  I  A  B  E  T  E  S  I  N  S  I  P  I  T  U  S
S  U  T  I  L  L  E  M  S  E  T  E  B  A  I  D  T
E  R  X  H  C  I  N  O  T  R  E  P  Y  H  L  L  M
X  Y  Y  R  Y  Y  B  T  W  V  L  N  W  I  R  D  P
E  B  V  T  D  P  D  Y  R  R  O  J  D  Q  P  M  G
R  T  C  P  I  W  E  X  T  I  N  D  R  J  M  Q  Q
C  G  X  I  J  C  J  R  T  M  L  K  J  P  Z  L  D
I  G  V  V  T  X  I  A  N  E  J  B  T  Y  X  X  T
S  N  R  T  K  O  R  X  S  A  L  B  D  L  N  M  W
E  V  Z  D  R  D  M  Y  O  R  T  D  L  Y  L  Z  N
J  L  R  J  Y  L  N  S  R  T  N  R  D  Y  B  J  P
M  M  Y  H  Z  D  D  J  O  T  R  N  E  Z  R  W  L
V  Q  E  P  R  X  G  T  K  O  Z  E  J  M  V  P  M
B  D  V  O  M  X  K  T  T  D  P  Z  T  W  I  R  M
W  W  M  V  N  M  Z  L  N  R  N  Y  V  A  R  A  Y
M  E  B  P  J  V  Y  Z  Y  G  W  D  H  G  W  Y  M
```

	CLUE	ANSWER
1	Solution with low solute and high water levels	_____
2	Activity that can increase sweating and water loss	_____
3	Caused by a mutation in the epithelial sodium channel	_____
4	Caused by a mutation in Aquaporin 2	_____
5	Water balance problems result from uncontrolled hyperglycemia	_____
6	Caused by dietary high salt intake	_____
7	Caused by over-hydration	_____
8	Caused by low water intake	_____
9	Solution with a high concentration of impenetrable solutes	_____

NOTES

CHAPTER 10

Blood: Hematopoiesis, Clotting, and the Immune System

Table of Contents

Blood cells circulate through every living tissue in our bodies. In humans, fetal blood is formed in the yolk sac by 1 month of age, and as we develop, blood formation processes moves to the liver, the spleen, and finally, as we continue into the 4th month of gestation, to the bone marrow. As we will see in this chapter, blood cell formation and functions in clotting, oxygen delivery, and immunity all require various micronutrients. Deficiencies in these vitamins and minerals can impair all aspects of the blood, throughout development and into adulthood. Keep this in mind as you read the chapter—consider how each micronutrient we discuss needs to be at an optimal level to maintain optimal blood formation and function, and how impairment of blood cells, by the very fact that blood is needed by every other system, can have widespread effects in the body.

BLOOD CELL FORMATION

Consider this: the stem cells in our bone marrow must continue to produce new blood cells throughout our lifetime, whether it be 50, 75, or even 100+ years! How does the hematopoietic system maintain pluripotent stem cells, which continue to proliferate and produce all lineages of our blood cells for 50+ years? As discussed in Chapter 7, on

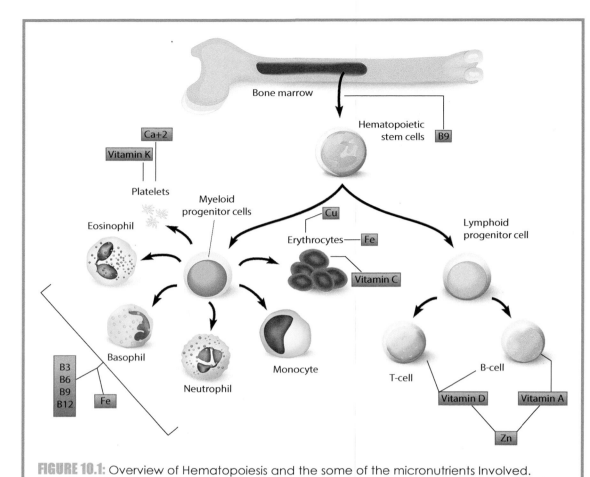

FIGURE 10.1: Overview of Hematopoiesis and the some of the micronutrients Involved. From the fetal period, until the end of life, the bone marrow hematopoietic system must continue to supply our bodies with all of the blood cells.

© Designua/Shutterstock.com

developmental biology, remember that folate, B12 and B6 (at a minimum) are needed to keep cells proliferating. These processes are important during fetal development, but as regards hematopoietic system, continue to be important throughout adulthood. As shown in Table 7.1, deficiency of B6, B9, and B12 all result in types of anemia—because these micronutrients are needed for one-carbon metabolism, which make the nucleotides and amino acids for proliferating cells. As we won't discuss this again in this chapter, make sure you remind yourself of all that can happen to mess up folate, B6 and B12 metabolism, and of all of the other micronutrients that facilitate one-carbon metabolism in our bodies. As shown in Figure 10.1, multiple micronutrients are needed in addition to B9, B6, and B12 for development and functioning of the different blood cell types. In addition (and not shown on Figure 10.1), these cells actively need all of the micronutrients for the TCA and ETC cycles, for cell signaling, and for antioxidant defense. Again, reviewing the previous chapters on these will help you to appreciate all of the needs of our hematopoietic system.

TABLE 10.2: Genetic conditions of Iron Metabolism. All conditions can be found on the NIH Genetics Home Reference web page. https://ghr.nlm.nih.gov/

Genetic conditions of Iron Metabolism	Gene involved	Phenotype
Iron refractory iron deficiency anemia	TMPRSS6	Anemia that does not respond to iron treatment (rare)
Hemochromatosis	Type I-Classic form, HFE mutation Type II-Hepcidin mutation Type III: Transferrin receptor mutation Type VI: ferroportin mutation	Iron overload and accumulation
Hereditary ceruloplasmin deficiency	Ceruloplasmin	Iron accumulation Tremors, ataxia Anemia

Iron metabolism and hematopoiesis

The micronutrient we will revisit now is iron. Our body makes around 2 million red blood cells *per second*, and for this it needs about 560 *quadrillion* molecules of hemoglobin, each with one iron-heme molecule at its center [5]. Suffice to say, we need a lot of iron to keep this process going.

As it happens, iron metabolism is not as simple as "it gets into the body, and goes to the red blood cells." There are quite a few steps, for that to happen. Iron is in a ferric state (Fe^{+3}) when it is bound to proteins, in our gut or blood, but it needs to be in a ferrous state (Fe^{+2}) within cells (Figure 10.2). As we initially discussed in Chapter 3 (Digestion), ferric iron is reduced to ferrous iron by the enzyme reductase duodenal cytochrome b (Dcytb), which requires vitamin C [6]. This enzyme uses vitamin C to provide an electron, which reduces the charge from Fe^{+3} to Fe^{+2} (if you think about it—it makes sense that one electron with a negative charge, reduces the positive charge by one). However, ascorbic acid (AA) was oxidized to dehyroascorbic acid (DHA) in the process, and it must actively be regenerated by other antioxidant systems. In the case of the enterocyte, it appears that the thioredoxin reductase (TR) enzyme is the key enzyme at work (Figure 10.2) [6]. As you hopefully recall

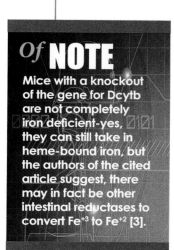

Of **NOTE**

Mice with a knockout of the gene for Dcytb are not completely iron deficient-yes, they can still take in heme-bound iron, but the authors of the cited article suggest, there may in fact be other intestinal reductases to convert Fe^{+3} to Fe^{+2} [3].

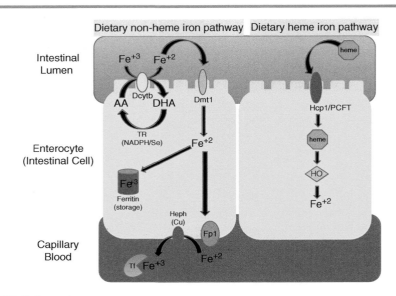

FIGURE 10.2: Iron absorption and metabolism. Iron travels within the gut and blood, and bound to proteins in these compartments, in a ferric (Fe(III) or Fe^{+3}) state, but is in our cells in a ferrous (Fe(II) or Fe^{+2}) state. The complex transfer between these states as iron crosses the enterocytes and goes into the bloodstream, and there other micronutrients needed for this process is shown. Dcytb: duodenal cytochrome b; TR: thioredoxin reductase; Dmt1: divalent metal transporter 1; Hcp1/PCFT: heme carrier protein 1 (also referred to as the proton-coupled folate transporter); Fp1: ferroportin; Heph: hephaestin; Tf: transferrin.

from Chapter 6, TR requires NADPH and selenium for full activity, and now we add these two micronutrients into our blood system requirements.

Getting back to iron, in the Fe^{+2} state, iron can now bind to the DMT1 receptor and be transported into the enterocyte. At this point, a decision must be made by the enterocyte: will iron be stored locally in ferritin, used by the enterocyte for its iron-containing enzymes or transported out of the cell to other tissues? The decision made depends on the body's sensing of iron availability, which it does in a very clever way. It turns out that the enzyme aconitase has two functions. The first, which you hopefully remember from Chapter 4, is as the enzyme that converts citrate to isocitrate in the TCA cycle (Figure 4.2). This iron-containing enzyme is busy making energy for the cell when iron stores are high. But when iron levels drop, iron falls off of aconitase, and the enzyme takes on a new function—that of an "iron sensing RNA-binding protein" or IRP (Figure 10.3). Aconitase can bind to "iron response elements," or IREs in either the 3' (tail) or 5' (front or head) of the RNA. It does this for the mRNAs of several iron regulatory proteins, including DMT1, transferrin receptor, and ferritin (Figure 10.3). When iron stores are low, aconitase binds to ferritin mRNA in its 5' end, and translation of ferritin mRNA is blocked meaning that ferritin protein is no longer made. This allows iron coming

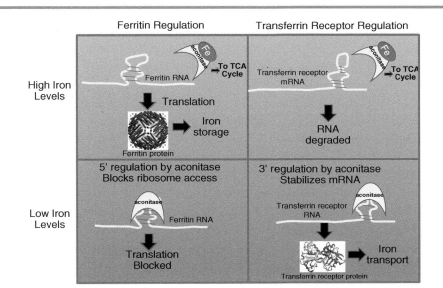

Ferritin Regulation   Transferrin Receptor Regulation

FIGURE 10.3: Translational Regulation of Ferritin and Transferrin. When iron levels are high, iron is bound to aconitase and it is functioning in the TCA cycle. When iron is low, aconitase acts as an iron responsive RNA-binding protein. When aconitase binds in the 5' end of mRNA, translation is blocked, as shown for ferritin. When aconitase binds in the 3' end of an mRNA, the mRNA is stabilized and then can be translated, as shown for transferrin receptor. Although not shown, DMT1 mRNA is also regulated by stabilization when iron stores are low, turning on the ability of the cell to make this protein.

© molekuul_be/Shutterstock.com

in by digestion to be released and no longer stored. Concurrently, aconitase binds to the 3' end of the mRNAs for both DMT1 and transferrin, which stabilizes these mRNAs, allowing the mRNA to be translated, and effectively increases the levels of these protein, which leads to increased iron uptake and transport [7]. Isn't that a neat system? If you think about how this system might have evolved, and why, you can appreciate how important iron homeostasis is to our bodies.

Let's get back to iron entry into the cell. As iron comes into an enterocyte, the decision is made whether to store iron as ferritin (which will be available if iron needs to be stored) or to transport it out of the cell. When iron is stored, it is converted back to the Fe^{+3} state by the ferroxidase center of ferritin [8]. When iron is transported out of the cell, it also needs to be converted back to the Fe^{+3} state, but this occurs after transport through ferroportin, by the copper-containing hephaestin protein (Figure 10.2). Fe^{+3} now binds to transferrin and can be transported to its target tissues, where it is taken up by the transferrin receptor. Remember that the amount of transferrin receptor on a cell membrane is regulated locally by the aconitase enzyme in that cell, ultimately determining how much transferrin receptor is available for iron uptake on a cell by cell basis.

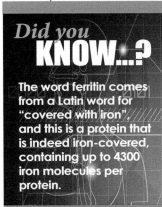

Did you
KNOW...?

The word ferritin comes from a Latin word for "covered with iron", and this is a protein that is indeed iron-covered, containing up to 4300 iron molecules per protein.

Cancer and red meat

There is a strong association between the intake of red meat and colorectal cancer. Some believe it is due to the degradation of heme in enterocytes, as the process produces carbon monoxide and N-nitroso compounds, which can bind DNA and may increase mutation rates. White meats have 10-fold lower heme levels than red meats [1].

Dietary iron can also be bound to heme protein, and in this case takes a different route to get into enterocytes (Figure 10.2). In duodenal cells, the protein Heme carrier protein-1 (HCP1) is a low affinity receptor for heme. However, HCP-1 is highly expressed in the intestine so even though the receptor has a low affinity for heme, plenty of heme is taken in by individual enterocytes. Here's the interesting part: we know of HCP1 already, but by another name—PCFT, or the proton-coupled folate transporter. It turns out that the intestinal heme transporter is a stronger transporter for folate, but gets the job done for both substances. It's an interesting dual use for a single protein (we seem to be getting a lot of that in this chapter, huh?). Once inside the cell, heme is oxidized to get the iron out of the molecule by the enzyme heme oxidase (HO) (Figure 10.2). Fe^{+2} now can be transported or stored in the regular ways during the daily turnover of iron between storage, transport, and use.

One of the primary sites of iron delivery is to the red blood cell progenitor/stem cells. Here the transferrin receptor binds to transferrin-iron complex in the blood, and through endocytosis, takes transferrin-iron into the cell within an endosome. Within the progenitor cells, most studies now suggest that DMT1/Dcytb complex release Fe^{+3} and convert it back to Fe^{+2} for release into the cytoplasm and uptake by enzymes that need it, including those involved in the electron transport cycle, the TCA cycle, and most importantly, for the purpose of this discussion, hemoglobin synthesis [9](Figure 10.4).

Before we talk about hemoglobin as a functional iron-containing molecule, let's talk about recycling of iron within cells, as this becomes somewhat important later on when we talk about conditions that prevent iron from getting out of cells. First, iron is recycled from iron-containing proteins when the proteins are degraded within lysosomes (Figure 10.4). To get the iron back out of the cell and into circulation, ferroportin is used (as in intestinal cells), but with a new partner, ceruloplasmin. Ceruloplasmin also does double duty—as a copper carrier protein in the bloodstream, and here, as a membrane associated protein working alongside of ferroportin as a ferro-oxidase, converting Fe^{+2} to Fe^{+3}, with the use of the copper-cofactor to transfer electrons [5]. A similar process happens in macrophages that phagocytize (i.e., eat!!) old red blood cells—the hemoglobin is metabolized, and heme protein is oxidized by HO, and finally exported to the bloodstream by the transferrin-ceruloplasmin complex (Figure 10.4). Finally and importantly as we'll see later, as excess iron is toxic to cells, several mechanisms prevent cells from picking up too much of it. Transferrin receptor might be made and at the cell surface, but not available for picking up transferrin—due to co-binding by the HFE protein (Figure 10.4). This protein senses levels of iron in the cell, and colocalizes with the transferrin receptors when iron levels are sufficient preventing further uptake [10].

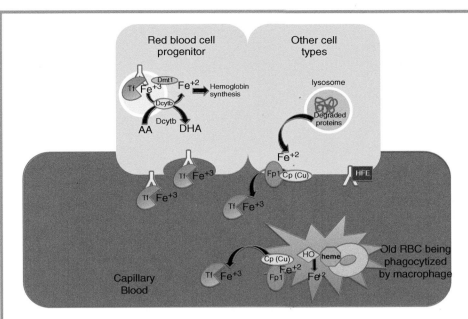

FIGURE 10.4: Metabolism of iron in red blood cells, and red blood cell progenitors (stem cells). Transferrin receptor (Tf) picks up transferrin-iron complex which is taken into the cell by endocytosis. Then, within the endosome, Fe^{+3} is oxidized to Fe^{+2} using the same process as uptake of iron by intestinal cells. The iron is then available for hemoglobin synthesis. Old red blood cells are phagocytized by macrophages, which results in released heme protein, and through heme oxidase (HO) release of Fe^{+2}. The Fe^{+2} can be released back into circulation by ferroportin, this time working with the copper-containing ceruloplasmin to convert Fe^{+2} to Fe^{+3}. The same mechanism (ferroportin-ceruloplasmin) is at work in other cell types where iron gets recycled. Iron uptake is regulated by the iron sensor HFE which blocks the transferrin receptor from binding the transferrin-iron complex when there is too much iron in the cell already.

© Raimundo79/Shutterstock.com

OXYGEN DELIVERY TO TISSUES

Before leaving the topic of red blood cells, let's talk about their role in our bodies. Most student learn very early in their education that blood carries oxygen, and it is the red blood cells that perform this duty, traveling from the lungs to pick up oxygen diffusing through the air sacs, and then transporting that oxygen to the rest of the needy tissues in the body (Figure 10.5). The globin family of proteins, are one of the earliest protein types that evolved in oxygen-living cells. This is thought to be because O_2 respiring organisms needed a way to carry oxygen in its O_2 form to different parts of an increasingly complex body [11]. The hemoglobin protein is produced in a multiple step process, which involves coordinated mitochondrial assembly of the heme moiety, and translation and folding of the protein globin units. The assembled complex is now ready for carrying oxygen. Without going too much into the chemical reactions that take place between oxygenation of hemoglobin

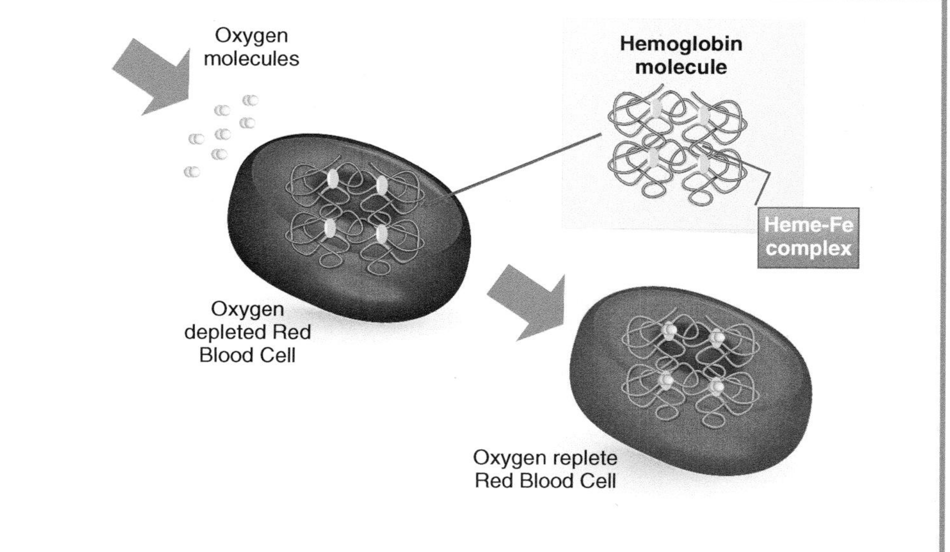

FIGURE 10.5: Hemoglobin in the red blood cell picks up molecular oxygen and deposits it in tissues for use in respiration. Hemoglobin has heme-iron molecules at its core.

© Designua/Shutterstock.com

and release of O_2 to tissues, suffice to say that iron plays a pivotal role in this process. The ability of iron to switch between the Fe^{+2} and Fe^{+3} states allows for uptake and release of O_2 within the core of the molecule [11]. As an aside, the well-known gene condition, sickle cell anemia results when a mutation in hemoglobin prevents full oxidation/reduction potential of the red blood cell due to a change in the hemoglobin structure [11].

In summary for this section, which was packed (meaty one might say…referring to the high level of heme in red meats!), iron metabolism is tightly controlled, both in uptake of iron from diet and by tissues from the blood, and in use or deposition of iron from stores. This is mainly because iron itself is so reactive and because of that, toxic unless kept bound to proteins and in nonreactive states. However, iron's reactivity is the very reason that hemoglobin can function to carry oxygen—so our cells, because of their need for oxygen for respiration, and iron for many iron-containing proteins take the good with the bad, and make the best of it.

CLOTTING

Clotting, or more formally coagulation, is the process by which liquid blood turns to a fibrous gel to plug a hole in a blood vessel with a clot or (formally, thrombus) (Figure 10.6). Vitamin K is needed for coagulation—and in fact got its name that way—from the Danish word *"koagulation."* As you will see, other micronutrients are needed to ensure that the process of clotting, and the dissolution of the clot

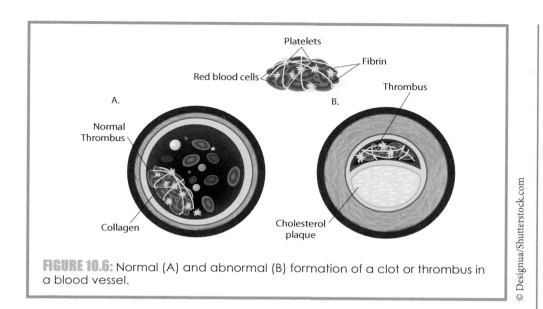

FIGURE 10.6: Normal (A) and abnormal (B) formation of a clot or thrombus in a blood vessel.

© Designua/Shutterstock.com

proceed quickly, efficiently, and correctly. As you already know, abnormal clotting can occur when cholesterol plaques form in vessels (as in the condition, atherosclerosis, Figure 10.6).

The highly regulated process of coagulation is shown on Figure 10.7. As once can see, coagulation actu`ally has three parts—an intrinsic pathway, an extrinsic pathway, and a common pathway. The intrinsic pathway is activated by inflammation, and serves to produce a bigger overall clot size (i.e., involved in thrombosis, but not hemostasis) [12]. As might be expected, individuals with a mutation of Factor XI from the intrinsic pathway, or Factor XII (which we did not include in our diagram), have minimal bleeding in response to tissue damage, but still have overall clotting defects [12]. The extrinsic pathway, which is activated by tissue damage, serves to stop bleeding, and individuals with mutations in any of the factors in the extrinsic pathway show bleeding disorders in response to cuts or lesions to their vessels. Both pathways converge on the common pathway, in which activated thrombin cleaves fibrinogen to produce fibrin, and activated Factor 13a facilitates cross-linking of the fibrin to form the clot.

However, what is more salient to our discussion of Figure 10.7 are the boxes with vitamin K and Ca^{+2} in them, indicating factors in the blood clotting process, which require carboxylation by vitamin K-dependent enzymes, and calcium binding as part of the overall process. Let's look at these more in depth.

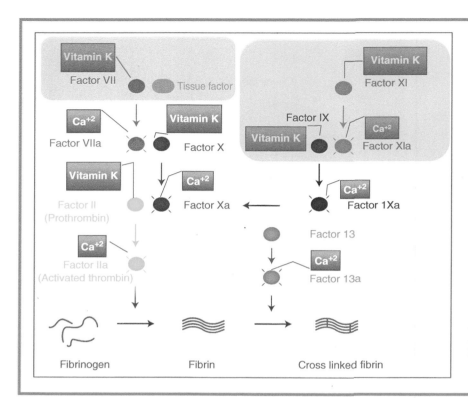

FIGURE 10.7: Vitamin K and Calcium-Dependent clotting factors. Note that Factor 13 does not require gamma glutamyl carboxylase activity, as it is a transglutaminase, but it does need calcium as a co-factor. Protein C, Z, and S (not shown) are also Vitamin K-dependent anti-coagulation factors. The extrinsic pathway is denoted by the light pink box. This pathway is activated when there is tissue damage. The intrinsic pathway is denoted by a light blue box. This pathway is more involved in inflammation and immune function. The rest of the process is called the common pathway, as it is common to both start points.

© joshya/Shutterstock.com

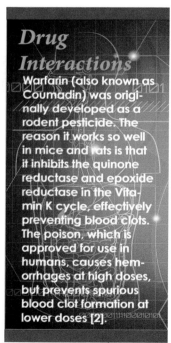

Drug Interactions

Warfarin (also known as Coumadin) was originally developed as a rodent pesticide. The reason it works so well in mice and rats is that it inhibits the quinone reductase and epoxide reductase in the Vitamin K cycle, effectively preventing blood clots. The poison, which is approved for use in humans, causes hemorrhages at high doses, but prevents spurious blood clot formation at lower doses [2].

Vitamin K cycle

In preparation for this discussion, please look back at Figure 8.7, which shows the vitamin K cycle. This same cycle is needed for coagulation. All of the proteins shown in Figure 10.7 with "Vitamin K" attached to them, as those that need to undergo vitamin K-dependent carboxylation. The vitamin K-dependent gamma glutamyl carboxylase enzyme, using the vitamin K vitamer hydroquinone as a cofactor, attaches a carboxyl group to a glutamate ("gla") amino acid in each protein. The process can occur multiple times within a protein—for example, in Factor VII, there are 10 vitamin K-dependent carboxylation events on "gla" amino acids [13]. This gla-carboxylation process is an evolutionarily ancient one—more primitive animals, including sea snails utilize vitamin K-dependent carboxylation to promote calcium-binding by proteins, both within a clotting-like system, and outside of it [14]. The vitamin K cycle requires NADPH to form dihydroquinone, so any deficiency of niacin could affect vitamin K-dependent carboxylation. Thus, vitamin-K dependent carboxylation is one of the cornerstones of the clotting process, by preparing clotting factors for calcium-mediated interactions, as we will see in the next section.

Calcium

Calcium ions participate in both protein interactions and cellular signaling during coagulation. We will talk both about the calcium-binding clotting factors, and the processes of cell-signaling that occur upon activation of the extrinsic pathway of coagulation.

First, let's start with tissue damage, leading to a hole in a capillary or other vessel. This damage results in exposure of collagen, which is normally in the extracellular matrix of the endothelial cells lining the vessel (**Figure 10.6**). Platelet receptors bind to this collagen, which starts a signaling cascade resulting in platelet activation. The signaling cascade involves, among other processes discussed in Chapter 5, calcium waves from stored vesicles containing calcium—and is an essential component of platelet activation, with as much as a 10-fold elevation in cytosolic calcium levels during platelet activation [15]. Ultimately, interaction of the platelets with the collagen at the site of injury adheres the platelets to that region of the vessel, localizing the clotting response, and resulting in shape changes in the platelet, which facilities clumping, and prepares platelet receptors for interaction with clotting factors, and with other platelets to form a tight clot [15].

In addition to signaling, calcium plays a key role in protein–protein interactions of the vitamin-K dependent clotting factors (Figure 10.7). Let's use Factor VII as an example, as it was also discussed under the vitamin K section. As discussed above, Factor VII has 10 carboxylated "gla" residues [13]. Interestingly, just seven of these post-translationally modified amino acid residue in the protein are critical for both the structural integrity of Factor VII and its function, although calcium can interact as all 10 carboxylated amino acids [13]. Also of interest, if there is sufficient magnesium, and not enough calcium, magnesium can substitute in 2–3 of these regions, and may actually enhance the activity of Factor VII in this conformation [13]. Both the tissue factor binding domain and the protease domain of Factor VII require a calcium ion for full activity, which both of these activities being a critical step in the initiation of coagulation activity during tissue damage (Figure 10.7). Of note, while magnesium may strengthen some activities, it appears that in a situation of high magnesium levels, Mg^{+2} ions will compete with calcium for binding to the carboxylated proteins, reducing the overall clotting time. However, in the presence of lower than normal calcium (hypocalcaemia), magnesium may substitute for some positions in the gla-carboxylated proteins and enhance coagulation [16, 17]. This balance between plasma Ca^{+2} and Mg^{+2} ions is critical for normal clotting reactions.

To summarize clotting—as discussed above, we need clots to repair damages to our vessels, and this process requires both calcium and vitamin K (along with B3 needed for the vitamin K cycle). Clotting itself is tightly regulated, but

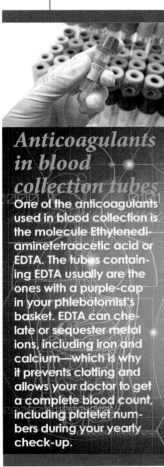

Anticoagulants in blood collection tubes

One of the anticoagulants used in blood collection is the molecule Ethylenediaminetetraacetic acid or EDTA. The tubes containing EDTA usually are the ones with a purple-cap in your phlebotomist's basket. EDTA can chelate or sequester metal ions, including iron and calcium—which is why it prevents clotting and allows your doctor to get a complete blood count, including platelet numbers during your yearly check-up.

can become pathogenic when platelets adhere to cholesterol deposits or plaques. In these cases, clotting must be controlled, usually through direct inhibitor of vitamin K-dependent carboxylation (such as with the drug Warfarin [2]) or by directly blocking the enzymatic activity of some of the clotting factors. As calcium levels are so tightly controlled in blood, it would be unusual to prescribe any calcium-lowering drug, as the effects would be wide-spread to bone and other calcium-requiring tissues. Of note, vitamin E can act as an anticoagulant, but it is thought to act by blocking or interfering with normal vitamin K uptake, rather than a direct effect on the clotting process [18].

THE IMMUNE SYSTEM

In addition to erythrocytes (red blood cells) and platelets, there are a whole slew of white blood cells that form our bodies' defense system. We will spend some of this section discussing the role of oxidative processes myeloid cells, namely eosinophils, basophils, neutrophils, and monocytes/macrophages, or our innate immunity system (Figure 10.1). We will also discuss how vitamins A and D and the mineral zinc modulate the adaptive immune responses by B- and T-cells.

A through D, to zinc

As early as 1928, just after vitamin A was characterized, the vitamin was recognized to be an immunity booster, providing resistance to infections, especially in studies where animals on vitamin A replete diets were compared to animals on a vitamin A-deficient diet [19]. Yet still today, many more products tout vitamin C as an immunity supplement, as compared to vitamin A. Let's begin this section, and then you can decide for yourselves which vitamins you think are best for boosting your immune system.

Getting back to vitamin A, remember that its vitamer, retinoic acid, acts as a coregulator of DNA transcription with the RAR and RXR zinc-finger transcription factors, and in fact, this is one of the places where zinc comes into play—we'll discuss its role a bit later. Vitamin A, in the form of retinol, bound to retinol binding protein travels in the blood, targeting vitamin A-dependent tissues, including special immunity areas in our guts called Peyer's patches. The cells in these patches, called dendritic cells can convert retinol to retinoic acid, using the enzyme retinol dehydrogenase (RDH)—a B3-requiring enzyme. Once formed, retinoic acid is used as a coregulator with the RAR/RXR heterodimer to activate a set of genes in these dendritic cells, ultimately providing "docks" for T-cells to bind to (or "home") to our gut enterocytes, which gives protective immunity against the bugs that we ingest [20]. There is some controversy as to whether retinoic acid also can contribute to T-cell differentiation or T-cell activation and/or tolerance [20], and as this is not an immunology text, we'll leave the controversy alone for now, and settle just on

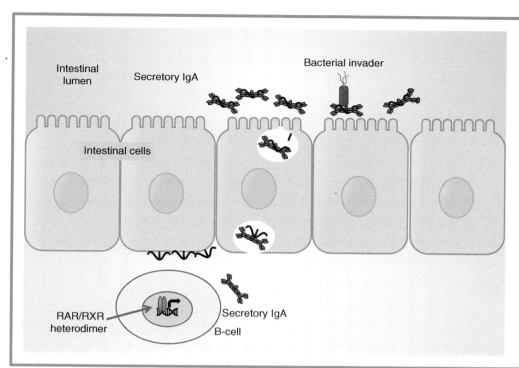

© ellepigrafica/Shutterstock.com

FIGURE 10.8:
Role of Vitamin A in secretory IgA production. RAR/RXR heterodimers stimulate transcription of the IgA genes (heavy and light chains). When IgA is secreted from the recruited B-cells, it can contribute to mucosal immunity in our guts.

its role in homing the immune cells to the gut where they are needed. Importantly, retinoic acid does act directly on B-cells, our antibody-producing cells, inducing receptors that allow B-cells to home to the gut [21]. Once there, transcriptional regulation within the nuclei of B-cells, by retinoic acid/RAR/RXR complexes, mediates what is called "class switching." This class-switching allows the B-cells to produce IgA immunoglobulin—the type that mediates the immune responses of the gut mucosa [21] (Figure 10.8). Thus, you can think of vitamin A as a key player in gut mucosal immunity, and possibly important systematically, due to its need by vitamin D and VDR (as you'll see below).

It might be surprising to some that vitamin D, with its major role in calcium and phosphorus regulation also plays a major role in the immune system. Interestingly, vitamin D, acting as a steroid hormone through VDR/RXR heterodimers mediates immune suppression, rather than immune activation. Of note, vitamin D's role in immunity, or at least in host defense, dates prior to its role in bone mineralization—cartilaginous fishes use calcitriol as a xenobiotic defense mechanism [22], suggesting that its immune roles were required even before its skeletal roles, making vitamin D a primary micronutrient when thinking about immunity.

Now I have to admit that I left a little something out when we discussed calcitriol production in the kidney (Chapter 8). That is to say that it turns out the kidney isn't the only place where we can make the active vitamin D vitamers—one of the other places where

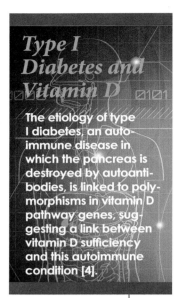

Type I Diabetes and Vitamin D

The etiology of type I diabetes, an auto-immune disease in which the pancreas is destroyed by autoanti-bodies, is linked to poly-morphisms in vitamin D pathway genes, sug-gesting a link between vitamin D sufficiency and this autoimmune condition [4].

it can be made is in our immune cells. In particular, the 1-α-hydroxylase enzyme is actually expressed in both dendritic cells and macrophages—likely therefore able to infiltrate mucosal and nonmucosal regions in our bodies allowing our bodies to localize the production of active vitamin D [23]. The reason this becomes import-ant is when we look back in history and consider how phototherapy or cod liver oil (both increasing circulating vitamin D levels) were used to treat diseases such as lupus and rheumatism [24]. Both of these are diseases that might be considered to be developed due to overactive immune systems. Indeed, multiple studies have shown that VDR signaling differentiates T-cells to T-regulatory cells and reduces B-cell activation—both of which will result in a suppressing of the immune re-sponse [24, 25] (Figure 10.9). Vitamin D deficiency or genetic variations in several vitamin D pathway enzymes and proteins are linked to several autoimmune dis-eases, and in some cases, vitamin D supplementation can alleviate the symptoms (examples of these papers, of which there are many are cited here: [24, 26–29]. This author thinks it is also quite interesting that vitamin D has been linked to antimicrobial immune responses as well [30], and therefore may possess both an immune stimulatory and immune-suppressant activity, dependent on the immune cell type (neutrophils versus T- and B-cells) and immune response (innate versus adaptive). What a unique set of roles vitamin D plays in our immune system!

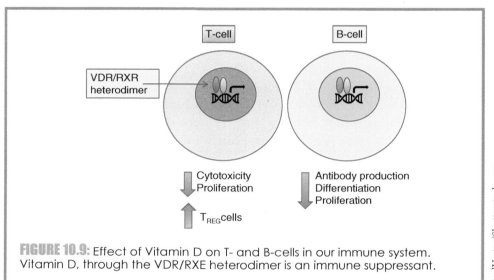

FIGURE 10.9: Effect of Vitamin D on T- and B-cells in our immune system. Vitamin D, through the VDR/RXE heterodimer is an immune suppressant.

ZINC VERSUS VITAMIN C AND THE COMMON COLD

Both vitamin A and vitamin D require zinc, as the transcription factors they work through are zinc-finger transcription factors. Remember that for these transcrip-tion factors, zinc acts as a structural cofactor, forming the "fingers" of amino acids that grab the DNA double helix (take a look back at Figure 1.5). So, is zinc also needed by our immune system? In a word—YES!

The best example one can give is the role of zinc lozenges treatment for the common cold. This author keeps a supply of the zinc-containing, fast dissolving tablets in her medicine cabinet and chews on one or two when she feels a cold coming on. What you say—not a vitamin C-containing supplement? No, because in fact there is little evidence that vitamin C cures the common cold [31], but the evidence for zinc treatment results in reduced severity and days of sickness by up to 3 days, as demonstrated by a very recent meta-analysis, are quite strong [32]. How does zinc do this? It is thought zinc facilitates vitamins A and D genomic effects, but also likely acts through the hundreds of other factors that require Zn as a structural cofactor. In fact, one of these, called thymulin, is secreted by the thymus and appears to regulate T-cell immunity [33]. However, in the words of one author the "unique properties of zinc may have significant therapeutic benefits in humans diseases," [33] and in the words of this author—more research is needed to fine tune zinc as a treatment option for boosting or suppressing immunity.

IMMUNITY AND OXIDANTS

Before concluding this section, we must consider the role of some micronutrients in oxidative mechanisms used by our innate immune cells, namely macrophages, eosinophils, and basophils. These so-called "professional phagocytes" utilize oxidants to kill off the junk they have eaten or more appropriately, phagocytized. To kill these bugs, the cells must make bleach (NaClO, sodium hypochlorite) and to do this they require NADPH for NADPH oxidase and iron as the heme group in myeloperoxidase (Figure 10.10) [34]. This use of oxidative mechanisms by our innate immunity system is one of the reasons why we need to keep our antioxidants in check with the oxidants—those coming from the environment and those generated within.

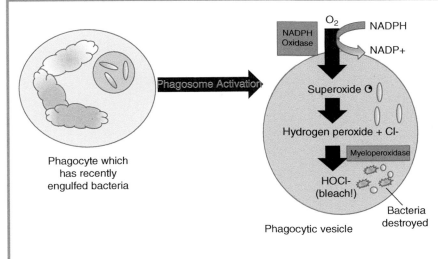

FIGURE 10.10: Professional phagocytes use oxidants to kill off invaders. You can tell a phagocyte by its segmented nucleus (pink), and the presences of phagosomes—which are lysosomal pockets containing phagocytized "bugs" (in green). NADPH oxidase produces superoxide using NADPH. Myeloperoxidase contains heme, meaning that this process also requires iron. The final product in the reaction is bleach (HOCl-), which kills the phagocytized bacteria.

MICRONUTRIENT DEFICIENCIES, TOXICITIES, AND GENETIC CONDITIONS AFFECTING BLOOD AND IMMUNITY

The blood system with stem cells, red blood cells, platelets, and immune cells is quite complex. In addition to relying on energy metabolism pathways, and on one-carbon metabolism for growth and differentiation, blood cells have specific micronutrient needs for their individual "specialties." Furthermore, many specific genes play key roles in iron metabolism, clotting, and immune function—and we will discuss those genes coding for proteins that interact with or require micronutrients for their activities.

Take a look back at Figure 10.1 and the micronutrients listed there. Now, look at the individual listings for these micronutrients in the back of this book. Which ones have blood-specific effects listed for dietary deficiency or toxicity? Hopefully you found that iron, zinc, B6, B9, B12, vitamin A, and vitamin K deficiencies are associated with problems with hematopoiesis, iron metabolism, clotting, and immunity. For example, the classic deficiency symptom for dietary iron deficiency is iron-deficiency anemia. Iron deficiency is the most common deficiency, worldwide, with effects mainly seen in the elderly women and children [35]. This condition is mainly treated with dietary iron supplementation, but in the case of one rare genetic disease, supplementary iron does not cure the anemia (Table 10.1). Variants in the gene TMPRSS6, which codes for a membrane protein that regulates a protein called hepcidin lead to low of iron uptake from small intestine. Although we didn't speak about hepcidin previously, it is secreted from liver and blocks uptake of dietary iron when liver stores are high. In the TMRPSS6 variant, hepcidin is continuously secreted [35]. As also shown in Table 10.1, variations in the hepcidin gene itself—especially those which inactivate the protein, can result in iron overload, as there is no ability of the liver to sense and respond to iron stores. This condition, called hemochromatosis can be caused variations in the genes encoding several iron-monitoring proteins in our bodies [35]. For each of the genes involved in hemochromatosis, take a look at where each protein is located and its function, and then consider why a variation in that protein might affect iron regulation. Finally, variants in the ceruloplasmin gene cause anemia with iron overload—because iron cannot get out of some cells (iron overload) and into others (red blood cells). In some of these cases of genetic disease, dietary iron intake must be assessed first to determine if there is a dietary or genetic cause, before any treatment can begin.

Let's look more closely now at dietary vitamin K intake, and associated genetic causes of vitamin K-dependent clotting disorders. First, while gut bacteria can synthesize vitamin K, it is still important to get additional vitamin K through the diet (or supplements), as the microbial synthesis is not sufficient. Interestingly, in

2001, the Food and Nutrition Board concluded that we do not know enough about vitamin K needs to establish an RDA—thus an AI is used (see supplemental page on vitamin K). In adults, vitamin K deficiency is extremely rare, but we know that most infants (unless their parents refuse it) get a vitamin K shot at birth [36]. Why you ask—because most neonates do not have sufficient microbial colonization of their intestines at birth, combined with low placental transport of vitamin K, and therefore low overall stores. Without this vitamin K shot, many newborns and infants up to 1 year might suffer from vitamin K-related bleeding disorder—fortunately a disorder that is cured by the single vitamin K shot [36]. However, some individuals suffer from a lifelong condition of vitamin K deficiency, which is caused by variants/mutations in either gamma glutamyl carboxylase, or epoxide carboxylase (Table 10.2). This condition, called vitamin K-dependent clotting factor deficiency (VKCFD) type I (gamma glutamyl carboxylase) or type II (epoxide carboxylase) lead to clotting disorders with low- to no carboxylation of the clotting factors requiring vitamin K-dependent carboxylation for their activity (shown in Figure 10.7) [37]. It is worth mentioning here that while dietary hypo- or hypercalcemia does not appear to affect clotting (at least symptomatically *in vivo*), variations in the genes coding for most of the calcium-binding clotting factors cause various types of hemophilia (Table 10.2). Multiple variants that affect the Gla carboxylated domains have been identified in these proteins—as an example, this article describing a variant in a Chinese patient where a glutamine at

VKCFD Type I and Type II Although we are only talking about the clotting and bone effects of this condition, take a look at the reference sited for these studies and you will find out that the list of Vitamin K dependent carboxylated proteins numbers 7 blood clotting proteins, 2 bone proteins, and 6 "other" proteins. What do these other proteins do and how do the symptoms of VKCFD relate to lack of carboxylation on these other proteins?

TABLE 10.2: Genetic Conditions of Blood Clotting and associated factors. All condition are described in the text with further information found on the Genetic's Home Reference web page: https://ghr.nlm.nih.gov/

Genetic conditions of Blood Clotting	Gene involved	Phenotype
Vitamin K-dependent coagulation factor deficiency TypeI	Gamma Glutamyl Carboxylase	Bleeding Bruising Skeletal deformities
Vitamin K-dependent coagulation factor deficiency TypeII	Epoxide Reductase	Bleeding Bruising Skeletal deformities
Individual blood factor hemophilia	Each bloodf actor e.g. IX, II	Bleeding Bruising Some due to inadequate carboxylation

position 27 in the protein was altered to a valine by a DNA mutation in Factor IX [38]. Since the glutamine residue was no longer at position 27, the protein was not properly carboxylated, and the individual was a hemophiliac [38].

Finally let's consider the dietary and genetic conditions affecting immunity. As you hopefully read in the appendix of the textbook, zinc deficiency is associated with lower overall immunity, and at this point you should understand why. Basically, to reiterate, zinc is needed as a structural cofactor both for thymulin, and for the zinc-finger transcription factors that mediate responses to retinoic acid and calcitonin. We've already discussed the need for vitamin A in mucosal immune response, and vitamin D for immune suppression (and autoimmunity being associated with low vitamin D). Now take a look at Table 10.3, which shows that genetic variations in ZnT8, a zinc transporter expressed only in the pancreas, is associated with type I Autoimmune-associated Diabetes [39]. This makes some sense—as it would be the local pancreatic zinc needed by zinc-dependent transcription factors that would be affected by these mutations. However, while variants in vitamin A associated genes have not (yet) been associated with immune status (at least to this author's knowledge and an extensive PubMed search), variants in vitamin D-associated genes have been found in several conditions of autoimmune disease (examples [4, 27]), Table 10.3.

The vitamin A, D, and zinc deficiencies affect acquired immunity, but there are conditions that affect innate immunity, or our phagocytes. For example, while B3 deficiency does not appear to overtly affect NADPH oxidase, which is actually a

TABLE 10.3: Genetic conditions affecting immune cells. All conditions are described in the text with further information found in the Genetics Home Reference web page: https://ghr.nlm.nih.gov/

Genetic condition affecting Immunity	Gene involved	Phenotype
Type I Diabetes	Zinc transporter ZnT8	Autoimmunity
Autoimmune Diseases (multiple types)	Vitamin D pathway genes	Autoimmunity
Chronic Granulomatous Disease	(NADPH Oxidase complex) cytochrome b-245 Subunit (CYBB) Cytochrome b-245 alpha (CYBA) (flavoprotein) Neutrophil cytosolic factor 1 (NCF1) Neutrophil cytosolic factor 2 (NCF2) Neutrophil cytosolic factor 4 (NCF4)	Increased Infections
Myeloperoxidase Deficiency	Myeloperoxidase (MPO)	Staph and Yeast Infections

complex of proteins, mutations in some of the protein subunits affect the ability to bind or enzymatically modify NADPH [40] (Table 10.3). Similarly, some variants in the myeloperoxidase gene (MPO) affect heme binding in the protein—leading to little or no peroxidase activity and impaired neutrophil function [41] (Print (Table 10.3).

In summary, major deficiency (and toxicity) of micronutrients needed by the various systems in our blood lead to dysfunction—and this can be caused by dietary factors, or genetic factors (or perhaps a combination of both). Regardless, the blood and immune systems are needed throughout the entire body to monitor infections, repair tears in vessels, and send oxygen to our tissues. Keeping this system in peak performance will keep all of our organs and body systems working well too.

CHAPTER SUMMARY

From stem cell proliferation to killing by our immune cells, our blood cells perform a multitude of functions, and require many different micronutrients. Keeping these micronutrient needs in balance within our diets, and if needed, through supplements helps to ensure that all of our tissues reap the benefits of blood!

- Hematopoietic stem cells maintain the ability to make new blood cells throughout our lives, but to do this require many different micronutrients for proliferation and differentiation processes.
- Iron metabolism utilizes several iron-containing proteins to do "double-duty" in iron transport, oxidation/reduction, and iron stores sensing.
- The clotting process requires vitamin K as a cofactor for gamma glutamyl carboxylation, which prepares clotting factors for calcium binding. Calcium and magnesium balance within the blood plasma are also critical.
- Our innate and adaptive immune system responses require both fat and water-soluble vitamins, and minerals such as zinc and iron.

POINTS TO PONDER

- What other enzymes have iron response elements in their RNA like ferritin and transferrin do? Are they all regulated by aconitase?
- Check out the current literature on vitamins A and D as possible treatments for cancer. There are opposing opinions with different cancers either benefitting or being prevented by different supplements. What do you think are the reasons for these differences?
- Can you think of a reason for taking vitamin C for blood vessel health? What about vitamin E?

References

1. Hooda, J., A. Shah, and L. Zhang. (2014). Heme, an essential nutrient from dietary proteins, critically impacts diverse physiological and pathological processes. *Nutrients* **6**(3): 1080–1102.
2. Whitlon, D.S., J.A. Sadowski, and J.W. Suttie. (1978). Mechanism of coumarin action: Significance of vitamin K epoxide reductase inhibition. *Biochemistry* **17**(8): 1371–1377.
3. Gunshin, H., et al. (2005). Cybrd1 (duodenal cytochrome b) is not necessary for dietary iron absorption in mice. *Blood* **106**(8): 2879–2883.
4. Hussein, A.G., R.H. Mohamed, and A.A. Alghobashy. (2012). Synergism of CYP2R1 and CYP27B1 polymorphisms and susceptibility to type 1 diabetes in Egyptian children. *Cell Immunol* **279**(1): 42–45.
5. Drakesmith, H., E. Nemeth, and T. Ganz. (2015). Ironing out Ferroportin. *Cell Metab* **22**(5): 777–787.
6. Lane, D.J. and D.R. Richardson. (2014). The active role of vitamin C in mammalian iron metabolism: much more than just enhanced iron absorption! *Free Radic Biol Med* **75**: 69–83.
7. Zhang, D.L., M.C. Ghosh, and T.A. Rouault. (2014). The physiological functions of iron regulatory proteins in iron homeostasis - an update. *Front Pharmacol* **5**: 124.
8. Bradley, J.M., N.E. Le Brun, and G.R. Moore. (2016). Ferritins: Furnishing proteins with iron. *J Biol Inorg Chem* **21**(1): 13–28.
9. Koury, M.J. and P. Ponka. (2004). New insights into erythropoiesis: The roles of folate, vitamin B12, and iron. *Annu Rev Nutr* **24**: 105–131.
10. Zhang, A.S., et al. (2003). Mechanisms of HFE-induced regulation of iron homeostasis: Insights from the W81A HFE mutation. *Proc Natl Acad Sci U S A* **100**(16): 9500–9505.
11. Bonaventura, C., et al. (2013).Molecular controls of the oxygenation and redox reactions of hemoglobin. *Antioxid Redox Signal* **18**(17): 2298–2313.
12. Long, A.T., et al. (2016). Contact system revisited: An interface between inflammation, coagulation, and innate immunity. *J Thromb Haemost* **14**(3): 427–437.
13. Gajsiewicz, J.M. and J.H. Morrissey. (2015). Structure-function relationship of the interaction between tissue factor and Factor VIIa. *Semin Thromb Hemost* **41**(7): 682–690.
14. Bandyopadhyay, P.K. (2008).Vitamin K-dependent gamma-glutamylcarboxylation: An ancient posttranslational modification. *Vitam Horm* **78**: 157–184.
15. Stalker, T.J., et al. (2012). Platelet signaling. *Handb Exp Pharmacol* (210): 59–85.
16. Huntsman, R.G., B.A. Hurn, and H. Lehmann. (1960). Paradoxical effect of magnesium ions on blood coagulation. *Nature* **185**: 852.
17. Huntsman, R.G., B.A. Hurn, and H. Lehmann. (1960). Observations on the effect of magnesium on blood coagulation. *J Clin Pathol* **13**: 99–101.

18. Card, D.J., et al. (2014). Vitamin K metabolism: current knowledge and future research. *Mol Nutr Food Res* **58**(8): 1590–1600.

19. Green, H.N. and E. Mellanby. (1928). Vitamin a as an anti-infective agent. *Br Med J* **2**(3537): 691–696.

20. Bono, M.R., et al. (2016). Retinoic acid as a modulator of T cell immunity. *Nutrients* **8**(6).

21. Mora, J.R. and U.H. von Andrian. (2009). Role of retinoic acid in the imprinting of gut-homing IgA-secreting cells. *Semin Immunol* **21**(1): 28–35.

22. Mazzaferro, S. and M. Pasquali. (2016). Vitamin D: A dynamic molecule. How relevant might the dynamism for a vitamin be? *Nephrol Dial Transplant* **31**(1): 23–30.

23. Hewison, M., et al. (2007). Extra-renal 25-hydroxyvitamin D3-1alpha-hydroxylase in human health and disease. *J Steroid Biochem Mol Biol* **103**(3–5): 316–321.

24. White, J.H. (2012). Vitamin D metabolism and signaling in the immune system. *Rev Endocr Metab Disord* **13**(1): 21–29.

25. Danner, O.K., et al. (2016). Vitamin D3 suppresses Class II invariant chain peptide expression on activated B-lymphocytes: A plausible mechanism for downregulation of acute inflammatory conditions. *J Nutr Metab* **2016**: 4280876.

26. Zhang, H.L. and J. Wu. (2010). Role of vitamin D in immune responses and autoimmune diseases, with emphasis on its role in multiple sclerosis. *Neurosci Bull* **26**(6): 445–454.

27. Eloranta, J.J., et al. (2011). Association of a common vitamin D-binding protein polymorphism with inflammatory bowel disease. *Pharmacogenet Genomics* **21**(9): 559–564.

28. Laird, E., et al. (2014). Vitamin D deficiency is associated with inflammation in older Irish adults. *J Clin Endocrinol Metab* **99**(5): 1807–1815.

29. Mansournia, N., et al. (2014). The association between serum 25OHD levels and hypothyroid Hashimoto's thyroiditis. *J Endocrinol Invest* **37**(5): 473–476.

30. Kroner Jde, C., A. Sommer, and M. Fabri. (2015). Vitamin D every day to keep the infection away? *Nutrients* **7**(6): 4170–4188.

31. Hemila, H. and E. Chalker. (2013). Vitamin C for preventing and treating the common cold. *Cochrane Database Syst Rev* (1): CD000980.

32. Hemila, H., et al. (2016). Zinc acetate lozenges for treating the common cold: An individual patient data meta-analysis. *Br J Clin Pharmacol* **82**(5): 1393–1398.

33. Prasad, A.S. (2008). Clinical, immunological, anti-inflammatory and antioxidant roles of zinc. *Exp Gerontol* **43**(5): 370–377.

34. Kalyanaraman, B. (2013). Teaching the basics of redox biology to medical and graduate students: Oxidants, antioxidants and disease mechanisms. *Redox Biol* **1**: 244–257.

35. Gozzelino, R. and P. Arosio. (2016). Iron homeostasis in health and disease. *Int J Mol Sci* **17**(1).

36. Lippi, G. and M. Franchini. (2011). Vitamin K in neonates: Facts and myths. *Blood Transfus* **9**(1): 4–9.
37. Napolitano, M., G. Mariani, and M. Lapecorella. (2010). Hereditary combined deficiency of the vitamin K-dependent clotting factors. *Orphanet J Rare Dis* **5**: 21.
38. Wang, N.S., et al. (1990). Factor IX Chongqing: A new mutation in the calcium-binding domain of factor IX resulting in severe hemophilia B. *Thromb Haemost* **63**(1): 24–26.
39. Yi, B., G. Huang, and Z. Zhou. (2016). Different role of zinc transporter 8 between type 1 diabetes mellitus and type 2 diabetes mellitus. *J Diabetes Investig* **7**(4): 459–465.
40. Segal, B.H., et al. (2000). Genetic, biochemical, and clinical features of chronic granulomatous disease. *Medicine (Baltimore)* **79**(3): 170–200.
41. Romano, M., et al. (1997). Biochemical and molecular characterization of hereditary myeloperoxidase deficiency. *Blood* **90**(10): 4126–4134.

Blood Micronutrients and Enzymes

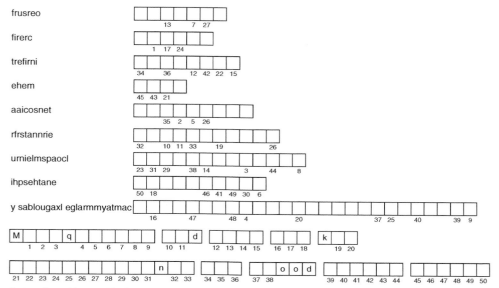

frusreo

⬚⬚⬚⬚⬚⬚⬚
     13   7 27

firerc

⬚⬚⬚⬚⬚⬚
1 17 24

trefirni

⬚⬚⬚⬚⬚⬚⬚⬚
34   36   12 42 22 15

ehem

⬚⬚⬚⬚
45 43 21

aaicosnet

⬚⬚⬚⬚⬚⬚⬚⬚
   35 2 5 26

rfrstannrie

⬚⬚⬚⬚⬚⬚⬚⬚⬚⬚
32   10 11 33   19   26

urnielmspaocl

⬚⬚⬚⬚⬚⬚⬚⬚⬚⬚⬚⬚
23 31 29   38 14   3   44   8

ihpsehtane

⬚⬚⬚⬚⬚⬚⬚⬚⬚⬚
50 18   46 41 49 30 6

y sablougaxl eglarmmyatmac

⬚⬚⬚⬚⬚⬚⬚⬚⬚⬚⬚⬚⬚⬚⬚⬚⬚⬚⬚⬚⬚⬚
  16   47   48 4   20   37 25   40   39 9

M			q								d							k	
1	2	3		4	5	6	7	8	9	10	11	12	13	14	15	16	17	18	19	20

										n						o	o	d											
21	22	23	24	25	26	27	28	29	30	31		32	33		34	35	36		37	38		39	40	41	42	43	44		45	46	47	48	49	50

Instructions: Unscramble the words that are either blood micronutrient forms or enzymes involved in blood clotting or blood formation. Put the numbers in the boxes to form a phrase, which is meaningful to the blood system.

NOTES

CHAPTER 11

Skin: Structure, Function, and Wound Healing

Table of Contents

The skin, or integumentary system is the largest organ in the body, basically providing an external wrap, holding in all of the other organs in our body. Skin serves as a site for vitamin D synthesis via photoisomerization of 7-dehydrocholesterol (see Chapter 8), and as a place of water exchange and temperature homeostasis through sweating (see Chapter 7). In this chapter, we will examine the roles of the micronutrients that act directly on keratinocytes in the epidermis, fibroblasts in the dermis/hypodermis, and hair follicles that protrude through all of the layers. As shown in Figure 11.1, the three layers make up the organ called "skin," and contain proliferating and differentiating keratinocyte cells, as well as specialized melanocytes, hair follicles, sweat, and sebaceous glands. The skin care cream/supplement industry is estimated to grow to a market share of $154 billion by the year 2021 [2], and so we will end our chapter discussing what current research tells us about whether supplements can alleviate visible skin conditions such as psoriasis, acne, wrinkles, and hair loss.

VITAMINS A AND D, WITH THYROID HORMONE AND BIOTIN

The skin, like all other actively metabolizing organs, requires the energy system, cell signaling machinery, and blood and immune systems for full function. Please refer back to those systems again and consider their roles in the cells of the skin. There are also micronutrients that are uniquely needed for skin keratinocyte proliferation, differentiation, and for the production of extracellular matrix proteins, which constitutes the dermis (next section). For the keratinocytes, which, depending on their differentiation state produce the specialized keratins that make up the different layers of the epidermis, we need the gene regulatory actions of vitamins A, D, and thyroid hormone (iodine)—all of which require zinc for their zinc-finger receptors. Let's look at each of these more closely.

Vitamin A—an elixir for your skin?

While the vitamer retinoic acid (cis- and trans- forms) and its receptors (RAR and RXR) undoubtedly regulate multiple genes in keratinocytes, the most cell-specific of these are likely the different keratin genes expressed in skin and hair. The keratin protein family comprise up to 54 different proteins, each with a unique cellular expression [3, 4]. The proteins form a helical filament that

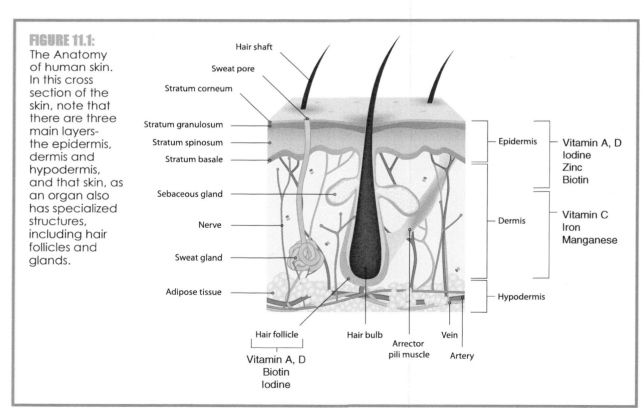

FIGURE 11.1:
The Anatomy of human skin. In this cross section of the skin, note that there are three main layers- the epidermis, dermis and hypodermis, and that skin, as an organ also has specialized structures, including hair follicles and glands.

© ksenia_bravo/Shutterstock.com

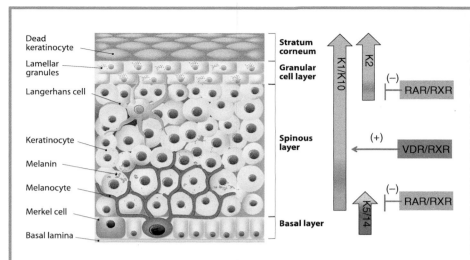

FIGURE 11.2: The Skin Epidermis. The epidermis has four main layers, and includes some specialized cells, such as melanocytes (for skin color), merkel cells (for touch reception) and Langerhans cells (for immune surveillance). Keratinocytes make up the majority of the cells in the epidermis. The keratin expression profiles were added using information in a paper by Torma (2011) and Ramat et al., (2009).

provides structural integrity, impermeability, and torsion strength to skin, hair, and nails (as well as claws, scales, horns, and other structures that humans don't have, but other animals do). As shown in Figure 11.2, different keratins are produced in different layers of the epidermis, and interestingly, while you (and I) might have thought that the RXR/RAR transcription factor would increase expression of the keratins in different levels, in this (simplified) version of the skin and keratin expression, retinoic acid on its own mainly serves to reduce the expression of specific keratins (such as K2, K5, and K14), which acts in promoting proliferation of the basal layers, and reducing thickness of the epithelial layers [3]. This scenario makes sense when you consider the condition of hypervitaminosis A, which is characterized by hyperplasia (too much proliferation), or hypovitaminosis A, which is characterized by rough, dry skin (too much differentiation). Technically, this all gets complicated by the fact the *vitamer type* of retinoic acid matters, since we know that all-trans retinoic acid is specific for RAR, while RXR can bind to 9-cis retinoic acid, but not all-trans retinoic acid. Gene expression pathways are complicated, and while the description above is likely over-simplified, for the purpose of this section, it is true. One might consider the rest of what is shown in Figure 11.2, namely that when vitamin A isn't turning keratin genes off, it is working with vitamin D to turn them on (i.e., keratins 1 and 10)[3, 4]. The shift to vitamin D-mediated gene expression is one of reduced proliferation and increased differentiation. Let's talk for a bit on vitamin D synthesis in the skin, which we visited in Chapter 8, but need to add now.

Sunny vitamin D synthesis

It turns out that most of the circulating vitamin D (25-hydroxy-D3 and 1,25-hydroxy-D3) cannot actually reach the uppermost, or even the middle layers of the epidermis by simple diffusion through capillaries into the keratinocytes [5].

So how does vitamin D get in? It doesn't have to, because the skin is the only organ that can synthesize vitamin D, *de novo*, from 7-dehydrocholesterol. As you learned in Chapter 8 (Figure 8.1) cholecalciferol is transported out to circulate to the liver and kidney for its two-step conversion to active calcitriol, all the while bound to the vitamin D binding protein (DBP) while in circulation. But in the skin, some of the cholecalciferol hangs around, and is converted to calcidiol, and then calcitriol, locally, by the actions of the 25- and 1-alpha hydroxylase enzymes—which are produced by the keratinocytes [5, 6]. In summary, with this local synthesis, the skin has its needed vitamin D locally, and does not have to wait around for production to occur in another organ, assuming you get enough sunlight and B3 so that the enzymes have substrate and coenzyme to work with.

Thyroid hormone—combating dry, itchy skin

One of the first signs of an abnormal thyroid axis is dry, scaly, and itchy skin (Figure 11.3). Indeed, multiple studies have demonstrated that thyroid hormone, acting through the thyroid hormone receptors (THR), in concert with retinoic acid and RXR can directly regulate keratin genes[7]. Specifically, keratins 5, 10, and 14 are downregulated in the presence of thyroid hormone and retinoic acid in epithelial cells [8], and considering Figure 11.2, this suggests a reduction of overall proliferation and increased differentiation to mature keratinocytes, similar to the effect of retinoic acid alone. In addition, thyroid hormone directly stimulates proliferation of dermal fibroblasts and the expression of collagen mRNA [7], which may make skin appear "plumper." The effect on collagen synthesis and overall epidermal differentiation certainly appears to play a role in wound healing, with topical application of T3 promoting improved healing in rat studies, and oral T3 improving the appearance of scars in humans [7].

Biotin—the skin, nail, and hair vitamin

Biotin deficiency is not usually a problem in modern society—most individuals get sufficient amounts from the diet, because the requirement of 30 μg/day can be achieved with a well-balanced diet of fruits, vegetables,

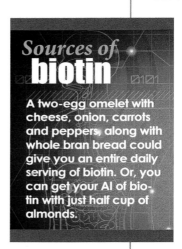

Sources of biotin

A two-egg omelet with cheese, onion, carrots and peppers, along with whole bran bread could give you an entire daily serving of biotin. Or, you can get your AI of biotin with just half cup of almonds.

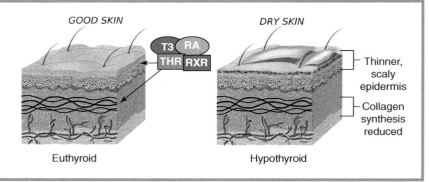

FIGURE 11.3: Thyroid hormone and skin thickness. Thyroid hormone through its receptor, along with retinoic acid and RXR, increases epidermal thickness (especially the stratum corneum), and healthy skin differentiation. It also increases collagen synthesis in the dermis.

GOOD SKIN — T3 RA / THR RXR — Euthyroid

DRY SKIN — Thinner, scaly epidermis — Collagen synthesis reduced — Hypothyroid

© Cessna152/Shutterstock.com

and lean proteins. However, over-the-counter supplements containing biotin are still a hot item, mainly because of the claim of biotin being the hair and skin vitamin. What is the evidence, and how does it work? There are four major carboxylases in energy metabolism pathways that require biotinylation for activity: acetyl CoA carboxylase, which is needed to produce malonyl CoA, pyruvate carboxylase, which is needed in gluconeogenesis, propionyl CoA carboxylase, which produces methylmalonyl CoA after the metabolism of fatty acids, allowing the byproducts to be used (after several more metabolic steps) in the TCA cycle, and finally methylcrotonoyl CoA carboxylase, needed for leucine metabolism. While we have not talked about all of the specific pathways these carboxylases are in, suffice to know for this chapter that the biotinylated carboxylases are involved in every pathway—carbohydrate, fat, and protein—needed for normal metabolism, especially in fast growing tissues such as the skin. Thus, biotin, and the activity of the enzyme holocarboxylase synthetase, which adds biotinylation to the carboxylases, is essential (Figure 11.4). Of note, while we don't need a lot of a biotin in our diets, our bodies ensure that biotin is readily available by recycling proteins that contain biotin using the enzyme biotinidase (Figure 11.4). Also of note, histones can be biotinylated, and although some of the published data is being criticized based on the techniques used at the time which may have lead to false positives, some biotinlyation is still detected using current technologies and thus something to consider [9]. As we saw in Chapter 5, secondary

Speaking of eggs…

The need for biotin wasn't discovered until researchers figured out what caused "egg-white injury"—a condition of severe dermatitis, hair loss with lack of muscle coordination. It turns out that avidin, a component of egg whites, binds irreversibly to biotin, basically causing a biotin deficiency when too many raw egg whites are consumed. So, get your biotin from cooked eggs, not raw eggs.

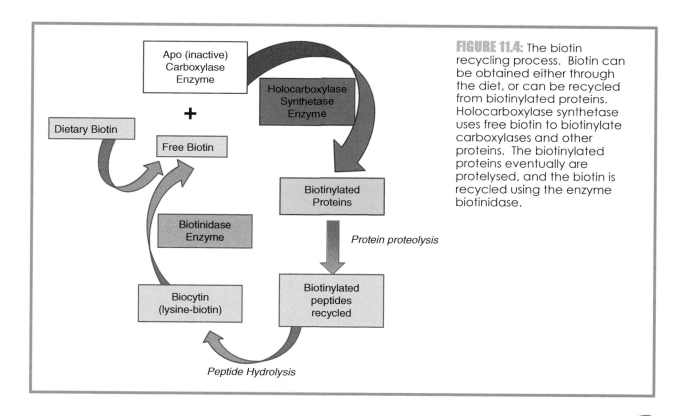

FIGURE 11.4: The biotin recycling process. Biotin can be obtained either through the diet, or can be recycled from biotinylated proteins. Holocarboxylase synthetase uses free biotin to biotinylate carboxylases and other proteins. The biotinylated proteins eventually are protelysed, and the biotin is recycled using the enzyme biotinidase.

modification of proteins, including histones, can affect their normal function. Thus, it is possible that biotinylation of histones can lead to changes in gene regulation. In skin, changes in biotin levels have the potential to affect biotin-mediated gene regulation. Indeed, data coming from a lab whose results are not considered to be in question show that in intestinal cells, the biotin receptor-SMVT is under biotinylated histone control [10]. This is an interesting story, because as the level of biotin increases in the cell, so does the level of biotinylation at histones located within the SMVT gene, causing reduced expression. As biotin levels drop, so do the levels of biotinylated histones around SMVT, and expression of SMVT gene and protein increase, bringing more biotin into the cells[10]. However, there have as yet been no additional reports of biotinlyation of SMVT in skin, or any skin-specific biotinylation of histones in other skin-specific genes. Based on this, for now we can only speculate that gene regulatory activity is modulated by biotin—and that this may be the reason why biotin in "the skin vitamin." However, the most efficacious role for biotin is in fatty acid, protein, and carbohydrate metabolism as mediated through the biotinylated carboxylases in these pathways, which are important for proliferating cells such as keratinocytes.

PSORIASIS, AND ACNE—CAN SUPPLEMENTS HELP?

Let's end this section by looking at the large number of products for skin care that seem to target conditions such as psoriasis and acne—and ask the question, can micronutrient supplementation help with any of these more visible conditions of our skin?

First, let's look at psoriasis. One of the best-known treatments for this condition is UV-light or "phototreatment." Let's think about why this treatment might work—psoriasis is characterized by dry, itchy skin that is also inflamed. At a cellular level, there is hyperproliferation of the keratinocytes, without proper differentiation. Most of the phototreatments used UV-B light, rather than UV-A light, and although different wavelengths are used, most fall within the same wavelengths 295–300 nm that is optimal for the synthesis of previtamin D [11]. Are you thinking what I'm thinking (and the referenced paper proposes . . .) . . . that phototherapy may actually be stimulating local vitamin D synthesis right where the skin needs it. In fact, increases in vitamin D after phototherapy have been documented [11]. We know that calcitriol promotes keratinocyte differentiation, and that psoriasis patients generation show lack of differentiation—so it makes sense that treatment of the area with more vitamin D would work. Does systemic or topical vitamin D treatment also work? In a word, YES [11]. However, topical vitamin D creams/ ointments are preferred so that only the region that needs it is treated, eliminating the possibility of vitamin D toxicity.

Let's move on to acne. Topical retinoids—such as tretinoin and isotretinoin are marketed under trade names such as Retin-A™ or Accutane™, are approved treatment for severe acne. Acne is a condition of the sebaceous glands, and the most common skin condition of adolescence—affecting approximately 80% of teenagers at some time in their teen years [12]. Topical retinoids are thought to work by increasing skin turnover, and this makes sense, as vitamin A would stimulate proliferation of the basal layer of cells—stimulating more skin/keratinocyte proliferation. However, the caution with this treatment is that while the skin is the target—these are given as topical preparations, there is a chance for birth defects if individuals become pregnant when on these treatments. Therefore all females on topical retinoids for the treatment of acne are coprescribed birth control.

There are other skin conditions, such as UV exposed skin, dermatitis, and age spots, and some of these also respond to micronutrient supplements, while others don't. Rather than go through a long list of these, I'll leave it up to you to investigate conditions you or one of your family members are interested in.

THE DERMIS AND HYPODERMIS

The dermis and hypodermis are sometimes overlooked in skin health, but are important to the overall thickness of our protective barrier, as well as a place where the hair follicles and sweat glands reside. Hormones, growth factors, vitamins, and minerals that are not synthesized in the epidermis, must also diffuse through the dermis from the capillaries that are located in the hypodermis and dermis. The main cell type of the dermis is the dermal fibroblast, which as we saw above, can be stimulated by thyroid hormone to proliferate and produce collagen. Recall from Chapter 8, that collagen mRNA is translated into collagen protein strands which undergo vitamin C and iron-dependent hydroxylation for formation of the triple helical strands that represent the mature collagen fibril that makes up the extracellular matrix of the dermis and in bone (Figure 8.6). As early as 1953, a study using guinea pigs (which you should remember the need to have vitamin C in their diet, as they have a GULO gene mutation) on a vitamin C sufficient versus vitamin C deficient diet indicated that vitamin C was needed for fibroblast proliferation and over all wound healing [13]. Subsequent studies in humans have shown mixed results, and mainly have examined vitamin C in its antioxidant, rather than coenzymatic roles [14].

Wrinkles—how can we prevent or remove them?

From young skin problems to those of the older group, we need to talk about wrinkles. As you can see from Figure 11.5, wrinkles derive from both dermal and epidermal issues. Collagen and elastin fibrils are broken or degraded in the dermis, while the epidermis sags, and may be thinner with aging. In an article appropriately titled "Old Skin," Dr Savin, the author, describes the epidermis of young and old skin that was not exposed to Sun as similar, with the older individuals have a slight thinning overall with the stratum corneum thickening slightly. He goes on to discuss the fact that the "elastic recoil" is lost in old skin so that it no longer "snaps back in place"

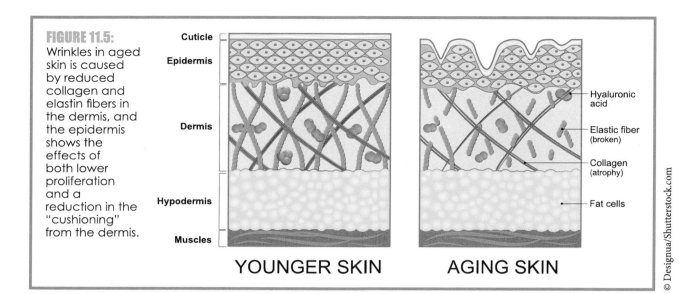

FIGURE 11.5:
Wrinkles in aged skin is caused by reduced collagen and elastin fibers in the dermis, and the epidermis shows the effects of both lower proliferation and a reduction in the "cushioning" from the dermis.

Cuticle
Epidermis
Dermis
Hypodermis
Muscles

Hyaluronic acid
Elastic fiber (broken)
Collagen (atrophy)
Fat cells

YOUNGER SKIN   AGING SKIN

© Designua/Shutterstock.com

[15]. This makes sense when looking at wrinkled versus young skin (Figure 11.5). Given that no one wants old-looking skin (or at least cosmetic companies believe this to be true), wrinkle creams are everywhere on pharmacy shelves—so what's in them and do they work? Some creams have vitamin A derivatives—similar to those found in acne treatments. These seem to be marketed toward "photodamaged" wrinkled skin—or skin that has crevices, yellowed/rough skin, or bleached skin, due to sun damage. While there is some evidence that the creams containing tretoinin, which is also used to treat acne, may work, the overall evidence is weak for major effects of vitamin A derivatives such as retinyl acetate or retinyl palmitate on damaged skin [16]. Other creams containing topical vitamin C have also been suggested, and from a biological standpoint it might make sense—can we repair collagen in the dermis? In human dermal fibroblast cultures (these are the cell types that make collagen in our dermis), treatment with vitamin C in fibroblast obtained from young individuals (3–8 day old) and older individuals (> 78 years old) increased proliferation rates—in other words, with extra vitamin C, the 78 year old fibroblasts grew faster (although not as fast as an eight year old fibroblasts) [17]—amazing! The ex vivo treatment (i.e., in a petri dish) also increased total collagen synthesis by 2-fold in both young and old fibroblasts [17]. So could vitamin C work on skin still attached to a human—it seems a possibility. In a more recent study, serum vitamin C levels were inversely correlated with wrinkle appearance—in other words, individuals that had enough dietary vitamin C were less likely to have wrinkles [18]. Furthermore, a newer study still showed that a drink containing vitamin C, vitamin E, lycopene (a vitamin A vitamer), and other nutraceuticals appeared to reduce the depth of wrinkles and to increase collagen deposition in the dermis [19]. This is an interesting formulation as it has both vitamin A and vitamin C—perhaps both are needed for full wrinkle ablation. In this area, more work needs to be done to prove that the vitamin C or vitamin A (or combo) creams really are efficacious for treating or preventing wrinkles.

Wound healing and often overlooked mineral, manganese

Students often confuse manganese with magnesium—similar names, and both are minerals with a +2 oxidation state—even Wikipedia states in the manganese entry "Manganese (Mn) is not to be confused with Magnesium (Mg)" [20]. As we will see in the nervous system, there are even some enzymes that can use either Mg or Mn as a cofactor. However, Mn is its own mineral, and any chapter on skin should not leave out the important role of Mn as a cofactor for the enzyme prolidase. Prolidase is a dipepsidase, which means it cleaves a two amino acid peptide from a protein undergoing degradation (recycling by the cell). The catch is, that that dipepsidase only cleaves dipeptides that have a proline at the end (Figure 11.6). Prolidase utilizes Mn in its substrate-binding core to hold the dipeptide in place and facilitates cleavage. So why is prolidase unique? Because while many endo- and exopeptidases can chop up proteins, only prolidase can chop up dipeptides that contain proline or hydroyxproline [21]. This means that to recycle a protein like collagen, you must have prolidase around. In a genetic condition called "prolidase deficiency," wound healing is impaired, likely due to the inability to both degrade the broken collagen chains, and to recycle the proline within them to make new collagen during the healing process [21]. Patients with this condition have ulcerated skin lesions that do not heal properly. Interestingly from a biological standpoint, prolidase activity is also associated with some cancers, perhaps as they begin to degrade the extracellular matrix to metastasize. There is the possibility that blocking prolidase activity, perhaps through manganese deficiency could prevent metastasis in these cases [21].

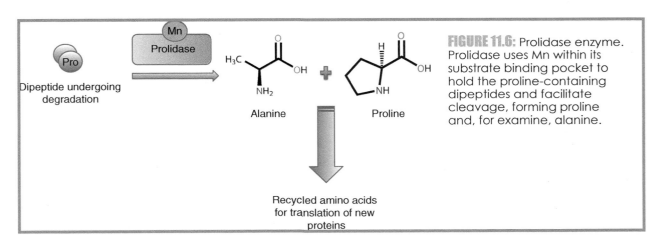

FIGURE 11.6: Prolidase enzyme. Prolidase uses Mn within its substrate binding pocket to hold the proline-containing dipeptides and facilitate cleavage, forming proline and, for examine, alanine.

© Leonid Andronov/Shutterstock.com

HAIR

Hair—some have it, some try to get rid of it, and some try to get more of it. As we all know, there are multiple products that claim to increase, decrease, or remove hair. Shampoos contain "keratin protein" to increase thickness of the hair-but do they work? Well, this section will not try to critique shampoo manufacturers on that point-you can make your own decision there. But we will discuss what vitamins and minerals specifically stimulate (or reduce) hair growth, at the level of the hair follicle.

We've already discussed biotin—the hair, nail, and skin vitamin, in the context of the skin, and the same functions of biotin there appear to be for hair (and nails) as well. The author herself took biotin supplements for a while and could see noticeable improvements in her nails (strength and length) and hair (growth). A recent analysis of biotin serum levels in women complaining of hair loss found that only 13% of women with hair loss had optimal circulating biotin levels—49% were in the suboptimal and 38% were in the deficient range [22]. Biotin supplementation has been helpful for patients with brittle nails in multiple studies [23]. So let's get on the biotin bandwagon!! Biotin is cheap to buy, and has no upper toxicity limit, so technically, you can take it at a high level for a long time with little to no side effects. You can try it for a while, but this author does not recommend for everyone—again, you probably should only take it if you know that you are getting suboptimal levels of dietary biotin. This is why she stopped taking it—remember that biotin can affect gene expression throughout the body, so it probably should be not "taken lightly."

Did you KNOW?

Different countries have different levels of supplementation for infant formulas. In Japan, some infant formulas are not supplemented with biotin, and there is documented biotin deficiency in that country [1].

Vitamin D supplementation seems to have the most scientific evidence behind it for hair follicle health (Figure 11.1). In a study from 2012, treatment of dermal papillae cells (which are found at the base of the follicle) with calcitriol for up to 72 hours can induce follicular "hair" growth in culture, and if those cells are transplanted onto rats, more hair follicles grow out of the calcitriol-treated cells than the nontreated cells [24]. So, what is vitamin D doing? Inducing keratin genes among other things! Studies have shown that vitamin D treatment can induce keratin 15—the hair "regeneration" keratin, as well as a multiple of other keratins and signaling pathways—all leading to hair/follicle growth (Figure 11.1) [3, 25]. In fact, females with low circulating levels of vitamin D are more likely to present clinically with female pattern hair loss [26], and individuals with rickets often show hair loss as one of the symptoms [27].

Fun FACT

Although we don't always think about the hair in our ears—the "inner hair cells" which are needed for hearing also require TH for growth and functioning. These are actually specialized nerve cells, but are hair-like structures.

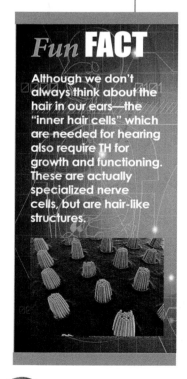

One of the symptoms of hypothyroidism is also thinning hair or lower than normal hair growth. In fact, like in the epidermis, thyroid hormone also modulates hair growth by directly stimulating keratin 15 gene expression and the proliferation of hair follicle cells [25]. This means that hair growth requires iodine, as a component of thyroid hormone, and retinoic acid, as a needed heterodimer for the thyroid hormone receptor (**Figure 11.1**). A new thyroid hormone analogue, "Eprotirome" promotes hair growth in cultured human scalp hair, suggesting it may be a treatment for baldness, alopecia, or other hair conditions [28]. A mouse model lacking both types of the main thyroid hormone receptors (TRα and TRβ), while not completely bald, do show slowed hair growth after dilapidation with reduced follicular cell proliferation overall [29].

To summarize, hair, like skin require many of the same micronutrients, which induce different keratins and stimulate follicular cell proliferation so that we have hair where we want it, and hopefully not stimulate hair growth where we don't want it.

CHAPTER SUMMARY

The maintenance of youthful, healthy skin is not only desired by many but also necessary for this organs role as a protective barrier for our bodies. Micronutrients play a key role in maintaining the continued renewal of skin, hair, and nails throughout our lifetime.

- Vitamin A and its derivatives work to maintain basal cell proliferation. It may also be useful for acne and wrinkle prevention. Vitamin A works with vitamin D and thyroid hormone to improve skin at all layers.
- Vitamin D is needed for differentiation of the keratinocytes, and for hair keratin synthesis. The skin also serves as the site for de novo synthesis of vitamin C from 7-DHC.
- The direct role for biotin in skin is likely through energy metabolism or biotinylation and regulation of gene expression, but more work is needed to understand the latter mechanism.
- Vitamin C, along with iron as a cofactor, promotes collagen triple helix formation in the dermis. This provides the dermis with "cushioning" and may be important in the prevention of wrinkles.
- Manganese is needed for collagen recycling during wound healing.

POINTS TO PONDER

- What other skin conditions might respond to micronutrient intervention? Are any conditions caused by too much of a micronutrient?
- There are genetic conditions that can lead to hair loss and skin conditions, and for the most part we did not discuss them in this chapter. Look in the literature and see if you can find any genetic skin, hair, or nail conditions related to or requiring the micronutrients that we discussed.
- Biotin is the hair, skin, and nail vitamin—just look at any bottle of biotin supplement and you'll see that or similar wording. What genes do you think might have targeted biotinylation of histones and how would you do this sort of experiment?

References

1. Wakabayashi, K., et al. (2016). Serum biotin in Japanese children: Enzyme-linked immunosorbent assay measurement. *Pediatr Int*, **58**(9): 872–876.
2. Trefis.com. (2014). *Size of the global skin care market from 2012 to 2021 (in billion U.S. dollars)*. The Statistics Portal. Available from: Retrieved October 28, 2016, from https://www.statista.com/statistics/254612/global-skin-care-market-size/.
3. Ramot, Y., et al. (2009). Endocrine controls of keratin expression. *Bioessays*, **31**(4): 389–399.
4. Torma, H. (2011). Regulation of keratin expression by retinoids. *Dermatoendocrinol*, **3**(3): 136–140.
5. Lehmann, B. (2005). The vitamin D3 pathway in human skin and its role for regulation of biological processes. *Photochem Photobiol*, **81**(6): 1246–1251.
6. Lehmann, B. (2009). Role of the vitamin D3 pathway in healthy and diseased skin–facts, contradictions and hypotheses. *Exp Dermatol*, **18**(2): 97–108.
7. Safer, J.D. (2011). Thyroid hormone action on skin. *Dermatoendocrinol*, 2011. **3**(3): 211–215.
8. Ohtsuki, M., et al. (1992). Regulation of epidermal keratin expression by retinoic acid and thyroid hormone. *J Dermatol*, **19**(11): 774–780.
9. Gravel, R.A. (2014). Holocarboxylase synthetase: A multitalented protein with roles in biotin transfer, gene regulation and chromatin dynamics. *Mol Genet Metab*, **111**(3): 305–306.
10. Gralla, M., G. Camporeale, and J. Zempleni. (2008). Holocarboxylase synthetase regulates expression of biotin transporters by chromatin remodeling events at the SMVT locus. *J Nutr Biochem*, **19**(6): 400–408.
11. Juzeniene, A., et al. (2016). Phototherapy and vitamin D. *Clin Dermatol*, **34**(5): 548–555.
12. Purdy, S. and D. de Berker. (2011). Acne vulgaris. *BMJ Clin Evid*, **2011**.
13. Von Numers, C. (1953). The role of vitamin C in the mucopolysaccharide metabolism of the skin; studies on free mucopolysaccharides and mast cells in the intact skin and during wound healing in normal and scorbutic guinea-pigs. *Ann Med Exp Biol Fenn*, **31**(4): 398–408.
14. Lorencini, M., et al. (2014). Active ingredients against human epidermal aging. *Ageing Res Rev*, **15**: 100–115.
15. Savin, J.A. (1981). Old skin. *Br Med J (Clin Res Ed)*, **283**(6304): 1422–1423.
16. Babamiri, K. and R. Nassab. (2010). Cosmeceuticals: the evidence behind the retinoids. *Aesthet Surg J*, **30**(1): 74–77.
17. Phillips, C.L., S.B. Combs, and S.R. Pinnell. (1994). Effects of ascorbic acid on proliferation and collagen synthesis in relation to the donor age of human dermal fibroblasts. *J Invest Dermatol*, **103**(2): 228–232.
18. Cosgrove, M.C., et al. (2007). Dietary nutrient intakes and skin-aging appearance among middle-aged American women. *Am J Clin Nutr*, **86**(4): 1225–1231.

19. Jenkins, G., et al. (2014). Wrinkle reduction in post-menopausal women consuming a novel oral supplement: A double-blind placebo-controlled randomized study. *Int J Cosmet Sci*, **36**(1): 22–31.

20. *Manganese*. [cited 2016 November 1]; Available from: https://en.wikipedia .org/wiki/Manganese.

21. Kitchener, R.L. and A.M. Grunden. (2012). Prolidase function in proline metabolism and its medical and biotechnological applications. *J Appl Microbiol*, **113**(2):. 233–247.

22. Trueb, R.M. (2016). Serum biotin levels in women complaining of hair loss. *Int J Trichology*, **8**(2): 73–77.

23. Cashman, M.W. and S.B. Sloan. (2010). Nutrition and nail disease. *Clin Dermatol*, **28**(4): 420–425.

24. Aoi, N., et al. (2012). 1alpha,25-dihydroxyvitamin D3 modulates the hair-inductive capacity of dermal papilla cells: Therapeutic potential for hair regeneration. *Stem Cells Transl Med*, 2012. **1**(8): 615–26.

25. Paus, R., et al. (2014). Neuroendocrinology of the hair follicle: Principles and clinical perspectives. *Trends Mol Med*, **20**(10): 559–570.

26. Banihashemi, M., et al. (2016). Serum vitamin D3 level in patients with female pattern hair loss. *Int J Trichology*, **8**(3): 116–120.

27. Azemi, M., et al. (2014). Vitamin D—dependent rickets, type II case report. *Mater Sociomed*, **26**(1): 68–70.

28. Olah, A., et al. (2016). The thyroid hormone analogue KB2115 (eprotirome) prolongs human hair growth (anagen) ex vivo. *J Invest Dermatol*, **136**(8): 1711–1714.

29. Contreras-Jurado, C., et al. (2014). Impaired hair growth and wound healing in mice lacking thyroid hormone receptors. *PLoS One*, **9**(9): e108137.

Micronutrients in the skin

Can you unscramble the tiles below to reveal the secret message?
Use the empty boxes to arrange the letter blocks in the correct order. Good luck!

a c i t	e a s e	n o i c	l e c	n o c y	r e n t	a c i
r o t i	d i n	r i o l	f e r a	o n	b a s a	t e d
i f f e	c r e a	r o l i	s e s	R e t i	i n c	l l p
t i o n	w h i	l a t i	l c e	s k e

Hint: The block with the capital letter in it starts the phrase. Empty boxes are the spaces bewteen words, and all of the groups of 4 letters or letters and spaces stay together to form the phrase. Place these together to form a phrase of 11 words.

_____

_____

CHAPTER 12

The Nervous and Sensory Systems

Table of Contents

THE CENTRAL AND PERIPHERAL NERVOUS SYSTEMS

I've left the best or at least the most complicated for last—the central and peripheral nervous systems. The central nervous system (CNS) consists of the brain and spinal cord, while the peripheral nervous system (PNS) consists of all of the nerves and ganglia outside of the brain and spinal cord, including those for our five senses (Figure 12.1). As we'll see in this chapter, multiple micronutrients and biochemical pathways are at play in the CNS and PNS, such that deficiency and toxicity of most of these will cause nervous system effects such as confusion, loss or increase in sensory information, problems with balance and motor control, or even neuron death. Before getting into the specific micronutrient pathways at play, let's discuss some of the basics of the nervous system, including the different types of cells in our nervous systems, and the role of the blood-brain barrier.

Fun FACT

Many people have studied Albert Einstein's brain. A 2014 article in the journal *Brain* showed that Dr. Einstein had a larger connection between the two hemispheres. This connection, called the corpus callosum is composed of nerve fibers, suggesting that the two sides of Dr. Einstein's brain may have communicated better and/or faster than "normal" people [4].

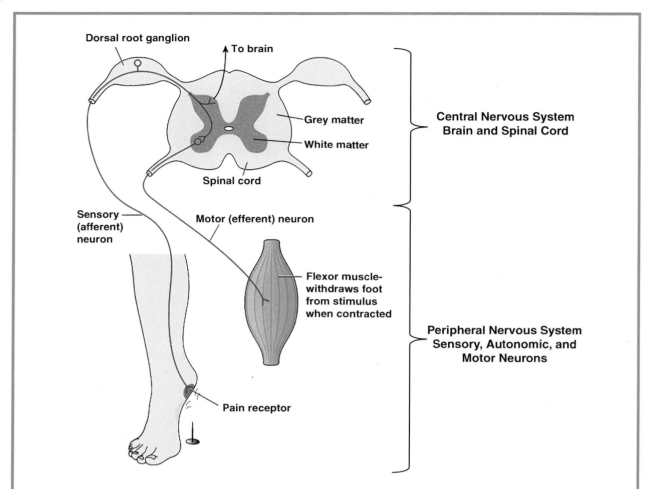

FIGURE 12.1: The central and peripheral nervous systems. The central nervous system (CNS) contains neurons and neuroglial cells in the brain and spinal cord, while the peripheral nervous system is further subdivided into sensory nerves (sight, hearing, touch, etc), autonomic nerves (breathing, digestion etc) and motor neurons (muscle innervation). The autonomic nerves arise from cranial nerves (not shown) which make up the parasympathetic fibers (regulating involuntary processes), while the sympathetic fibers branch off from grey matter in the spinal cord, and regulate our "fight or flight" responses. Taste and smell functions occur within the autonomic nervous system sensory nerves, and are one of the few areas that are not considered involuntary for this system.

© Blamb/Shutterstock.com

The CNS and PNS are composed of neurons and neuroglial cells—and each of these are further subspecialized (Figure 12.2). Nerve cells, or neurons are excitable cells of the CNS and PNS that transmit signals through electrical or chemical signals. As we'll see, ion pumps in the cell membranes of neurons produce voltage-gradients or differential charges between the inside and outside of the cells. Neurons often have dendritic branches (also called dendritic "trees") that extend from the cell body and receive signals from the neighboring neurons. On the other side of the cell body, neurons have a single axon, which may travel one meter or more before reaching its terminal in the spinal cord or peripheral target organ. Neurons can produce different chemical signals (neurotransmitters) or protein signals (neuropeptides)

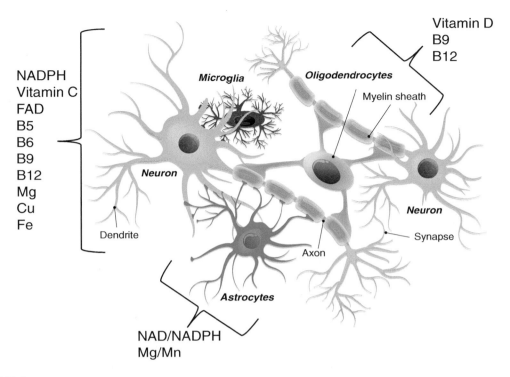

NEURONS AND NEUROGLIAL CELLS

Vitamin D
B9
B12

Microglia

Oligodendrocytes

Myelin sheath

NADPH
Vitamin C
FAD
B5
B6
B9
B12
Mg
Cu
Fe

Neuron

Neuron

Dendrite

Synapse

Axon

Astrocytes

NAD/NADPH
Mg/Mn

© Designua/Shutterstock.com

FIGURE 12.2: Cell types of the nervous and sensory systems, and micronutrients associated with these cell types. Neurons are responsible for transmitting the chemical and/or electrical messages while the glial cells are supporting cells of the nervous system—both types require micronutrients. Astrocytes associated with capillaries make up the blood-brain barrier of the nervous system.

to transmit their messages. The axon of neurons are either myelinated or unmyelinated—allowing for either rapid "jumping" of the signal, or slower waves of signal, respectively in the myelinated or unmyelinated axons. The oligodendricytes of the CNS (or Schwann cells of the PNS) provide the myelin wrapping, which will be discussed later. As we will also see in the chapter, the astrocytes of the CNS and PNS provide important supporting roles, including formation of the blood-brain barrier, metabolic support of the neurons, and recycling/uptake/release of glutamate. Finally, the microglia cells are the macrophages of the CNS, providing a "cleanup" function, and immune surveillance for the rest of the cells in the brain and spinal cord.

As mentioned above, astrocytes form the blood-brain barrier for the CNS, by maintaining tight junctions that allow passive diffusion of things such as lipid-soluble chylomicrons, glucose, water, salts, and amino acids. Thus, fat-soluble vitamins and some ions such as calcium, sodium, and potassium can enter the CNS by this route. However, both vitamin D and vitamin A enter the brain through the cerebral-spinal fluid, bound to their serum binding proteins, DBP and RBP, respectively [5, 6]. For the water-soluble vitamins and minerals, specific transport systems exist. For example, the riboflavin transport (RF2) is found on brain capillary endothelial cells, suggesting that B2 enters the brain using an active transport mechanism [7]. Iron is bound to transferrin receptor and is endocytosed by the endothelial astrocytes, which act to transport iron to neurons and other glia, likely through cerebral-spinal fluid [8, 9]. Suffice to say that there are mechanisms for transport past the blood-brain barrier for all the needed micronutrients. Let's get to the meat of this chapter—what we need the micronutrients for!

ION CHANNELS AND SIGNAL TRANSMISSION FROM AXONS TO DENDRITES

Nerve impulses travel down the axon, and then jump across the synapse to be transmitted by the post-synaptic cell. How exactly does this happen and where are micronutrients involved? First, let's look at the synapse (Figure 12.3). The synapse is composed of the axon of the pre-synaptic neuron, and one of the dendrites of the post-synaptic neuron, with a synaptic cleft in between. Electrical messages travel down the axon through a series of sodium and potassium channels that create gradients of charge along the membrane of the axon. Some voltage-gated channels are also calcium channels and allow waves of calcium to travel across the axon terminal. These calcium waves result in the release of synaptic vesicles containing neurotransmitters into the synaptic cleft, and with binding to ligand-gated channels, propagation of the signal through the next neuron. What I've written here is a highly simplified version of what really goes on—but it gets to

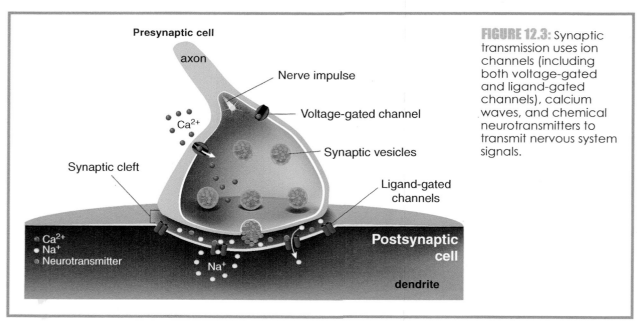

FIGURE 12.3: Synaptic transmission uses ion channels (including both voltage-gated and ligand-gated channels), calcium waves, and chemical neurotransmitters to transmit nervous system signals.

© Designua/Shutterstock.com

the issue at hand—ion channels and mineral micronutrients are required to propagate excitatory signals in the nervous system.

Ion channels in the nervous system transport calcium (Ca^{+2}), sodium (Na^+), potassium (K^+), and chloride (Cl^-), and in doing so, change the membrane potential where they are opened, propagating the electrochemical signal [10]. There are multiple types of each—some that we have seen before such as the calcium channel TRPV6, and the calcium sensing receptor CaSR, and others that we have not discussed, such as the voltage-gated sodium channel (VGSC). Let's look at this one in more depth. When the axon is at rest, the VGSC gate for sodium is closed (Figure 12.4). As a negative charge starts to propagate down the axon, the VGSC

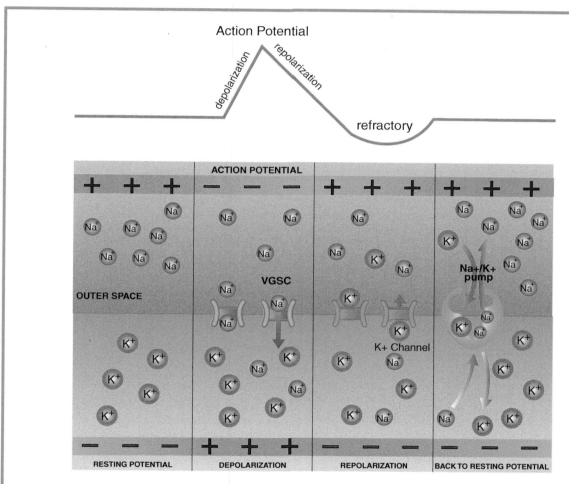

FIGURE 12.4: Sodium and potassium channels mediate action potentials in nerve. Top: cartoon showing the electrical impulse recording of an axon. Bottom, cartoon of an axon. As the electrical wave approaches, the voltage gated sodium channels (VGSC) open, allowing the flow of sodium inside the cell. This causes the inside of the membrane to be more positively charged than the outside. During repolarization, potassium channels pumps potassium outside of the cell. The action of the sodium/potassium pump finally brings the membrane back to resting potential, waiting for the next signal.

© extender_01/Shutterstock.com

opens, letting sodium ions flow into the cell, and changing the inside of the cell to a more positive state. The changing charge on the inner membrane of the nerve cell is what propagates the action potential. Once enough charge has accumulated, the gate closes and become inactivated, which blocks any more Na⁺ from flowing in. The membrane is now depolarized. Potassium channels open, which pump potassium from the intracellular to the extracellular environment, leading to repolarization, followed by the action of the Na⁺/K+ ATPase pump, which pumps sodium ions back out, and potassium ions in, allowing the membrane to return to its resting potential, ready for another signal.

Isn't it odd to think about the fact that these action potentials, and the opening and closing of ion channels is all happening in your brains and your PNS right now—each taking just a few milliseconds to complete so that you can get on with reading your chapter. Let's get on with it then!

MICRONUTRIENTS, NEUROTRANSMITTERS, AND NEUROPEPTIDES

As you'll see in this section, both vitamins and minerals are needed to synthesize many of our neurotransmitters as well as to amidate (put an amino group on) some of the neuropeptides that we've already talked about (e.g., TRH and vasopressin). In fact, it is hard to come up with a part of the CNS and PNS that doesn't require micronutrients for its daily activities. It's impossible in fact!

One of the more interesting of these is the link between the neurotransmitter glutamate, with the amino acid glutamine, and alpha-ketoglutarate in the TCA cycle. According to one review article, the amino acid glutamine is the most abundant amino acid in our plasma, and does enter the CNS through the glutamine/neutral amino acid transporter SNAT1 (sodium-coupled neutral amino acid transporter 1) [11]. Once within the CNS, glutamine can be converted to glutamate by the enzyme phosphate-activated glutaminase (PAG) (Figure 12.5). This is a key step and the start of the glutamate/GABA-glutamine cycle [12], as neurons do not synthesize pyruvate carboxylase and thus, cannot synthesize glutamate/GABA directly from glucose precursor. Glutamate is released from synaptic vesicles, and works as a neurotransmitter, but the excess is picked up by astrocytes, which utilize the glutamate either to make more amino acid glutamine or to shuttle the glutamate into the TCA cycle by converting it to alpha-ketoglutarate (alpha-KG) [12]. Two enzymes are key in this astrocyte-specific process—Glutamine synthetase and glutamate dehydrogenase.

Do you remember…?
Which other enzymes use Mg⁺² as an ATP bridge?

Glutamine synthetase (GS) is a 12-subunit enzyme, which requires two positively charged metal cofactors for function. Interestingly, GS can use either Mn⁺² or Mg⁺², using one as an ATP bridge (similar to the

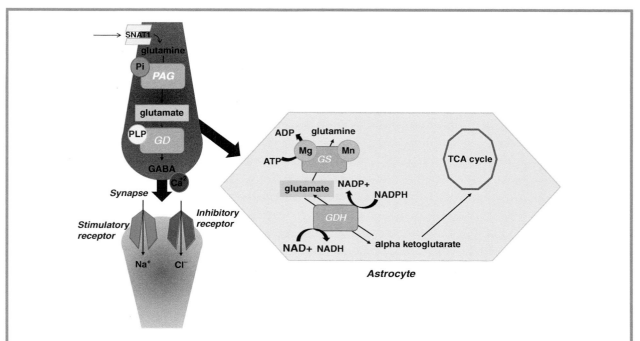

FIGURE 12.5: The astrocyte TCA cycle, and neuron glutamate production pathways are linked. Glutamine is transported into neurons by the SNAT1 transporter, and then can be converted to glutamate or GABA by the Phosphate activated glutaminase (PAG) and glutamate decarboxylase (GD) enzymes respectively. Note that PAGE requires inorganic phosphate, while GD is a B6-requiring enzyme. Calcium is needed to facilitate vesicle release of either glutamate or GABA. GABA can bind to either stimulatory receptors which co-transport sodium, or inhibitory receptors which co-transport chloride ions. The glutamate/GABA-glutamine cycle works between glutaminergic neurons (those that use glutamine/glutamate and GABA) and astrocytes. As shown, astrocytes can take up excess glutamate, and either convert it to the amino acid glutamine via the enzyme Glutamine synthtase, which requires 2 Mg, or 2Mn or one of each mineral, as well as ATP, or it can recycle glutamate into the TCA cycle using the enzyme glutamate dehydrogenase, which needs B3, and makes alpha ketoglutarate, which can enter the TCA cycle for energy production.

ATP-bridge functions of Mg^{+2} that we discussed in Chapter 4), and one as a structural cofactor. Interestingly, at least one study has reported that Mn^{+2} and Mg^{+2} can associate freely (i.e., either two of one of these, or one of each), with little to no effect on the overall tertiary structure of the enzyme [13]. Alternatively, glutamate can be shuttled to the TCA cycle, via the enzyme glutamate dehydrogenase. This enzyme is a B3-requiring enzyme, and can perform the reaction between glutamate and alpha-KG in either direction (Figure 12.5) [14]. Instead of being released into the synapse, glutamate can also be directly converted to the neurotransmitter GABA (gamma amino-butyric acid) by the enzyme glutamate decarboxylase (GD, also called glutamic acid decarboxylase-GAD). This enzyme requires B6, in the vitamer form PLP for full activity. GABA is an interesting neurotransmitter in that there are both inhibitory and stimulatory receptors found on post-synaptic neurons—meaning that depending on the receptor, GABA can either send an inhibitory signal or a stimulatory signal downstream [12]. Note, as shown

What's in a name?

Stiff person syndrome is an auto-immune disorder in which the person has antibodies against the PLP-binding domain in GD. This results in progressive muscular rigidity [1]. There is, unfortunately, no cure, and while several possible treatments are being tried, none work to relieve all of the symptoms.

on Figure 12.5, the two different types of receptors are actually ligand-gated (with GABA being the ligand) ion channels—sodium release being the positive or stimulatory signal, and chloride release being the inhibitory signal.

Fun FACT

High levels of tryptophan in your Thanksgiving turkey could lead to more serotonin synthesis—giving you that sleepy, happy feeling. Serotonin can be used to make melatonin, which can make you sleepy. Tryptophan is also the starting substrate for de novo niacin synthesis, and B3 is also needed for neurotransmitter synthesis. All in all, turkey is a great way to make lots of neurotransmitters!

Neurons also specifically synthesize other neurotransmitters, including acetylcholine, dopamine, serotonin, and norepinephrine—all of which require various vitamins and minerals for synthesis (Figure 12.6). For example, acetylcholine is the product of the choline acetyltransferase enzyme (ChAT), with the substrates of acetyl coA and choline. Remember that acetyl coA is made from vitamin B5, while choline is one of our required nutrients, but not considered a vitamin as we do make plenty of it from other nutrients. Dopamine and serotonin have similar synthetic pathways, with different starting amino acids. While serotonin requires tryptophan as the starting material, and the enzyme tryptophan hydroxylase, dopamine is synthesized from tyrosine, using the enzyme tyrosine hydroxylase. As you can see on Figure 12.6, both of these enzymes require iron as a cofactor, and the cosubstrate BH4 (tetrahydrobiopterin) [15]. We've not talked about BH4 before, but it turns out that this substrate requires folate, in the form tetrahydrofolate for synthesis. Thus, we add in B9 as a requirement for both serotonin and dopamine synthesis. But we are not done—synthesis of the dopamine and serotonin neurotransmitters is a two-step process, and at this second step, both intermediates 5-HT and L-Dopa can use the aromatic L-amino acid decarboxylase enzyme (AADC) [15]. AADC requires both Mg^{+2} and

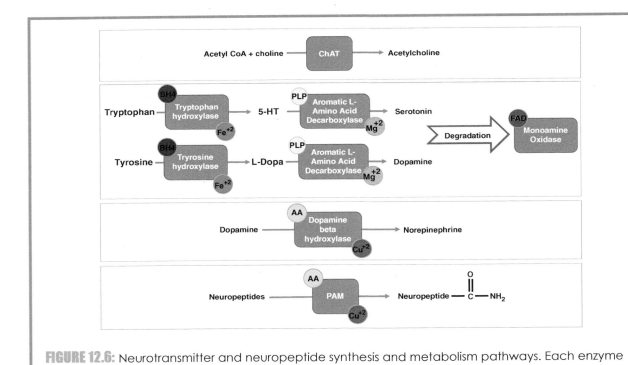

FIGURE 12.6: Neurotransmitter and neuropeptide synthesis and metabolism pathways. Each enzyme and the required micronutrients are further discussed in the text.

B6 in the form PLP. Given the name of the enzyme you probably should have guessed that it required B6—remember that any time you see an enzyme that deals with amino acids in some way or form, you should predict that B6 is a coenzyme, and here it is in AADC as you should have predicted. Both dopamine and serotonin can be referred to as "monoamines," as they have single "amine" groups in their structures (which I didn't show, but you can take my word for). This is important when it comes to the last enzyme in our pathway—monoamine oxidase (MAO). This enzyme comes in an "A" form and a "B" form, with different forms in different parts of the nervous system, but for our purposes, is important to note because it can degrade monoamines—rendering them inactive. As shown on Figure 12.6, MAO is a flavoprotein, requiring FAD in its active site as a coenzymatic vitamer [16]. MAO enzymes are the targets of many neuropsychiatric drugs, which act to inhibit the enzyme from degrading serotonin and dopamine—both of which have been associated with "happy" and "active/nondepressive" behaviors [16]. Finally, not all dopamine is released into the synapse—neurons of the autonomic nervous system use the enzyme dopamine beta hydroxylase to convert dopamine to norepinephrine. Dopamine beta hydroxylase is a copper cofactor-dependent enzyme that also utilizes vitamin C to maintain copper in a +2 state [17]. Another copper-dependent enzyme should also be mentioned, and that is peptidylglycine alpha-amidating monooxygenase (PAM) [18]. First, while we've talked about the neuropeptides vasopressin and TRH before, it should be established that neuropeptides are different from neurotransmitters in that neuropeptides are made of amino acids linked together in a small protein, or peptide. They are usually cleaved from a larger "pro-peptide" molecule, but that part of the story is beyond what we need to know for this text. For us, the key part comes when neuropeptides gain their full activity—and this happens through amidation, or addition of an amide group by the enzyme PAM. As shown on Figure 12.6, PAM requires both copper as a cofactor, and like dopamine beta-hydroxylase, vitamin C in the form, ascorbic acid, as a coenzyme [17, 18]. With this final enzyme, we end our foray into neuropeptide and neurotransmitter metabolism—can you go back now and list all of the micronutrients needed?

AS MICRONUTRIENTS GO DOWN, NEUROLOGICAL DISEASE GOES UP

From the last section, it should be fairly evident that micronutrients are key to synthesis and metabolism of both neurotransmitters and neuropeptides. Deficiency in any of these—especially the vitamin coenzymes can have widespread effects on the nervous system (Table 12.1). Let's take a look at some of these. First, let's remember some material way back in Chapter 2—the original condition name for beriberi in poultry was neuritis—because the chickens were acting a bit nuts when they were not getting sufficient thiamine, but the original thought was that the neurological condition was caused by a virus infecting the nervous system—hence, neuritis. Likewise, the symptoms of pellagra are remembered as the "Four D's"—diarrhea, dermatitis, dementia, and death. Scurvy is usually thought of in relation to crazed pirates—likely made crazy by lack of vitamin C during sea voyages. If you

TABLE 12.1: Vitamin nutritional deficiencies linked to neurological conditions. Can you add in the enzymes that need each of these vitamins?		
Deficiency	**Condition**	**Nervous System Symptoms**
Niacin	Pellagra	Dementia (remember the 4 D's)
Riboflavin	Ariboflavinosis	Migraines
Thiamine	Wernicke-Korsakoff Syndrome	Ataxia, confusion, hallucinations, memory loss
B6	No official name	Seizures (thought to be due to lack of GABA)
Vitamin C	Scurvy	Emotional changes (think crazed pirates!)

look closely at Table 12.1, most of the links between the vitamin deficiency and the outcome—for example, scurvy and emotional instability—make sense. Vitamin C is needed for norepinephrine synthesis and for neuropeptide amidation, so low levels could affect both of these processes. Sure enough—mice with a deletion of the sodium dependent vitamin C transporter type 2 (SVCT2), which is the vitamin C transporter for brain, show lower levels of serotonin and norepinephrine [19].

But what about thiamine? Which enzyme did we discuss in the last section that is a thiamine-dependent enzyme? Huh? We didn't. There are four known thiamine dependent enzymes, and these were mainly discussed in Chapter 4—pyruvate dehydrogenase, alpha-KG dehydrogenase, branched chain amino acid dehydrogenase, and transketolase. Yet, the symptoms of Beriberi and Wernicke-Korsakoff syndrome can be neurological in nature—including ataxia, confusion, hallucinations and complete memory loss [20]. Wernicke-Korsakoff is frequently caused by alcoholism, and as we saw in Chapter 3, the expression of the thiamine receptor ThTr1, in intestine can be downregulated by alcohol, leading to nutritional B1 deficiency [21]. But why is a B1 deficiency linked to neurological conditions? The best explanation is that the four enzymes involved are key to the TCA cycle, amino acid metabolism, and the pentose phosphate shunt—and as we did discuss in the last section of this chapter, we need the integrated TCA cycle, and amino acid metabolism to integrate with neurotransmitter synthesis between neurons and astrocytes. In individuals with beriberi, or Wernicke-Korsakoff deficiency, this integration is likely not fully functional, and deficits in glutamate/GABA synthesis may occur.

We also saw that a lot of minerals were needed as neuronal enzymatic cofactors. Indeed, although not listed in a separate table, conditions such as hypomagnesemia, copper deficiency, and iron deficiency are also associated with neurological conditions. One of the more interesting (in this author's opinion) is the possible link between the idiopathic condition "restless leg syndrome" and iron deficiency. The most frequent association between individuals who have this condition and any diagnostic tests is that of iron deficiency—cerebrospinal fluid ferritin levels are up to 65% lower in patients with restless leg syndrome than with age-matched controls [22]. While there is still discussion in the literature as to whether low systemic or nervous-system specific iron levels is the cause or the effect, it is clear that iron supplementation can relieve the symptoms [22].

There are also a number of genetic conditions—many affecting the very enzymes that synthesize neurotransmitters—that have neurological symptoms, and relevant to this chapter, can sometimes be "cured" by supplementing with vitamins or minerals. While there is not a comprehensive list prepared, it is recommended that you might check on some of these yourself, using the Genetics Home Reference web page (https://ghr.nlm.nih.gov/). Let's discuss a few of these here. First is a riboflavin connection. While ariboflavinosis is listed on Table 12.1, migraines are not a common condition for overt riboflavin deficiency. However, they may be one of the symptoms of a slight deficiency, as supplementation with B2 can reduce the frequency of migraines and the severity of their symptoms [23]. A genetic mutation in the brain riboflavin transporter, RF2, can lead to a condition called Fazio-Londe Syndrome, which is characterized by paralysis of the facial nerves, and palsy, and can be treated with high dose riboflavin supplements [24]. One might expect, if riboflavin uptake into the brain were the issues, that these patients would also have migraines as one of their symptoms. Alas, they do not . . . so genetically, at this time we cannot make the association of migraines and low riboflavin levels. A second genetic condition worth mentioning in this context is Menke's disease. This is a condition in which there is an inherited mutation of the copper cellular transporter ATP7A. Menke's is characterized by mental retardation, seizures, and ataxia—likely due to defective copper availability for enzymes such as PAM, and dopamine beta-hydroxylase—both of which need copper as a cofactor. One can likely go through the enzymes listed in the previous section, identify genetic conditions associated with mutations in those enzymes, and determine if vitamin or mineral supplementation would be of help for any of all of the conditions. It is interesting to note here that in many cases, simply over-supplementing (over and above the RDA) with a B-vitamin may relieve some neurological symptoms. So, the next time your brain isn't behaving, consider which B-vitamin (or vitamin C) you might be missing . . . and check out the scientific literature to see if it might help!

THE SENSES

We often take our senses for granted, but imagine living in a world where one or more of them were missing? What would it be like not to smell fresh baked cookies, or taste the chocolate from them melting on your tongue? What if you could not

Vitamin A	Sodium	B6	Sodium	Sodium
B3	Potassium	B12	Calcium	Calcium
Zinc	Chloride	Calcium	Potassium	
	Calcium	Potassium	Zinc	
		Sodium	Fluoride	
			Chloride	

FIGURE 12.7: The five senses and associated micronutrients.

© Subidubi/Shutterstock.com

feel the touch of a soft blanket, or hear the concertos of Mozart? Of course some people are missing one of their senses—up to 0.1% of children born in the US have a hearing loss, while 3% of Americans aged 40 and over are legally blind and up to 17% report some vision problem that impairs their ability to see by age 65 [25]. While many sensory system conditions are genetic in nature, some are directly caused by a lack of, or toxicity of micronutrients. In this section, we will examine how micronutrients shape our sensory system, and what happens to vision, hearing, smell, taste, or touch when one goes above or below the recommended daily requirements for a micronutrient. Figure 12.7 provides an overview of the five sensory systems and the micronutrients that play key roles in each.

Sight

Early Egyptians knew that liver (a great source of vitamin A, as it is stored there) could restore night vision in those suffering from loss. In fact, it is likely common knowledge to most people that vitamin A is important to vision, and in this section we will discuss in detail why it is important, how carotenes from food like carrots, for example can become part of our vision system, and what happens when we are deficient in vitamin A vitamers, including carotenes and non-vitamin A carotinoids. However, vitamin A is not the only micronutrient needed to maintain eye health—minerals and other vitamins are needed to transmit signals through the optic nerve and back to the brain, and to convert the vitamin A vitamers into the correct forms that our photoreceptor cells can use.

The central molecules in vision are the vitamin A-complexed opsin proteins. While the role of vitamin A is usually discussed in the rod cells (night vision, or low light

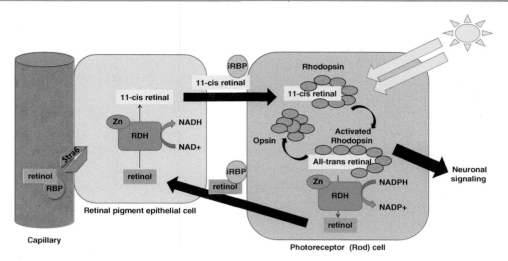

FIGURE 12.8: The vision cycle. Retinol, bound to retinol binding protein (RBP) travels through the serum. RBP binds to its receptor, Stra6, and is taken into the retinal pigment epithelial cell. Retinol is converted to 11-cis retinal by retinol dehydrogenase (RDH) which requires NAD+ as an enzymatic co-enzyme and zinc as a structural co-factor. 11-cis-retinal is transported across the intercellular space to the photoreceptor cell where it complexes with opsin to form rhodopsin. Rhodopsin is activated by light, which photoisomerizes the 11-cis retinal to all-trans retinal, and starts neuronal signaling through the option nerve to the brain cortex. Retinal is recycled by RDH to form retinol, which is transported back to the retinal pigment epithelial cell to begin the cycle again.

conditions), in fact, both the cones and the rods utilize 11-cis retinal complexed with opsins to detect light and color. In humans, the color opsins include long, medium, and short wave color detector pigments, along with rhodopsin, for night vision and melanopsin, which works to control circadian rhythm through light [26]. All of these essentially utilize a similar process, which is shown for rhodopsin in Figure 12.8.

Retinol is transported to the capillary of the eye bound to retinol binding protein (RBP). RBP binds to its receptor Stra6, which is found throughout the body, including on the retinal pigment epithelial cells (Figure 12.8). However, vision requires 11-cis retinal, so the retinol that is absorbed must be converted to retinal using the enzyme we've seen before—retinol dehydrogenase. This enzyme is unique in actually being able to work in both directions. As shown in Figure 12.8, retinol dehydrogenase can also convert retinal back to retinol in the photoreceptor cells. But we are getting ahead of ourselves . . . Once the 11-cis retinal is formed, it can be transported through the intercellular matrix to the photoreceptor cells (in this case, the rod cells) by binding to the interstitial retinal binding protein iRBP [27]. The 11-cis retinal then complexes with the "empty" opsin protein, forming rhodopsin (in a rod cell), or one of the other pigment opsins (in a cone cell). Rhodopsin with its vitamin A acting as a structural coenzyme is poised and ready for the signal, which is light. Upon reaching the photoreceptor cell, the photons in light cause a photoisomerization of (changes the structure of) 11-cis retinal

Did you
KNOW...?

There are at least 8 different RDH enzymes, and other related enzymes—all involved in converting forms of vitamin A. However (and thankfully) for our purposes, we will keep the enzyme name more general and just call it "RDH"

to all-trans retinal. This structural change in the retinal moiety leads to an opening or relaxing of the structure of the rhodopsin molecule, and nerve transmission-resulting in vision. Note that rhodopsin, and all of the other opsins are G-protein coupled proteins [26]—so that the structural change in the protein causes a signaling cascade in the photoreceptor cell, opening and closing of ion-gated channels, and propagation of a nerve signal down the axons, as we have discussed in the previous sections of this chapter.

Vitamin A in development

Matthew-Woods Syndrome is a genetic condition caused by a mutation in the Stra6 gene. The most striking phenotype of this syndrome is microphthalmia, or "small eye." In some cases the eyes can be completely missing. This condition is due to lack of retinoic acid, which is needed for eye development [2].

What is neat about vision is that the photoreceptor cells are able to work with the retinal pigment epithelium to recycle the vitamin A vitamers and reuse it in more opsin molecules (Figure 12.8). However, vision requires the most vitamin A when compared to the daily needs of other organs in our body, and therefore, the eye is most sensitive to the effects of deficiency of this micronutrient. Nutritional blindness, due to vitamin A deficiency is still the most frequent cause of blindness worldwide, with an estimated 250,000–500,000 children becoming blind due to vitamin A deficiency each year [28]. Blindness in these children is actually due to a condition termed xerophthalmia, which is characterized by dryness of the cornea and abnormalities of the conjunctiva. While we have just spent time talking about the role of vitamin A in color and light detection, for children with vitamin A deficiency, blindness is caused by a lack of retinoic acid and its need by the corneal epithelial cells [29]. With xerophthalmia, the cornea and conjunctival epithelial cells are highly keratinized with low basal cell proliferation. Adults developing vitamin A deficiency, which could be due to steatorrhea (excess fat in the stool) or even intestinal parasites, complain of not being able to drive at night, or not being able to see the stars—common complaints for night blindness. Both xerophthalmia (if caught early) and night blindness conditions are reversible, and treatable by increasing vitamin A intake either in diet or through supplements.

Non-vitamin A carotinoids in vision and eye health

There are several carotinoids that cannot be converted to vitamin A in any form, yet still seem to have beneficial effects for our eye health and vision, and these are worth mentioning. In particular, lutein, which is found in high levels in green leafy vegetables such as kale, and zeaxanthin, which gives corn kernels, and saffron their yellow color, accumulate in an area of the eye called the macula. The macula of the eye is also slightly yellow in appearance—do a Google™ search of a normal eye and you will easily see this. Interestingly, these xanthophyll carotinoids, as they are called are also present in the retina of the eye, and serve an important purpose—namely in shielding the rest of the pigmented epithelium from ultraviolet blue rays, reducing glare and also enhancing color vision [30]. Low intake of lutein and zeaxanthin, and low macular concentrations of the carotinoids are associated with increased probability of age-related macular degeneration (AMD), and multiple studies show that supplementation with these carotinoids appears to both prevent, and in some cases treat AMD cases, especially those in the early stages [30]. So, eating your carrots, corn, saffron, and green veggies are great for keeping your eyes healthy, and your vision strong.

Hearing

The sense of hearing is one that comes about from changes in pressure, fluid flow, and the propagation of sound waves through a fluid called the endolymph. These changes allow sensory neuron hair cells within our cochlea to detect movement or waves through the endolymph, resulting in neurotransmitter release and transmission of the signal. All of this happens because of mineral ions and water balance, while disruption of water levels and ion balance within the endolymph can and does result in hearing loss.

Endolymph is unusual compared to other fluid compartments in that there is a high potassium (K+) content and low sodium (Na+) content (Figure 12.9) [31]. How is this gradient generated and maintained? Specifically through potassium channels, which leak K+ into the endolymph, and Na/K ATPase, pumps, which take up potassium from the interstitial spaces (basolateral side of the cell) for eventual release into the endolymph [31]. To counter potassium transport, the epithelial

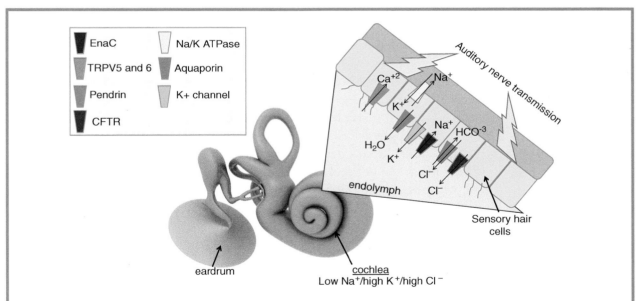

FIGURE 12.9: Ear endolymph ion and water balance utilizes various channels and pumps. The endolymph of the cochlea is unusual compared to other body fluid compartments in having high K+ and low Na+. This ratio is actively maintained with pumps, channels and aquaporins as shown. The movement of the endolymph, which can be caused by sound waves activates sensory hair cells which open calcium channels, release neurotransmitters and transmits auditory sensory information. References supporting this figure can be found in the text.

sodium channel (ENaC) and possibly other sodium channels, take up Na+ from the endolymph for release by the Na/K ATPase on the other side of the cell [32]. Concurrently, chloride channels, such as the cystic fibrosis transmembrane receptor (CFTR) and pendrin, can move chloride ions out into the endolymph [32]. Interestingly, pendrin can move either chloride ions or iodine ions, depending on the tissue (in the thyroid it is the protein responsible for moving iodine into the colloid for incorporation into thyroid hormone). Finally, calcium influx to the sensory hair cells, notably through the TRPV5 and TRPV6 calcium channels occurs with hair movement, and starts the process whereby a rise in cellular calcium levels signals auditory transmission [33]. Interestingly, vitamin D levels influence levels of TRPV5 and 6 in parts of the ear [33], and at least one study has shown a link between vitamin D levels, osteoporosis, and hearing loss [34].

Is there any evidence that dietary ion intake can influence hearing? In Meniere's disease, a condition of "ear ringing" or tinnitus, a low salt diet protects and even treats the condition [32]. PubMed searches at the time of this writing for other nutritional interventions, particularly those to treat mineral ion deficiency or toxicity that could impair hearing loss were unsuccessful. However, variations in many of the channels, receptors, and proteins discussed above are known to result in hearing loss or impairment [35], confirming the role of these ion transporters in auditory sensory transmission.

Touch

We are bombarded with touch, or even the lack of touch, but how does our bodies utilize micronutrients to transmit the sensation of touch, pain, and pressure? Touch remains, according to one author, the least understood of our senses [36], but we do know that ion channels are again involved in transmitting signals of touch, pain, and pressure to our central nervous systems. Within the skin, pressure, heat, pain, or slight deformation/stretching of the skin results in ion channel activation, leading to touch detection by the CNS (Figure 12.10). For fine touch, this process appears to be regulated by voltage-gated sodium and potassium channels [36], which release sodium into the axon of the nerve, and pump potassium out, causing a propagating action potential to travel along the axon, similar to what was shown in Figure 12.4. For both pain and pressure, members of the transient receptor potential vanilloid channel family (TRPV), which includes the intestinal and ear calcium channel (TRPV5 and TRPV6), mediate calcium-based signaling in response to sensed pressure, or, in the case of TRPV1, which can bind to capsaicin, signaling in response to specific external stimuli [36]. The only micronutrient deficiencies documented to affect the sensation of touch are dry beriberi, which likely affects peripheral nerve "health" through energy metabolism, and B12 or B6 deficiency, which may lead to toxic increases in homocysteine, impairing peripheral sensory nerves.

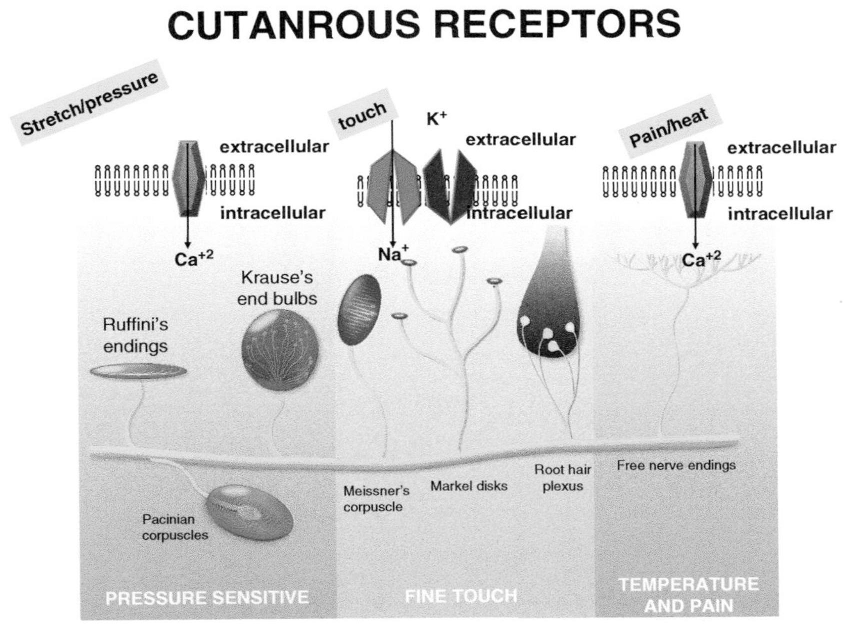

CUTANROUS RECEPTORS

FIGURE 12.10: Touch and pain receptors in our skin. All of these specialized nerve cells transmit the sensation of touch, pressure and pain using ion channels. The ion channels at the cell membranes of the various peripheral nerves are shown above the specialized nerve cells. We understand the least about touch, and how it is conveyed.

© pinta.t.s/Shutterstock.com and © Designua/Shutterstock

Taste

Tasting the coffee you are drinking while reading this text, or the pizza that you had for dinner, involves an organ called the tongue. The tongue and parts of the mouth, contain specialized sensory neurons to transmit the signals of sweet, sour, bitter, salty, and umami (savory) to the CNS—and of course requires micronutrients for detecting and transmitting taste perception (Figure 12.11). While we use our vision and sense of smell to determine if we want to eat something, the ultimate test and conclusion is made by our taste buds. Our taste buds are composed of up to 80 polarized (directionally-placed) sensory nerve cells, which have specialized nerve fibers and receptors responsible for sensing the taste of anything we put in our mouths. In total, our mouth (including the tongue, pharynx, epiglottis, palate, and larynx) contains up to 5000 taste buds [37].

Before getting to the taste buds themselves, it is important to talk about the saliva in our mouth. Saliva is produced with specific ionic and protein compositions, providing a solution in which food partially dissolves, and taste particulates can stimulate taste receptors. When we detect food, our mouth waters—saliva is produced. Saliva contains ions Na^+, K^+, Ca^{+2}, Zn^{+2}, Cl^-, F^-, and lots of water, proteins, fats, amino acids, as well as a myriad of other things [38]. The three major salivary glands—the

Fun FACT

The myth of the four areas of taste on our tongue is really a misinterpretation of some older data. A German scientist, D.P. Hanig published a 1901 paper in which he described the results of human volunteer studies, which showed greater sensitivity to sweetness at the tip of the tongue, saltiness toward the middle and bitter or sour on the sides and back of the tongue, respectively. These results were interpreted by Dr. E.G. Boring, a historical psychologist, into a figure called "Boring Figure" (I'm not kidding)—which you might know as the tongue map. It wasn't until 1974 when a female scientist, Dr. Virginia Collins reexamined Hanig's data, and concluded that while some regions are more sensitive for specific tastes than other, all regions of the tongue can detect all types of tastes. Despite this, the tongue map is still being taught, almost 50 years later [3]!

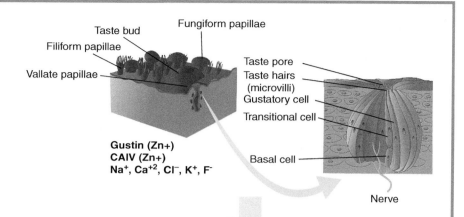

Filiform papillae
Vallate papillae
Taste bud
Fungiform papillae

Taste pore
Taste hairs (microvilli)
Gustatory cell
Transitional cell

Basal cell

Nerve

Gustin (Zn+)
CAIV (Zn+)
Na^+, Ca^{+2}, Cl^-, K^+, F^-

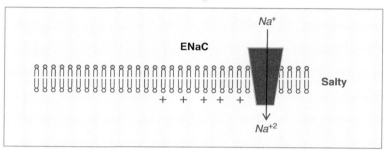

Na^+

ENaC

Salty

+ + + + +

Na^{+2}

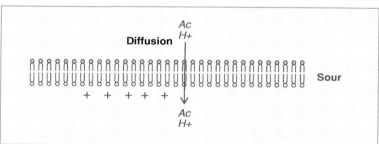

Ac
$H+$

Diffusion

Sour

+ + + + +

Ac
$H+$

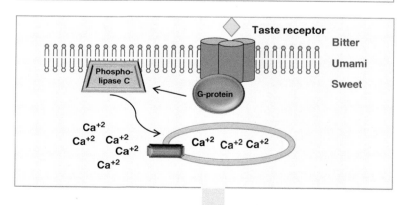

Taste receptor

Bitter

Umami

Sweet

Phospho-lipase C

G-protein

Ca^{+2}
Ca^{+2} Ca^{+2}
Ca^{+2}
Ca^{+2}

Ca^{+2} Ca^{+2} Ca^{+2}

Neurotransmitter release

FIGURE 12.11: Micronutrients involved in taste perception. Gustin protein—or carbonic anhydrase VI is a secreted zinc-containing enzyme which can convert water and CO2 to bicarbonate and protons—and plays a role in taste perception for bitter compounds. Carbonic anhydrase IV is found in sour receptors and may be responsible for perception of carbonation. It also contains zinc in its active site. The taste buds each contain up to 80 taste cells, with receptors for salty, bitter, umami, and sweet.

© Designua/Shutterstock.com

sublingual, submandibular, and the parotid glands produce saliva, and utilize, as you hopefully have guessed by now, ion channels, aquaporins, and calcium signaling. We won't go into the specifics here, as it is much the same as the other times we have discussed it (such as for the ear, and for water balance itself). However, there is one protein component of saliva worth mentioning—the Zn-containing protein carbonic anhydrase VI, affectionately known by the name "gustin" (Figure 12.12) [37]. Gustin has been implicated in the growth and maintenance of taste buds, and in one paper, individuals with a polymorphism in the gustin gene had a decreased ability to taste bitter compounds, and showed fewer numbers of "normal looking" taste buds on their tongue [39]. Zinc supplementation can help individuals with this polymorphism to have a stronger sensation of taste for bitter compounds, as zinc sits at the active site of the gustin enzyme (and all carbonic anhydrase forms), and supplementation enhances zinc's interaction with the protein [37]. Carbonic anhydrase enzymes perform the reaction: $CO_2 + H_2O \leftrightarrow HCO^- + H^+$, and gustin is the only known carbonic anhydrase enzyme that is secreted rather than found intracellularily [37]. For saliva, it is thought that the balance between the forward and reverse reactions can control sensitivity to taste by the levels of water/CO_2 production, or bicarbonate/proton production. Another nonsecreted, intracellular carbonic anhydrase, CAIV is expressed in sour-detecting taste cells, and may be one of the ways that we detect (and enjoy) carbonated beverages [40]. So, for saliva, zinc is an important micronutrient that enhances taste sensitivity, especially in carries of the gustin gene polymorphism.

As shown on Figure 12.11, taste perception occurs through a combinatorial activation of taste receptors, which are present at different concentrations within our taste buds. In other words, the reason for the "regions" of taste that are still described in classrooms worldwide, is that certain areas of the tongue have more of one receptor type than another—but to our knowledge, none of the mechanisms on Figure 12.11 are devoid in any areas of the tongue and mouth that contain taste buds. We can perceive salty even at the tip of our tongues to some degree, or bitter and sweet in the middle—go ahead and try it with some sour gummys or salty potato chips and you will see. Micronutrients are involved in the actual sensing of these tastes. For example, our favorite Na^+ channel, the epithelial sodium channel ENaC detects sodium ions in our saliva (which must be above the normal level of sodium that is maintained there), causing a depolarization of the membrane of the taste receptor cell, and neurotransmitter release. Interestingly, individuals with a polymorphism of their ENaC gene, which leads to a less active channel have reduced overall taste perception for salt [41]. This could mean that they might over-salt foods to get the same salt taste. Could individuals with this variant be contributing to the epidemic of hypernatremia (salt toxicity)? Moving on to sour tastes, diffusion of protons (H^+ moieties which are part of acids) is the mechanism for tasting bitter substances, again following by depolarization of the membrane of the taste receptor cell and neurotransmitter signaling (Figure 12.11). There is some evidence for a specific sour receptors, but to date, the findings

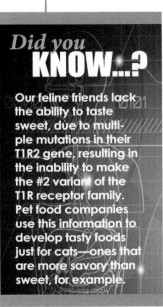

Did you KNOW...?

Our feline friends lack the ability to taste sweet, due to multiple mutations in their T1R2 gene, resulting in the inability to make the #2 variant of the T1R receptor family. Pet food companies use this information to develop tasty foods just for cats—ones that are more savory than sweet, for example.

© ellepigrafica/Shutterstock.com

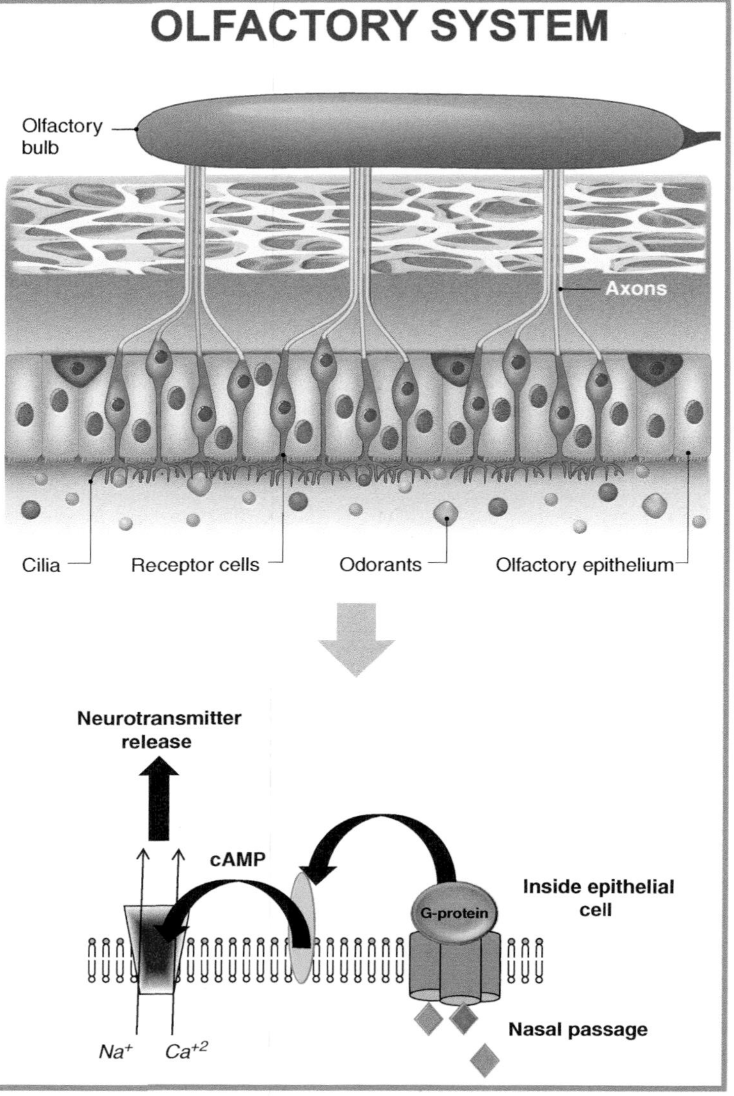

OLFACTORY SYSTEM

FIGURE 12.12: Odor detection by the nose. The nasal epithelium contains hundreds of receptors for odorant molecules. The majority of these are G-protein coupled receptors which cause sodium/calcium uptake and neurotransmitter release for propagation of the sensory signal.

have not been fully characterized [41]. For sweet, bitter, and umami (savory) taste, members of the G-protein coupled taste receptor families T1R and T2R can detect the taste molecules (such as sugars, sugar alcohols, and amino acids, such as glutamate—which is responsible for much of our savory taste detection) and convert the binding of these molecules to the receptor into a G-protein-activated signaling pathway, which ultimately involves calcium release, followed by neurotransmitter release and signaling. There are actually multiple forms (genes) of the T1R and T2R receptors, allowing fine-tuned detection of sweet, bitter, and savory flavors [41]. There are also a lot of different gene polymorphisms within the taste receptors, suggesting that different people may have different abilities to detect tastes—and this likely accounts for many of our food preferences, and perhaps even the occurrence of a "sweet tooth" [41]. However, maintaining dietary levels of zinc, salts, calcium,

© Designua/Shutterstock.com

and other ions are key to maintaining taste sensations. So, go ahead, have the double pepperoni pizza, cola, and chocolate chip cookie—but make sure you can fully enjoy it by getting your RDA of micronutrients first!

Smell

Our noses contain hundreds of variants of specialized odorant receptors, each with the ability to detect a particular odor molecule [42]. The odor receptors, are G-protein linked transmembrane receptors (Figure 12.12), and signal through adenylate cyclase and cAMP to activate sodium/calcium channels and stimulate neurotransmitter release [42]. These G-protein-linked receptors were originally discovered in 1991, and are the most well characterized of the odorant receptors. Two other types of odorant receptors, the trace-amine-associated receptors and the MS4A receptor family also appear to be involved in smell detection, but are not as well characterized in terms of signaling and any ion involvement [42], so we won't discuss them further.

Before leaving the sense of smell, it is important to mention the possible role of thiamine in this sense—but perhaps more in maintaining neuronal viability (life!) than the actual smell transmission. Individuals with Korsakoff's syndrome, which is usually characterized by psychiatric disorders, may also have a dampened sense of smell. A PubMed™ search reveals 11 different publications and clinical reports of Korsakoff patients with olfactory problems—including one showing that the deficit in odor discrimination is only slightly better than patients with frontal lobe damage [43]. For smell, this is essentially where our story ends. Short and sweet (smelling)!

CHAPTER SUMMARY

The cells of the CNS and PNS utilize ions, vitamins, and other mineral cofactors such as iron to perform daily tasks, including movement, breathing, digestion and memory.

- Micronutrients are key to neuropeptide amidation and neurotransmitter synthesis.
- In most vitamin deficiencies, reintroducing the vitamin, or even initially over supplementing with the vitamin can relieve the neurological symptom.
- The process of vision utilizes both vitamins and minerals, including integration of the retinal vitamers of vitamin A into opsin to form the sensory molecule for vision.
- Hearing is controlled by fluid balance and changes in waves, pressure, and flow of the endolymph. Ion channels and aquaporins maintain proper ion and water concentrations.
- Touch is the least understood of our senses, but involves ion channels to transmit sensory touch, pain, and pressure information to the CNS.

- Taste and smell are linked by the fact that odorant and taste particles activate receptors that signal neurotransmitter release. However, there are many more odorant receptor genes, than taste receptor genes—at least in humans.

POINTS TO PONDER ☑☑☑☑☑☑☑1111☑☑☑☑☑☑

- What might be the effect of B-vitamin toxicity on the nervous system? Can you think of any condition or situation where this is a problem?
- Homocysteine is thought to be a toxic byproduct, and is usually "cleaned up" by the folate one-carbon metabolism cycle. However, high homocysteine is linked to neurological conditions—can you figure out which ones? Do they respond to folate supplementation?
- We did not discuss the role of antioxidants in the nervous system, and senses, but the genetic condition AVED is due to low Vitamin E. Look up its symptoms and think about how Vitamin E deficiency in the nervous system could impair its functioning.
- One symptom of hypervitaminosis A is diplopia, or double vision. Can you speculate on what might cause this?
- Touch is the least understood of the senses. How could you design an experiment to test if whole body sodium levels could influence fine touch sensation?
- ENaC is used by many of our sensory neurons. What might be the effect (if any) on the sensory abilities for people with Liddle syndrome?

References

1. Ali, F., et al. (2011). Stiff-person syndrome (SPS) and anti-GAD-related CNS degenerations: Protean additions to the autoimmune central neuropathies. *J Autoimmun* **37**(2): 79–87.

2. Golzio, C., et al. (2007). Matthew-Wood syndrome is caused by truncating mutations in the retinol-binding protein receptor gene STRA6. *Am J Hum Genet* **80**(6): 1179–87.

3. Dowdey, S. (2007). How Taste Works. 10 November, 2016; [Available from: HowStuffWorks.com.; http://health.howstuffworks.com/mental-health/human-nature/perception/taste.htm.

4. Men, W., et al. (2014). The corpus callosum of Albert Einstein's brain: Another clue to his high intelligence? *Brain* **137**(Pt 4): e268.

5. Alonso, M.I., et al. (2011). Cerebrospinal fluid control of neurogenesis induced by retinoic acid during early brain development. *Dev Dyn* **240**(7): 1650–9.

6. Katikaneni, L.P., et al. (1987). High levels of group-specific component (vitamin-D-binding protein) in the cerebrospinal fluid of infants aged less than 2 months. *Biol Neonate* **52**(5): 250–5.

7. Patel, M., et al. (2012). Molecular and functional characterization of riboflavin specific transport system in rat brain capillary endothelial cells. *Brain Res* **1468**: 1–10.

8. Descamps, L., et al. (1996). Receptor-mediated transcytosis of transferrin through blood-brain barrier endothelial cells. *Am J Physiol* **270**(4 Pt 2): H1149–58.

9. Moos, T., et al. (2007). Iron trafficking inside the brain. *J Neurochem* **103**(5): 1730–40.

10. Waszkielewicz, A.M., et al. (2013). Ion channels as drug targets in central nervous system disorders. *Curr Med Chem* **20**(10): 1241–85.

11. Xiao, D., et al. (2016). The glutamine-alpha-ketoglutarate (AKG) metabolism and its nutritional implications. *Amino Acids* **48**(9): 2067–80.

12. Bak, L.K., A. Schousboe, and H.S. Waagepetersen. (2006). The glutamate/GABA-glutamine cycle: Aspects of transport, neurotransmitter homeostasis and ammonia transfer. *J Neurochem* **98**(3): 641–53.

13. Boksha, I.S., et al. (2002). Glutamine synthetase isolated from human brain: octameric structure and homology of partial primary structure with human liver glutamine synthetase. *Biochemistry (Mosc)* **67**(9): 1012–20.

14. McKenna, M.C., et al. (2016). Glutamate oxidation in astrocytes: Roles of glutamate dehydrogenase and aminotransferases. *J Neurosci Res* **94**(12): 1561–71.

15. Pearl, P.L. (2013). Monoamine neurotransmitter deficiencies. *Handb Clin Neurol* **113**: 1819–25.

16. Gaweska, H. and P.F. Fitzpatrick. (2011). Structures and mechanism of the monoamine oxidase family. *Biomol Concepts* **2**(5): 365–77.

17. Klinman, J.P. (2006). The copper-enzyme family of dopamine beta-monooxygenase and peptidylglycine alpha-hydroxylating monooxygenase: resolving the chemical pathway for substrate hydroxylation. *J Biol Chem* **281**(6): 3013–6.

18. Kumar, D., R.E. Mains, and B.A. Eipper. (2016). 60 YEARS OF POMC: From POMC and alpha-MSH to PAM, molecular oxygen, copper, and vitamin C. *J Mol Endocrinol* **56**(4): T63–76.

19. Meredith, M.E. and J.M. May. (2013). Regulation of embryonic neurotransmitter and tyrosine hydroxylase protein levels by ascorbic acid. *Brain Res* **1539**: 7–14.

20. Sharp, C.S., M.P. Wilson, and K. Nordstrom. (2016). Psychiatric Emergencies for Clinicians: Emergency Department Management of Wernicke-Korsakoff Syndrome. *J Emerg Med* **51**(4): 401–4.

21. Subramanian, V.S., et al. (2010). Effect of chronic alcohol feeding on physiological and molecular parameters of renal thiamin transport. *Am J Physiol Renal Physiol* **299**(1): F28–34.

22. Koo, B.B., K. Bagai, and A.S. Walters. (2016). Restless legs syndrome: Current concepts about disease pathophysiology. *Tremor Other Hyperkinet Mov (N Y)* **6**: 401.

23. Namazi, N., J. Heshmati, and A. Tarighat-Esfanjani. (2015). Supplementation with riboflavin (vitamin B2) for migraine prophylaxis in adults and children: A review. *Int J Vitam Nutr Res* **85**(1–2): 79–87.

24. Varadarajan, P., V. Thayanathi, and L.C. Pauline. (2015). Fazio Londe syndrome: A treatable disorder. *Ann Indian Acad Neurol* **18**(1): 87–9.

25. Pleis, J.R. and M. Lethbridge-Cejku. (2007). Summary health statistics for U.S. adults: National Health Interview Survey, 2006. Vital Health Stat 10, (235): 1–153.

26. Zhong, M., et al. (2012). Retina, retinol, retinal and the natural history of vitamin A as a light sensor. *Nutrients* **4**(12): 2069–96.

27. Bridges, C.D., et al. (1984). Visual cycle in the mammalian eye. Retinoid-binding proteins and the distribution of 11-cis retinoids. *Vision Res* **24**(11): 1581–94.

28. Global prevalence of vitamin A deficiency in populations at risk 1995–2005, W.H. Organization, Editor. 2009, *WHO Global Database on Vitamin A Deficiency*, Geneva, Switzerland.

29. Duignan, E., et al. (2015). Ophthalmic manifestations of vitamin A and D deficiency in two autistic teenagers: Case reports and a review of the literature. *Case Rep Ophthalmol* **6**(1): 24–9.

30. Scripsema, N.K., D.N. Hu, and R.B. Rosen. (2015).Lutein, Zeaxanthin, and meso-Zeaxanthin in the Clinical Management of Eye Disease. *J Ophthalmol* **2015**: 865179.

31. Wangemann, P. (2006). Supporting sensory transduction: Cochlear fluid homeostasis and the endocochlear potential. *J Physiol* **576**(Pt 1): 11–21.

32. Mori, N., et al. (2016). Ion transport its regulation in the endolymphatic sac: Suggestions for clinical aspects of Meniere's disease. *Eur Arch Otorhinolaryngol.*

33. Yamauchi, D., et al. (2005). Vitamin D upregulates expression of ECaC1 mRNA in semicircular canal. *Biochem Biophys Res Commun* **331**(4): 1353–7.

34. Jung, D.J., H.H. Cho, and K.Y. Lee. (2016). Association of bone mineral density with hearing impairment in postmenopausal women in Korea. *Clin Exp Otorhinolaryngol.*

35. Angeli, S., X. Lin, and X.Z. Liu. (2012). Genetics of hearing and deafness. *Anat Rec (Hoboken)* **295**(11): 1812–29.

36. Lumpkin, E.A., K.L. Marshall, and A.M. Nelson. (2010). The cell biology of touch. *J Cell Biol* **191**(2): 237–48.

37. Fabian, T.K., et al. (2015). Molecular mechanisms of taste recognition: Considerations about the role of saliva. *Int J Mol Sci* **16**(3): 5945–74.

38. Greabu, M., et al. (2009). Saliva—a diagnostic window to the body, both in health and in disease. *J Med Life* **2**(2): 124–32.

39. Melis, M., et al. (2013). The gustin (CA6) gene polymorphism, rs2274333 (A/G), as a mechanistic link between PROP tasting and fungiform taste papilla density and maintenance. *PLoS One* **8**(9): e74151.

40. Cummins, E.P., et al. (2014). Carbon dioxide-sensing in organisms and its implications for human disease. *Cell Mol Life Sci* **71**(5): 831–45.

41. Bachmanov, A.A., et al. (2014). Genetics of taste receptors. *Curr Pharm Des* **20**(16): 2669–83.

42. Dey, S. and L. Stowers. (2016). Think you know how smell works? Sniff again. *Cell* **165**(7): 1566–7.

43. Hulshoff Pol, H.E., et al. (2002). Odor discrimination in patients with frontal lobe damage and Korsakoff's syndrome. *Neuropsychologia* **40**(7): 888–91.

Micronutrient-Deficiency in the Nervous System

Can you find all the hidden words in this word search?
words can go in the following directions: → ← ↓ ↑

```
P  E  L  L  A  G  R  A  U  Y  D  K  J  D  W
F  N  R  R  C  G  C  I  B  C  B  X  I  E  G
S  E  K  N  E  M  W  N  S  B  D  E  A  R  E
E  F  L  X  E  G  V  E  H  Q  F  E  W  D  T
V  O  V  B  Q  W  E  P  S  U  M  Z  Q  N  B
F  B  U  J  B  Y  N  O  S  H  K  K  M  E  E
Q  G  U  H  M  Y  D  R  C  F  U  R  A  P  R
V  I  X  A  B  R  N  E  U  S  I  B  C  C  I
B  E  B  P  L  M  A  D  R  Y  D  G  S  K  S
T  Q  N  Y  K  F  Z  I  V  G  O  W  H  P  E
W  I  L  B  O  N  S  S  Y  N  U  Q  V  M  R
T  Y  N  E  D  N  O  L  -  O  I  Z  A  F  I
X  Z  D  J  M  D  H  P  K  Z  Z  D  P  N  B
A  L  I  D  D  L  E  B  A  H  H  W  O  W  K
I  W  E  R  N  I  C  K  E  N  G  U  G  E  I
```

PELLAGRA	BERIBERI	FAZIO-LONDE
PENDRED	LIDDLE	MENKES
SIDEROPENIA	WERNICKE	SCURVY
WILSONS		

NOTES

APPENDIX

CALCIUM

Forms

- Divalent metal- ionized Ca^{2+}

Sources

- Good food sources: Milk & dairy products (yogurt-415mg/8oz verses 2% milk-293mg/8oz), Seafood, especially salmon, sardines (w/ bone), clams, some vegetables especially, turnip, kale, mustard greens, broccoli, cauliflower (leafy vegetables contain oxalates that bind Ca^{2+}), Legumes and legume products (tofu), Ca^{2+}-supplemented foods
- Drugs: antacids

DRI

- Adult males 1000 mg/day
- Adult females 1000 mg/day
- Adults over 71 1200 mg/day
  - UL = 4000 mg/day
- The average US female is not meeting DRI requirements. It is rare that adults over 71 are meeting their requirement. Most women and girls are below to EAR level as well

Absorption/Digestion/Metabolism

- Two main transport processes:
  - Energy dependent, saturable transport via TRPV6
  - Unsaturable, passive & paracellular absorption (absorption between cells)
- Factors improving Ca+ absorption
  - $1,25(OH)_2D_3$
    - genomic and non-genomic mechanisms
  - Lactose ($\uparrow$ Ca solubility) – better diffusion in infants

- o   Sugars & sugar alcohols (xylitol)
- o   Phe, Trp, Ala, His can activate Ca sensing receptor
- Factors inhibiting Ca+ absorption
  - o   Phytate (in corn, wheat, wild rice) - binds Ca $\rightarrow\downarrow$ availability
  - o   Fiber – $\downarrow$ absorption through Small Intestine
  - o   Oxalate (in spinach, rhubarb, chocolate, okra, beets, celery, berries, nuts) - chelates Ca $\rightarrow \downarrow$ fecal excretion
  - o Mg^{2+}, Zn^{2+}, Fe^{2+}- Excess of these cations compete for absorption.
  - o   Unabsorbed FAs in GI track can form insoluble Ca-FA complexes in the lumen, and inhibit Ca absorption

Deficiency/Toxicity

- Deficiency
  - o   Those at risk: Postmenopausal women and seniors (thin, inactive, or aged females), Amenorrheic women and the female athlete triad (combination of eating disorder, amenorrhea, and osteoporosis), People w/ lactose intolerance, Vegetarians - high-fiber/high-phytate diets (decreased Ca absorption), Smokers, Alcoholics, Those with family history/genetic disposition—SNPs in the FDPS gene associated with lower Bone mineral density (Levy, 2009) Toxicity
  - o $\downarrow$ Ca^{2+} affects mostly bone and muscle
    - ■   Rickets (in children)- growth cartilage fails to mature & mineralize normally
    - ■   Hypocalcemia- asymptomatic to severe symptoms, including seizures, tetany, or arrhythmias
    - ■   Osteomalcia (decreased minerals in bone)- muscle weakness, bone pain, fractures
    - ■   Long term low Ca intakes are associated w/ hypertension, colon cancer, and obesity
- Toxicity
  - o   UL 19+ male/female - 4000 mg/d
  - o   Signs of toxicity: hypercalcemia, deposition of Ca in soft tissues, constipation, potential for kidney stones (hypercalciuria, >4 mg/kg BW/d)
  - o   Oxalates bind to calcium which contributes to kidney stones

COPPER

Forms:

- Cu+2 and Cu+1
  - Note that pennies today are made mostly from zinc, but a 1965 penny contained mostly copper and today could be worth as much as 3 cents!

Sources

- Shellfish, green leafy vegetables, nuts, tomatoes, potatoes, pumpkin

DRI

- RDA of 0.9 mg/day for adults (men and women are identical)
  - Lower for children and infants
  - Slightly higher for lactating women

Absorption/Digestion/Metabolism

- Two apical copper transporters Ctr1 (copper transporter 1) and DMT1 (may also transports other divalent metals—cadmium, iron, manganese)
- Like iron, Cu+2 is reduced to Cu+1 by CytoB (Dyctb)
- ATOX1, a cellular copper chaperone delivers copper from Ctr1 to ATP7A, which transports copper from the enterocyte to the plasma.
  - Mutation in ATP7A results in Menke's syndrome (genetic copper deficiency)
- Once in plasma, like zinc, copper is bound by albumin and transported to the liver
  - Once in the liver, copper is incorporated into ceruloplasmin (using ATP7B) for circulation to tissues
    - Mutation of ATP7B results in Wilson's Disease
    - Some scientific questions of whether ceruloplasmin is really *that* important for copper transport, as individuals with mutations in ceruloplasmin actually have altered iron metabolism

- High Zinc levels results in low copper absorption
  - Metallothionein (produced in response to high metal in general)
  - Binds metal within the enterocyte, blocking it from entering circulation
  - Metal is lost in feces when enterocyte is sloughed off

Deficiency/Toxicity

- Deficiency
  - Rare and most individuals do get the required intake level.
    - Deficiency symptoms determined from genetic deficiency
  - Anemia, cardiac enlargement, skeletal defects, reproductive failure, low aortic elasticity, altered pigmentation, neutropenia
    - Some symptoms such as irregular heartbeat and altered glucose utilization may occur before overt deficiency
- Toxicity
  - UL = 10 mg/d
    - Not studied extensively.
    - GI discomfort with as little as 5mg/day.
    - Acute liver failure for one individual with extreme intake

FLUORIDE

Forms:

Ionic form is F^-. Fluoride is the thirteenth most abundant element in the earth's crust. Can be found in association with calcium (CaF_2), magnesium (MgF_2), aluminum (AlF_2), and sodium (NaF_2)

Sources:

Fluoride concentration in most foods is very low, and could depend on the concentration in drinking/irrigation water used with the food. Tea and marine fish have natural fluoride, but most intake occurs from fluoridated water, and dental products.

DRI:

Females and young males (<19) have an AI of 3 mg/day, while older males have a slightly higher intake level of 4 mg/day. The AI for children is lower (range 0.01-2 mg/day). The UL is established as 10 mg/day for adults and up to 10 mg/day for children. The UL was established based on the risk for fluorosis.

Absorption/Digestion/Metabolism

- 80-90% of ingested fluoride is absorbed passively. If calcium is ingested together with fluoride, then only 50-70% is absorbed as calcium interfere with absorption by forming insoluble CaF_2.
    - In the stomach, HF (hydrofluoric acid) easily passes through the gastric lining (40% absorbed here)
    - No evidence for any active transport mechanism
- Excreted mainly through the kidneys
    - Acidity of the urine affects fluoride absorption/retention

Deficiency/Toxicity

- Deficiency
  - Causes dental caries
  - Osteoporesis is associated with low F (Boulétreau PH, Bost M, Fontanges E, *et al* (June 2006). "Fluoride exposure and bone status in patients with chronic intestinal failure who are receiving home parenteral nutrition". *Am. J. Clin. Nutr.* 83 (6): 1429–37)

- Toxicity
  - Dental Fluorosis
    - Occurs pre-eruptively in developing teeth during enamel formation
    - Can be mild, moderate or severe
  - Acute Toxicity
    - Life threatening—can occur in the average home due to overuse of dental products accompanied by fluoride in the water
    - Nausea and vomiting, excessive salivation, sweating, headache, diarrhea, weakness
    - Spasm or convulsions can occur, accompanied by hypotension and cardiac arrhythmias
      - Due to hyperkalemia and hypocalcemia
  - Chronic Toxicity
    - Skeletal Fluorosis
      - Initially an increase in bone density
      - Then increase in calcification of bone, with joint stiffness
      - Finally bony outgrowths, and calcification of ligaments and joints
    - Bone fractures-controversial
      - Some studies support this, while others (above) show the opposite

IODINE

Forms:

Found and functions in its ionic form, iodide (I^-). Also found as iodate (IO^{-3}) which is added to bread as a "dough improver"

Sources

Most food sources are low. Fish, shellfish and seaweed have highest natural amounts as these organisms concentrate iodine from seawater. Iodized salt provides 71 µg/1.5 grams of salt

DRI

Adult daily recommended intakes of 150 µg/day (just ½ teaspoon of iodized salt) or 1 3 oz filet of haddock. Pregnancy and lactating women need up to 290 µg/day while children and infants need less. Surveys of average intakes by NHANES indicate that average intake in the US is sufficient at 138-353 µg/day.

Absorption/Digestion/Metabolism

- Iodide ion can be absorbed by passive diffusion. If iodate or iodine is ingested, it is reduced to iodide ion by GSH (glutathione)
- Na/I transporter in the thyroid takes up iodine
    o Can be inhibited by perchlorate (EPA regulated substance)
- Synthesis of thyroid hormones requires pendrin glycoprotein which "pumps" iodide to the follicular lumen (colloid)
    o Thyroid peroxidase oxidizes iodide which is coupled to thyroglobulin, in either a monoiodo (MIT) or diiodo (DIT) form, eventually forming T3 and T4
- T3 and T4 are released from the colloid, and then travel to tissues using transthyretin with retinol binding protein, thyroid binding globulin, or albumin

- o The iodine from used T3 and T4 can recycled or excreted upon breakdown and degradation of T3/T4

Deficiency/Toxicity

- Deficiency
  - o Now called "Iodine Deficiency Disorders" as Goiter is a symptom
    - Goiter is caused by reduced accumulation of iodine, and production of T3/T4, which leads to increased TSH synthesis by the pituitary gland, leading to hyperplasia of the thyroid
    - Cretinism—neurological (mental retardation, deaf mutism, motor spasticity) or myxedematous (hypothyroid with growth retardation, but less severe)
    - Spontaneous abortion, stillbirth, congenital abnormalities, and perinatel/infant mortality increased with hypothyroidism
    - Could less severe IDD cause attention deficit and/or hyperactivity disorders?
    - Hypothyroidism-Hashimotos Autoimmune Thyroiditis
      - Not due to iodine deficiency, but due to autoantibodies against thyroid
      - Fatigue, cold sensitivity, constipation, mental slowness, reduced cardiac function and increased cholesterol
- Toxicity
  - o UL = 1100 µg/day based on effects of increasing TSH and increased risk for developing hypothyroidism
  - o Hyperthyroidism
    - Graves Disease—autoantibodies against TSH receptor
      - Leads to continuous stimulation of the thyroid gland
      - Weight loss, heat intolerance, irritability, tachycardia, muscle, tremor, nervousness
      - Radioactive iodine can be used as treatment-destroys the gland (but then the patient becomes hypothyroid)
    - Jod-Basedow phenomenon
      - Iodine-induced hyperthyroidism
      - Occurs when there is a steep increase in dietary iodine following deficiency
    - Wolff-Chaikoff effect
      - High iodine intake followed by hypothyroidism
      - This known effect can be used to treat hyperthyroidism, as a high dose of iodine can shut down the production of TH transiently (about 10 days)

IRON

Forms

- Fe^{2+} (Ferrous), Fe^{3+} (Ferric)
- 2–4 g/70 kg BW—related to BW, physiological conditions, age, gender, pregnancy, state of growth
  - "Functional Iron" >65% of body Fe is found in hemoglobin, ~10% as myoglobin, 1–5% as part of enzymes in the blood or in storage
  - "Transport Iron"—transferrin
  - "Storage Iron"—Ferritin (and hemosiderin)
    - Hemosiderin is a minor component, mostly found in iron overload or cell damage.

Sources

- Two forms of dietary iron
  - Heme iron
    - Derived from hemoglobin and myoglobin in meat, fish, poultry (up to 60%)
  - Nonheme iron
    - Plant foods: beans, nuts, fruits, vegetables, tofu, dairy products (poor)

DRI

- Note that the DRI is very different for men and women

Age/gender group	RDA (mg/d)
Men 19+ years	8
Women 19-50 years	18
Women 50+ years	8
Pregnant Women	27

Absorption/Digestion/Metabolism

- Heme Iron Absorption
    - Binds to heme carrier protein 1 (hcp1) on brush border membrane (which it turns out is also a folate receptor!!)
    - Heme is hydrolyzed to Fe+2 by heme oxygenase
- Nonheme Iron Absorption
    - Fe+3 is converted to Fe+2 by duodenal cytochrome b (DcytB).
    - Fe+2 can be absorbed using the di-metal transporter DMT1
- The iron pool has two fates:
    - Incorporation into ferritin, as storage
    - Export to the bloodstream by ferroportin
        - Fe+2 is converted back to Fe+3 by the action of either hephaestin or ceruloplasmin
        - Fe+3 is transported to tissues in a complex with transferrin.
- Interaction with Other Nutrients
    - Vitamin C enhances Fe absorption and maintains Fe.
        - Releases Fe^{3+} from ferritin, and reduces to Fe^{2+}
    - Copper
        - Hephaestin and ceruloplasmin can act as ferroxidases.
        - Oxidation of Fe^{2+} (ferrous iron) into Fe^{3+} (ferric iron) is necessary for transport in the plasma in association with transferrin, which can carry iron only in the ferric state
    - Zinc
        - Excess intake of NHI from supplements, may inhibit Zn absorption
    - Calcium
        - Ca intake decreases the NHI absorption
    - Retinoic acid
        - The combination of vitamin A and Fe supplements ameliorate anemia more effectively
    - Lead (Pb)
        - Inhibits the activity of aminolevunic acid dehydratase, required in heme synthesis
    - Selenium (Se)
        - Fe deficiency is associated with decreased Se and Se-dependent enzymes

Deficiency/Toxicity

- Deficiency
    - Pallor, fatigue, irritability, dizziness, hair loss, etc.
        - Progressive deficiency results in iron-deficiency anemia

- Deficiency—who is at risk?
  - Infants and children (6 mo – 4 yrs)
    - Low Fe content of milk, rapid growth rate, and insufficient body reserves of Fe
  - Adolescents
    - Rapid growth, high needs of expanding RBC mass
  - Females of childbearing age
    - Menstrual losses
  - Pregnant women
    - Expanding blood volume, the demands of the fetus
  - People with bleeding or inflammatory diseases
    - Hemorrhage, renal disease, renal replacement therapy, decreased GI transit time, steatorrhea, parasites
  - Vegetarians
  - People who engage in regular intense exercise
- Treatment of Deficiency
  - Heme iron most bioavailable, so could consider more meat, poultry, and fish
  - Ferrous salts, esp. $FeSO_4$—a 300 mg tablet contains 60 mg Fe^{2+} and should be taken 3–4 x /d with meals.
    - Absorption enhanced with vitamin C
  - IV administration for severe cases
- Toxicity
  - UL = 45 mg/d—excess Fe from high-dose supplements = GI distress, constipation, nausea
  - Fe overload
    - Determined by $\uparrow$ serum [ferritin] or >62% Tf saturation
    - Can occur with hemolytic anemia, or ineffective erythropoiesis
  - Hereditary hemochromatosis
    - Increased iron absorption/storage due to genetic mutation in the HFE gene

MAGNESIUM

Forms

- Divalent metal ion (Mg+2)
- 4th most abundant cation in the body, and 2nd most abundant intracellular cation
- Total body content of Mg+2 is ~24 grams, mainly on bone

Sources

- In lots of different food sources—almost all, but most abundant in whole grain cereals, legumes, nuts (brazil nuts are highest) and chocolate.
- Milk of magnesia—used as an antacid and laxative

DRI

- Adult males, 400-420 mg/day while females are lower at 310-320/day
- More than 50% of the population may have intakes below the EAR.
  - Mainly due to processed foods, which have reduced Mg+2

Absorption/Digestion/Metabolism

- Absorbed along the entire intestinal track
- Paracellular (between cells, passive) pathway, requires transepithelial concentration gradient (with charge) and higher concentrations
- Transcellular (through cells) pathway occurs via TRPM6 (transient receptor potential melastin) channel. Low Mg+2 induces expression of TRPM6, and increased absorption of Mg+2
  - EGF (epidermal growth factor) stimulates TRPM6 trafficing to the cell membrane, but colon cancer patients treated with anti-EGF antibodies (a form of chemotherapy), may develop hypomanesemia due to low Mg+2 absorption.

- Kidney is primary organ involved in Mg+2 homeostasis
    - Again, TRPM6 channel is involved in lumen absorption, and a Mg+2/2Na+ antiporter system transports Mg+2 to the blood

Deficiency/Toxicity

- Deficiency
    - Can be caused by vomiting, diarrhea, ulcerative colitis, and draining of intestinal or biliary fistula
    - Celiac's disease or other malabsorption syndromes can cause Mg+2 deficiency
    - Mg+2 deficiency by certain drugs, including aminoglycosides, cisplatin, cyclosporine (cancer therapies)
    - Mg+2 depletion causes hypokalemia, hypocalcemia, neuromuscular hyperexcitivity, electrocardiogram abnormalities and arrhythmias.
- Toxicity
    - UL established, especially for pharmacological use (i.e. Milk of Magnesia, renal failure patients)
    - But in patients without kidney failure, toxicity would normally not occur
    - Diarrhea is one symptom

MANGANESE

Forms:

- Mn+2, Mn+3, Mn+7
  - Mn+2 can compete with Mg+2 in some biological systems
  - Mn+2 is the oxidation state used functionally in the body-the other oxidation states are toxic as strong oxidizers

Sources

- Brown rice, ready-to-eat cereal, tea, green leafy vegetables, tree nuts, legumes

DRI

- AI (as no RDA levels have been set) of 2.3 mg/day for males and 1.8 mg/day for females
  - Lower for children and infants
  - Slightly higher for lactating women

Absorption/Digestion/Metabolism

- DMT1 (also transports other divalent metals—cadmium, iron, copper, zinc)
  - Rats with mutant DMT1 have reduced manganese update in the intestine
- Mn is transported to the liver using α2-macroglobin (Mn+2) or transferrin (Mn+3 –little used)
- High Iron, Zinc or Copper levels results in low Mn absorption
  - Due to metallothionein (see fact sheet on Copper for mechanism)
- No storage pool, except perhaps intracellular through metallothionein

Deficiency/Toxicity

- Deficiency
    - Reduced growth, weak bone (due to role in cartilage formation-glycosyltransferases and xylosyltransferase), reduced reproduction (unknown reason for this), malformations in offspring, impaired glucose tolerance (pyruvate carboxylase, and phosphoenolpyruvate carboxylase)
- Toxicity
    - UL = 11 mg/d
        - Considered the least toxic mineral.
        - Vegetarians usually consume *at least* this much per day with no adverse effects
            - 25 days of 15 mg/day resulted in high Mn-SOD levels
        - Toxicity rarely occurs via oral intake, but from industrial and auto exhaust emissions.
            - Pancreatitis, and neurological disorders (like Parkinson's and schizophrenia)
            - Exposure is regulated by OSHA

OTHER TRACE MINERALS

Forms:

- The term "ultra-trace" element only began to appear in the 1980's
- Four elements are considered nutritionally ultra-trace
    - Cobalt, iodine, molybdenum, and selenium
    - See individual pages for iodine and selenium
- Boron and Chromium are not yet considered nutritionally essential, but may have health benefits
- Silicon can have some bioactivity
- Nickel and Vanadium appear to be essential in animal studies
- Arsenic-bioactive, but required?

Sources:

- Molybdenum: plant foods are major source
- Chromium: plants?
- Boron: All plant foods
- Cobalt: Non-ruminant herbivores produce vitamin B12 from bacteria in their colons which again make the vitamin from simple cobalt salts. Humans must obtain cobalt for B12 in this form
- Silicon: Beer is a great source of silicon!
- Nickel: chocolate and nuts
- Vanadium: grains, mushrooms, parsley

DRI:

Molybedunum: Males and females ages 14+, 45µg per day

Absorption/Digestion/Metabolism

Absorption, digestion and metabolism of these nutritional trace minerals are not well-studied.

Deficiency/Toxicity

- Deficiency
    - No molybdendum deficiency has been unequivocally identified in humans other than those nourished by parenteral nutrition, or rare genetic defects
    - Chromium deficiency has been attributed to only three people on long-term parenteral nutrition
    - Nickel: impaired reproduction, conception, bone health, and lipid metabolism (animal studies)
    - Silicon may be associated with bone mineral density

- Toxicity
    - Increased silicon in drinking water associated with decreased Alzheimers, but no toxicity has been established
    - No toxicity for molybdenum although an UL is established

PHOSPHORUS

Forms and Discovery

- Often found associated w/ cations
  - (Mg^{2+},Ca^{2+})
- Found as free phosphate (PO_4)$^{3-}$ or bound (ester or anhydride linkage) in circulation and tissues
- $H_2PO_4^-$ and HPO_4^{2-} - the two major inorganic forms in aqueous environments

Sources

- Animal products > plant foods
- Dairy products > meats, poultry, fish > eggs
  - In meat mostly as organic compounds, hydrolyzed to HPO_4^{2-} - >70% absorption
- Cereals, nuts, legumes, grains
- Coffee & tea – small amount
- Soft drinks
  - phosphoric acid (H_3PO_4)
- Supplements
  - phosphate

DRI

- 1997 RDA for adults = 700 mg/d
  - Based on serum [phosphate] to meet cellular and skeletal needs

Absorption/Digestion/Metabolism

- Active Transport
  - Low P_i (inorganic phosphate) stimulates active Vitamin D synthesis (via increasing 1, 25-hydroxyvitamin-D_3-1α-hydroxylase
  - Na^+-dependent P_i cotransporter type IIb (NaPi-IIb) in brush border membrane of small intestine

- Facilitative Diffusion
  - Occurs when phosphorus levels are high
- Excretion through urine and sweat
  Other
  - PTH—decreaed Ca^{++} → increases PTH from parathyroid → inreases P from bone to blood and increased P in blood → ↑ P excretion in urine
  - Calcitonin- increased Ca^{++} → ↑ calcitonin from thyroid → ↑ reabsoprtion of P in the kidney → bone formation
  - Alkaline phosphatase- cleaves ester bonds in the gut and to increase available P for absorption
  - Vitamin D-calcitriol binds VDR → increases intestinal P absorption and increases P from bone

Deficiency/Toxicity

- Deficiency
  - Hypophosphatemia
    - loss of appetite, anemia, muscle weakness, bone pain, rickets (in children),
    - osteomalacia (in adults), increased susceptibility to infection, numbness and tingling of the extremities, and difficulty walking.
    - Severe hypophosphatemia may result in death.
  - 'Refeeding syndrome'
    - Malnourished patients fed with high CHO loads → causes a rapid fall in P, Mg, and K the blood. High demand to make ATP which pulls out P
  - Hypophosphatemic rickets (*aka* Dent's syndrome) –
    - A X-linked recessive genetic disorder causing a defect in the re-absorption of P in the kidneys leading to excess P loss from the body and inadequate bone mineralization.
    - Consequence of genetic mutations in the renal chloride channel CLCN5 which encodes a kidney-specific voltage gated chloride channel – leads to dysfunctions in proximal tubular endocytosis → decreased endocytosis of PTH → increased PTH in tubular binding to PTHII receptors →endocytosis of NaP_iII co-transporters → decreased P reabsorption
- Toxicity
  - No evidence of adverse effects
  - UL set at 4 g/d
    - based on UL of normal serum [Pi]
  - Chronic hyperphosphatemia symptoms:
    - Convulsions, Arrythmias, Tetany and numbness/parasthesias in hands, feet, around mouth and lips "CATS go numb"
    - Managed by reducing P intake and giving oral phosphate binders (Ca^{2+} or Mg^{2+} salts)

SELENIUM

Forms

Se^{-2} (selenide or H_2Se, hydrogen selenide), SeO_3^{-2} (selenite, with H_2SeO_4, selenous acid), and SeO_4^{-2} (selenate, with H_2SO_4, selenic acid). The major forms in cells are selenoamino cids, with selenium forming covalent bonds with carbons. SeCys (selenocysteine) is encoded by DNA/mRNA, and SeMet (selenomethionine) is found in plant, but can be incorporated into animal proteins

Sources

Food sources vary, based on availability of selenium in soil (for plants) and livestock diets. Nuts, especially Brazil nuts are a good source. Garlic, onions, and broccholi plants are "selenium accumulator plants" and will accumulate large amounts of Se if grown in Se-rich soils.

DRI

Males and females have an RDA of 55 μg/day with an increase for pregnant or lactating females to 60-70 μg/day. Children are lower at 15-40 μg/day. According to intake data, most Americans (and other countries) may be consuming 2-5 times the RDA, but the UL is 400 μg/day for males and females. There are lower IL for infants and children.

Absorption/Digestion/Metabolism

- Passive diffusion for inorganic selenium
  - Selenium is converted to H_2Se (selenide)
    - May be further reduced by NADPH and GSH to selenite
- Selenium-Met and Selenium-Cys are absorbed via amino acid transporters
  - Sel-Met and Sel-Cys can be used in place of methionine and cysteine in selenoproteins
    - There is a special tRNA$^{Ser/SeCys}$
      - Encoded by UGA (TGA)—usually serves as a stop codon! Secondary structure in the RNA itself instructs the incorporation of selenium

- Use requires selenophosphate syntase (SPS) to make the tRNA$^{Ser/SeCys}$

Deficiency/Toxicity

- Deficiency
  - Juvenile Cardiomyophathy (Keshan Disease)
    - Prevalent in China
    - Multi-focal myocarditis in children 2-10 years old
  - Kashin-Beck Disease
    - Osteoarthropathy in epiphyseal cartilage, and growth plates
    - Could also be related to impaired thyroid function
  - Possible role in preventing carcinogenesis
    - Anti-tumor effects of supplementation
- Toxicity
  - Selenosis
    - Neuropathy (first seen in grazing cattle)
    - Severe GI disturbances
    - Acute Respiratory failure, myocardial infarction and renal failure if prolonged
  - High selenium intake linked to diabetes risk

SODIUM, POTASSIUM AND CHLORIDE

Forms and History

- Na+ ion (with chloride) constitute the major electrolytes in plasma
- K+ is located in cells and extracellular fluids
- Cl⁻ is the most abundant anion in the ECF
  - Neutralizes Na^+ to maintain electrolyte balance
- The body contains 100 g of sodium, 95 g of chloride and 140 g of potassium
  - ~1/3 of the sodium is sequestered in the skeleton
  - ~60-70% of potassium is in skeletal muscles
- The English word *salary*, derives from *salarium*, the wafers of salt sometimes given to Roman soldiers along with their other wages.
  - The chemical abbreviation for sodium is a contraction of the element's Latin name *natrium*

Sources

- Sodium
  - Mostly consumed as NaCl
  - 1 tsp salt contains 2,300 mg Na (=5,827 mg NaCl)
  - Cured meats, processed foods, canned vegetables, snacks, condiments (400 – 1,000 mg Na)
    - Up to 75% Na intake from processed foods
    - Natural sources – vegs, milk, eggs (40 – 150 mg Na)
- Potassium
  - Abundant in unprocessed foods (with phosphate and citrate)
    - papaya (~780 mg), bananas (~450 mg), prune juice, cantaloupe, honeydew, mango – very high in K, Legumes, nuts and seeds, peanut butter , Milk and yogurt
- Chloride
  - Almost all the dietary Cl consumption is associated w/ Na in the form of salt (~60% in NaCl)
  - Eggs, meats seafood

DRI

- Sodium
  - 2010 DRI is 1.5 grams Na/day (AI)
    - Most consume 3 -18 g NaCl/d (1.2 – 7.1 g Na/d)
    - Need at least ~ 85 mg Na/day to match obligatory losses
- Chloride
  - AI: 2.3 g/d
- Potassium
  - AI : 4.7 g/d
    - Average intake of Americans - ~ 3.3 g

Absorption/Digestion/Metabolism

- Sodium/Potassium ATPase and sodium/chloride transporters in small intestine regulates entry of Na+ and K+ into and out of cells (both for absorption into cells, and out into blood, and within tissues)
  - Na/K ATPase is found on basolateral side of SI, and pumps Na+ out, and K+ in
- Other transporters include Na/glucose transporters, Na/H transporters, Na/amino acid transporters.
- Liddle Syndrome-due to mutation in epithelial Na channel
  - Results in increased Na^{+2} retention/decreased urinary excretion
  - Mutation causes increased activity of the channel, so more Na^{+2} back into the plasma
- Absorbed Na^+ is transported freely in the blood
  - Primarily controlled by Arginine Vasopressin, and the Renin-Angiotensin-Aldosterone system.
- High K → ↓ urinary Ca excretion
  - Can replace NaCl in the diet with KCl to reduce urinary Ca excretion
  - Potassium citrate can prevent Na-induced urinary Ca excretion → ↓ bone resorption
- Blood pressure medications including angiotensin converting enz inhibitors, and angiotensin receptor blockers
  - ↑ urinary K excretion
  - Diuretics - ↑ Na and water excretion

Deficiency/Toxicity

- Deficiency
  - Sodium
    - Blood [Na+] < 135 mEq/L = Hyponatremia
      - Muscle cramps, nausea, vomiting, dizziness, shock, coma, death
    - Can happen acutely due to water intoxication, excessive losses, and/or inappropriate AVP secretion
  - Potassium
    - Hypokalemia (< ~3.5 mM): $\uparrow$ BP, $\uparrow$ urinary Ca excretion, $\uparrow$ bone resorption, $\downarrow$ bone formation
    - Cardiac arrhythmias, muscular weakness, hypercalciuria, glucose intolerance, mental disorientation due to significant fluid loss (vomiting or diarrhea, diuretic meds) or refeeding syndrome
  - Chloride
    - Deficiency does not occur under normal conditions
    - Deficiency results GI tract disturbance –diarrhea and vomiting
    - Convulsions at really low levels

- Toxicity
  - Sodium
    - UL : 2.3 g Na/d
    - Patients with hypertension and kidney disease – on Na restricted diet (2 g – still higher than AI which is 1.5g)
  - Potassium
    - No UL
    - Hyperkalemia by high dose of dietary supplements— Cardiac arrest
  - Chloride
    - Toxicity is not a problem—regulated and excreted
    - UL is 3.6 grams (related to Na^+)

ZINC

Forms

- Zn+2 (only one state, unlike Copper and Mn)
- Following K+ and Mg+, Zinc is the most common intracellular metal ion.
  - Usually found in association with a metalloenzyme (over 200 known)

Sources

- Shellfish, liver, beef, poultry, fortified cereal, legumes, nuts, yogurt

DRI

- RDA of 11 mg/day for adults (men and women are identical)
  - Lower for children and infants
  - Slightly higher for lactating women

Absorption/Digestion/Metabolism

- Transcellular movement, using zinc transporters ZIP4 and ZnT5
  - Acrodermatitis enteropathica (AE) patients have a ZIP4 mutation
    - Dermatitis around orifices, and limbs, night blindness, impaired taste, hypogonadism, alopecia, poor growth, immune deficiency
    - Increased zinc supplementation for treatment (death without treatment)
- Paracellular movement in between cells (high concentration only)
- ZnT1 transporter moves Zinc from the enterocyte to the blood, where it is bound with Albumin for transport to the liver
  - Upon reaching the liver, Zinc is repackaged with α2-macroglobin, and released into the blood.
  - There are up to 200 Zinc transporters which may be involved in tissue uptake from plants, nemotodes, insects and mammals.
    - About 24 of these are found in humans

- ZIP transporters go from the extracellular to the cytosol
- ZnT transporters go from the cytosol to the extracellular
  - Zinc containing vesicles (zincosomes) store zinc in cells

Deficiency/Toxicity

- Deficiency
  - Seen in populations that consume a lot of phytate (interferes with absorption) and/or low meat
  - Loss of appetite, poor growth, alopecia, immune dysfunction, hypogonadism, poor wound healing, abnormal taste
- Toxicity
  - UL = 40 mg/d
    - Determined by reduction of Cu/Zn SOD activity (by resultant copper deficiency)

VITAMIN A

Forms and Discovery

- Retinoids—Preformed Vitamin A
  - o Retinol, retinal, retinoic acid
- Carotinoids—Pro Vitamin A
  - o β-carotene, α-carotene, β-cryptoxanthin
- Carotinoids that are NOT precursors to Vitamin A
  - o Lycopene, canthaxanthin, lutein

Sources

- Preformed Vitamin A
  - o Animal sources: Liver, Giblets (Retinyl Esters)
  - o Plant Sources: Pumpkin, Sweet Potatos, Carrots, Squash (Carotenoids)
  - o Fortified margarine and other oils
- Pro Vitamin A
  - o β-carotene (carrot, sweet potatoes, cantaloupe, squash) - exhibits the greatest provitamin A activity
  - o α-carotene (carrots, sweet potatoes, broccholi)
  - o β-cryptoxanthin (tomato)
  - o lycopene (watermelon, tomato)
  - o zeaxanthin (peppers, corn, potatoes, & eggs),
  - o lutein (kale, beets, kiwi, & eggs)

DRI

In discussing Vitamin A, we use "retinol activity equivalents" with 1 RAE = 1 μg retinol, 12 μg of β-carotene, 24 μg α-carotene, and 24 μg β-cryptoxanthin
- Adult males 900 RAE
- Adult females 700 RAE
  - o UL = 3000 RAE
- The current DRI was established in 2001, and was due to new research showing that the 1989 levels were inadequate, as dietary carotenoids were not as bioavailable as β-carotene in oil.
- Up to 59% of the US population does not meet the recommended amount of daily Vitamin A, although they are within the EAR value.

Absorption/Digestion/Metabolism

- Retinyl ester from animal sources are cleaved by retinyl ester hydrolases in the intestines to produce retinol and a fatty acid
  - Requires bile acids
- β-carotene from plant sources is cleaved into two molecules of retinal by β-carotene 15, 15'-monooxygenase (BCMOI) in the intestines, but also some uncleaved β-carotene is transferred to tissues such as liver, adipose and brain for cleavage.
- Other AdMet-see figure 30-11 and lecture slide
- <u>Interactions with other nutrients</u>
  - Vitamin E
    - High β-carotene - ↓ plasma Vit E concentration
  - Vitamin K
    - Excess Vit A interferes with Vit K absorption.
  - Protein
    - inadequate protein intake → ↓ carotenoid dehydrogenase
  - Zinc Deficiency
    - Decreased synthesis of RBP4 and TTR
  - Iron
    - Vit A deficiency is associated w/ microcytic iron deficiency anemia.
    - Vit A + iron supplements seems to reduce anemia more effectively than either iron or vit A alone
  - Vit D & Calcium
    - Excess retinol may impair Vit D and Calcium absorption

Deficiency/Toxicity

- Deficiency
  - Ocular (night blindness, for example). Night blindness can turn into xerophtalmia with drying of the cornea (xerosis), and can lead to full blindness
  - Reduced immunity
  - Hyperkeratosis, including intestinal epithelium and skin involvement
- Toxicity
  - Rare
  - Liver involvement (Vitamin A intoxication)
  - Fetal abnormalities
  - Hypervitaminosis A - nausea, vomiting, double vision, headache, dizziness, and dry skin
    - Chronic Toxicity: Retinol (~3-4× the RDA for months or years) can cause hypervitaminosis A - anorexia, dry itchy flaky skin, alopecia (hair loss), ataxia, bone & muscle pain, conjunctivitis (pink eye)
  - No UL for carotenoids

VITAMIN B1 (THIAMINE)

Forms and Discovery

- Thiamine or thiamin, Vitamin B_1, aneurin (Europe)
- Thiamine exists as free thiamin and as various phosphorylated forms:
  - thiamin monophosphate (TMP)
  - thiamin pyrophosphate (TPP) **Predominant form
    - AKA thiamin diphosphate (ThDP)
  - thiamin triphosphate (TTP)
- Discovered due to its deficiency disease (BeriBeri)

Sources

- whole grains, enriched or fortified grains, yeast, wheat germ
- meat (pork), legumes, nuts, green vegetables (peas, asparagus & okra)
- milk and fruit (poor sources)

DRI

- RDA (1998) for men 14+ yr is: 1.2 mg/d
- RDA (1998) for women 19+ yr 1.1 mg/d

Absorption/Digestion/Metabolism

- TPP is hydrolyzed by intestinal phosphatases to free thiamin prior to absorption
  - Anti-thiamin factors:
    - thiaminases cleave thiamin- making it inactive
    - found in the animal flesh of some raw fish (freshwater- tuna, carp, mackerel, herring) and shellfish (mussels)
    - thermolabile- cooking the fish inactivates the thiaminases
  - Thiamin antagonists
    - Caffeine and tannic acid (tea)

- Active transport mechanism for intestinal absorption by ThTr1 and ThTr2 (thiamin/H$^+$ antiport carrier system)
  - Passive diffusion at high concentrations
- 90% of thiamin is transported in blood, and then phosphorylated in liver to TPP

Deficiency/Toxicity

- Beriberi (wet, dry, acute)
- Wernicke-Korsakoff Syndrome
- Rogers Syndrome
- Toxicity is not a problem—high doses used for treatment of some diseases

VITAMIN B2 (RIBOFLAVIN)

Forms and Discovery

- Also called: vitamin B_2, Vitamin G
- Forms-FAD and FMN (flavoproteins)
- Originally isolated as a fluorescent fraction from milk

Sources

- Good sources: Milk/dairy - as riboflavin
- Legumes & green vegetables (spinach), grains (whole and fortified)- as FMN or FAD
    - 1.5 cups of sliced almonds yields 1.4mg of riboflavin
- Heat stable and light sensitive

DRI

- RDA (1998) for men 14+ yrs is 1.3 mg/d
- RDA (1998) for women 19+ yrs is 1.1mg/d
- Why higher in men versus women?
    - Riboflavin is important in energy metabolism. Thus, the recommended intake varies according to energy intake/need

Absorption/Digestion/Metabolism

- Riboflavin that's attached non-covalently to proteins is digested by hydrochloric acid, by other gastric and by intestinal enzymes.
- FAD and FMN are digested in the intestinal lumen
- Metals (such as Cu^{2+}, Zn^{2+}, Fe^{2+}, Mn^{2+}) can bind to riboflavin and FMN $\rightarrow \downarrow$ riboflavin absorption.
- Alcohol ingestion $\rightarrow \downarrow$ riboflavin digestion & absorption
- In small intestine, riboflavin uses both Na+-dependent absorptive and at high doses, passive absorption
- In intestinal cells, it is converted back to FMN by flavokinase, requiring Zn+2 and ATP

Deficiency/Toxicity

- Ariboflavinosis (deficiency)
  - Severe deficiency can impair the synthesis of vitamin B6, and niacin
- No human toxicity ever reported

VITAMIN B3 (NIACIN)

Forms and Discovery

- AKA: vitamin B_3, nicotinic acid, or nicotinamide
- NAD is found primarily in its oxidized form (NAD^+), whereas NADP is found in its reduced form (NADPH).
- Niacin was discovered through the condition pellagra.
  - Original preparation of niacin made by oxidizing nicotine using nitric acid
  - The resulting name 'niacin' was derived from nicotinic acid + vitamin.
  - Pellagra was prevalent in the Southern US where corn was a main dietary staple in the early 1900s
  - Corn contains a relatively unavailable form of niacin, unless treated with alkaline solution

Sources

- Best sources: fish (tuna & halibut), meat (beef, poultry, pork)
- Live animals have NAD & NADP, however, following the slaughter, it's hydrolyzed to free nicotinamide
- Enriched cereals, bread products, whole grains, seeds, & legumes
- Coffee & tea
- In supplements – as nicotinamide

DRI

- "Niacin Equivalents" is used since we can synthesize niacin from tryptophan.
- RDA for men 14+ yrs: 16 mg of NE/d
- RDA for women 14+ yrs: 14 mg of NE/d
- 60 mg of Tryptophan can generate 1 mg of niacin - 1 niacin equivalent (NE)

Absorption/Digestion/Metabolism

- Gut—Na-dependent active absorption at low concentration
- Gut—Passive Diffusion at high concentration
- In the plasma, niacin is found as nicotinamide, and some nicotinic acid. Nicotinamide moves across the cell membrane by passive diffusion
- The metabolism of niacin takes place in the liver, with conversion to N-methyl nicotinamide and final excretion by the kidney
- NAD salvage and de-novo pathway

Deficiency/Toxicity

- Pellegra (deficiency)
  - •The 4 D's: Dermatitis, Dementia, Diarrhea, & Death
- Flushing/skin irritation (toxicity)
  - UL 35 mg/d (adults)

VITAMIN B5 (PANTOTHENIC ACID)

Forms and Discovery

- Pantothenic Acid or Pantothenate
    - Pantoic acid + β-alanine = Pantothenic acid
    - Pantothenic acid + β-mercaptoethylamine = Pantetheine
    - Pantetheine + 3'-phospho-ADP = Coenzyme A (CoA)
    - CoA + acetate = Acetyl CoA (Acetyl-CoA)
    - CoA + LCFA = Long chain fatty acyl CoA
- Humans cannot make PA
- From the Greek word "pantos" meaning "everywhere"

Sources

- Present in all plant and animal foods.
- Good sources: liver, egg yolks, legumes
    - PA is contained in foods in various bound forms (including CoA, CoA esters, acyl carrier protein, & glucose)
- Lost (~35-75%) in highly processed foods (refining, freezing and canning)
    - A typical US diet provides at least 2 x AI
    - In supplements, found as calcium pantothenate or as pantothenol (*aka* pantenol)

DRI

- AI for men and women 14 + yrs is 5 mg/d
    - This level based on the amt needed to replace urinary excretion
    - assumed bioavailability of 50%

Absorption/Digestion/Metabolism

- Absorbed principally in the jejunum
- Passive diffusion at high concentrations

- Na⁺-dependent multivitamin transporter (SMVT) at low concentrations
  - The heart, muscle, brain, kidney, & liver cells uptake PA by sodium-dependent active transport (SMVT)
  - PA shares intestinal SMVT w/ biotin & lipoic acid

Deficiency/Toxicity

- Deficiency is rare (lots of food sources!)
  - Deficiency has been reported in conjunction with severe malnutrition
  - Symptoms: vomiting, fatigue, weakness, irritability
- Some conditions that may increase the need for PA include alcoholism, diabetes mellitus, and inflammatory bowel diseases.
- Burning feet syndrome (during WWII)
  - Numbness of the toes and a sensation of burning in the feet
  - Can be corrected w/ calcium pantothenate administration
- Toxicity rare
  - No upper limit established
  - Intakes of 100 mg (20x AI) increase the excretion of niacin

VITAMIN B6 (PYRIDOXINE)

Forms and Discovery

- The vitamin was identified in 1934, and confirmed the structure in 1938
- The pyridoxal (PL) and pyridoxamine (PM) forms were identified in the mid-1940s
- There are actually six vitamers (forms): pyridoxine (PN), pyridoxal (PL), pyridoxamine (PM), pyridoxine 5' phosphate (PNP), pyridoxal 5' phosphate (PLP), pyridoxamine 5' phosphate (PMP)

Sources

- All six vitamers are found in food
  - Plant Sources: PN, PNP, and PN-glucosides
    - Whole grains, starchy vegetables, bananas, nuts, fortified cereals
  - Animal sources: PLP, PMP
    - Meat, fish, poultry
- PN hydrochloride is found in supplements or fortified foods.
- B6 present in foods can be lost through processing (heating, canning, milling, sterilization, and freezing)

DRI

- The 1998 RDA for men/women 19–50 years = 1.3 mg/d
- Requirement is somewhat related to protein intake
  - RDA higher for those >50 years and men
- NHANES data from 2003-2004 suggests that a higher RDA of 3–4.9 mg/d should be instituted

Absorption/Digestion/Metabolism

- Vitamers that are phosphorylated (PNP, PLP, PMP) must be dephosphorylated prior to absorption
  - This requires the action of alkaline phosphatase and zinc.
  - Alkaline phosphatase enzyme found at the brush border membrane hydrolyzes the phosphate

- PN glucosides are hydrolyzed by glucosidase
- PL and PM are absorbed primarily in jejunum via passive diffusion
- PN is absorbed by a specialized, Na^+-dependent carrier-mediated system
- PLP is the main vitamer (60–90%) found in the systemic blood
  - Most of PLP is bound to albumin in the plasma
  - From the plasma, the unphosphorylated vitamers (PL, PN, PM) may be taken up by RBCs, converted to PLP, and bound to Hgb
    - PNP and PMP are converted to PLP by an FMN-dependent oxidase (PNP oxidase, or PMP oxidase)
    - PL is phosphorylated by PL kinase (pyridoxal kinase).
- Most PLP (~75%) is in skeletal muscle, bound to glycogen phosphorylase
- Excess PL can be oxidized in liver to 4-pyridoxic acid and excreted in urine.
  - Requires aldehyde dehydrogenase and NAD in tissues
  - Requires aldehyde oxidase and FAD in the liver and kidneys

Deficiency/Toxicity

- Deficiency is rare
  - In the 1950s, severe heat treatment of infant milk caused deficiency in infants
    - Heat processing resulted in pyrodoxyl-lysine (a RXN b/w PLP and lysine)
    - Signs: sleepiness, fatigue, cheilosis, glossitis, stomatitis, neurological problems (seizure, convulsions)
- Other effects (rare)
  - Impaired NAD synthesis from Trp → impaired NAD-dependent metabolism
  - Impaired heme synthesis makes paler RBC → hypochromic, microcytic anemia
  - Hyperhomocyteinuria
- Aging alters metabolism—at risk for deficiency
- Alcohol can inhibit conversion of PN and PM to PLP
- Women on oral contraceptives may not maintain sufficient B6 levels (PLP form)
- Toxicity:
  - UL adults 100 mg/d
  - Signs of toxicity: unsteady gait, neuropathy (due to loss of myelination and sensory fibers in nerves)
    - Pharmacological doses of vitamin B6 have been used for the treatment of several conditions including hyperhomocysteinemia, carpal tunnel syndrome, premenstrual syndrome, muscular fatigue, numbness

Other

- Hyperhomocysteinemia
  - Could be caused by low B6 levels
- Hypophosphatasia
  - Genetic inactivation of tissue alkaline phosphatase

VITAMIN B7 (BIOTIN)

Forms and Discovery

- Discovered due to "egg white injury"
  - Eating raw eggs results in hair loss and dermatitis.
    - Avidin—forms the tightest noncovalent bond found in nature
    - Avidin, a glycoprotein in raw egg whites, irreversibly binds to biotin, and prevents its absorption (and ↓ bioavailability); heat labile
    - Streptavidin—bacterial analog of avidin
    - Tamavidin—avidin-like protein in tamogitake mushrooms
  - A substance (now called biotin) in liver could cure this condition (in 1931)
- Structure was determined in the early 1940s
- Protein bound, or as biocytin

Sources

- Good sources: egg yolks, liver, soybeans, yeast
  - NOT in veggies, fruits, meats
- Also produced by bacteria in the colon

DRI

- AI for men/women 19+ years is 30 μg/day
- RDA not determinable due to:
  - Insufficient information about biotin requirements
  - Uncertain contribution of intestinal bacteria synthesis
  - Uncertain about bioavailability of biotin in some foods

Absorption/Digestion/Metabolism

- Biotin in food is bound to proteins → digestive proteolysis yields biocytin
- Biocytin is digested by biotinylase yielding biotin and lysine

- Biotinidase is found on the BBM and in pancreatic and intestinal juices
  - Biotinidase deficiency
    - Autosomal recessive
    - Neurocutaneous disorder
- Transport in the intestine occurs via the sodium-dependent multivitamin transporter (SMVT) (also transports pantothenic acid and lipoic acid)
  - SMVT is expressed in tissues for cellular uptake
    - Monocarboxylate transporter I (MCT1) is a lymphocyte biotin transporter that may work in nerve cells as well
  - Passive diffusion at high concentration

Deficiency/Toxicity

- Deficiency can be due to prolonged intake of egg whites, infants on formula w/o biotin (Japan), short gut syndrome patients w/o supplementation
- Symptoms include thinning of hair, loss of hair color, dermatitis, neurological symptoms including depression, lethargy, hallucinations, and paresthesias of arms/legs
- No toxicity has been reported; no upper limit has been established
  - In people w/o disorders of biotin metabolism, doses of up to 5 mg/day are tolerated

Other

- Holocarboxylase synthase deficiency

VITAMIN B9 (FOLATE)

Forms and Discovery

- Discovered due to megaloblastic anemia (along with Vitamin B12)
- Folic Acid (oxidized form) and Folate (reduced form), Dihydrofolate (more reduced), Tetrahydrofolate (most reduced)
- Methylated forms of THF

Sources

- Mushrooms, green vegetables (spinach, cabbage, broccoli, brussel sprouts), legumes (lima & kidney beans), fruits (oranges & strawberries), and liver
- Fortified grains and other foods/supplements (folate form)
- Bacteria in gut synthesize folate

DRI

- RDA for men/women 14 + yrs is 400 µg DFE/d
  - 1 DFE =
    1 mg of food folate
    0.6 mg of folic acid from fortified food or supplement
    0.5 mg of synthetic folate supplement taken on an empty stomach
- DFE calculation for food = mg food folate (natural) + (1.7 × mg folic acid (added))

Absorption/Digestion/Metabolism

- Polyglutamate forms in foods must be hydrolyzed to the monoglutamate form (folate) by glutamate carboxypeptidase II (GCPII)
  - Enzyme can be impaired by alcohol, and enzymatic inhibitors found in legumes, lentils, cabbages, and oranges
- Active Transport in intestine by Sodium-dependent, carrier-mediated transporters, Folate binding proteins
- Passive Transport at high concentrations
- Genetic defects in transport and metabolism

Deficiency/Toxicity

- Deficiency associated with increased cancer, and neural tube defects in fetuses
- Dementia, anemia
- Hyperhomocysteinemia
- Toxicity—associated with insomnia and GI upset

VITAMIN B12 (COBALAMIN)

Forms and Discovery

- Discovered due to megaloblastic anemia (along with Folate)
- Cobalt-containing vitamin
- Cobalamin, methylcobalamin, cyanocobalamin, 5'-deoxyadenosylcobalamin

Sources

- Animal products, as B12 comes from gut bacteria
- Plants do not contain B12 unless contaminated with manure

DRI

- RDA for men/women 14+ yrs is 2.4 μg/d
- In the US, inadequate absorption causes most of B12 deficiency rather than inadequate intake.
    - Loss of parietal cells which secrete IF (aging)
    - Reduced pepsin production (aging)
    - Gastic bypass surgery

Absorption/Digestion/Metabolism

- Ingested protein-bound cobalamins in foods must be released from the proteins/polypeptides
    - Digested by the gastic proteolytic enzyme pepsin and hydrochloric acid in the stomach
    - Intrinsic factor with haptocorrins "R" proteins (most B12 is absorbed by this pathway)
        - B12 released from proteins in the stomach, where it binds haptocorrins
        - R-B12 complex moves to small intestine where R is released and B12 binds IF

- There are two pathways of vitamin B12 absorption.
  - Passive diffusion (<1% of intake)
  - Cubilin associated with the AMN protein
- Impaired absorption can be caused by Gastric atrophy, Achlohydria (lack of HCl in the stomach), antacids, pancreatic insufficiency, tapeworms
- Unlike the other water soluble vitamins, B12 is stored and retained in the body for long periods of time. (even years)
  - Liver is primary storage site

Deficiency/Toxicity

- UL not determinable
  - No adverse effects have been associated with the massive doses of B12
- Megaloblastic anemia—deficiency which is similar to that for folate deficiency
- Neurologic disease affecting the spinal cord, peripheral nerves and brain (usually occurs after anemia)
- Masking of B12 deficiency by folate sufficiency

VITAMIN C

Forms and Discovery

- Most animals make Vitamin C
    - Exceptions are humans and guinea pigs
    - Notable experiments on scurvy/guinea pigs by Szent-Gyorgyi
    - Humans and guinea pigs lack active gulonolactone oxidase enzyme
- Ascorbic Acid (AA) and Dihydroascorbic Acid (DHA)

Sources

- Good sources: asparagus, papaya, broccoli, brussels sprouts, peppers, tomatoes, oranges, strawberries, grapefruit, lemons and limes (red peppers > oranges)
- Fruit and veggies juices from the above sources
- Fortified foods

DRI

- RDA for men 19-30 years 90 mg/d
- RDA for women 19-30 years 75 mg/d
- Smokers 19 years and older 125 (males), 110 (females)
    - 100 - 200 mg daily intake produces plasma concentrations of ~1 mg/dL

Absorption/Digestion/Metabolism

- Sodium (Na) coupled transporters SVCT1 and SVCT2
    - SVCT1 is the main intestinal transporter
    - SVCT2 is the main tissue transporter (very high in brain, eye)
- Excessive iron in the intestinal tract can destroy Vit C (but anecdotally, Vitamin C can help with iron absorption)
- The highest concentrations of Vit C are found in the adrenal and pituary glands (~30-50 mg/100 g wet tissue).
- The liver contains the most Vit C (based on total weight)

- The maximal body pool is ~ 1500 mg. (~ 3% of body pool of ascorbic acid turns over each day)

Deficiency/Toxicity

- Deficiency-Scury
  - ○ effects on collagen synthesis, oxidation states
- High Vitamin C interferes with
  - ○ Warfarin (controversal)
  - ○ Certain laboratory tests (including serum bilirubin, serum creatinine, and the fecal occult blood test)
- Tolerable upper intake level (UL): men/women 19-30 yrs 2000 mg/d
  - ○ Toxic levels can be obtained only from supplements, which often contain 1000mg
  - ○ Symptoms of Toxicity are:
    - ■ Abdominal pain & osmotic diarrhea
      - • Osmotic diarrhea occurs when unabsorbed, water-soluble solutes remain in the bowel, where they retain water
    - ■ Kidney stones
      - • one of the metabolites of vitamin C is oxalate which is a main component of many kidney stones
    - ■ Interfere with Fe and Cu metabolism

Other

- Substances that lower effective Vitamin C levels
  - ○ Estrogen-containing contraceptives are known to lower vitamin C levels in plasma and white blood cells
  - ○ Aspirin (increases excretion)

VITAMIN D

Forms and Discovery

- Pre-vitamin D_2 "ergosterol" $\Rightarrow$ ergocaciferol (produced by phytoplankton, yeast, fungi, using UV light)
- Pre-vitamin D_3 "pre-calciferol" (produced by animals from sunlight)$\Rightarrow$ cholecalciferol (see pathway for production)
- Calcidiol (25-(OH) D_3) is converted to 1,25-(OH)$_2$ D_3 Calcitriol-the active form active form (genomic actions)
- Cats and Dogs cannot synthesize Vitamin D, while humans can

Sources

- Primarily in animal food sources – liver, beef, veal, eggs (yolk), dairy products, some fatty fishes, fish oils, fish eggs
- Vit D fortified foods - milk, yogurt, cheese, margarine, OJ

DRI

- New DRI for both calcium and Vitamin D published in 2011
  - Set with the assumption that dietary intake is only source (since amount varies with UVB exposure)
  - 600 IU/day (higher for older adults—see meta-analysis from class)
- See commentary in textbook on controversy regarding Vitamin D intake recommendations

Absorption/Digestion/Metabolism

- Vitamin D_3 is synthesized in the basel and spinosum strata of the skin starting with 7-dehydrocholesterol (7-DHC)
  - UVB radiation converts 7-DHC to pre-vitamin D_3
  - Normal body temperatures then complete the process, converting to Vitamin D_3
  - Vitamin D_3 is transported from the skin to the bloodstream (and from

liver and kidney as calcidiol and calcitriol, respectively) bound to Vitamin D-binding protein (VDBP)
- In the liver, Vitamin D_3 is converted to calcidiol by 25-hydroxylase
- In the kidney, calcidiol is converted to calcitriol by 1-hydroxylase
- Uptake in the diet is similar to other fat-soluble vitamins, requiring bile salts, chylomicrons, and lipoproteins
  - Vitamin D_3 and Vitamin D_2 can both be converted to calcitriol
- Stored in adipose tissue (for winter)
  - large pool of $25(OH)D_3$ in the blood
- Interactions with other Nutrients
  - Regulates calcium and phosphorus concentrations
  - Iron
    - Deficiency can impair fat soluble vitamin absorption.
  - Vit K
    - Vitamin D stimulates expression of BGP (osteocalcin) and MGP

Deficiency/Toxicity

- Deficiency
  - Rickets
  - Osteomalacea
- Toxicity
  - Hypercalcemia

VITAMIN E

Forms and Discovery

- α-tocopherol (most active), β-tocopherol, γ-tocopherol, δ-tocopherol, α-tocotrienol, β-tocotrienol
- Discovered in 1936
- Vit E was isolated from wheat germ and named 'α-tocopherol'
  - Greek "tokos"-childbirth + "phero"-to bear—deficient rats were infertile

Sources

Oil-rich seeds/nuts, corn and soybean oils, peanut butter, eggs, some vegetables, and meat

DRI

- Most recent recommendations from 2000
  - Based on red cell hemolysis data from Vitamin E deficient and supplemented humans
  - Based on α-tocopherol intake only
  - 15 mg/day
  - Most US individuals average ~6-8 mg/day, especially those on low fat diets
- UL-1000 mg/day

Absorption/Digestion/Metabolism

- Absorption similar to other fat soluble vitamins and lipids in general
  - Bile salt micelles
  - Incorporated into chylomicrons and enters intercellular space, then bloodstream
  - Finally delivered to the liver, and incorporated into VLDLs
- Liver secretes VLDLs carrying Vitamin E into the bloodstream and transported to tissues

- o   This process is crucial to maintaining normal plasma Vitamin E levels
- o   α-tocopherol transfer protein (α-TTP) is essential
    - ▪ Familial ataxia with isolated Vitamin E deficiency (AVED) caused by absence of functional α-TTP
    - ▪ Neurological disorders, and low serum Vitamin E levels
    - ▪ Can be normalized with high supplements of Vitamin E
- • Interactions with other Nutrients
    - o   Vit C
        - ▪ AA reduces vit E radical to regenerate vit E.
    - o   Poly Unsaturated FAs
        - ▪ The requirement for the vit E increases or decreases as the degree of unsaturation of FAs in tissues rises or falls.
        - ▪ Dietary fat improves absorption
    - o   β-carotene
        - ▪ Vit E inhibits β-carotene absorption and its conversion to retinol in the intestine
    - o   Vit K
        - ▪ high vit E can impair vit K absorption
        - ▪ In the vit K cycle, vit E or α-tocopheryl quinone may block regeneration of the reduced form of vit K.

Deficiency/Toxicity

- • Deficiency
    - o   Associated with increased RBC hemolysis, especially in lab tests where RBS are exposed to hydrogen peroxide
    - o   Malabsorption syndromes associated with neurological defects (similar to genetic familial isolated vitamin E deficiency)
    - o   Low vitamin E status associated with heart disease
- • Toxicity
    - o   very rare and does not seem to accumulate in the body and there is no single "storage organ" for Vitamin E
    - o   Increased blood coagulation time/hemorrhage

VITAMIN K

Forms and Discovery

- Phylloquinone (major form from diet), menaquinone (synthesized by bacteria or from phylloquinone in animal tissues) and menadione (synthetic)
- Discovered as a "koagulation" factor; hence Vitamin "K"

Sources

- The main sources - Leafy green vegs (collards, spinach, kale),broccoli
    - Good sources - Veg oils (soybean, rapeseed & canola oils) & margarine
- In plant foods - as phylloquinone (the majority of the vit K in the US diet)
- In animal foods (such as eggs, chicken, livers, etc.) - as a mixture of menaquinones
- Bacteria in the GI tract (esp. the colon) provide menaquinones for humans – conflicting information on whether this is a substantial source

DRI

- Due to lack of data, AI is used
    - AI for 19 + yrs male = 120 µg/d
    - AI for 19 + yrs female = 90 µg/d

Absorption/Digestion/Metabolism

- Phylloquinone is absorbed from the duodenum and jejunum
    - Within the intestinal cells, phylloquinones are incorporated into the chylomicron → lymph system → circulation → transport to tissues
- MKs synthesized by intestinal bacteria are absorbed from the ileum and colon
- In the liver, absorbed menadiones are alkylated along w/ phylloquinone and MKs, incorporated into VLDLs, and carried to extrahepatic tissues in LDLs and HDLs

Deficiency/Toxicity

- Deficiency-hemorrhagic disease
  - VKDB (infants)
  - Vitamin K-dependant coagulation factor deficiency (genetic)
- High Vitamin K interferes with Warfarin
- No Upper Limit has been established
  - Although the natural K_1 and K_2 forms are nontoxic, the synthetic form K_3 (menadione) has shown toxicity.
    - synthetic menadione at high doses may cause liver damage and hemolytic anemia

PUZZLE ANSWERS

CHAPTER 1: CROSSWORD

	ACROSS	ANSWER
2	B7	Biotin
6	B9	Tetrahydrofolate
11	Vitamin A	Retinoic Acid
12	B3	Nicotinamide Adenine Dinucleotide

	DOWN	ANSWER
1	B5	Pantothenic Acid
3	B1	Thiamine pyrophosphate
4	B2	Flavin Mononucleotide
5	Vitamin E	Tocopherol
7	Vitamin K	Menaquinone
8	B6	Pyridoxal
9	Vitamin D	Calcitriol
10	B12	Cobalamin

CHAPTER 2: WORD SEARCH

	CLUE	ANSWER
1	Sea captain with first clinical study	Lind
2	Female scientist who helped discover vitamin A	Davis
3	Secret rat colonies at the University of Wisconsin	McCollum
4	Nobel prize for anti-neuritic factor	Eijkmann
5	Coined the word "vitamins"	Funk
6	Discovered the anti-scorbic vitamin	Von Szent-Gyorgyi
7	Discovered carotinoids	Kuhn
8	Discovered the quinone chemistry of fat-soluble vitamin	Doisy
9	Discovered growth stimulating role of thiamine	Hopkins
10	Worked on flavins	Karrer
11	Goiter is caused by iodine deficiency	Chatin
12	Iron deficiency causes anemia	Davies
13	A member of the 1941 Food and Nutrition Board	McCollum
14	Convened the National Nutrition Conference for Defense	Roosevelt
15	Created golden rice	Paine

CHAPTER 3: SCRAMBLED DOUBLE PUZZLE

1 ENTEROCYTES
2 PASSIVE DIFFUSION
3 ACTIVE TRANSPORT
4 MICELLES
5 CHYLOMICRONS
6 PROTON-COUPLE FOLATE TRANSPORTER
7 SODIUM MULTI-VITAMIN TRANSPORTER
8 HAPTOCORRIN
9 CUBIN
10 DUODENUM
11 TRANSIENT RECEPTOR POTENTIAL MELASTATIN
12 AVIDIN
13 THIAMINASES
14 GOITERGENS
15 PHOSVITIN

Phrase: A healthy digestive tract promotes micronutrient absorption.

CHAPTER 4: FALLING PHRASES

Carbohydrates, fat, and protein all require thiamine, riboflavin, niacin, and pantothenic acid for metabolism.

CHAPTER 5: WORD SEARCH

	CLUE	ANSWER
1	Cell membrane component involved in signaling	Phosphatidylinositol
2	Dumbbell-shaped calcium binding protein	Calmodulin
3	Phosphorylates proteins	Kinase
4	Removes phosphate groups from proteins	Phosphatase
5	Protein modification that requires B5	Acetylation
6	Protein modification that requires B7	Biotinylation
7	Vitamin A vitamer involved in gene regulation	Retinoic Acid
8	Vitamin D vitamer that binds to VDR	Calcitriol
9	Protein deacetylases that require NAD+	Sirtulin
10	Needed by VDR and RXR as a structural cofactor	Zinc
11	Enzyme that uses B7 as a coenzyme	Holocarboxylase Synthetase
12	Name of cellular structures involved in non-genomic vitamin D signaling	Caveolae
13	Thyroid hormone requires this micronutrient	Iodine

CHAPTER 6: ANAGRAMS

ANAGRAM	TERM or PHRASE
TOAD SAINT NIX	ANTI-OXIDANTS
COBRA TEAS	ASCORBATE
MACE GLAMOR PHOTO	GAMMA TOCOPHEROL
ISLE MENU	SELENIUM
A DRENCHED EXIT RIOTUS	THIOREDOXIN REDUCTASE
TOENAIL THUG	GLUTATHIONE
A DISCO INTRO	CAROTINOIDS
HENNA AX ZIT	ZEAXANTHIN
ARCADE FLIERS	FREE RADICALS
A CIRCA HYDRID DISCO DO	DIHYDROASCORBIC ACID
A DIMERIZED SPOUSE TUX	SUPEROXIDE DISMUTASE
AS CAT ALE	CATALASE

CHAPTER 7: CROSSWORD

ACROSS		ANSWER
	1	Methytetrahydrofolate reductase
	4	Neural tube defect
	5	Cobalamin
	7	One carbon metabolism
	9	Homocystein
	10	Sideroblastic anemia
	11	Goiter
	12	Calcium waves
DOWN		
	2	Serine hydroxymethyltransferase
	3	Deiodinase
	6	Blindness
	8	Dihydrofolate

CHAPTER 8: CRYPTOGRAM PUZZLE

Phrase: Calcitonin secretion occurs when there is high blood calcium, while parathyroid secretion occurs when calcium levels are too low.

CHAPTER 9: WORD SEARCH

	CLUE	ANSWER
1	Solution with low solute and high water levels	Hypo-osmotic
2	Activity that can increase sweating and water loss	Exercise
3	Caused by a mutation in the epithelial sodium channel	Liddle Syndrome
4	Caused by a mutation in Aquaporin 2	Diabetes Insipitus
5	Water balance problems result from uncontrolled hyperglycemia	Diabetes Mellitus
6	Caused by dietary high salt intake	Hypernatremia
7	Caused by over-hydration	Water Toxicity
8	Caused by low water intake	Dehydration
9	Solution with a high concentration of impenetrable solutes	Hypertonic

CHAPTER 10: SCRAMBLED DOUBLE PUZZLE

Scrambled Words:
ferrous
ferric
ferritin
heme
aconitase
transferrin
ceruloplasmin
hephaestin
gamma glutamyl carboxylase

Phrase: Menaquinone and iron are key micronutrients for blood system health.

CHAPTER 11: SCRAMBLED PHRASE

Retinoic acid increases basal cell proliferation, while calcitriol increases keratino-cyte differentiation.

CHAPTER 12: WORD SEARCH

```
P  E  L  L  A  G  R  A  +  +  +  +  +  D  +
+  +  +  +  +  +  +  I  +  +  +  +  +  E  +
S  E  K  N  E  M  +  N  +  +  +  +  +  R  +
+  +  +  +  +  +  +  E  +  +  +  +  +  O  +
+  +  +  +  +  +  +  P  +  +  +  +  +  N  B
+  +  +  +  +  +  +  O  S  +  +  +  +  E  E
+  +  +  +  +  +  +  R  C  +  +  +  +  P  R
+  +  +  +  +  +  +  E  U  +  +  +  +  I
+  +  +  +  +  +  +  D  R  +  +  +  +  B
+  +  +  +  +  +  +  I  V  +  +  +  +  E
W  I  L  S  O  N  S  S  Y  +  +  +  +  R
+  +  +  E  D  N  O  L  .  O  I  Z  A  F  I
+  +  +  +  +  +  +  +  +  +  +  +  +  +
+  L  I  D  D  L  E  +  +  +  +  +  +  +
+  W  E  R  N  I  C  K  E  +  +  +  +  +
```

INDEX

vitamin B2 (riboflavin), 286
vitamin B3 (niacin), 288
vitamin B5 (pantothenic acid), 290
vitamin B6 (pyridoxine), 292
vitamin B7 (biotin), 294
vitamin B9 (folate), 296
vitamin B12 (cobalamin), 298
vitamin C, 300
vitamin D, 53, 302
vitamin E, 51, 304
vitamin K, 306
fortified and enriched foods, 24
overview, 11
fortified foods
brown *versus* white rice, 20
nutrition research and, 23–25
four D's. *see* pellagra
free radical, 103–104
Funk, Casimir, 21

ion channels and signal transmission
    axon, 228, 229
    dendrites, 228
    sodium and potassium channels, 229, *229*
    synapse, 228, *228*
    voltage-gated sodium channel (VGSC), 229, *229*
iron
    digestion and, 43, *43*
    divalent metal transporter (DMT1), 42–43, *43*, 52
    overview, 267
iron-deficiency anemia, 202
iron metabolism and hematopoiesis
    ceruloplasmin, 192, *193*
    dietary iron, 192
    enterocyte, 189
    ferritin, 190, 191, *191*
    ferroportin, 192, *193*
    heme carrier protein-1 (HCP1), 192
    heme oxidase (HO), 192, *193*
    hemoglobin, 192
    iron response elements (IREs), 190
    iron sensing RNA-binding protein (IRP), 190
    reductase duodenal cytochrome b (Dcytb), 189, *190*
    thioredoxin reductase (TR), 189
    transferrin, 191, *191*
iron response elements (IREs), 190
iron sensing RNA-binding protein (IRP), 190
isotonic/iso-osmotic conditions, *171*
isotretinoin, 216

K

kakke, 19
keratin, 213
keratinocytes, 212
kidney-renin-angiotensin system, 177
Koch, Robert, 19
Korsakoff's syndrome, 245
Krebs cycle, *64,* 64–66

L

L-glutamyl-L-cysteinylglycine, 109. *see also* glutathione
        (GSH)
Liddle syndrome, 52, 182
Lind, James, 19
lipid bylayers and receptor signaling
    cell signaling and calcium waves, 88, 88–91, *89*
    phospholipids, 87–88, *88*

lipid metabolism, 72–75, *73, 74*
liver
    nutrition research about, 18
    overview, 2, 4
lutein, 238
lycopene, 116

M

macrominerals, 7, 9
macronutrients, defined, 1
magnesium, 197, 266
malate dehydrogenase, 66
manganese (Mn), 219, *219*, 268
matrix gla protein (MGP), 144, 154
McCollum, Elmer Verner, 20
Meniere's disease, 240
Menke's disease, 235
metabolism. *see also* digestion; energy; individual names
        of minerals and vitamins
    amino acid, 76–81, *77, 78, 79, 80*
    carbohydrate, *69,* 69–72, *71*
    fat, 75–76, *76*
methionine cycle, 128, 138
methionine synthase (MS), 127, *131*
methylation, 93
methylene tetrahydrofolate reductase (MTHFR),
        126, 127, 130, *131*
methyl groups, 94
methyl THF, *126*
micelles, 37, 38
micronutrient-associated conditions
    calcium, phosphorus, and vitamin D, 156–159
    genetic conditions affecting, 160–161
    vitamin K, vitamin C, iron, copper, niacin, 159
micronutrients
    abnormal micronutrient absorption, 45–53, *46, 47,*
        48, 50
    in bone, 153–156
        fluoride, 155–156
        vitamin K-dependent carboxylation,
            154–155
    deficiencies, toxicities, and genetic conditions
        affecting blood and immunity,
        202–205, *203, 204*
    deficiency of, and fat/carbohydrate metabolism,
        75–76, *76*
    defined, 1

oxidative distress disorders, 118
oxidative phosphorylation, 66–68, *67*
oxidative stress, 103
oxygen delivery, to tissues, *193*, 193–194
oxygen free radical, *104*

P

pantothenic acid
    acetyl-CoA, 62
    bile acid CoA ligase gene, 51
    CoA, 63
    digestion and, 36
    vitamin B5 (pantothenic acid), overview,
        289–290
passive diffusion, *34*, 34–37, *35, 37*
patents, on foods, 25
pellagra, 233
pendrin, 240
pentose phosphate pathway, 71, 72
peptidylglycine alpha-amidating monooxygenase
        (PAM), 233
peripheral nervous system (PNS),
        225–227, *226*
Peyer's patches, 198
phosphate-activated glutaminase (PAG),
        230, *231*
phosphate-regulating endopeptidase (PHEX), 161
phospholipase C (PLC), 148
phospholipids, 87–88, *88*
phosphorus, 272
phosphorylation, 92
photoisomerization, 237–238
phototreatment, 216
plasma osmolarity, 180, 182
platelets, 197
PLP
    digestion and, 36, *37*
    energy and, 73, 76–79, *77*
PMP, 36, *37*
PNP, 36, *37*
post-translational modifications (PTMs), 92–95
potassium, 277
precalciferol, 144
professional phagocytes, 201, *201*
prolidase
    deficiency, 219, *219*
    definition, 219

protein
    amino acid metabolism, 76–81, *77, 78, 79, 80*
    minerals forms and functions, 8
    modification of intracellular proteins, 92–95
proton-coupled folate transporter (PCFT), 173
pseudoaldosteronism, 52
psoriasis, 216
public policy, nutrition research and, 23–25
PubMed˚, 245
pyridoxine
    PLP, 36, *37*, 73, 76–79, *77*
    PMP, 36, *37*
    PNP, 36, *37*
    vitamin B6 (pyridoxine), overview, 291–292
pyruvate dehydrogenase complex, 6, *6*, 62–64, *63*

R

racemase enzymes, 78
RALDH
    CYP26, levels of, *133*
    retinoic acid, 132
reactive oxygen species (ROS), 103, 105
receptor potential vanilloid channel family
        (TRPV), 240
Recommended Daily Allowances (RDAs), 10, *11*
reduced folate carrier (RFC), *131*, 173
reductase duodenal cytochrome b (Dcytb),
        189, *190*
restless leg syndrome, 235
retinaldehyde dehydrogenase (RALDH), 114
retinoic acid, 131–134, 198, 199
retinoic acid receptor (RAR), 33
retinoid X receptor (RXR), 147
retinol, 237, *237*
retinol binding protein (RBP), 237
retinol dehydrogenese (RDH), 114, 198, 237
reverse T3, 135
rhodopsin, 237, 238
riboflavin
    digestion and Solute Carrier Protein (SLC) family
        of vitamin transporters, 40, *41*
    riboflavin transport (RF2), 228
rice
    brown *versus* white, 19, 20, *24*
    golden, *24,* 24–25
rickets, 51
RNA, modification of, 94–95

Roger's syndrome, 50
Roosevelt, Franklin D., 24
RXR, 134

S

S-adenosyl methionine (SAM), 127
Said, Hamid, 41
sailors, scurvy and, 18–19
scurvy, 18–19, 233
selenium, 274
selenoprotein, 107
semidehydroascorbate (SDA), 106, 107
senses
    hearing, *239,* 239–240
    non-vitamin A carotinoids, in vision and eye health,
        238–239
    overview, 235–236, *236*
    sight, 236–238, *237*
    smell, 245
    taste, 241–245, *242, 243*
    touch, 240, *241*
serine hydroxymethyltransferase (SHMT), *126,* 127, *131*
serotonin, 232, 233
sickle cell anemia, 194
sight, 236–238, *237*
signaling, 87–91, 88, 89
silicon, 269–270, *270*
single nucleotide polymorphisms (SNPs), *160*
single nucleotide variants (SNVs), *160*
skeletal system,genetic conditions, *160*
skin
    biotin, 214–216, *215*
    dermis and hypodermis, 217–219, *218, 219*
    hair, 219–221
    human, anatomy of, 211–212, *212*
    psoriasis, and acne, 216–217
    sunny vitamin D synthesis, 213–214
    thyroid hormone, 214, *214*
    vitamin A, 212–213
smell, 245
SOD1, 116–118
SOD2, 116–118
SOD3, 116–118
sodium (Na), 177
sodium and potassium channels, 229, *229*
sodium dependent vitamin C transporter type 2
        (SVCT2), 234

sodium-iodide symporter (NIS), 136
Solute Carrier Protein (SLC) family of vitamin
        transporters, 39–40, *41*
stable oxygen molecule, *104*
stem cells, 187
steroid and xenobiotic receptor (SXR), 154
steroid hormone receptor, 148
succinate dehydrogenase, 66, 67
sunny vitamin D synthesis, 213–214
superoxide dismutases (SOD), 116–118
sweet tooth, 245
synapse, 228, *228*
Szent-Gyorgyi, Albert, 61

T

taste
    buds, 241, 244
    carbonic anhydrase enzymes, 244
    ENaC, 244
    G-protein-activated signaling pathway, 244
    gustin, *242, 243*
    micronutrients involved in, 241, *242,* 244
    sweet tooth, 245
    zinc supplementation, 243
TCA cycle, *64,* 64–66, 153, 231, *231*
5' tetrahydrofolate (THF), 126, *127*
thiamine
    chemical structure, 21
    genetics of vitamin absorption and, 50, *50*
    rice and, 19, 20
    Solute Carrier Protein (SLC) family of vitamin
        transporters, 39, *41*
thiamine diphosphate (ThDP), 35
thioredoxin reductase (TR), 107, 189
thyroid hormone, 95, *97,* 214, *214*
thyroid hormone receptor (THR), 153, 214
thyroid stimulating hormone (TSH), 135, 137
thyrotropin releasing hormone (TRH), 135
thyroxine (T4), 134
Tolerable Upper Intake Level (UL), 10, *11*
touch, 240, *241*
toxicity. *see* deficiency/toxicity
TPP, 35, 63
trace minerals, 7, 9
transaminases, 76–77
transferrin, 191, *191*
transient receptor potential (TRP), 146